T0211047

Lecture Notes in Computer Science 10488

Commenced Publication in 1973
Founding and Former Series Editors:
Gerhard Goos, Juris Hartmanis, and Jan van Leeuwen

More information about this series at http://www.springer.com/series/7408

Stefano Tonetta · Erwin Schoitsch
Friedemann Bitsch (Eds.)

Computer Safety, Reliability, and Security

36th International Conference, SAFECOMP 2017
Trento, Italy, September 13–15, 2017
Proceedings

 Springer

Editors
Stefano Tonetta (iD)
Fondazione Bruno Kessler
Trento
Italy

Friedemann Bitsch (iD)
Thales Deutschland GmbH
Ditzingen
Germany

Erwin Schoitsch (iD)
AIT Austrian Institute of Technology
Vienna
Austria

ISSN 0302-9743   ISSN 1611-3349 (electronic)
Lecture Notes in Computer Science
ISBN 978-3-319-66265-7   ISBN 978-3-319-66266-4 (eBook)
DOI 10.1007/978-3-319-66266-4

Library of Congress Control Number: 2017949512

LNCS Sublibrary: SL2 – Programming and Software Engineering

This Springer imprint is published by Springer Nature
The registered company is Springer International Publishing AG
The registered company address is: Gewerbestrasse 11, 6330 Cham, Switzerland

Preface

This volume contains the papers presented at SAFECOMP 2017, the 36th International Conference on Computer Safety, Reliability, and Security, held in Trento, Italy, in September 2017.

The European Workshop on Industrial Computer Systems, Technical Committee 7 on Reliability, Safety, and Security (EWICS TC7), established the SAFECOMP conference series in 1979. It has since then contributed considerably to the progress of the state of the art of dependable computer systems and their application in safety-related and safety-critical systems, for the benefit of industry, transport, space systems, health, energy production and distribution, communications, smart environments, buildings, and living. It covers all areas of dependable systems in the "Smart World of Things", influencing our everyday life. Embedded systems, cyber-physical systems, (industrial) Internet of Things, autonomous systems, systems-of-systems, safety and cybersecurity, digital society and transformation are some of the keywords. For all the upcoming megatrends, safety, reliability, and security are indispensable – SAFECOMP addresses them properly from a technical, engineering, and scientific point of view, showing its increasing relevance for today's technology advancements.

We received a good number of high-quality submissions (65), and the international Program Committee, more than 50 members from 14 countries, worked hard to select 22 for presentation and for publication in the SAFECOMP 2017 proceedings (Springer LNCS 10488). The review process was thorough with at least three reviewers with ensured independency. Three renowned speakers from the international community were invited to give a keynote: Marcel Verhoef, "From Documents to Models: Towards Digital Continuity"; John McDermid, "Safety of Autonomy: Challenges and Strategies"; and Radu Grosu, "CPS/IoT: Drivers of the Next IT Revolution". As in previous years, the conference was organized as a single-track event, allowing intensive networking during breaks and social events, and participation in all presentations and discussions.

This year we had again five high-quality workshops in parallel the day before the main conference, ASSURE, DECSoS, SASSUR, TELERISE (for the first time co-located with SAFECOMP), and TIPS. These workshops differed according to the topic, goals, and organizing group(s), and are published in a separate SAFECOMP workshop proceedings volume (LNCS 10489).

We would like to express our gratitude and thanks to all those who contributed to making this conference possible: the authors of submitted papers and the invited speakers; the Program Committee members and external reviewers; EWICS and the supporting organizations; and last but not least, the Local Organization Committee, who took care of the local arrangements, and the Publication Chair for finalizing this volume.

We hope that the reader will find these proceedings interesting and stimulating.

September 2017
Erwin Schoitsch
Stefano Tonetta

Organization

EWICS TC7 Chair

Francesca Saglietti   University of Erlangen-Nuremberg, Germany

Conference Co-chairs

Stefano Tonetta   FBK Fondazione Bruno Kessler, Italy
Erwin Schoitsch   AIT Austrian Institute of Technology, Austria

Program Co-chairs

Erwin Schoitsch   AIT Austrian Institute of Technology, Austria
Stefano Tonetta   FBK Fondazione Bruno Kessler, Italy

Publication Chair

Friedemann Bitsch   Thales Deutschland GmbH, Germany

Local Organizing Committee

Annalisa Armani   FBK Fondazione Bruno Kessler, Italy
Silvia Malesardi   FBK Fondazione Bruno Kessler, Italy
Stefano Tonetta   FBK Fondazione Bruno Kessler, Italy

Workshop Chair

Erwin Schoitsch   AIT Austrian Institute of Technology, Austria

International Program Committee

Thomas Arts   Quviq, Sweden
Peter G. Bishop   Adelard, UK
Friedemann Bitsch   Thales Deutschland GmbH, Germany
Jean-Paul Blanquart   Airbus Defence and Space, France
Sandro Bologna   Associazione Italiana esperti in Infrastrutture Critiche (AIIC), Italy
Andrea Bondavalli   University of Florence, Italy
Jens Braband   Siemens AG, Germany
António Casimiro   University of Lisbon, Portugal
Peter Daniel   EWICS TC7, UK
Ewen Denney   SGT/NASA Ames Research Center, USA

Felicita Di Giandomenico	ISTI-CNR, Italy
Wolfgang Ehrenberger	Hochschule Fulda, Germany
John Favaro	Intecs SpA, Italy
Alberto Ferrari	United Technologies Research Center (UTRC) – Advanced Laboratory on Embedded Systems (ALES), Italy
Francesco Flammini	Federico II University of Naples, Italy
Barbara Gallina	Mälardalen University, Sweden
Ilir Gashi	CSR, City University London, UK
Janusz Górski	Gdansk University of Technology, Poland
Jérémie Guiochet	LAAS-CNRS, France
Wolfgang Halang	Fernuniversität Hagen, Germany
Maritta Heisel	University of Duisburg-Essen, Germany
Chris Johnson	University of Glasgow, UK
Bernhard Kaiser	Berner&Mattner, Germany
Karama Kanoun	LAAS-CNRS, France
Joost-Pieter Katoen	RWTH Aachen University, Germany
Tim Kelly	University of York, UK
Floor Koornneef	Delft University of Technology, The Netherlands
Timo Latvala	Space Systems Finland Ltd., Finland
Zhendong Ma	AIT Austrian Institute of Technology, Austria
Silvia Mazzini	Intecs, Italy
John McDermid	University of York, UK
Frank Ortmeier	Otto-von-Guericke Universität Magdeburg, Germany
Philippe Palanque	University Toulouse, IRIT, France
Michael Paulitsch	Thales Austria GmbH, Austria
Holger Pfeifer	fortiss GmbH, Germany
Thomas Pfeiffenberger	Salzburg Research Forschungsgesellschaft m.b.H, Austria
Peter Popov	City University London, UK
Laurent Rioux	Thales R&T, France
Alexander Romanovsky	Newcastle University, UK
Matteo Rossi	Politecnico di Milano, Italy
Kristin Yvonne Rozier	Iowa State University, USA
John Rushby	SRI International, USA
Francesca Saglietti	University of Erlangen-Nuremberg, Germany
Christoph Schmitz	Zühlke Engineering AG, Switzerland
Erwin Schoitsch	AIT Austrian Institute of Technology, Austria
Christel Seguin	Office National d'Etudes et Recherches Aérospatiales, France
Amund Skavhaug	The Norwegian University of Science and Technology, Norway
Oleg Sokolsky	University of Pennsylvania, USA
Wilfried Steiner	TTTech Computertechnik AG, Austria
Mark-Alexander Sujan	University of Warwick, UK
Stefano Tonetta	Fondazione Bruno Kessler, Italy

Martin Törngren	KTH Royal Institute of Technology, Stockholm, Sweden
Mario Trapp	Fraunhofer Institute for Experimental Software Engineering, Germany
Elena Troubitsyna	Åbo Akademi University, Finland
Tullio Vardanega	University of Padua, Italy
Marcel Verhoef	European Space Agency, The Netherlands
Helene Waeselynck	LAAS-CNRS, France

Sub-reviewers

Rob Alexander	University of York, UK
Mehrnoosh Askarpour	Politecnico di Milano, Italy
Philipp Berger	RWTH Aachen University, Germany
Pierre Bieber	Office National d'Etudes et Recherches Aérospatiales, France
Sofia Cassel	KTH Royal Institute of Technology, Stockholm, Sweden
Luigi Di Guglielmo	United Technologies Research Center (UTRC), Italy
Orlando Ferrante	United Technologies Research Center (UTRC), Italy
Simon Foster	University of York, UK
Robert Heumüller	Otto-von-Guericke Universität Magdeburg, Germany
Dubravka Ilic	Space Systems Finland Ltd., Finland
Sebastian Junges	RWTH Aachen University, Germany
Romain Laborde	University Toulouse, IRIT, France
Lola Masson	LAAS-CNRS, France
Behrang Monajemi	Berner&Mattner, Germany
Sebastian Nielebock	Otto-von-Guericke Universität Magdeburg, Germany
Robert Palin	University of York, UK
Junkil Park	University of Pennsylvania, USA
Masoumeh Parseh	KTH Royal Institute of Technology, Stockholm, Sweden
Stephane Paul	Thales R&T, France
Inna Pereverzeva	Åbo Akademi University, Finland
Irum Rauf	Åbo Akademi University, Finland
Thomas Santen	Technische Universität Berlin, Germany
Valerio Senni	United Technologies Research Center (UTRC), Italy
Thierry Sotiropoulos	LAAS-CNRS, France
Lars Svensson	KTH Royal Institute of Technology, Stockholm, Sweden
Thanassis Tsiodras	European Space Agency, The Netherlands
Nelufar Ulfat-Bunyadi	University of Duisburg-Essen, Germany
Pieter van Gelder	Delft University of Technology, The Netherlands
Kimmo Varpaaniemi	Space Systems Finland Ltd., Finland
Eugene Vasserman	Kansas State University, USA
Matthias Volk	RWTH Aachen University, Germany

Supporting Institutions

European Workshop on Industrial Computer
Systems Reliability, Safety and Security

Fondazione Bruno Kessler

Austrian Institute of Technology

Thales Deutschland GmbH

Lecture Notes in Computer Science (LNCS),
Springer Science + Business Media

European Space Agency

Austrian Association for Research in IT

Austrian Computer Society

European Research Consortium
for Informatics and Mathematics

ARTEMIS Industry Association

Electronic Components and Systems
for European Leadership - Austria

German Computer Society

European Network of Clubs for Reliability
and Safety of Software-Intensive Systems

European
Network of
Clubs for
REliability and
Safety of
Software

IEEE SMC Technical Committee on
Homeland Security (TCHS)

Associazione Italiana per l'Informatica e il
Calcolo Automatico

Verband österreichischer Software Industrie –
Austrian Software Industry Association

Invited Talks

Safety of Autonomy: Challenges and Strategies

John McDermid

University of York, UK
john.mcdermid@cs.york.ac.uk

Abstract. Robots and autonomous systems have been in use for some time - for example in factories and in urban railways. However there is now an unprecedented level of activity in robotics and autonomy, with applications ranging from domestic and healthcare robots to driverless cars. Whilst, in some cases, safety is being assessed thoroughly, in many situations these applications cannot effectively be addressed using standard methods. Challenges include demonstrating the safety of artificial intelligence (AI), especially learning or adaptive systems and the effectiveness of image analysis and scene under-standing. At a broader level there are difficulties for standards and regulations that, in some cases, have historically sought to exclude the use of AI. The talk will discuss some of these challenges and consider solution strategies, including approaches to dynamic assessment of safety.

CPS/IoT: Drivers of the Next IT Revolution

Radu Grosu

Institute of Computer Engineering, Vienna University of Technology, Austria
radu.grosu@tuwien.ac.at

Abstract. Looking back at the time Bill Gates was one of his brilliant students, Christos Papadimitriou a Harvard professor and world-renowned computer scientist, concluded that one of the greatest challenges of the academic community is to recognising when an IT revolution is on its way. He did not see the PC revolution coming, but his student did. Since then several others happened, such as the Internet and the Mobiles revolutions. Another imminent one is in the making: The CPS/IoT revolution.

Cyber-physical systems (CPS) are spatially-distributed, time-sensitive, and multi-scale, networked embedded systems, connecting the physical world to the cyber world through sensors and actuators. The Internet of Things (IoT) is the backbone of CPS. It connects the swarm of Sensors and Actuators to the nearby Gateways through various protocols, and the Gateways to the Fog and the Cloud. The Fog resembles the human spine, providing fast and adequate response to imminent situations. The Cloud resembles the human brain, providing large storage and analytic capabilities.

Four pillars, Connectivity, Monitoring, Prediction, and Optimisation drive the CPS/IoT. The first two have been already enabled by the technological developments over the past years. The last two, are expected to radically change every aspect of our society,. The huge number of sensors to be deployed in areas such as manufacturing, transportation, energy and utilities, buildings and urban planning, health care, environment, or jointly in smart cities, will allow the collection of terabytes of information (Big-Data), which can be processed for predictive purposes. The huge number of actuators will enable the optimal control of these areas and drive market advantages.

Despite of all these optimistic predictions, a main question still lingers: Are we ready for the CPS/IoT revolution? In this talk, I will address the grand challenges that stand in our way, but also point out, the great opportunities of CPS/IoT.

Contents

Safety and Security

Dynamic Fault Trees

Model-Based Safety Analysis for Vehicle Guidance Systems

Majdi Ghadhab[1], Sebastian Junges[2], Joost-Pieter Katoen[2], Matthias Kuntz[1], and Matthias Volk[2(✉)]

[1] BMW AG, Munich, Germany
[2] RWTH Aachen University, Aachen, Germany
matthias.volk@cs.rwth-aachen.de

Abstract. This paper considers the design-phase safety analysis of vehicle guidance systems. The proposed approach constructs dynamic fault trees (DFTs) to model a variety of safety concepts and E/E architectures for drive automation. The fault trees can be used to evaluate various quantitative measures by means of model checking. The approach is accompanied by a large-scale evaluation: The resulting DFTs with up to 300 elements constitute larger-than-before DFTs, yet the concepts and architectures can be evaluated in a matter of minutes.

1 Introduction

Motivation. Cars are nowadays equipped with functions, often realised in software, to e.g., improve driving comfort and driving assistance (with a tendency towards autonomous driving). These functions impose high requirements on functional safety. To meet these requirements, it is crucial to execute these functions with a sufficiently low probability of undetected dangerous hardware failures. ISO 26262 [1] is the basic norm for developing safety-critical functions in the automotive setting. It enables car manufacturers to develop safety-critical devices—in the sense that malfunctioning can harm persons—according to an agreed technical state-of-the-art. The safety-criticality is technically measured in terms of the so-called Automotive Safety Integrity Level (ASIL). This level takes into account driving situations, failure occurrence, the possible resulting physical harm, and the controllability of the malfunctioning by the driver. The result is classified from ASIL QM (no special safety measures required) up to ASIL D (with ASIL A, B, C in between). This paper considers the design-phase safety analysis of the *vehicle guidance* system, a key functional block of a vehicle with a high safety integrity level (ASIL D, i.e., 10^{-8} residual hardware failures per hour). The crux of our approach is to: (1) construct dynamic fault trees [2] (DFTs) from system descriptions and combine them (in an automated manner) with hardware failure models for several partitionings of functions on hardware, and (2) analyse the resulting overall DFTs by means of probabilistic model checking [3].

© Springer International Publishing AG 2017
S. Tonetta et al. (Eds.): SAFECOMP 2017, LNCS 10488, pp. 3–19, 2017.
DOI: 10.1007/978-3-319-66266-4_1

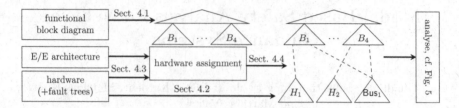

Fig. 1. Overview of the model-based safety approach

A Model-Based Approach. Figure 1 summarises the approach of this paper. The failure behaviour of the functional architecture, given as a functional block diagram (FBD), is expressed as a two-layer DFT: the upper layer models a system failure in terms of block failures B_i while the lower level models the causes of block failures. The use of DFTs rather than static fault trees allows to model warm and cold redundancies, spare components, and state-dependent faults; cf. [4]. Each functional block is assigned to a hardware platform for which (by assumption) a DFT is given that models its failure behaviour. Depending on the partitioning, the communication goes via different fallible buses. From the partitioning, and the DFTs of the hardware and the functional level, an overall DFT is constructed (in an automated manner) consisting of three layers: (1) the system level; (2) the block level; and (3) the hardware level. Details are discussed in Sect. 4.

Analysis. We exploit probabilistic model checking (PMC) [3] to analyse the DFT of the overall vehicle guidance system. It can be used as a black-box algorithm— no expertise in PMC is needed to understand its outcomes—and supports *various metrics* that go beyond reliability and MTTF [5]. In contrast to simulation, where results are obtained with a given statistical confidence, PMC provides *hard guarantees* that the safety objectives are met. This is important as ISO 26262 requires metrics to be objectively assessable: "metrics are verifiable and precise enough to differentiate between different architectures" [1, 5:8-2]. Whereas most ISO 26262-based analyses focus on single and dual-point of failures, PMC naturally supports the analysis of *multi-point of failures* of the vehicle guidance system's DFT. This is highly relevant, as "[for systems where the] concept is based on redundant safety mechanism, multiple-point failures of a higher order than two are considered in the analysis" [1, 5:9-4].

Contributions. The main contribution of this paper is two-fold: We report on the usage of dynamic fault trees for safety analysis in a potential automotive setting. While standard fault tree analysis is part of the ISO 26262, the usage of DFTs in this field is new. The paper shows how additional features help to create faithful models of the considered scenarios. These models are then used to analyse the given scenarios. To increase the applicability of DFTs as a method for probabilistic safety assessment in an industrial setting, we give concrete building blocks to work with, e.g. redundancy and faults covered by fallible safety mechanisms.

A clear benefit of the usage of DFTs is that all these methods are integrated in existing off-the-shelf analysis tools, which provide sound error bounds. This reduces the amount of domain specific knowledge in the analysis, and thus supports a more model-oriented approach. In this paper, we utilise this to investigate the effect of different hardware partitioning on a range of metrics. The generated fault trees are to the best of our knowledge the largest real-life ones in the literature – larger trees have only been artificially created for scalability purposes [6]. In particular, this paper is the first to consider the model-checking based approaches for DFT analysis on real-life case studies.

Related Work. Earlier work [7] considers an automotive case study where functional blocks are translated to static fault trees without treating the partitioning on hardware architectures. The effect of different topologies of a FlexRay bus has been assessed using FTA in [8]; and identified the need for modelling dynamic aspects. The analysis of architecture decisions under safety aspects has been considered in e.g. [9] using a dedicated description language and an analytical evaluation. Safety analysis for component-based systems has been considered in [10], using state-event fault trees. Qualitative FTA has been used in [11] for ISO 26262 compliant evaluation of hardware. Different hardware partitionings are constructed and analysed using an Architecture Description Language (ADL) in [12]. ADL-based dependability analysis has been investigated for several languages, e.g., AADL [13], UML [14], Arcade [15], and HiP-HOPS [16]. These approaches typically have a steeper learning curve than the use of DFTs. The powerful Möbius analysis tool [17] has recently been extended with dynamic reliability blocks [18]. Model checking for safety analysis has been proposed by, e.g., [19]; which focuses on AltaRica, and does not cover probabilistic aspects.

Remark. The proposed concepts and architectures are exemplary. No implication on actual safety concepts or E/E architectures implemented by BMW AG can be derived from these examples. The same remark applies on any quantity (failure rates, obtained metrics, ...) presented in this paper.

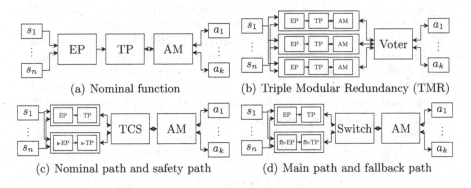

(a) Nominal function

(b) Triple Modular Redundancy (TMR)

(c) Nominal path and safety path

(d) Main path and fallback path

Fig. 2. Different functional block diagrams for vehicle guidance

2   Vehicle Guidance

The most challenging safety topic in the automotive industry is currently the driving automation, where the driving responsibility is moving partly or even entirely from the driver to the embedded vehicle intelligence. Rising liability questions make it crucial to develop functional safety concepts adequately to the intended automation level and to provide evidence regarding the integrity and the reliability of these concepts.

2.1   Scenario

As a real-life case study from the automotive domain, we propose to consider the functional block diagram (FBD) in Fig. 2(a) representing the skeletal structure of automated driving. Data collected from different sensors (cameras, radars, ultrasonic, etc.) are synthesised and fused to generate a model of the current driving situation in the Environment Perception (EP). The model is used by the Trajectory Planning (TP) to build a driving path with respect to the current driving situation and the intended trip. The Actuator Management (AM) ensures the control of the different actuators (powertrain, brakes, etc.) following the calculated driving path. Thus, the blocks in the FBD fulfil tasks: The tasks are realised by (potentially redundant) functional blocks, connected by lines to depict dataflow. These diagrams are *not* reliability block diagrams in which the system is operational as long as a path through operational blocks exist. According to the automation level, the vehicle guidance function must be designed as *fail-operational*, that is, the system should safely continue to operate for a certain time after a failure of one of its components.

2.2   Modelling of Safety Concepts

Functional Safety Concepts. Based on the criticality of the vehicle guidance function, especially when the driver is out-of-the-loop, ASIL D applies to it. Different design patterns have been developed and implemented in safety-critical systems with fail-operational behaviour and high safety levels, cf. e.g. [20]. The variety of possibilities is illustrated by the following three concepts:

SC1- Triple Modular Redundancy (TMR), Fig. 2(b): The nominal function for vehicle guidance is replicated into three paths each fulfilling ASIL B. A Voter, fulfilling ASIL D, ensures that any incorrect path is eliminated.

SC2- Nominal path and safety path, Fig. 2(c): Consists of two different paths, a nominal path (n-Path) and a safety path (s-Path) in hot-standby mode. The n-Path provides a full extent trajectory with ASIL QM and the s-Path a reduced extent trajectory but with highest safety and integrity level ASIL D. The safety trajectory is generated from a reduced s-EP (safety Environment Perception) and s-TP (safety Trajectory Planning). The Trajectory Checking and Selection (TCS) verifies whether the trajectory calculated by the n-Path is within the safe range calculated by the s-Path or not. In the case of failure, the s-Path takes over the control and the safe trajectory with reduced extent is followed by the AM. In this case, we consider the system to be *degraded*.

SC3- Main path and fallback path, Fig. 2(d): Similar to SC2 although the main path (m-Path) is now developed according to ASIL D in order to detect its own hardware failures and signalise them to the Switch. The Switch then commutates the control of the AM to a fallback path (fb-Path) with ASIL B. In this case, we consider the system to be *degraded*.

Technical Safety Concepts and Partitioning on E/E Architecture. The next design step consists of extending the nominal E/E architecture for vehicle guidance and partitioning the blocks of every safety concept on its elements. The nominal E/E architecture is represented in Fig. 3(a). The vehicle guidance function is implemented on an ADAS-platform (Advanced Driver Assistance System) which is connected to all used sensors. A number of dedicated ECUs (Electronic Control Unit) control the actuators. On an I-ECU (Integration ECU), additional, non-dedicated actuation functions can be implemented. Naturally, implementing all blocks from the safety concepts on the ADAS in Architecture A defeats the purpose of the redundant paths.

Figure 3 gives further illustrative examples for E/E architectures for the different safety concepts: For SC1, Architecture B (Fig. 3(b)) allows an implementation of the three redundant paths on separate ADAS-cores. The Voter is implemented on the I-ECU. For SC2, the following two implementations both yield ASIL D for the safety path, each with TCS and AM on the I-ECU: (1) Executing the nominal path on one ADAS and redundant execution of the s-Path on two ADAS-cores in *lock-step mode*, using Architecture B. (2) *Encoded execution* [21] of the s-Path on a single ADAS+-core in Architecture C (Fig. 3(c)), the + refers to the additional hardware resources to run an encoded s-Path. An E/E architecture for SC3 could run on Architecture C, where the m-Path is implemented on $ADAS_1$ and the fb-Path on $ADAS_2$. Alternatives are considered in our experiments in Sect. 5.

Hardware Platforms and Faults. We assume that all hardware platforms can completely recover from transient faults (e.g. by restarting the affected path),

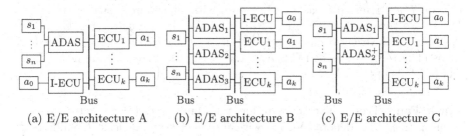

(a) E/E architecture A   (b) E/E architecture B   (c) E/E architecture C

Fig. 3. Different E/E architectures

so that only transient fault directly leading to a failure of the system are of importance. As transient faults disappear quickly, the probability for another fault occurring in presence of a transient fault is negligible. It is thus reasonable to assume that during a transient fault, no other faults occur [1].

2.3   Measures

The safety goal for the considered systems is to avoid wrong vehicle guidance. As the system is designed to be fail-operational, the system should be able to maintain its core functionality for a certain time. The safety goal is violated, if e.g. two out of three TMR paths or both the n-Path and the s-Path fail. The goal is also violated if e.g. a failure of the n-Path is not detected. The safety goal is classified as ASIL D. We stress that safe faults do not need to be considered. For ease of notation we define the *complement* of probability p as $1 - p$.

Several measures allow insights in the safety-performance of the different safety concepts: *System integrity* refers to the probability that the system safely operates during the considered operational lifetime. To obtain the average failure-probability per hour, the complement of the integrity is scaled with the lifetime (to determine the failures in time, FIT). Besides the integrity, the mean time to failure (MTTF) is a standard measure of interest. We expect that only a reduced functionality is provided in the degraded states: The following measures reflect insights also relevant for customer satisfaction: (1) the probability at time t that the system provides the full functionality, (2) the fraction of system failures which occur without going to a degraded state first, (3) the expected time to failure upon entering the degraded state, (4) the criticality of a degraded state, in terms of the probability that the system fails within e.g. a typical drive cycle, and (5) the effect on the overall system integrity when imposing limits on the time a system remains operational in a degraded state. It is important to consider the robustness or *sensitivity* of all measures w.r.t. changes in the failure rates.

3   Technical Background

3.1   Fault Trees

Fault trees (FTs) are directed acyclic graphs (DAG) with typed nodes. Nodes of type T are referred to as "a T". Nodes without children (successors in the DAG), are *basic events* (BEs, Fig. 4(a)). Other nodes are *gates* (Fig. 4(b)–(h)). A BE *fails* if the event occurs; a gate fails if its *failure condition* over its children holds. The *top level event* ($\mathsf{TLE}(F)$) is a specifically marked node of a FT F. $\mathsf{TLE}(F)$ fails iff the FT F fails.

Static Fault Trees. The key gate for static fault trees (SFTs, gates (b)–(d)) is the *voting* gate (denoted VOT_k) with *threshold* k and at least k children. A VOT_k-gate fails, if k of its children have failed. A VOT_1 gate equals an OR-gate, while a VOT_k with k children equals an AND-gate.

(a) BE (b) VOT$_k$ (c) OR (d) AND (e) SEQ (f) PAND (g) SPARE (h) FDEP

Fig. 4. Node types in ((a)–(d)) static and (all) dynamic fault trees

Dynamic Fault Trees. As SFTs are not expressive enough for a faithful model, cf. e.g. [22], dynamic fault trees (DFTs) additionally allow the following gates:

Sequence-Enforcers. The sequence enforcer (SEQ, Fig. 4(e)) restricts the order in which BEs can fail; its children may only fail from left-to-right. Contrary to a widespread belief, SEQs cannot be modelled by SPAREs (introduced below) [22]. SEQs appear in [1, 10-B.3], where they are indicated by the boxed L.

Priority-and. The (binary) priority-and (PAND, Fig. 4(f)) fails iff all children failed and the right child did not fail before the left child.

Spare-Gates. Spare-gates (SPARE, Fig. 4(g)) model spare-management and support warm and cold standby. Warm (cold) standby corresponds to a reduced (zero) failure rate. Likewise to an AND, a SPARE fails if all children have failed. Additionally, the SPARE *activates* its children from left to right: A child is activated as soon as all children to its left have failed. By activating and therefore using a child the failure rate is increased. The children of the SPAREs are assumed to be roots of independent subtrees, these subtrees are called *modules*. Upon activation of the root of a module, the full module is activated.

Functional Dependencies. Functional dependencies (FDEP, Fig. 4(h)) ease modelling of feedback-loops. FDEPs have a *trigger* (a node) and a *dependent event* (a BE). Instead of propagating failure upwards, upon the failure of the trigger, the dependent event fails. FDEPs are syntactic sugar in SFTs, but not in DFTs [6].

Activation Dependencies. To overcome syntactic restrictions induced by SPAREs and to allow greater flexibility with activation, we use *activation dependencies* (ADEPs), as proposed in [22, Sect. 3E]. If the *activation source* is activated, this is propagated to the *activation destination*. ADEPs are typically used in conjunction with an FDEP, where the activation sources are the dependent events and the activation target is the trigger.

3.2 Analysing DFTs by Model Checking

Both the measures of interest (Sect. 2.3) and the dynamic extensions to fault trees refer to different states in the model. It is therefore natural to make these states explicit with a state-based model. Markov models have been long used in model checking and performance evaluation as such state based models [23].

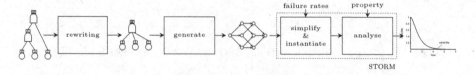

Fig. 5. Overview of the STORM-dft approach

STORM (see http://www.stormchecker.org) is the state-of-the-art tool for the automatic analysis of DFTs via a conversion to Markov Automata (MA) [5]. The tool chain is depicted in Fig. 5. As a first step, we *rewrite* the given FT: Whereas an FT has a lot of structural requirements that make it a good and readable fault tree, cf. [24], these requirements are counterproductive in terms of automated analysis: Consider e.g. superfluous levels of ORs in the FT. DFTs can automatically be rewritten using the techniques from [6] to make them more suitable for analysis purposes. STORM translates the rewritten DFT into a (deterministic) parameterised MA: This is the computationally most expensive step. STORM then reduces the parameterised MA to a parametric continuous time Markov chain (CTMC). Next, the parametric CTMC is instantiated to a CTMC by considering concrete values for all failure rates: Thus, the model construction is invoked only once for multiple sets of failure rates. The last step executes the model-checking routine with a property to produce the required result.

Properties. STORM takes a wide variety of measures, corresponding to continuous stochastic logic properties with reward extensions [3]. Most relevant are:

Reach-Avoid Probability. Given sets of target states and bad states, this measure gives the probability to reach the target state without visiting a bad state meanwhile. If the bad set is empty, this is *reachability*.

Time-Bounded Reach-Avoid Probability. Given an additional deadline, it gives the probability to reach a target state (avoiding bad states) within the deadline.

Expected Time. Given a set of target states that are eventually reached, it gives for each state the expected time to reach the target.

Evidence. Some measures require the evaluation of degraded system states on the earliest moment that certain nodes in the FT already failed. Typically, the original DFT is also analysed, and the complete state space has been constructed before. Thus, it is beneficial to deduce measures for the degraded system on the original state space. Using *evidence* allows defining degraded states as initial states in the underlying model to ease analysis. Given evidence in the form of a set of BEs considered as already failed, all possible orderings (traces) in which they failed are considered. Following these traces from the initial state of the model yields a set of states S; based on the evidence, the system is in one of these states. For all states in S, we obtain values for the measures via model checking. Evidence in the form of gates is conceptually equivalent, but realised via backward-search.

Transient Faults. After the occurrence of a transient fault, the system either fails directly, or the fault disappears and the system returns to its previous state. Transient events are thus considered in each state, but are only added to the underlying MA if they lead to the failure of the TLE.

Approximate Reliability. To alleviate the state space explosion problem, we lifted the idea for sound over- and under-approximation of the MTTF [5] to reliability. The central observation is that typically only a fraction of the state space is relevant to obtain tight bounds for the property at hand. Thus, only a fraction of the state space needs to be constructed: A safe over-approximation of the complement of the reliability consists in assuming that each terminal state in the partial state space corresponds to the failure of the TLE, whereas an under-approximation simply assumes that the TLE cannot fail if it has not failed in one of the terminal states.

4   Methodology

This section describes details for the approach from Fig. 1.

4.1   From Functional Block Diagrams to Functional Fault Trees

Definition 1 (Block diagram). *A block diagram $\mathcal{D} = (Blc, \triangleright)$ is a finite directed graph. The vertices are called* blocks, *the edges are called* channels.

Formally, the input for this step is any block diagram, the output is a FT F with *dummy events* for each hardware piece: $\{f_x \mid x \in Blc \cup \triangleright\} \subseteq F_{BE}$.

The *functional FT*, i.e. the system and the block level, is created manually: This has several advantages, most importantly: (1) There is no need to formalise the semantics of the FBD and its implicit assumptions, e.g. different failure behaviour of voters or edges with different meaning in FBD, and adaptions can be made by hand. (2) Constructing the FT is an important step in the development-*process* of safety-critical systems [1].

For the considered scenarios, the TLE is assumed to represent the safety-critical failure of the system. A *task-based* partitioning of the FT is helpful: The TLE is assumed to fail if any of the tasks can no longer be executed. The tasks fail if no block can realise the task anymore. Dataflow is encoded by encoding an error in the input as a fault. The failure behaviour of a single block is precisely expressed as a fault tree (referred to as *block fault tree*). A typical example is depicted in Fig. 6(a): The hardware-failure is a dummy event, to be

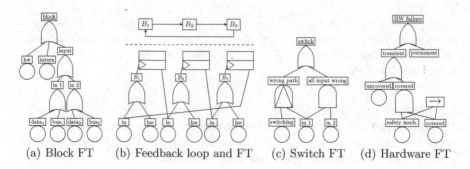

(a) Block FT   (b) Feedback loop and FT   (c) Switch FT   (d) Hardware FT

Fig. 6. Illustrative fragments of the fault trees

connected with the hardware FT, and internal failures can be used for sub-blocks or for additional descriptions. The input fails if either of the two input channels fail: The channels fail if either the hardware for the channel fails or the block creating the input fails, dummies for bus hardware and data flow, respectively. It is important to support feedback loops, which are realised by the use of FDEPs, as in [24]. The structure (simplified) is depicted in Fig. 6(b): For three blocks as shown on top, the three FTs are connected via FDEPs. If e.g. B_1 fails, the failure is propagated to the input of B_2, etc. The use of FDEPs prevents that cyclic dependencies yield cyclic FTs, and is very flexible. The scheme can be used as-is for hierarchical descriptions of both tasks and functional blocks. For the safety concepts, the following remarks apply.

Triple Modular Redundancy. For the Voter input failures, rather than an OR over the inputs as in Fig. 6(a), a VOT$_2$ is used. The block fails if two inputs fail.

Fallback and Cold-Redundancy. The fallback-path is in cold standby: Using a SPARE instead of an AND to encode the failure of all blocks fulfilling a task ensures the activation of the fallback-path.

Path Switching. The Switch (SC3) may fail. This only leads to failure when the path has to be switched. This is reflected by the FT in Fig. 6(c): the Switch fails if it either uses the wrong path or if all input is wrong. The path is wrong if the switching mechanism fails before the primary input fails, i.e., it can no longer switch to an operational path. The scheme can be extended to more paths.

4.2 Fault Trees for Hardware

We support arbitrary (D)FTs to model the hardware failures. We briefly illustrate how to integrate coverage and both transient and permanent faults, as in [1, 10:B]. The DFT is depicted in Fig. 6(d). Faults are either transient or permanent faults. Each type has its own corresponding safety mechanism. A transient fault occurs if either the fault is not covered by the safety mechanism or the fault is covered but the safety mechanism has failed before. The latter is modelled with use of a SEQ, it cannot be modelled faithfully by a static FT.

4.3 Hardware Assignment and E/E Architecture

Definition 2 (Hardware assignment). *Given a block diagram* $\mathcal{D} = (\mathsf{Blc}, \rhd)$, *a set of hardware-platforms* H *and a set of buses* Bus, *a* hardware-assignment *is a function* $h \colon \mathcal{D} \to H \cup \mathsf{Bus}$ *s.t.* $h(\mathsf{Blc}) \subseteq H$ *and* $h(\rhd) \subseteq \mathsf{Bus}$.

Typically, we only want to assign blocks to hardware-platforms; the channel-assignment then follows from the E/E architecture. This can be captured by a simple set of rules, exemplified below: Any channel between two blocks assigned to the same hardware platform is realised by the internal infrastructure on the platform; it requires no additional hardware. All other channels are realised via the same bus, as typical in CAN or FlexRay. Formally, assume $\mathsf{Bus} = \{\mathsf{CAN}\} \cup \{c_p \mid p \in H\}$. For a fixed block-assignment, the channel-assignment between blocks s and t is thus $c_{h(s)}$ if $h(s) = h(t)$ and CAN otherwise.

4.4 Constructing a Complete Fault Tree

To merge the FTs, we take the disjoint union of the functional FT F with $\{f_x \mid x \in \mathsf{Blc} \cup \rhd\} \subseteq F_{\mathsf{BE}}$, and the hardware FTs $\{F_y \mid y \in H \cup \mathsf{Bus}\}$. For each $x \in \mathsf{Blc} \cup \rhd$, an FDEP with trigger $\mathsf{TLE}(F_{h(x)})$ and dependent event f_x is added, and an ADEP in the reverse direction. The ADEP ensures that the hardware FTs are correctly activated. For example, consider the block FT in Fig. 6(a) and the corresponding hardware FT in Fig. 6(d). The TLE "HW failure" of the hardware FT is connected to the dummy BE "hw" of the block FT with an FDEP.

4.5 Translating Measures

We translate the measures introduced in Sect. 2.3. The formal definition of the measures is given in Table 1. As we construct the FT such that the TLE corresponds to a violation of the safety goal, *(system) integrity* corresponds to reliability in FT analysis. Thus, the integrity is obtained by first computing the time-bounded probability to reach a state where the TLE has failed and then complementing this value. *FIT* computation is realised by post-processing. The *MTTF* corresponds to the expected time until a state is reached where the TLE has failed. In the considered DFTs, the expected time is always defined. For degraded states, for (1) we compute the complement of the time-bounded reachability probability for reaching a failed or degraded state and call this *Full Function Availability* (FFA), for (2) we compute the time-bounded reach-avoid probability avoiding degraded states and reaching the TLE failure and call this *Failure Without Degradation* (FWD), for (3) we compute the expected time from the moment of degradation to a failure. We scale these with the probability to reach such a state. The result is the *Mean Time from Degradation to Failure* (MTDF). Furthermore, for (4) we compute the reliability from the moment of degradation: we take the minimum over all states and call the complement the *Minimal Degraded Reliability* (MDR) and for (5) we compute the time-bounded reachability to a TLE failure with a drive cycle as deadline starting from the

Table 1. Definition of measures

	Measure	Model Checking Queries
System	integrity	$1 - P(\lozenge^{\leq t} \text{ failed})$
System	FIT	$\frac{1}{\text{lifetime}} \cdot \left(1 - P(\lozenge^{\leq \text{lifetime}} \text{ failed})\right)$
System	MTTF	$\mathsf{ET}(\lozenge \text{ failed})$
Degradation	FFA	$1 - P(\lozenge^{\leq t} \text{ (failed} \vee \text{degraded)})$
Degradation	FWD	$P((\neg\text{degraded}) \, \mathsf{U}^{\leq t} \, (\neg\text{degraded} \wedge \text{failed}))$
Degradation	MTDF	$\Sigma_{s \in \text{degraded}} \left(P(\neg\text{degraded } \mathsf{U} \, s) \cdot \mathsf{ET}^s(\lozenge \text{ failed})\right)$
Degradation	MDR	$\text{argmin}_{s \in \text{degraded}} \left(1 - P^s(\lozenge^{\leq t} \text{ failed})\right)$
Degradation	SILFO	$1 - \left(FWD + \Sigma_{s \in \text{degraded}} \left(P(\neg\text{degraded } \mathsf{U}^{\leq t} \, s) \cdot P^s(\lozenge^{\leq \text{drivecycle}} \text{ failed})\right)\right)$

moment we reach a degraded state. We scale this with the probability to reach a degraded state in time, and add the FWD. We call the complement *System Integrity under Limited Fail-Operation* (SILFO). Sensitivity analysis is realised by a series of experiments with different failure rates.

5   Experiments

The goal of the presented experiments is to show the applicability of the proposed methodology on systems and concepts similar to those from Sect. 2.2.

5.1   Set-up

All experiments are executed on a 2.9 GHz Intel Core i5 with 8 GB RAM. We consider the three safety concepts. For each SC, we construct a functional FT. We include four sensors, of which two are required for safe operation, and four actuators, which are all required for safe operation.

Different Partitioning Schemes. For each concept, we vary the baseline partitions from Sect. 2.2. For each concept, we additionally use (1) the nominal architecture and (2) remove the I-ECU from the architecture; reassigning the components to ADAS_2. For some combinations, we vary the hardware, by e.g. considering a redundant bus or introducing more hardware platforms. We additionally scale the number of sensors and actuators and the required number of sensors for safe operation.

Failure Rates. For presentation purposes we assume the following failure rates, which do not necessarily reflect reality and especially do not reflect any system from BMW AG. We assume that functional blocks, e.g. EP, are free of systematic faults. Sensors, actuators, and ECUs have failure rates of $10^{-7}/\text{h}$. In the ADAS hardware platforms transient (permanent) faults occur with rate $10^{-4}/\text{h}$

$(10^{-5}/h)$, respectively. All faults can be detected by a safety mechanism covering 99%/90%/60% (for ASIL D/B/QM) of the faults, which fails with rate $10^{-5}/h$. For ADAS+, failure rates increase by a factor 10 and coverage becomes 99.9%.

Tool-Support. Both the generation of the FT corresponding to the safety concepts as well as their analysis are supported by a Python toolchain. For a FBD and block trees for each block, dependencies based on the data flow in the FBD are automatically inserted. Give an E/E architecture, a partitioning, hardware FTs and the functional FT, the complete FT is automatically generated. The analysis of DFTs as in Fig. 5 is completely automated. We additionally add templates for the hardware FTs, such that changes in coverage or failure rates require only single parameters to be changed.

5.2 Evaluation

An overview of (a selection of) considered scenarios and the corresponding DFTs and CTMCs can be found in Table 2. Each scenario is defined by the safety concept, the used architecture with possible adaptions and the fraction of sensors and actuators which have to be operational (columns 2–6). The next three columns give the number of basic events, dynamic gates and the total number of nodes in the DFT. The last three columns contain the number of states and transitions in the CTMC after applying reduction techniques and the percentage of degraded states in the CTMC. The analysis results for the measures from Sect. 4.5 are given in Table 3. Notice that SC1 does not have degraded states. The times for generating the model and computing each measure are given in Table 4. Figure 7 illustrates the obtained measures for a variety of concepts and architectures. The complement of the integrity is given in Fig. 7(a) and FIT in Fig. 7(b). Figure 7(c) considers SC2 and SC3 on Architecture C: The straight lines were obtained by the baseline failure rates for the hardware components, whereas the dashed (dotted) lines were obtained assuming an increased (decreased) coverage according to an increased (decreased) ASIL level. The graph in Fig. 7(d) displays the SILFO for the safety concepts with degraded states and a drive cycle of one hour. Moreover, computing an approximate integrity allowing a 3% relative error on the largest scenario could be computed within 22 s (requiring only 324,990 states).

5.3 Analysis of Results

Table 2 indicates that reduction techniques successfully alleviate the state space problem: Depending on the scenario, the generated state space remains small even for hundreds of elements. Naturally, latent faults increase the state space, but then the effectiveness of the approximation increases. Most of the considered measures can be computed within seconds even on the largest models. However, MTDF and SILFO are computationally more expensive, as model checking queries have to be performed for each degraded state. For SILFO, the failure

Table 2. Model characteristics

Scenario						DFT			CTMC		
	SC	Arch.	Adap.	Sens.	Act.	#BE	#Dyn.	#Elem.	#States	#Trans.	Degrad.
I	SC1	B	—	2/4	4/4	76	25	233	5,377	42,753	—
II	SC2	B	—	2/4	4/4	70	23	211	5,953	50,049	19.35%
III	SC2	C	ADAS+	2/4	4/4	57	19	168	1,153	7,681	16.65%
IV	SC3	C	—	2/4	4/4	57	21	170	385	1,985	12.47%
V	SC2	A	—	2/4	4/4	58	19	185	193	897	0.00%
VI	SC2	B	removed I-ECU	2/4	4/4	65	21	199	1,201	8,241	19.98%
VII	SC2	B	5 ADAS, 2 BUS	2/8	7/7	96	30	266	194,433	2,171,905	19.35%
VIII	SC2	B	8 ADAS, 2 BUS	6/8	7/7	114	36	305	3,945,985	66,225,665	10.90%

Table 3. Obtained measures with operational lifetime $= 10{,}000$ h and drive cycle $= 1$ h

Scenario		System			Degradation				
		1-integ.	FIT	MTTF	FFA	FWD	MTDF	MDR	SILFO
I	SC 1/B	1.58E-2	2.49E-6	85,658	–	–	–	–	–
II	SC 2/B	1.02E-2	1.13E-6	341,954	5.17E-2	9.98E-3	227,565	2.88E-1	9.98E-3
III	SC 2/C (ADAS+)	1.21E-2	1.66E-6	111,380	5.23E-2	1.07E-2	20,808	7.35E-1	1.07E-2
IV	SC 3/C	1.02E-2	1.13E-6	284,685	1.58E-2	1.02E-2	135,124	2.14E-1	1.02E-2
V	SC 2/A	5.99E-2	9.29E-6	69,177	5.99E-2	5.99E-2	0	0	5.99E-2
VI	SC 2/B (I-ECU)	1.12E-2	1.23E-6	344,309	5.27E-2	1.10E-2	230,976	2.05E-1	1.10E-2
VII	SC 2/B (5 ADAS)	1.71E-2	1.83E-6	280,228	5.83E-2	1.67E-2	173,305	3.66E-1	1.67E-2
VIII	SC 2/B (8 ADAS)	1.71E-2	1.83E-6	269,305	9.78E-2	1.64E-2	TO	4.34E-1	TO

Table 4. Timings

	I	II	III	IV	V	VI	VII	VIII
Model generation	1.02 s	1.02 s	0.38 s	0.33 s	0.34 s	0.40 s	25.13 s	632.89 s
System + FFA + FWD	0.02 s	0.02 s	0.00 s	0.00 s	0.00 s	0.00 s	1.46 s	46.67 s
MTDF	—	2.67 s	0.18 s	0.03 s	0.02 s	0.20 s	2892.42 s	>3600 s
MDR	—	0.60 s	0.11 s	0.02 s	0.02 s	0.11 s	26.07 s	781.93 s
SILFO	—	1.83 s	0.17 s	0.04 s	0.02 s	0.18 s	1694.91 s	>3600 s

probability within a drive cycle is orders of magnitude smaller than the FWD indicating that the duration of the drive cycle is insignificant for SILFO.

The variety of measures obtained allows some insights in the effect of different safety concepts that go beyond merely meeting specific targets. The MTTF indicates that system integrity of SC3/C and SC2/B are superior, with SC2/B slightly better than SC3/C. A similar claim can be deduced from Fig. 7(a). The differences between SC3/C and SC2/B are marginal. Figure 7(b) indicates that it is not always sufficient to look at the FIT as a measure as the value changes with the considered operation time. The sensitivity shows that the influence of the safety coverage in SC2 is higher than in SC3. Thus, the importance of fault coverage in platforms depends on the chosen architecture. SC2/B and SC3/C differ in their failure behaviour of degraded states as seen in Fig. 7(d). When limiting the driving time in the degraded state to one hour SC2/B offers a

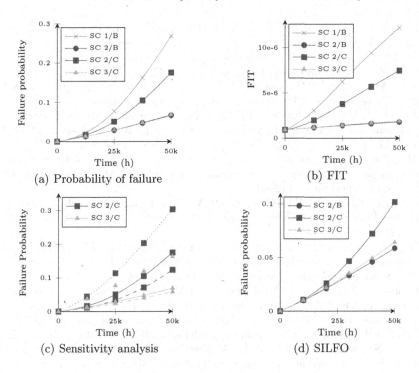

Fig. 7. Analysis results

better integrity than SC3/C, whereas in the overall integrity the difference is marginal.

6   Conclusion

We presented a model-based approach towards the safety analysis of vehicle guidance systems. The approach (see Fig. 1) takes the system functions and their mapping onto the hardware architecture into account. Its main benefit is the flexibility: new partitionings and architectural changes can easily and automatically be accommodated. The obtained DFTs were analysed with probabilistic model checking. Due to tailored state-space generation [5], the analysis of these DFTs—with up to 100 basic events—is a matter of minutes. Future work consists of involved error propagation schemes and a rigorous treatment of transient faults.

References

1. ISO: ISO 26262: Road Vehicles - Functional Safety (2011)
2. Dugan, J.B., Bavuso, S.J., Boyd, M.: Fault trees and sequence dependencies. In: Proceedings of RAMS, pp. 286–293 (1990)

3. Katoen, J.P.: The probabilistic model checking landscape. In: Proceedings of LICS, pp. 31–45. ACM (2016)
4. Ruijters, E., Stoelinga, M.: Fault tree analysis: a survey of the state-of-the-art in modeling, analysis and tools. Comput. Sci. Rev. **15–16**, 29–62 (2015)
5. Volk, M., Junges, S., Katoen, J.P.: Fast dynamic fault tree analysis by model checking techniques. IEEE Trans. Ind. Inform. (2017, to appear)
6. Junges, S., Guck, D., Katoen, J.P., Rensink, A., Stoelinga, M.: Fault trees on a diet: automated reduction by graph rewriting. Formal Asp. Comput. **29**(4), 651–703 (2017)
7. McKelvin, M.L., Sangiovanni-Vincentelli, A.: Fault tree analysis for the design exploration of fault tolerant automotive architectures. SAE International, SAE Technical Paper, pp. 1–8 (2009)
8. Leu, K.L., Chen, J.E., Wey, C.L. Chen, Y.Y.: Generic reliability analysis for safety-critical flexray drive-by-wire systems. In: Proceedings of ICCVE, pp. 216–221 (2012)
9. Rupanov, V., Buckl, C., Fiege, L., Armbruster, M., Knoll, A., Spiegelberg, G.: Employing early model-based safety evaluation to iteratively derive E/E architecture design. Sci. Comput. Program. **90**, 161–179 (2014)
10. Grunske, L., Kaiser, B., Papadopoulos, Y.: Model-driven safety evaluation with state-event-based component failure annotations. In: Heineman, G.T., Crnkovic, I., Schmidt, H.W., Stafford, J.A., Szyperski, C., Wallnau, K. (eds.) CBSE 2005. LNCS, vol. 3489, pp. 33–48. Springer, Heidelberg (2005). doi:10.1007/11424529_3
11. Adler, N., Otten, S., Mohrhard, M., Müller-Glaser, K.D.: Rapid safety evaluation of hardware architectural designs compliant with ISO 26262. In: Proceedings of RSP, pp. 66–72. IEEE (2013)
12. Walker, M., Reiser, M., Piergiovanni, S.T., Papadopoulos, Y., Lönn, H., Mraidha, C., Parker, D., Chen, D., Servat, D.: Automatic optimisation of system architectures using EAST-ADL. J. Syst. Softw. **86**(10), 2467–2487 (2013)
13. Bozzano, M., Cimatti, A., Katoen, J.P., Nguyen, V.Y., Noll, T., Roveri, M.: Safety, dependability and performance analysis of extended AADL models. Comput. J. **54**(5), 754–775 (2011)
14. Leitner-Fischer, F., Leue, S.: QuantUM: quantitative safety analysis of UML models. In: Proceedings of QAPL. EPTCS, vol. 57, pp. 16–30 (2011)
15. Boudali, H., Crouzen, P., Haverkort, B.R., Kuntz, M., Stoelinga, M.: Architectural dependability evaluation with Arcade. In: Proceedings of DSN, pp. 512–521. IEEE (2008)
16. Chen, D.J., Johansson, R., Lönn, H., Papadopoulos, Y., Sandberg, A., Törner, F., Törngren, M.: Modelling support for design of safety-critical automotive embedded systems. In: Harrison, M.D., Sujan, M.-A. (eds.) SAFECOMP 2008. LNCS, vol. 5219, pp. 72–85. Springer, Heidelberg (2008). doi:10.1007/978-3-540-87698-4_9
17. Courtney, T., Gaonkar, S., Keefe, K., Rozier, E., Sanders, W.H.: Möbius 2.3: an extensible tool for dependability, security, and performance evaluation of large and complex system models. In: Proceedings of DSN, pp. 353–358. IEEE (2009)
18. Keefe, K., Sanders, W.H.: Reliability analysis with dynamic reliability block diagrams in the Möbius modeling tool. ICST Trans. Secur. Saf. **3**(10), e3 (2016)
19. Bozzano, M., Cimatti, A., Lisagor, O., Mattarei, C., Mover, S., Roveri, M., Tonetta, S.: Safety assessment of AltaRica models via symbolic model checking. Sci. Comput. Program. **98**, 464–483 (2015)
20. Armoush, A., Salewski, F., Kowalewski, S.: Design pattern representation for safety-critical embedded systems. JSEA **2**(1), 1–12 (2009)

21. Ghadhab, M., Kaienburg, J., Süßkraut, M., Fetzer, C.: Is software coded processing an answer to the execution integrity challenge of current and future automotive software-intensive applications? In: Schulze, T., Müller, B., Meyer, G. (eds.) Advanced Microsystems for Automotive Applications 2015. LNM, pp. 263–275. Springer, Cham (2016). doi:10.1007/978-3-319-20855-8_21
22. Junges, S., Guck, D., Katoen, J.P., Stoelinga, M.: Uncovering dynamic fault trees. In: Proceedings of DSN, pp. 299–310. IEEE (2016)
23. Baier, C., Haverkort, B.R., Hermanns, H., Katoen, J.P.: Performance evaluation and model checking join forces. Commun. ACM **53**(9), 76–85 (2010)
24. Stamatelatos, M., Vesely, W., Dugan, J.B., Fragola, J., Minarick, J., Railsback, J.: Fault Tree Handbook with Aerospace Applications. NASA Headquarters (2002)

Rare Event Simulation for Dynamic Fault Trees

Enno Ruijters[1]([✉]), Daniël Reijsbergen[2], Pieter-Tjerk de Boer[3],
and Mariëlle Stoelinga[1]

[1] Formal Methods and Tools, University of Twente, Enschede, The Netherlands
{e.j.j.ruijters,m.i.a.stoelinga}@utwente.nl
[2] Laboratory for Foundations of Computer Science,
University of Edinburgh, Edinburgh, Scotland
daniel.reijsbergen@gmail.com
[3] Design and Analysis of Communication Systems,
University of Twente, Enschede, The Netherlands
p.t.deboer@utwente.nl

Abstract. Fault trees (FT) are a popular industrial method for reliability engineering, for which Monte Carlo simulation is an important technique to estimate common dependability metrics, such as the system reliability and availability. A severe drawback of Monte Carlo simulation is that the number of simulations required to obtain accurate estimations grows extremely large in the presence of *rare events*, i.e., events whose probability of occurrence is very low, which typically holds for failures in highly reliable systems.

This paper presents a novel method for rare event simulation of dynamic fault trees with complex repairs that requires only a modest number of simulations, while retaining statistically justified confidence intervals. Our method exploits the importance sampling technique for rare event simulation, together with a compositional state space generation method for dynamic fault trees.

We demonstrate our approach using three parameterized sets of case studies, showing that our method can handle fault trees that could not be evaluated with either existing analytical techniques, nor with standard simulation techniques.

1 Introduction

The rapid emergence of robots, drones, the Internet-of-Things, self-driving cars and other inventions, increase our already heavy dependence on computer-based systems even further. Reliability engineering is an important field that provides methods, tools and techniques to identify, evaluate and mitigate the risks related to complex systems. Moreover, asset management is currently shifting towards reliability-centered, a.k.a. risk-based, maintenance. This shift also requires a good understanding of the risk involved in the system, and of the effects of maintenance on the reliability. Fault tree analysis (FTA) is one of the most important techniques in that field, and is commonly deployed in industry ranging from railway and aerospace system engineering to nuclear power plants.

ⓒ Springer International Publishing AG 2017
S. Tonetta et al. (Eds.): SAFECOMP 2017, LNCS 10488, pp. 20–35, 2017.
DOI: 10.1007/978-3-319-66266-4_2

A fault tree (FT) is a graphical model that describes how failures propagate through the system, and how component failures lead to system failures. An FT is a tree (or rather, a directed acyclic graph) whose leaves model component failures, and whose gates model how failures propagate through the system, and lead to system failures. Standard (or: static) FTs (SFTs) contain a few basic gates, like AND and OR, making them easy to use and analyze, but also limited in expressivity. To cater for more complex dependability patterns, like spare management and causal dependencies, a number of extensions to FTs have been proposed.

One of the most widely used extensions is the dynamic fault tree (DFT) ·[7], providing support for common patterns in system design and analysis. More recently, maintenance has been integrated into DFTs supporting complex policies of inspections and repairs [9]. Both of these developments have increased the memory and time needed for analysis, to the point where many practical system cannot be analyzed on current systems in a reasonable time.

One approach to combat the complexity of analysis is to switch from analytic techniques to simulation. By not constructing the entire state space of the system, but only computing states as they are visited, memory requirements are minimal and computation time can be greatly reduced. This approach can be successfully applied to industrial systems [19], but presents a challenge when dealing with highly reliable systems: If failures are very rare, many simulations are required before observing any at all, let alone observing enough to compute statistically justified error bounds.

This problem in simulating systems with rare events can be overcome through rare-event simulation techniques, first developed in the 1950's [11]. By adjusting the probabilities to make failures less rare, and subsequently calculating a correction for this adjustment, statistically justified results can be obtained from far fewer simulations than would otherwise be needed.

We present a novel approach to analyze DFTs with maintenance through importance sampling. We adapt the recently-developed Path-ZVA algorithm [17] to the settings of DFTs. We retain the existing compositional semantics by Boudali et al. [4] already used in current tools [1]. Using three case studies, we show that our approach can simulate DFTs too large for other tools with events too rare for traditional simulation techniques. Thus, our approach has clear benefits over existing numerical tools, and tools without rare event simulation: We can analyze larger DFTs, producing results quicker and obtain narrow confidence intervals.

Related Work. Apart from DFTs and repairs, many more extensions have been developed. For an overview we refer the reader to [20]. Most current FTA formalisms support repairs using per-component repair times [23]. More complicated policies can be specified using repair boxes [2] or the Repairable Fault Tree extension [6], however both of these require exponentially distributed failure times of components where our approach allows Erlang distributions.

A wide range of analysis techniques exist as well, again summarized in [20]. Standard simulation methods date back to 1970 [24], continuing to be developed until the present day [19]. Rare event simulation has been used to estimate system reliability since 1980 [12] and is still applied today [15], although, to our surprise, we are not aware of any approach applying rare event simulation specifically to fault trees. An overview of importance sampling techniques in general can be found in [10].

Organization of the Paper. This paper first explains fault trees, DFTs, and repairable DFTs in Sect. 2. Section 3 describes rare event simulation, and the Path-ZVA algorithm used in our approach. Next, our adaptation of rare event simulation to DFTs is explained in Sect. 4. Our case studies with their results are shown in Sect. 5, before concluding in Sect. 6.

2   Fault Tree Analysis

Fault tree analysis is an industry-standard, widely used method for graphically modeling systems and conducting reliability and safety analysis [23]. Fault trees (FTs) model how component failures interact to cause system failures. They assist in the evaluation of a wide number of dependability metrics, including the system reliability (i.e., the probability that the system fails within its given mission time) and the availability (i.e., the average percentage of time that a system is up).

An FT is a directed acyclic graph where the leaves describe failures modes, called *basic events* (BEs), at a component level. *Gates* specify how the failures of their children combine to cause failures of (sub)systems. The root of the FT, called the *top level event* (TLE), denotes the failure of interest.

Standard, also called *static*, fault trees have boolean connectors as gates. These are the AND-, OR-, and VOT(k)-gates, which fail when all, any, or at least k of their children fail, respectively. The leaves of the tree are typically described with either simple probabilities describing the probability of failing within a time window of interest or the probability of being failed at any particular time, or with exponential failure rates describing the probability of failure before any given time. If components are repairable, the repair time in a standard fault tree is typically also given as an exponential rate.

An example of such a tree is shown in Fig. 1. This FT describes a case study from [9], modeling part of the interlocking system of a railway corridor. It consists of relay and high voltage cabinets, with redundancy to survive the failure of any single cabinet of each type. In the figure, the TLE is the OR-gate at the top. Its children are two VOT(2)-gates and an AND-gate. The leaves of the tree are the BEs describing the failures of individual relay and high voltage cabinets.

Classic quantitative analysis techniques for static fault trees include the computation of: The probability of the TLE before a given time (called the system *reliability*), the expected percentage of time the system is functioning (the *availability*), the components that make the largest contributions to these metrics,

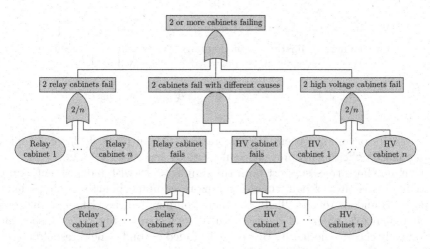

Fig. 1. Example fault tree of the relay cabinet case study. Due to redundancy, the system can survive the failure of any single cabinet, however two failures cause system unavailability. The number of cabinets varies, and is indicated by n.

and the sensitivity of these metrics to the parameters of the BEs. For a more complete overview of analysis techniques, we refer the reader to [20].

2.1 Dynamic and Repairable Fault Trees

Over the years, many extensions to FTs have been developed [20]. One of the most prominent extension is the *dynamic fault trees* (DFT) model [7]. DFTs introduce several new gates to cater for common patterns in dependability models: (1) The priority-AND (PAND) models order-dependent effects of failures. It fails if and only if its left child fails and then its right child. This is used e.g. to model the difference between a fire detector failing before or after a fire starts. (2) The SPARE gate, modeling a primary component with one or more spare elements. The spare elements can have different failure rates when they are in use, and can be shared between multiple gates. Shared spare elements can only be used by one gate at any time. (3) The functional dependency (FDEP) gate which causes all of its children to fail when its trigger fails. It is used e.g. to model common cause failures, such as a power failure disabling many components.

Many practical systems are not just built and then left on their own, instead repairs and maintenance are often performed to keep a system functioning correctly and correct failures when they occur. This maintenance is crucial to the dependability of the system, as it can prevent or delay failures. It is therefore important to consider the maintenance policy when performing reliability analysis.

Standard fault trees support only simple policies of independent repairs with exponentially distributed repair times starting immediately upon component failure [23]. Various extensions provide more complex policies, describing that

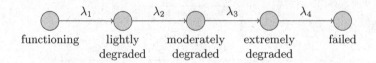

functioning   lightly   moderately   extremely   failed
degraded   degraded   degraded

Fig. 2. Basic event with multiple degradation phases.

some repairs occur in sequential order rather than in parallel [2], or complex maintenance policies with preventive inspections and repairs [18, 19].

Dynamic fault trees support both the simple model with independent, exponentially distributed repair times, and more complex policies with periodic inspections and/or repairs [9]. In the more complex policies, BEs can progress through multiple phases of degradation, as depicted in Fig. 2. An inspection periodically checks whether its BEs have degraded beyond some threshold phase, and returns them to their undegraded phase if they have. A periodic replacement simply returns its BEs to their undegraded phase periodically.

2.2 Compositional Semantics

The analysis used in this paper follows the compositional semantics in terms of input/output interactive Markov chains given in [4]. This compositional approach converts each element of the DFT (i.e., gate and basic event) to an I/O-IMC, and composes these models to obtain one large I/O-IMC for the entire DFT. Intermediate minimization helps keep the size of the state-space to a minimum allowing the analysis of larger models.

Input/Output Interactive Markov Chains. I/O-IMCs are a modeling formalism combining continuous-time Markov chains with discrete actions (also called *signals*). They have the useful property of being composable, as the signals allow several I/O-IMCs to communicate [4].

An example of this composition is shown in Fig. 3. The input signals (denoted by a '?') can only be taken when the corresponding output signal (denoted by '!') is taken. Internal actions (denoted by ';') and Markovian transitions (denoted by Greek letters) are taken independent of the other modules. If multiple non-Markovian transitions can be taken from a state, which transition is taken is nondeterministic.

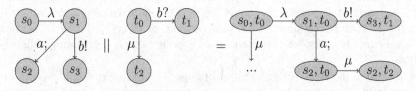

Fig. 3. Example of the partial parallel composition of two I/O-IMCs.

In the example, the component models all begin in their initial states. From t_0 the transition 'b?' cannot be taken unless the output transition 'b!' is also taken, so both initial states can only perform their Markovian transitions. Assuming the leftmost model takes its transition with rate λ first, the composition enters state s_1, t_0. From here, two options are possible: (1) the internal action 'a;' from s_1 to s_2 can be taken, leaving the rightmost model in state t_0, or (2) the output transition 'b!' from s_1 to s_3 can be taken together with the input transition 'b?' from t_0 to t_1. In the latter case, the composed model takes a transition 'b!' allowing it to be composed with yet more models, and enters state s_3, t_1, from which neither component model can take further transitions. If the internal action was taken, the transition from t_0 to t_2 with rate μ remains possible, leading to the terminal state s_2, t_2.

3   Rare Event Simulation

Performance measures in practical problems often depend on events which occur only rarely. Estimating probabilities of such rare events using standard stochastic simulation is not efficient: with a limited amount of available simulation runs, the event of interest will either not be observed at all, or not sufficiently often to draw statistically sound conclusions. To deal with this, rare-event simulation techniques have been developed, which modify the model or the simulation procedure in such a way that the event of interest occurs more frequently, and then compensate mathematically for this modification.

There are two main approaches to rare event simulation, namely *splitting* and *importance sampling*, both of which go back to the early days of computing [11]. In this paper, we use importance sampling; see [10] for a survey. In importance sampling, the probability distributions of the random variables in the model are modified to make the target event occur more frequently. Every time the simulator draws a sample from a random variable, a so-called *likelihood ratio* is updated, to keep track of the error being made. In standard simulation, the estimator for the target probability would be $\hat{\gamma} = \sum_{i=1}^{N} I_i$, where the sum is over all N samples or sample paths drawn, and I_i is the indicator of the target event having occurred on the ith sample(path). In importance sampling, the estimator is changed to $\hat{\gamma} = \sum_{i=1}^{N} I_i L_i$. Here L_i is the likelihood ratio of the ith sample(path), defined as its probability under the original probability measure divided by its probability under the modified measure.

Change of Measure. The challenge in importance sampling is to find a good way to change the probability distribution, also called a *change of measure* (CoM). Generally, transitions (e.g., component failures) that bring the system closer to the target state (e.g., system failure), should be made more likely and vice versa. However, a bad choice can lead to an estimator which is worse than the standard simulation, e.g., by putting too much emphasis on parts of the state space that are not relevant; this can even lead to estimators that are biased or have infinite variance. On the other hand, the theoretically optimal choice leads to an estimator with zero variance. Calculating a zero variance estimator, however, requires that we already know the probability of interest, and is therefore unfeasible.

The Path-ZVA Algorithm. Many different methods have been proposed to find a good change of measure; in this paper, we exploit the Path-ZVA algorithm [16,17]. This algorithm is well suited for DFT simulation since it works fully automated for a large class of Markov chain models with provably good performance, and it does not require the entire state space to be constructed. Rather, the only input needed is a function which, given a state, returns the outgoing transitions, together with the associated rates. The simulator can then estimate probabilities of events of the form "reaching state (or set of states) A, starting from state B, and before returning to state C", where C must be a state that is reached frequently. Also (but related) it can estimate the fraction of time the system spends in states (or set of states) A. In either case, an estimate and a confidence interval are returned. As such, these capabilities of Path-ZVA fit very well to estimating the unavailability of a system composed of several components, as typically described using dynamic fault trees, under the restrictions that there are repairs (so state C in the above can be the state where all components are up), and that all failure and repair processes are Markovian.

Like many other recent algorithms, the Path-ZVA algorithm starts with a numerical approximation of the probability of interest, and then computes a CoM from that approximation, using the formula that could be used for computing the zero-variance CoM if the true probability of interest were known. Some other examples of this approach in the context of modeling highly reliable Markovian systems include [3,14]. All of this builds on parameterizing the model's rates in terms of powers of some rarity parameter ϵ, an idea that goes back to [21] where a heuristic CoM was proposed.

In the case of Path-ZVA, the approximation of the probability of interest consists of summing the contribution of only the most important paths to the event of interest; hence the name Path-ZVA: zero-variance approximation based on exploring these dominant paths. Each possible path to the event of interest consists of a number of transitions of the Markov chain, each of which has a rate parameterized by ϵ. The dominant paths are those whose transitions have the lowest total power of ϵ and are thus dominant in the limit of small ϵ. These are found by running a graph analysis algorithm, which needs to explore only a small subset of the state space (typically several orders of magnitude smaller than the full state space). For more details see [17].

Under mild conditions, it can be proven that the method leads to estimators having the nice property of Bounded Relative Error. This means that as the event of interest gets rarer due to rates in the model being chosen smaller, the estimator's confidence interval width shrinks proportionally with the probability of interest, making its *relative* error bounded (cf. [13]).

Other Approaches. Compared to other importance sampling based approaches, (e.g. [5,14,21]) the Path-ZVA has the advantage of dealing well with models having so-called high-probability cycles and having provable efficiency properties in the limit of very small ϵ, thus avoiding the issues of bias and large or infinite variance mentioned above.

Splitting-based approaches have not been considered in this paper because they tend to be less suitable for models where the rare target event is reached via only a few transitions each having a low rate, since such models provide fewer points where sample paths can be split.

4   Rare Event Simulation for Fault Trees

To develop a rare event simulation technique for repairable FTs and DFTs, we need to convert the FT into a Markov chain. For this purpose, we follow the semantics of [4], describing the behavior of a DFT as an I/O-IMC. A major benefit of this approach is that the I/O-IMC is not constructed as one large model, but as a parallel composition of many smaller I/O-IMCs, each modeling one element (i.e., gate, basic event, or maintenance module) of the DFT.

Overall, given a DFT, our analysis technique consists of the following steps:

1. Use DFTCalc to compute I/O-IMCs for all elements of the DFT.
2. Perform a breadth-first search of the Markovianized composition (explained in Sects. 2.2 and 4.1) of these elements to identify the smallest number of rare transitions needed to reach a failed state, called d.
3. Continue the breadth-first search to find all paths that reach a failed state within d rare transitions.
4. Apply the Path-ZVA algorithm (explained in Sect. 3) to adjust the transition probabilities and compute the corresponding likelihood ratios. Since only the above-mentioned paths receive altered probabilities, the rest of the model can be computed on-the-fly.
5. Sample traces of the adjusted model, ending each trace when it returns to the initial state, storing the likelihood ratio, total time, and time spent in unavailable (i.e., failed) states.
6. Average the total time $\overline{D}$ and unavailable time $\overline{Z}$ of the traces, multiplied by the likelihood ratios. Now $\overline{Z}/\overline{D}$ is the output estimated unavailability.

4.1   Reducing I/O-IMCs to Markov Chains

In most settings, I/O-IMCs are analyzed by computing the parallel composition of the full system, and analyzing this model using a standard model checker [1]. Our setting often produces models too large to compute the full parallel composition, so we use Monte Carlo simulation in which we can compute visited states on-the-fly.

Our technique requires that the (composed) I/O-IMC be reduced to a Markov Chain, which means removing any non-Markovian transitions. In our process, while computing the outgoing transition from a state after composition, we immediately take any non-Markovian transition we encounter. Thus we are only left with states with only Markovian transitions, which can be used as an input for the Monte Carlo simulation.

This process leaves undefined which transition is taken in nondeterministic states. In most reasonable DFT models, the only source of nondeterminism is the order in which gates fail when an element has multiple parents. Such nondeterminism is spurious, in that it has no effect on the outcome of the analysis. It is therefore acceptable to leave the exact resolution undefined.

In models where nondeterminism can actually affect the results of the analysis, our determinisation is clearly not desirable. We therefore apply our analysis only on DFTs in which a syntactic check rules out the possibility of non-spurious nondeterminism. In particular, we require the children of PAND or SPARE gates to be entirely independent subtrees. We have found that in practice, most DFTs in the literature already satisfy this condition.

4.2   Tooling

For our analysis, we use the models of the DFT elements produced by DFTCalc, as well as its description of how to compose them. This way, we ensure that our semantics are identical to those used in the existing analysis.

DFTCalc produces IMCs for the DFT elements, and a specification describing how the IMCs are composed. It then uses the CADP [8] tool to generate the composed IMC which can be analyzed by a stochastic model checker.

FTRES instead uses the models and composition specification to generate the composition on the fly and apply the importance sampling algorithm to compute the unavailability of the model.

5   Case Studies

To investigate the effectiveness our method, we compare FTRES to both a standard Monte Carlo simulator (MC) without importance sampling built into FTRES, and to the DFTCalc tool, which evaluates DFTs numerically via stochastic model checking. We analyze three case studies, for a number of different parameters. The first case is an industrial case study from railway signaling [9]. The second and third cases model a fault-tolerant parallel processor (FTPP) [7] and a hypothetical example computer system (HECS) [22], both well-known benchmarks from the literature.

Experimental Setup. For each of the cases, we compute the unavailability (exact for DFTCalc, 95% confidence interval for FTRES and MC). We measure the time taken with a time-out of 48 h, and the memory consumption in number of states (which is negligible for MC). For DFTCalc we measure both peak and final memory consumption. Simulations by FTRES and MC were performed for 10 min.

For the railway cabinets and FTPP cases, we model the failure times of the basic events via an Erlang distribution where the number of phases P is a parameter ranging from 1 to 3 phases; clearly, $P = 1$ corresponds to the exponential distribution. For the HECS case, basic events are exponentially distributed.

All experiments were conducted on a dual 2.26 GHz Intel® Xeon® E5520 processor and 24 GB of RAM.

5.1 Railway Cabinets

This case models a redundant system of relays and high-voltage cabinets used in railway signaling and provided by the consultancy company Movares [9].

The FT, shown in Fig. 1, describes the relays and high voltage systems controlling a railway section. The relays are used to interface the electrically-powered systems such as switch motors with remote operating stations. They are also crucial for the safety of the trains, as they prevent multiple signals allowing trains onto already-occupied tracks, switches moving while trains are passing, and other safety violations. The high voltage cabinets provide power for local systems such as switches and signals.

We consider several variants of the FT for given parameter values. We augment the FT with a periodic inspection restoring any degraded basic events to perfect conditions. The time between executions of this action is governed by an Erlang distribution with two phases, and a mean time of half a year. We vary the number of cabinets in the system from 2 to 4.

Table 1 shows the results of the FTRES and DFTCalc and the MC tool. We note that, whenever DFTCalc is able to compute an analytic result, this result lies within the confidence interval computed by FTRES. We further see that the 2-phase models with 4 cabinets, and the 3-phase models with 3 or 4 cabinets could not be computed by DFTCalc within the time-out (times shown in Fig. 4), while FTRES still produces usable results. Finally, while the standard Monte Carlo simulation produces reasonable results for the smaller models, on the larger models it computes much larger confidence intervals. For the largest models, the MC simulator observed no failures at all, and thus computed an unavailability of 0.

Figure 6 shows the generated state spaces for both tools. Since FTRES only needs an explicit representation of the shortest paths to failure, it can operate in substantially less memory than DFTCalc. Although the final model computed by DFTCalc is smaller due to its bisimulation minimization, the intermediate models are often much larger.

5.2 Fault-Tolerant Parallel Processor

The second case study is taken from the DFT literature [7], and concerns a fault-tolerant parallel computer system. This system consists of four groups of processors, labeled A, B, C, and S. The processors within a group are connected by a network element, independent for each group. A failure of this network element disables all connected processors.

Table 1. Comparison of the unavailabilities computed by DFTCalc, FTRES, and MC simulation for the case studies with N cabinets/processor groups.

	N	P	Unavailability		
			DFTCalc	FTRES	MC
Railway cabinets	2	1	$4.25685 \cdot 10^{-4}$	$[4.256; 4.258] \cdot 10^{-4}$	$[4.239; 4.280] \cdot 10^{-4}$
	3	1	$7.71576 \cdot 10^{-4}$	$[7.713; 7.716] \cdot 10^{-4}$	$[7.694; 7.751] \cdot 10^{-4}$
	4	1	$1.99929 \cdot 10^{-3}$	$[1.998; 2.000] \cdot 10^{-3}$	$[1.999; 2.004] \cdot 10^{-4}$
	2	2	$4.55131 \cdot 10^{-8}$	$[4.548; 4.555] \cdot 10^{-8}$	$[1.632; 4.387] \cdot 10^{-8}$
	3	2	$6.86125 \cdot 10^{-8}$	$[6.846; 6.873] \cdot 10^{-8}$	$[0.673; 1.304] \cdot 10^{-7}$
	4	2	—	$[2.358; 2.394] \cdot 10^{-7}$	$[2.282; 3.484] \cdot 10^{-7}$
	2	3	$5.97575 \cdot 10^{-12}$	$[5.714; 6.252] \cdot 10^{-12}$	—
	3	3	—	$[5.724; 7.914] \cdot 10^{-12}$	—
	4	3	—	$[0.337; 1.871] \cdot 10^{-11}$	—
FTPP	1	1	$2.18303 \cdot 10^{-10}$	$[2.182; 2.184] \cdot 10^{-10}$	—
	2	1	$2.19861 \cdot 10^{-10}$	$[2.198; 2.199] \cdot 10^{-10}$	—
	3	1	$2.21420 \cdot 10^{-10}$	$[2.213; 2.215] \cdot 10^{-10}$	—
	4	1	$2.22979 \cdot 10^{-10}$	$[2.229; 2.230] \cdot 10^{-10}$	$[0; 2.140] \cdot 10^{-8}$
	1	2	$1.76174 \cdot 10^{-20}$	$[1.761; 1.763] \cdot 10^{-20}$	—
	2	2	$1.76178 \cdot 10^{-20}$	$[1.756; 1.770] \cdot 10^{-20}$	—
	3	2	—	$[1.673; 1.856] \cdot 10^{-20}$	—
	4	2	—	$[1.257; 2.553] \cdot 10^{-20}$	—
	N	k	DFTCalc	FTRES	MC
HECS	1	1	$4.12485 \cdot 10^{-5}$	$[4.118; 4.149] \cdot 10^{-5}$	$[2.615; 10.64] \cdot 10^{-5}$
	2	1	—	$[3.010; 3.061] \cdot 10^{-9}$	—
	2	2	—	$[8.230; 8.359] \cdot 10^{-5}$	$[0; 1.734] \cdot 10^{-4}$
	3	1	—	$[3.024; 3.213] \cdot 10^{-13}$	—
	3	2	—	$[8.853; 9.106] \cdot 10^{-9}$	—
	3	3	—	$[1.230; 1.261] \cdot 10^{-4}$	$[0; 1.267] \cdot 10^{-4}$
	4	1	—	$[1.328; 8.213] \cdot 10^{-17}$	—
	4	2	—	$[1.145; 1.270] \cdot 10^{-12}$	—
	4	3	—	$[1.744; 1.817] \cdot 10^{-8}$	—
	4	4	—	$[1.609; 1.667] \cdot 10^{-4}$	—

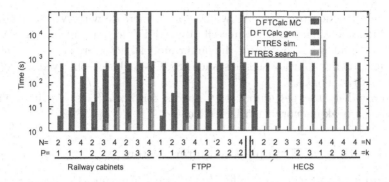

Fig. 4. Processing times for the different tools: Times for model generation and model checking for DFTCalc, and for the graph search and simulation for FTRES. Bars reaching the top of the graph reached the time-out. Most bars for the HECS case study omitted as they all timed out.

The system also has several workstations, each of which contains one processor of each group. A workstation normally uses processors A, B, and C. Processor S is used as a spare when one of the others fails. If more than one processor fails, the workstation is down (Fig. 5).

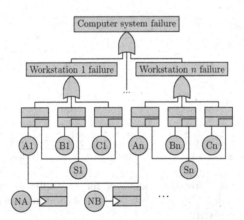

Fig. 5. DFT of the fault-tolerant parallel processor. Connections between the FDEP for B omitted for clarity, as well as the FDEPs for groups C and S.

Repairs are conducted by a periodic replacement which restores any degraded components to perfect condition. This replacement occurs at times following an Erlang distribution of four phases, with a mean time of 0.5 for each phase.

The numerical results and computation times for this case study can be found in Table 1 and Fig. 4 respectively. We note that the unavailability varies little when increasing the number of computer groups, as the dominant sources of failures are the network elements which do not increase with N. We again see that FTRES continues to perform well after DFTCalc runs out of time. We do see wider confidence intervals for the larger models, however the results remain usable for practical purposes. The standard MC simulation observed no failures for most of the models.

Figure 6 lists the generated state spaces for both tools. Again, FTRES requires less peak memory than DFTCalc.

5.3   Hypothetical Example Computer System

Our third example considers the Hypothetical Example Computer System (HECS) used in [22] as an example of how to model a system in a DFT. It consists of a processing unit with three processors, of which one is a spare, of which only one is required to be functional. It further contains five memory units of which three must be functional, two buses of which one must be functional, and hardware and software components of an operator interface.

We parameterize this example by replicating the HECS N times, and requiring k of these replicas to be functional to avoid the top level event. The basic events in this case remain exponentially distributed, and we add maintenance as a periodic replacement of all failed components on average every 8 time units (on a 2-phase Erlang distribution).

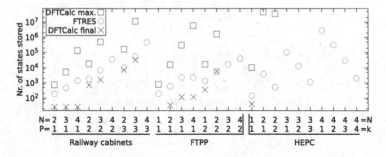

Fig. 6. Numbers of states stored in memory for the different cases with N cabinets/processor groups. For DFTCalc, both the largest intermediate and the final (minimized) state spaces are given.

As for the other cases, Table 1 lists the numeric values computed by the tools, while Figs. 4 and 6 show the processing time and state spaces computed, respectively. We notice that except for the simplest case, DFTCalc is unable to compute the availability within 48 h, and the MC simulator in many cases failed to observe any failures, and produced very wide confidence intervals in the cases where it did. FTRES, on the other hand, produced reasonable confidence intervals for all cases (although the interval for the $(4, 1)$ case is fairly wide, it also has the largest state space and a very small unavailability).

5.4   Conclusions on Case Studies

As the sections above show, FTRES outperforms DFTCalc for larger models, and traditional MC simulation for models with rare failures. In particular, FTRES:

- requires less memory than DFTCalc in every case, and requires less time for large models, while still achieving high accuracy.
- can analyze models larger than DFTCalc can handle.
- gives substantially more accurate results than MC in similar processing time.

6   Conclusion

We have presented FTRES, an efficient and novel approach for rare-event simulation of dynamic fault trees through importance sampling. We follow the compositional semantics of Boudali et al. [4] providing flexibility and extensibility. Our use of the Path-ZVA [17] algorithm allows us to store only a small fraction of the state space, ameliorating the problem of the state space explosion.

We have demonstrated through three case studies that our approach has clear benefits over existing numerical tools, and tools without rare event simulation: We can analyze larger DFTs, produce results quicker and obtain narrow confidence intervals.

As future work, we intend to extend the tool to support non-spurious nondeterminism, allowing the analysis of the full space of DFTs.

Acknowledgments. This research was partially funded by STW and ProRail under project ArRangeer (grant 12238) with participation by Movares, STW project SEQUOIA (15474), NWO project BEAT (612001303), NWO project SamSam (50918239) and the EU project grant SUCCESS (651.002.001/1467).

References

1. Arnold, F., Belinfante, A., Berg, F., Guck, D., Stoelinga, M.I.A.: DFTCALC: a tool for efficient fault tree analysis. In: Bitsch, F., Guiochet, J., Kaâniche, M. (eds.) SAFECOMP 2013. LNCS, vol. 8153, pp. 293–301. Springer, Heidelberg (2013). doi:10.1007/978-3-642-40793-2_27
2. Bobbio, A., Codetta-Raiteri, D.: Parametric fault trees with dynamic gates and repair boxes. In: Proceedings of the 2004 Annual IEEE Reliability and Maintainability Symposium (RAMS), pp. 459–465 (2004)
3. de Boer, P.T., L'Ecuyer, P., Rubino, G., Tuffin, B.: Estimating the probability of a rare event over a finite time horizon. In: Proceedings of the 2007 Winter Simulation Conference, pp. 403–411. IEEE Press (2007)
4. Boudali, H., Crouzen, P., Stoelinga, M.I.A.: A rigorous, compositional, and extensible framework for dynamic fault tree analysis. IEEE Trans. Depend. Secur. Comput. **7**(2), 128–143 (2010)
5. Carrasco, J.A.: Failure transition distance-based importance sampling schemes for the simulation of repairable fault-tolerant computer systems. IEEE Trans. Reliab. **55**(2), 207–236 (2006)

6. Codetta-Raiteri, D., Franceschinis, G., Iacono, M., Vittorini, V.: Repairable fault tree for the automatic evaluation of repair policies. In: Proceedings of the Annual IEEE/IFIP International Conference on Dependable Systems and Networks (DSN), pp. 659–668 (2004)
7. Dugan, J.B., Bavuso, S.J., Boyd, M.A.: Fault trees and sequence dependencies. In: Proceedings of the 1990 Annual IEEE Reliability and Maintainability Symposium (RAMS) (1990)
8. Garavel, H., Lang, F., Mateescu, R., Serwe, W.: CADP 2011: a toolbox for the construction and analysis of distributed processes. Int. J. Softw. Tools Technol. Transf. 15(2), 89–107 (2013)
9. Guck, D., Spel, J., Stoelinga, M.I.A.: DFTCalc: reliability centered maintenance via fault tree analysis (tool paper). In: Butler, M., Conchon, S., Zaïdi, F. (eds.) ICFEM 2015. LNCS, vol. 9407, pp. 304–311. Springer, Cham (2015). doi:10.1007/978-3-319-25423-4_19
10. Heidelberger, P.: Fast simulation of rare events in queueing and reliability models. In: Donatiello, L., Nelson, R. (eds.) Performance/SIGMETRICS 1993. LNCS, vol. 729, pp. 165–202. Springer, Heidelberg (1993). doi:10.1007/BFb0013853
11. Kahn, H., Harris, T.: Estimation of particle transmission by random sampling. In: Monte Carlo Method; Proceedings of the Symposium, 29–30 June–1 July 1949. National Bureau of Standards: Applied Mathematics Series, vol. 12, pp. 27–30 (1951)
12. Kumamoto, H., Tanaka, K., Inoue, K., Henley, E.J.: Dagger-sampling Monte Carlo for system unavailability evaluation. IEEE Trans. Reliab. R–29(2), 122–125 (1980)
13. L'Ecuyer, P., Blanchet, J., Tuffin, B., Glynn, P.: Asymptotic robustness of estimators in rare-event simulation. ACM Trans. Model. Comput. Simul. (TOMACS) 20(1) (2010). doi:10.1145/1667072.1667078. Article No. 6
14. L'Ecuyer, P., Tuffin, B.: Approximating zero-variance importance sampling in a reliability setting. Ann. Oper. Res. 189(1), 277–297 (2011)
15. Ramakrishnan, M.: Unavailability estimation of shutdown system of a fast reactor by Monte Carlo simulation. Ann. Nucl. Energy 90, 264–274 (2016)
16. Reijsbergen, D.P.: Efficient simulation techniques for stochastic model checking. Ph.D. thesis, University of Twente, Enschede, December 2013
17. Reijsbergen, D.P., de Boer, P., Scheinhardt, W., Juneja, S.: Path-ZVA: general, efficient and automated importance sampling for highly reliable Markovian systems. ACM Trans. Model. Comput. Simul. (TOMACS) (submitted)
18. Ruijters, E., Guck, D., Drolenga, P., Peters, M., Stoelinga, M.: Maintenance analysis and optimization via statistical model checking. In: Agha, G., Houdt, B. (eds.) QEST 2016. LNCS, vol. 9826, pp. 331–347. Springer, Cham (2016). doi:10.1007/978-3-319-43425-4_22
19. Ruijters, E., Guck, D., Drolenga, P., Stoelinga, M.I.A.: Fault maintenance trees: reliability centered maintenance via statistical model checking. In: Proceedings of the IEEE 62nd Annual Reliability and Maintainability Symposium (RAMS), January 2016
20. Ruijters, E., Stoelinga, M.I.A.: Fault tree analysis: a survey of the state-of-the-art in modeling, analysis and tools. Comput. Sci. Rev. 15–16, 29–62 (2015)
21. Shahabuddin, P.: Importance sampling for the simulation of highly reliable Markovian systems. Manag. Sci. 40, 333–352 (1994)
22. Stamatelatos, M., Vesely, W., Dugan, J.B., Fragola, J., Minarick, J., Railsback, J.: Fault tree handbook with aerospace applications. Office of safety and Mission Assurance NASA Headquarters (2002)

23. Vesely, W.E., Goldberg, F.F., Roberts, N.H., Haasl, D.F.: Fault Tree Handbook. Office of Nuclear Regulatory Reasearch, U.S. Nuclear Regulatory Commision (1981)
24. Vesely, W.E., Narum, R.E.: PREP and KITT: computer codes for the automatic evaluation of a fault tree. Technical report, Idaho Nuclear Corp. (1970)

Safety Case and Argumentation

Arguing on Software-Level Verification Techniques Appropriateness

Carmen Cârlan[1(✉)], Barbara Gallina[2], Severin Kacianka[3], and Ruth Breu[4]

[1] fortiss GmbH, Munich, Germany
carlan@fortiss.org
[2] Mälardalen University, Västerås, Sweden
barbara.gallina@mdh.se
[3] Technische Universität München, Garching, Germany
kacianka@in.tum.de
[4] Institut für Informatik, Innsbruck, Austria
ruth.breu@uibk.ac.at

Abstract. In this paper, we investigate the pondered selection of innovative software verification technology in the safety-critical domain and its implications. Verification tools perform analyses, testing or simulation activities. The compliance of the techniques implemented by these tools to fulfill standard-mandated objectives (i.e., to be means of compliance in the context of DO-178C and related supplements) should be explained to the certification body. It is thereby difficult for practitioners to use novel techniques, without a systematic method for arguing their appropriateness. Thus, we offer a method for arguing the appropriate application of a certain verification technique (potentially in combination with other techniques) to produce the evidence needed to satisfy certification objectives regarding fault detection and mitigation in a realistic avionics application via safety cases. We use this method for the choice of an appropriate compiler to support the development of a drone.

Keywords: Safety cases · Faults · Standard compliance · Verification techniques

1 Introduction

For the certification of safety-critical systems, safety engineers are frequently required to present a safety case of the system. A safety case is *a documented body of evidence that provides a convincing and valid argument that a system is adequately safe for a given application in a given environment* [3]. The certification authority investigates the confidence in the claims of a safety case, namely the probability of the claim being true [3]. This probability depends on how uncertainties regarding the safety case (e.g., regarding the evidence expected to support the claims) are handled. For example, one uncertainty regards the correctness of the implementation. This uncertainty lays in the verification procedure and is caused by (1) uncertainty in the correct implementation of the

© Springer International Publishing AG 2017
S. Tonetta et al. (Eds.): SAFECOMP 2017, LNCS 10488, pp. 39–54, 2017.
DOI: 10.1007/978-3-319-66266-4_3

verification tool – *Can the output of the tool be trusted?*, (2) uncertainty in the rationale of the verification technique – *Is this the right way for verifying the fulfillment of system requirements?* [7]. Thus, in order to employ a state-of-the-art verification tool, the engineer needs to assess the *appropriateness* of the technique it implements. A technique is *appropriate* if it provides *trustworthy* and *relevant* verification results. Considerable research effort has been put into the investigation of arguing tool assurance (i.e., integrity and qualification according to standard) [7]. Safety standards provide certain objectives techniques must satisfy. These objectives are typically used in industry in form of checklists for the selection of verification techniques. However, the standards do not clarify (1) why the objectives contribute to demonstrate the confidence in results and (2) how they relate to the characteristics of the verification technique that must achieve them. For example, before DO-333 [22], it was unknown (1) what was the relevance of this objective for the system's safety, and (2) how the testing structural coverage objective could be addressed with a formal verification technique. This problem has been dealt with by supplements providing guidance on how to adapt these innovative technologies to a DO-178C project (e.g., DO-333 Formal Methods Supplement). However, the creation of such supplements can take years. One of the main causes for this is that little is known about arguing whether a technique is appropriate to support a given activity. The appropriateness of a technique is its quality to satisfy the corresponding objectives. Thus, in this paper, we take on the problem of *appropriately employing verification techniques for the construction of systems according to a specific level of stringency, specified via an assurance level (AL)*.

This paper's contribution at tackling this problem is three-fold. First, we offer an alternative for the pondered selection of verification techniques. *Pondered selection* means a selection of techniques, based on how they are contributing to typical systematic failure avoidance. We achieve this by extending the Structured Assurance Case Metamodel (SACM) [19]. Second, we describe relationship types between heterogeneous verification results collaborating to the achievement of one safety goal. Third, based on this meta-model, we provide safety case patterns for arguing the appropriateness of a certain technique.

In Sect. 2, we provide the context of our problem statement. In Sect. 3, we present our metamodel. Then, in Sect. 4, we present a set of safety case patterns that help with the pondered selection of a certain verification technique for the performance of a certain activity. We evaluate our approach by instantiating the proposed metamodel to assess the appropriateness of the results from a compiler, performed on a drone (see Sect. 5). The last two sections contain related work and conclusions.

2   Background

The development of safety-critical systems is guided by standards. In avionics, it is recommended that software developers reach the objectives defined in the **DO-178C** de-facto standard [21]. DO-178C is technology-independent, abstractly defining development and verification activities to be performed. For each activity, it defines a set of objectives that need to be satisfied by concrete verification techniques. How these objectives are to be fulfilled is up to concrete means of compliance. A means of compliance is the technique that the developer uses to satisfy the objectives stated in the standard [21]. The certification authority needs to agree on the means of compliance proposed by the developer. Techniques of the software verification process need to be proposed during the certification liaison process. The verification process has two purposes: (1) show that the system implements its safety requirements and (2) detect and report faults that may have been introduced during the software development processes. DO-178C focuses on analysis, reviews and software testing techniques for performing verification activities. Whereas its supplement DO-333 [22] provides guidance for using formal methods (e.g., abstract interpretation, model checking, theorem-proving and satisfiability solving) in the certification of airborne systems. The supplement modifies DO-178C objectives, activities, and software life cycle data to address when formal methods are used as part of the software development process.

The Object Management Group offers a standardized modeling language for describing safety cases: the **Structured Assurance Case Metamodel (SACM)** 2.0 [19]. SACM contains a structured way of describing evidence-related efforts, namely the Artefact Metamodel. The Artefact Metamodel contains classes depicting the following: artefacts, participants, resources, activities, and techniques. The *Activity* class represents units of work related to the management of *ArtefactAssets*. The *Technique* class describes the techniques performing the activities. For example, the *Verification of Low-level Requirements* activity, from DO-178C/DO-333, may be performed either via a testing technique (e.g., unit testing) or a formal analysis technique (e.g., theorem proving). There are three types of evidence in safety cases, namely *direct*, *backing* and *reinforcement* [24]. Whereas direct evidence refers to proofs that the system under certification meets the safety goal, the backing evidence proves that the direct evidence can be used in the argumentation with confidence [1,16]. In order to justify the confidence, the relevance of the evidence serves as a proof of safety claim's satisfaction [24]. The relevance of an evidence type is assessed by documenting the *role* and *limitations* of the underlying technique. Such limitations may be that the verification technique is not able to cover the entire input space or to identify deep faults due to insufficient unrolling. This information helps to make an informed decision when choosing a type of evidence for satisfying a certain claim [16].

3   Pondering the Selection of Verification Techniques

In this section, we propose guidelines for the selection of techniques in order to fulfill verification objectives of DO-178C/DO-333. We propose a metamodel that offers a description of standard-mandated compliance and considers the relationships between standard objectives, software verification techniques and safety evidence. Our metamodel extends the SACM Artefact Metamodel. We refine the *Technique* and *Activity* classes in the SACM metamodel, by *Verification Technique* and, respectively, *Verification Activity* classes (see Fig. 1).

Next, we will explain the attributes pallet of our proposed SACM *Verification Technique* class, depicted in Fig. 1. These attributes enable the characterization of the appropriateness of a verification technique. Some of the attributes come from the objectives a technique needs to fulfill in order to be employed for a DO-178C/DO-333-compliant activity (e.g., structural coverage). Additional attributes are taken from specialized literature depicting safety verification techniques (e.g., works such as [2,23]). These attributes are taken into consideration during safety assurance, but have not been documented in the standard and are typically not included in checklists, since they are considered implicit attributes (e.g., technique soundness). Explicitly addressing these attributes helps at taking an informed decision and to build a convincing argument for the technique appropriateness. For some of the described attributes, we provide enumerations of the values the attributes can take. The permitted values are extracted from the standard.

Any verification technique has a certain name, which uniquely identifies it (see *techniqueName* attribute). Verification techniques address different verification objectives because of their different rationale. Thus, the *Verification Tech-*

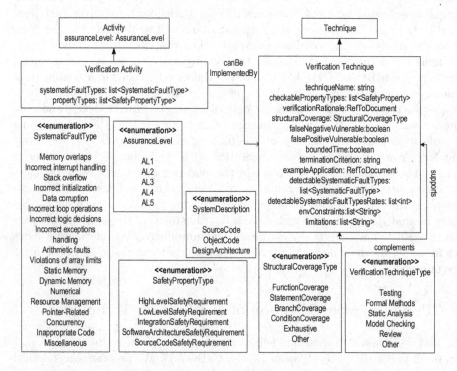

Fig. 1. A meta-model for depicting verification techniques and activities

nique class should contain an attribute referencing a description of the rationale (see the *verificationRationale* attribute). Documenting the context is required when assessing how appropriate the technique is and indicates the feasibility of the technique's application. For instance, the *exampleApplication* attribute, referencing projects which already made use of the technique, can only be used if the verification's context is similar. The context includes the constraints on the environment of the system (see *envConstraints*) [4]. This attribute ensures that the technique is appropriate for verifying the system, in the context in which the system is supposed to work.

No unique technique can cover all objectives of the verification process. For example, the rationale of **testing** techniques is to execute the code to reveal faults. However, testing has its limitations. One limitation is that testing techniques may detect concurrency faults, but overall, the level of confidence about the quality of the code is not high. This is due to the fact that concurrent software is inherently non-deterministic. Thus, it is necessary to describe the objectives of the verification technique, namely the types of properties it can check (see *checkablePropertyTypes* attribute). The *checkablePropertyTypes* attribute enumerates all the standard-mandated properties the respective technique can cover.

Static analysis takes all thread execution pathways and deployment scenarios into account. Thus, **static analysis** verification techniques are more appropriate for discovering and diagnosing concurrency faults. Hence, it is important to know to what extent the scope may be verified by the technique (i.e., number of explored states or loop unrolling). Thus, we add to the *VerificationTechnique* class the *structuralCoverage* attribute. Static analysis techniques have the benefit of verifying the system's code exhaustively. However, they also have their limitations, which need to be specified, understood and assessed for the fulfillment of an objective (see *limitations* attribute). In the *Verification Technique* class we suggest possible limitations of verification techniques. One possible limitation is the detection of false negatives (see attribute *falseNegativeVulnerable*). This does not affect the certification process per se, but it delays the process, since the safety engineer might investigate an error which does not exist. Another limitation may be that a verification technique verifies a property and may say that the property is satisfied, when it is not. Such techniques are unsound. We capture this limitation in the *falsePositiveVulnerable* boolean attribute. Example of false-positives is when a test result wrongly indicates that a particular condition or attribute is present. Unsound techniques cannot be used in the verification process of safety-critical systems, since they may be harmful. For example, the consequences of falsely confirming that a state is reachable may be catastrophic. Thus, verification techniques that have the *falsePositiveVulnerable* attribute set to "true" may not be used for employing safety verification activities. Furthermore, a frequent type of limitation, which is specific to model checking techniques, is the fact that the verification might not terminate in due time. In such cases, model checking cannot be set to explore all the states due to their large number: large number of states makes the verification last longer than feasible (see the boolean *boundedTime* attribute). If the *boundedTime* attribute is true, the *terminationCriterion* attribute should also be set, in order to know when the verification is supposed to stop and to know up to which length counterexamples have been searched.

The verification process is described by DO-178C as a process for discovering faults. Thus, in order to analyze a verification technique, it is important to know what types of faults it may uncover - *detectableSystematicFaultTypes* (e.g., arithmetic faults, violations of array limits). In studies presenting tools checked against benchmarks, there is a so called defect rate, which refers to the percentage of erroneous tests. The *detectableSystematicFaultTypesRates* attribute of the *Verification Technique* class offers a quantitative assessment of how a selected technique is better than others. Each element from the *detectableSystematic-FaultTypesRates* list corresponds to the element with the same position from the *detectableSystematicFaultTypes* list.

This metamodel describes a set of traces between two different aspects of safety argumentation artefacts: the verification activity and the verification technique (see Fig. 1). These traces enable the assessment of the appropriateness of a technique for performing some activity. The *Verification Activity* class, depicted in Fig. 1, offers a general structure for depicting any verification activities in DO-178C. The attributes of this class are derived from the structure of these verification activities. As presented in [11], every development activity, including verification activities, has an assurance level. In the context of DO-333 it is called assurance level (AL). Thus, we add to the *Activity* class the *assuranceLevel* attribute. The *Activity* class also depicts the typical faults that are to be identified and mitigated during the referred activity type (see the attribute *systematicFaults*). The *propertyTypes*, which must be achieved by the verification process, given the assurance level, are indicated by *Tables A 3–6*, in DO-178C. A verification technique is appropriate to perform a certain verification activity (see *canBeImplementedBy* relationship), if the technique is able to check *at least some* of the *propertyTypes* required by the activity to be checked (i.e., the set *checkablePropertyTypes* of the technique is at least a subset of the *propertyTypes* set of the activity), applicable by the *assuranceLevel*. Also, the technique should be able to detect *at least some* of the *systematicFaultTypes* specified by the activity (i.e., the set *detectableSystematicFaultTypes* of the technique is at least a subset of the *systematicFaultTypes* set of the activity). However, a technique may only be able to check *certain* properties or to identify *certain* faults. Different techniques may be combined in order to perform a verification activity. For example, in Cârlan et al. [6], we present a testing technique and a model checker collaborating for discharging verification goals.

Heterogeneous Verification Techniques. Evidence tends to be incomplete (e.g., a single test case, or model checking of a single property). In this situation, multiple items of evidence are needed. In Fig. 1, we document and reason about the relationships between the heterogeneous verification techniques generating evidence items. One type of relationships is *supports*. This relationship covers the case where a verification technique is used to assess the fulfillment of an objective by the results of another verification technique. Techniques in a *supports* relationship work orthogonally, addressing different concerns – one discharges safety goals, the other is used to verify the results discharging the safety goals, in order to assess the trustworthiness of the evidence provided by the first technique. Thus, a verification technique *supports* another if it is used to detect faults in the other's verification results, by providing *backing* evidence. For example, a model checking technique may support a static analysis technique by verifying the faults detected [5]. The other relationship type is *complements*. This relation represents two verification techniques that collaborate for providing relevant evidence for discharging together safety goals. On the one hand, a verification technique may complement another if it is used to detect the faults not identified by the other. On the other hand, a verification technique complements another technique if it is able to verify types of requirements which cannot be verified by the other technique. Both of the techniques provide *direct* evidence. For example, verifying a set of properties via bounded model checking, combined with testing [6].

4   A Pattern for Arguing Technique Appropriateness

In the system's safety cases, the developer has to argue that the verification results are *trustworthy* and *relevant*. As mentioned in Sect. 1, this enables the assessor to have confidence in the results. The techniques associated with the creation, inspection, review or analysis of assurance artefacts contribute to the level of relevance of the safety case evidence [8,19]. In this section, we offer a pattern for arguing the appropriateness of verification techniques, driven by the need to deliver relevant safety evidence. We call this argumentation structure the *technique appropriateness* argument pattern. Each element of the pattern relates to an attribute of our proposed metamodel. The attributes from the metamodel are italicized in the safety claims. The fact that the pattern is based on the metamodel eases the (semi-)automatic pattern instantiation.

The top-level goal of the pattern depicted in Fig. 2 is that the technique implemented by the tool employed in the execution/automation of a certain activity is appropriate for generating activity outputs ($G1$). Goal $G1$ may only be satisfied if the technique is sound ($C4$). In order to argue over the capabilities of a technique for discharging safety goals, one should explicitly state the verification scope and the environmental constraints ($C1$, $C2$). The fact that the verification technique has been previously used in other projects with similar environmental constraints may be used as justification for its appropriateness. Each verification technique needs to demonstrate the satisfaction of several goals (i.e., required objectives to be fulfilled and outputs to be provided), as defined in *Tables A 3–7*, from DO-178C ($C3$). The main goal of the performed verification activity is the verification of a certain type of requirements ($G3$), as recommended by the *assuranceLevel* ($C7$). One should argue this using the rationale of the technique ($G6.1$). The argumentation further developing goal $G6.1$ mirrors the verification steps (presented in [5]). When arguing over goal $G3$, it is relevant to cover the requirement types that are imposed by the activity type to be detected by the technique ($C6$). Each requirement type has different suitable verification techniques. Thus, the selected verification technique may not be able to cover all the requirement types ($G3.1$). When the technique cannot cover all the verification space (i.e., to have 100% structural coverage), another technique may be employed to cover the rest of the verification space, as stated in goal $G6.2$. However, this is an optional goal, since structural code coverage is not an applicable coverage criterion for all verification techniques (e.g., deductive verification). When arguing over goal $G1$, one should also consider the limitations (weaknesses) implied when employing the respective technique ($S4$). Techniques may work together to compensate for such limitations ($G4.1$, $G4.2$, $G4.3$). *Table A-7* from DO-178C and DO-333 recommends that any verification results should be verified ($G1.1$).

A considerable set of standard-mandated compliance requirements for verification techniques targets the detection of certain typical faults (see $G2$, in Fig. 2). Indeed, if a verification technique does not eliminate any fault, the performed verification activity does not increase the confidence in the claim [13]. While arguing for the main goal $G1$, the capability of detecting (some) typical faults is also relevant ($G2.1$). If the selected verification technique cannot detect some of expected fault types, it must be supported by another verification technique ($G2.2$). Whereas all the other sub-goals of $G1$ offer a *mere compliance* to standard-mandated objectives, this part of the safety argumentation ($G2.1$) offers *pondered compliance* (i.e., aware selection of techniques). The contribution to failure avoidance is two-fold (1) the coverage of the typical fault types that are imposed by the activity type - qualitative argument ($G5$) and (2) the number of detectable faults - quantitative argument ($J2$). The strength of the technique is given by the number of implementation problems (faults) types it can detect. For arguing the coverage of a typical fault type, an argument based on the *fault-based argumentation* pattern depicted in Fig. 3. The scope of the *fault-based argumentation* pattern is to offer a structure for arguing the selection of a certain technique, by stating its contribution to failure mode avoidance/reduction.

5   Example

In this section, we present our experience with selecting an adequate open-source compiler for a drone in compliance with DO-178C. In the context of safety critical projects, there are few compiler selection approaches [25]. DO-178C compliant software may not contain software faults that lead to failure. Compilers are designed to perform minimal static analysis on the program in order to detect software faults [17]. In a project involving high costs, where *time is money*, engineers should take advantage of the static analysis techniques provided "for free" by compilers. Cârlan et al. [5] present a code review workflow, which employs a set of static analysis for discharging safety goals. Instead of employing a large number of expensive static analysis, we want to also rely on the used compiler(s) for detecting some of the software faults and thus possibly reducing the size of

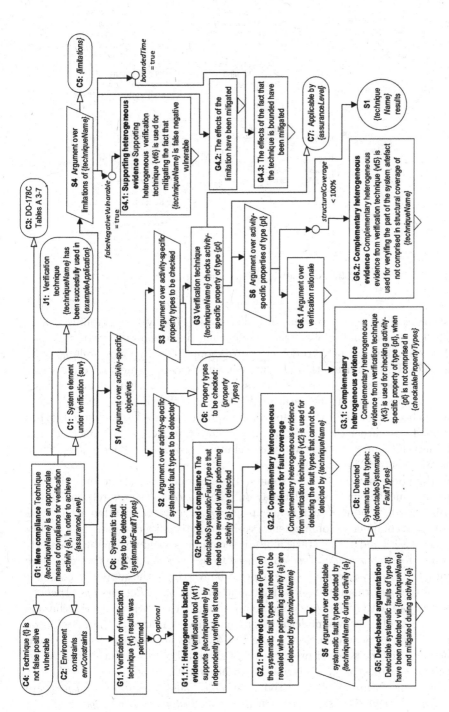

Fig. 2. Technique appropriateness argument pattern

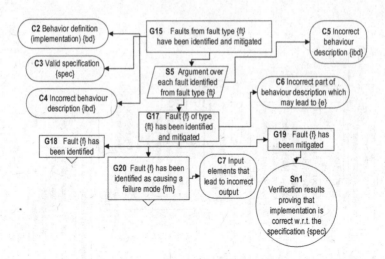

Fig. 3. The fault-based argumentation pattern

the static analysis set. According to Höller et al. [17], diverse compiling is able to detect a larger number of software faults than single compiling. For example, diverse compiling can help to detect up to about 70% of memory-related software faults. These indicate that (1) different compilers implement different static analysis techniques and (2) static analysis techniques underlying compilers may play a significant role in the verification process. Different static analysis techniques embedded in different compilers are appropriate to detect different types of faults. Thus, rather then selecting an adequate compiler, we will select a compiler which integrates a static analysis technique appropriate for *complementing* static analysis techniques.

As compilers may merely offer some simple static checks, a static analysis technique implemented by a compiler may only have a *complements* relationship to a verification technique, which is able to performing the verification activity. In order for the compiler to complement a verification technique to perform a particular activity, its underlying static analysis technique should be capable of detecting some of *systematicFaultTypes* that need to be detected during the respective activity. For brevity reasons, in this paper, we investigate the support a compiler offers for the performance of one activity, namely the *6.3.4 Reviews and Analyses of Source Code* activity. For the pondered selection of the static analysis technique underlying a compiler, we modeled this activity in accordance to the *Verification Activity* class, presented in Sect. 3 (see Fig. 4). This activity checks the system at source level. The types of properties that should be checked during this activity (*checkablePropertyTypes* attribute), together with the objectives to be fulfilled by the performance of this activity (see *detectableSystematicFaultTypes*) are taken from the DO-178C standard. The *detectableSystematicFaultTypes* attribute

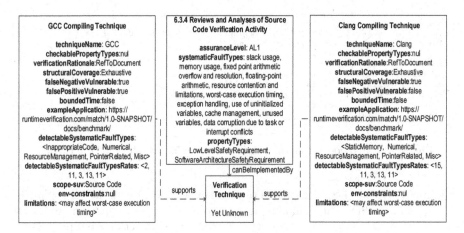

Fig. 4. A model for clang and gcc and the DO-178C 6.3.4 verification activity

is filled with information given by the *f. Accuracy and consistency* paragraph of the *6.3.4*.

The Battle Between clang and gcc. We have two candidate techniques for the role of compiler in our project, namely clang and gcc. We model the static analysis techniques implemented by these two compilers based on our proposed metamodel in Sect. 3. Compilers are able to check the entire code, with no exceptions, hence the *structuralCoverage* for both compilers is depicted as *Exhaustive*. We based our decision also on the experience of RV Team, while compiling the code from the Toyota Benchmark [23] with these two compilers (see the *exampleApplication* attributes). The *detectableSystematicFaultTypes* attribute, together with the *detectableSystematicFaultTypesRates* attribute for both of the models have been filled in with information from the same experience report. While selecting the appropriate static analysis, its impact on the worst-case execution timing should be considered and assessed (see *potentialDeficits* attribute). In Fig. 4, we see that both of the techniques are able to detect *systematicFaultTypes*, which should be detected during the *6.3.4* activity. This makes them equally appropriate candidates. However, while the technique implemented by the clang compiler may detect defects of type static memory (e.g., static buffer overrun/underrun), the technique in gcc compiler does not have this ability. In turn, the gcc technique is capable of finding imperfect code defects, such as dead code detection, floating-point arithmetic, use of uninitialized variables, unused variables and improper error handling. The selection is now reduced to selecting the type of defects that would have a bigger impact on the safety of the system under verification (in our example the drone). In our concrete case, static buffer overflows are a bigger concern than floating-point arithmetic defects, because they may lead the vehicle's software to crash. As learned from the Ariane 5 accident, buffer overflows may have devastating consequences on a flying system's safety [12]. As such, we selected the static analysis of clang compiler

```
// mList is declared as float mList[4];
void Turtle::velocityCallback(const geometry_msgs::Twist::ConstPtr& vel)
{ last_command_time_ = ros::WallTime::now();
  lin_vel_ = vel->linear.x;
  ang_vel_ = vel->angular.z;
  // remeber the last 5 velocities to replay them
  mList[0] = lin_vel_; mList[1] = mList[0];
  mList[2] = mList[1]; mList[3] = mList[2];
  // static buffer overflow
  mList[4] = mList[3]; }
```

Fig. 5. Mutated code of method that sets the velocity values for the turtle

and, implicitly, the clang compiler. From this experience, we learned that, in the selection of a verification technique, it is not only important what kind of faults a verification technique is able to detect, but also the impact of the type of fault on system safety.

Proving the Selection. In order to confirm that we chose the appropriate compiler, we compile a small sample of code in the environment in which we will compile the code for the drone, namely the robot operating system (ROS) [20]. To simplify the discussion, we show the problems on a much smaller ROS introductory example, *turtlesim*[1]. This example allows the user to control an animated turtle by sending it ROS messages. In principle the control software for the UAV[2] uses the same mechanisms and build environment. We mutated that code with four buffer overflow defects (see Fig. 5). We observe that, as our scope was to have a compiler supporting the detection of buffer overflow faults, clang was more appropriate, since it discovered all the four faults (see Fig. 6 for an example), whereas gcc was not able to discover any buffer overflow faults.

```
/home/user/catkin_ws/src/turtlesim/src/turtle.cpp:72:2: warning: array index
    4 is past the end of the array
    (which contains 4 elements) [-Warray-bounds]
      mList[4] = mList[3];
      ^         ~
/home/user/catkin_ws/src/turtlesim/include/turtlesim/turtle.h:79:3: note:
    array 'mList' declared here
  float mList[4];
  ^
1 warning generated.
```

Fig. 6. The error message given by clang. gcc does not point out the error

In Fig. 7, we show how clang compiler contributes at discharging the main goal of the *Technique appropriateness argument pattern.* Goal *G2.2.1* is to be further-developed by instantiating the *Fault-based argumentation pattern.* All

---

[1] http://wiki.ros.org/turtlesim, the source code can be found on github: https://github.com/ros/ros_tutorials.

[2] We used the Erlecopter: http://erlerobotics.com/blog/erle-copter/.

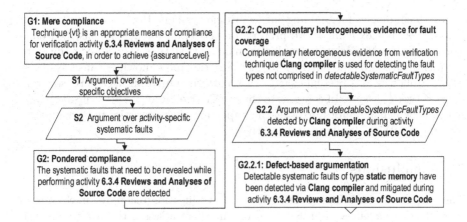

Fig. 7. Partial instantiation of *Technique appropriateness argument pattern*

the warnings from the compiler are to be documented and referenced in the documentation. We suggest building a test case for every warning. After dealing with these warning, in order to prove that they have been mitigated (see *G19* from the *Fault-based argumentation pattern*), we would run the test cases and reference their results.

6 Related Work

The problem of arguing compliance with standards by using patterns has been investigated quite heavily during the last decade. Habli et al. [15] and Denney et al. [7] present safety case patterns for the use of formal methods results for certification. Bennion et al. [2] present a safety case for arguing the compliance of the Simulink Design Verifier model checker to DO-178C. Gallina et al. [9] argue about adequacy of a model-based testing process. Cârlan et al. [5] offer a pattern which integrates static analysis results in an argument for the fulfillment of certain safety objectives. While all these works focus on a certain verification technique as strategy for discharging a safety goal, we offer a safety case pattern to argue the pondered selection of a verification techniques of any type for discharging a safety goal.

Similarly, the problems related to compliance of the certification artefacts and their confidence have also been tackled. Gallina et al. [10] proposes a process compliance pattern for arguing about reuse of tool qualification certification artifacts. One of the identified sub-goals for the claim of trustworthy performance of a certain tasks is that the guidance (how the activity should be performed) has been followed. We offer a reusable argumentation structure for the appropriateness of a technique for a certain activity. We argue that the technique implemented by that tool follows the guidance given by the standard. The problem of confidence in the certification artefacts has been addressed by Graydon et al. [14], who offer a framework for utilizing safety cases for the selection of certain technologies for building safety-critical systems. How to make a decision is, however, not explained. We propose one criterion for making justified decisions on used verification technologies, namely that they need to contribute to the identification or the mitigation of systematic faults known to affect systems' safety. Holloway [18] presents safety case patterns mirroring DO-178C software correctness objectives. In contrast to the work of Holloway, we present safety case patterns, which are built mirroring the important characteristics to be compliant with the DO-178C verification objectives.

7   Conclusions

The output of a tool implementing a certain verification technique may be used as evidence in a safety case. For this, one needs to assess if the respective verification technique is appropriate to generate results for supporting the truth of safety case claims. In this paper, we proposed a metamodel to provide guidelines for the pondered selection of appropriate verification technologies for performing standard-mandated verification activities. Based on this metamodel, we also presented a set of safety case patterns arguing the appropriateness of the verification techniques providing assurance evidence. As future work, we plan to validate our proposed pattern by applying it to argue about appropriateness of verification techniques used in the projects we currently work on. Also, we want to extend our approach in order to support (semi-)automatic creation of safety arguments based on the proposed metamodel.

Acknowledgements. This work has been partially sponsored by the Austrian Ministry for Transport, Innovation and Technology (IKT der Zukunft, Project SALSA) and the Munich Center for Internet Research (MCIR). The author B. Gallina is financially supported by the ECSEL JU project AMASS (No. 692474).

References

1. Ayoub, A., Kim, B.G., Lee, I., Sokolsky, O.: A systematic approach to justifying sufficient confidence in software safety arguments. In: Ortmeier, F., Daniel, P. (eds.) SAFECOMP 2012. LNCS, vol. 7612, pp. 305–316. Springer, Heidelberg (2012). doi:10.1007/978-3-642-33678-2_26
2. Bennion, M., Habli, I.: A Candid industrial evaluation of formal software verification using model checking. In: Companion Proceedings of the 36th International Conference on Software Engineering, pp. 175–184. ACM, New York (2014)
3. Bloomfield, R.E., Bishop, P.G.: Safety and assurance cases: past, present and possible future - an Adelard perspective. In: Dale, C., Anderson, T. (eds.) Making Systems Safer, pp. 51–67. Springer, London (2010). doi:10.1007/978-1-84996-086-1_4
4. Bourdil, P.A., Dal Zilio, S., Jenn, E.: Integrating model checking in an industrial verification process: a structuring approach. Working Paper or Preprint (2016). https://hal.archives-ouvertes.fr/hal-01341701
5. Cârlan, C., Beyene, T.A., Ruess, H.: Integrated formal methods for constructing assurance cases. In: Proceedings of International Symposium on Software Reliability Engineering Workshops, pp. 221–228. IEEE (2016)

6. Cârlan, C., Ratiu, D., Schätz, B.: On using results of code-level bounded model checking in assurance cases. In: Skavhaug, A., Guiochet, J., Schoitsch, E., Bitsch, F. (eds.) SAFECOMP 2016. LNCS, vol. 9923, pp. 30–42. Springer, Cham (2016). doi:10.1007/978-3-319-45480-1_3
7. Denney, E., Pai, G.: Evidence arguments for using formal methods in software certification. In: Proceedings of International Symposium on Software Reliability Engineering Workshops, pp. 375–380. IEEE (2013)
8. Gallina, B.: A model-driven safety certification method for process compliance. In: Proceedings of International Symposium on Software Reliability Engineering Workshops, pp. 204–209. IEEE (2014)
9. Gallina, B., Andrews, A.: Deriving verification-related means of compliance for a model-based testing process. In: Proceedings of IEEE/AIAA 35th Digital Avionics Systems Conference, pp. 1–6 (2016)
10. Gallina, B., Kashiyarandi, S., Zugsbratl, K., Geven, A.: Enabling cross-domain reuse of tool qualification certification artefacts. In: Bondavalli, A., Ceccarelli, A., Ortmeier, F. (eds.) SAFECOMP 2014. LNCS, vol. 8696, pp. 255–266. Springer, Cham (2014). doi:10.1007/978-3-319-10557-4_28
11. Gallina, B., Pitchai, K.R., Lundqvist, K.: S-TunExSPEM: Towards an extension of SPEM 2.0 to model and exchange tunable safety-oriented processes. In: Proceedings of the 11th International Conference on Software Engineering Research, Management and Applications. pp. 215–230. Springer SCI (2014)
12. Garfinkel, S.: History's worst software bugs (2005). http://archive.wired.com/software/coolapps/news/2005/11/69355?currentPage=all
13. Goodenough, J., Weinstock, C.B., Klein, A.Z.: Toward a theory of assurance case confidence. Technical report CMU/SEI-2012-TR-002, Software Engineering Institute, Pittsburgh, PA, USA (2012)
14. Graydon, G., Knight, J.: Process synthesis in assurance-based development of dependable systems. In: Proceedings of 8th European Dependable Computing Conference, pp. 75–84. IEEE (2010)
15. Habli, I., Kelly, T.: A generic goal-based certification argument for the justification of formal analysis. Electron. Notes Theor. Comput. Sci. **238**(4), 27–39 (2009)
16. Hawkins, R., Kelly, T.: A structured approach to selecting and justifying software safety evidence. In: Proceedings of 5th International Conference on System Safety, pp. 1–6. IET (2010)
17. Höller, A., Kajtazovic, N., Rauter, T., Römer, K., Kreiner, C.: Evaluation of diverse compiling for software-Fault Detection. In: Proceedings of the Design, Automation and Test in Europe Conference and Exhibition, pp. 531–536. IEEE (2015)
18. Holloway, C.M.: Explicate'78: uncovering the implicit assurance case in DO-178C. Technical report 20150009473, NASA Langley Research Center (2015)
19. Object Managment Group: Structured assurance case metamodel - SACM, version 2.0 Beta. Technical report (2016). http://www.omg.org/spec/SACM/2.0/Beta1/PDF/
20. Quigley, M., Gerkey, B., Conley, K., Faust, J., Foote, T., Leibs, J., Berger, E., Wheeler, R., Ng, A.: ROS: an open-source robot operating system. In: Proceedings of Open-Source Software Workshop International Conference on Robotics and Automation, vol. 3. IEEE (2009)
21. RTCA: DO-178C, software considerations in airborne systems and equipment certification. RTCA & EUROCAE (2011)
22. RTCA: DO-333 formal methods supplement to DO-178C and DO-278A. RTCA & EUROCAE (2011)

23. Shiraishi, S., Mohan, V., Marimuthu, H.: Test suites for benchmarks of static analysis tools. In: Proceedings of International Symposium on Software Reliability Engineering Workshops, pp. 12–15. IEEE (2015)
24. Weaver, R., McDermid, J., Kelly, T.: Software safety arguments: towards a systematic categorisation of evidence. In: Proceedings of the 20th International System Safety Conference. System Safety Society (2002)
25. Wei, C., Xiaohong, B., Tingdi, Z.: A study on compiler selection in safety-critical redundant system based on airworthiness requirement. Procedia Eng. **17**, 497–504 (2011)

Confidence Assessment Framework
for Safety Arguments

Rui Wang[(✉)], Jérémie Guiochet[(✉)], and Gilles Motet[(✉)]

LAAS-CNRS, Université de Toulouse, CNRS, INSA, UPS, Toulouse, France
{rui.wang,jeremie.guiochet,gilles.motet}@laas.fr

Abstract. Confidence in safety critical systems is often justified by safety arguments. The excessive complexity of systems nowadays introduces more uncertainties for the arguments reviewing. This paper proposes a framework to support the argumentation assessment based on experts' decision and confidence in the decision for the lowest level claims of the arguments. Expert opinion is extracted and converted in a quantitative model based on Dempster-Shafer theory. Several types of argument and associated formulas are proposed. A preliminary validation of this framework is realized through a survey for safety experts.

Keywords: Safety argument · Confidence assessment · Belief function theory

1 Introduction

Safety case is an important representative of structured arguments adopted for critical systems. It is used to formally present that a system is free from unacceptable risks. This justification often demonstrates the compliance of the system with safety regulation and includes a great amount of convincing evidence in parallel. Both developers of critical systems and regulation bodies have to spend time on evaluating such argumentation in order to produce trustful systems or make a justified decision for certification. Many works have been done to help this evaluation process. (1) Building a clear safety argument with a graphical representation of safety arguments [6,15]; (2) Adding confidence arguments to justify the confidence in safety arguments [2,12]; (3) Assessing the confidence in arguments with quantitative methods [7,8,11].

This paper focuses on the third perspective. A confidence assessment framework with specific steps based on Dempster-Shafer theory is proposed to facilitate the argumentation assessment process. It requires the safety experts' opinions only on the lowest level claims of safety arguments. Then, the proposed framework aggregates these opinions in a quantitative way to deduce the decision and the confidence in this decision for the top goal of the safety argument. We made a first experiment through a survey among safety experts and a preliminary validation of this framework is obtained.

This paper is organized as follows. In Sect. 2, the background on GSN and belief function theory is provided. In Sect. 3, the overview of the proposed safety

© Springer International Publishing AG 2017
S. Tonetta et al. (Eds.): SAFECOMP 2017, LNCS 10488, pp. 55–68, 2017.
DOI: 10.1007/978-3-319-66266-4_4

argument assessment framework is given. Two argument types with quantitative
confidence aggregation models are introduced. Afterwards, in Sect. 4, expert data
collection is realized through a survey. We present the survey implementation;
then its responses are analyzed. In Sect. 5 the related works are introduced.
Finally, the contributions of our approach are summarized and future works are
highlighted in Sect. 6.

2   Background

2.1   Safety Argumentation

Structuring an argument to convince regulation bodies is a main challenge for
critical systems. Many approaches, such as safety case [4,16], assurance case
[13], trust case [6], and dependability case [5], provide concepts and notations
for taking up this challenge.

Safety cases, a popular form of safety argumentation, could be defined as [4]
"a documented body of evidence that provides a convincing and valid argument
that a system is adequately safe for a given application in a given environment". A graphical argumentation notation, named as Goal Structuring Notation (GSN), has been developed [15] to represent the different elements of an
assurance case and their relationships with individual notations. GSN allows
the representation of the supporting evidence, objectives to be achieved, safety
argument, context, etc. An example of GSN is given in Fig. 1, which is derived
from the Hazard Avoidance Pattern [16]. The five main elements of GSN presented in this figure are: *goal* (e.g., G1): the claim about the system; *solution*
(e.g., Sn1): the reference to evidence item(s); *strategy* (e.g., S1): the nature of
inference that exists between a goal and its supporting sub-goal(s); *context* (e.g.,
C1): a reference to contextual information, or a statement.

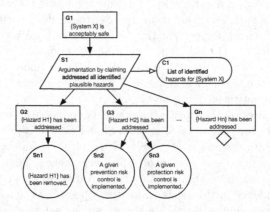

Fig. 1. GSN example adapted from Hazard Avoidance Pattern [16]

2.2   Dempster-Shafer Theory

Among uncertainty theories (such as probabilistic approaches, possibility theory, fuzzy set, etc.), Dempster-Shafer (D-S) Theory or evidence theory, was developed by Arthur Dempster and Glenn Shafer successively [18]. This theory offers a powerful tool to model human belief in evidence from different sources, and an explicit modeling of epistemic uncertainties, which is not the case in other theories. As presented later, we propose to use the D-S Theory as it allows uncertainty, imprecision or ignorance, i.e., "we know that we don't know" to be explicitly expressed.

Let X be a variable taking values in a finite set Ω representing a *frame of discernment*. Ω is composed of all the possible situations of interest. In this paper, we consider only binary frame of discernment, i.e. $\Omega_X = \{\bar{X}, X\}$. For instance, if X would be the state of a bulb, then $\Omega = \{on, off\}$. The *mass function* on Ω (m^{Ω}) is the mapping of the power set of Ω on the closed interval [0,1] that is, $2^{\Omega} \rightarrow [0, 1]$. The mass $m^{\Omega}(P)$ reflects the degree of belief committed to the hypothesis that the truth lies in P. The sum of the masses of all elements in the power set is equal to one. For instance, we can have the following assignment of belief: $m_1(\{on\}) = 0.5$, $m_1(\{off\}) = 0.3$, $m_1(\{on, off\}) = 0.2$. Note that $m_1(\{on, off\})$ does not represent the belief that the bulb might be in $\{on\}$ or $\{off\}$ state, but the degree of belief in the statement "we don't know".

More generally, an opinion about a statement X is assessed with 3 masses: *belief* $(bel_X = m(X))$, *disbelief* $(disb_X = m(\bar{X}))$, and the *uncertainty* $(uncer_X = m(\Omega))$. This leads to $m(X) + m(\bar{X}) + m(\Omega) = 1$ (*belief + disbelief + uncertainty = 1*). Thus we have:

$$\begin{cases} bel_X = m(X) \text{ represents the belief} \\ disb_X = m(\bar{X}) \text{ represents the disbelief} \\ uncer_X = m(\Omega) = 1 - bel_X - disb_X \text{ represents the uncertainty} \end{cases} \quad (1)$$

where bel_X, $disb_X$ and $uncer_X \in [0, 1]$.

3   Safety Argument Assessment Framework

In this section, we introduce an assessment framework for safety arguments, which allows (1) experts to provide their opinions on the lowest level claims of a structured safety argument based on available evidence (e.g. test reports, verification reports, etc.); and (2) to aggregate these opinions hierarchically until we obtain the opinion of the top claim of the argument. The opinion aggregation adopts a quantitative assessment method of argument confidence proposed in our previous works [19]. A new formula to calculate the degree of disbelief and uncertainty is provided in this paper.

3.1   Framework Overview

The proposed assessment framework of safety argument is summarized in Fig. 2 with an argument showing that *Goal B and Goal C support Goal A*. This schema also illustrates the three main steps:

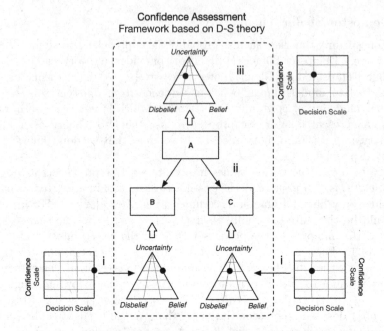

Fig. 2. Schema of the assessment framework for safety argument

i Transforming safety experts' opinions of a goal of a structured argument into a 3-tuple *(bel,uncer,disb)* representing *Belief, Uncertainty* and *Disbelief* in this goal. In Fig. 2, the process for B and C starts from using a scaled evaluation matrix and then an uncertainty triangle named Jøsang triangle [14]. We refer to the transformation expression between decision/confidence and belief functions proposed in paper [7]. The experts' opinion is presented in two dimensions: *decision* and *confidence in this decision.* Instead of the original proposal with belief function and plausibility function, we convert the opinion directly into (bel,uncer,disb), to make explicit the formal concepts.

ii Aggregating all the 3-tuple estimation of lower-level claims into the upper-level claim. This step is based on the confidence assessment method derived from the D-S Theory [19]. As shown in Fig. 2, the *Belief, Uncertainty* and *Disbelief* of B and C are aggregated to produce the three values of A. This aggregation requires some basic information on the argument, such as: the argument types, the weights of B and C, etc.

iii The last step presents the inverse process of Step 1, which aims to generate the opinion on A, i.e. the *decision* on A and the *confidence in this decision.*

This approach is detailed in Sects. 3.2 and 3.3. In Sect. 3.4, an application to an argument example helps for a better understanding of this assessment framework for safety argument.

3.2   Argument Types and Assessment

Like most of structured arguments, a GSN argument has a tree structure, which is composed of a top goal and branches of sub-goals. As described in [12], the assessment of the confidence in the top goal may be based on the estimation of the *trustworthiness* of each sub-goal and the *appropriateness* of the sub-goals in regard to the top goal. Thus, we propose two assessment parameters corresponding to these two aspects. Figure 3 shows an example of a simple argument: goal A is supported by two sub-goals B and C; the assessment parameters are annotated on this GSN argument and interpreted in the following way:

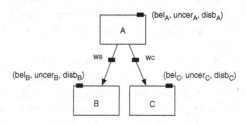

Fig. 3. An example of simple argument annotated with assessment parameters

- A 3-tuple *(bel,uncer,disb)*, such as $(bel_A, uncer_A, disb_A)$ (see the definition in Eq. (1)) represents the *trustworthiness* of a claim. They do not only assess the confidence in the claims, but also allow our degree of distrust and uncertainty in them to be explicitly expressed.
- w_B and w_C are the *disjoint contributing weights* of B and C, $w_B, w_C \in [0, 1]$ and $w_B + w_C \leq 1$. A *disjoint contributing weight* means the degree that B or C can independently contribute to the trustworthiness in A. It refers to the *appropriateness* of sub-goals.

In order to propagate the trustworthiness estimation from B and C nodes to A, we propose two argument types:

- Dependent argument (D-Arg): When the contribution (to the trustworthiness in A) of a sub-goal B depends on the trustworthiness in another sub-goal C, the argument $B + C \rightarrow A$ is called *dependent argument*. For example, an argument is *"B: Test process is correct"* and *"C: Test results are correct"* support *"A: System is acceptably safe"*. The contribution of C to the trustworthiness in A depends on the trustworthiness in B.
- Redundant argument (R-Arg): When sub-goals belonging to the same top goal have a certain degree of overlapping to contribute to the trustworthiness in the top goal, the argument is called *redundant argument*. For example, an argument is *"B: Formal verification is passed"* and *"C: Test is conclusive"* support *"A: System is acceptably safe"*. B and C are two different techniques to assure the system safety. Either of them can support A in certain degree without depending on the other one.

Based on these two argument types, we proposed in [19] the aggregation formulas to integrate the trustworthiness of sub-goals. The related formulas are presented as Eqs. (II) and (IV) in Table 1 for the dependent and redundant arguments, respectively. In this calculation, we introduce a factor to represent the degree of dependency and redundancy among sub-goals. For an argument such as *B and C support A*, this factor, representing the *degree of correspondence* of sub-goals B and C, is expressed as: $c_A = 1 - w_B - w_C$, where $c_A \in [0, 1]$. While c_A varies between 0 and 1, the two formulas (II) and (IV) lead to several special cases of argument types, which are also described in Table 1. In particular:

- Fully dependent argument (FD-Arg): For a *dependent argument*, when $c_A = 1$, i.e. $w_B = w_C = 0$, the argument is a *fully dependent argument*. B have a total interdependence on C. One sub-goals cannot contribute to the trustworthiness in A without the other one.
- Fully redundant argument (FR-Arg): For a *redundant argument*, when $c_A = 1$, i.e. $w_B = w_C = 0$, the argument is *fully redundant argument*. Either of B and C can contribute to the full trustworthiness in the top goal.
- Disparate argument (I-Arg): When the *correspondence* between B and C c_A decreases (i.e. w_B, w_A increase) to $c_A = 0$ (i.e. $w_B + w_C = 1$), the aggregation formulas of the dependent and redundant arguments become the same formulas ((III) in Table 1). B and C contribute independently to only one part of the trustworthiness in the top goal.

Except the above three special argument types, other arguments are either *partial dependent argument (PD-Arg)* or *partial redundant argument (PR-Arg)*.

Table 1. Comparison of two different argument types

Arg. types		c_A	w_B, w_C	Aggregation formula	
D-Arg	FD-Arg	1	0	$bel_A = bel_B bel_C$ $disb_A = disb_B + disb_C - disb_B disb_C$	(I)
	PD-Arg	↓	↓	$bel_A = bel_B w_B + bel_C w_C + bel_B bel_C c_A$ $disb_A = disb_B w_B + disb_C w_C + (disb_B + disb_C - disb_B disb_C)c_A$	(II)
	I-Arg	0	$\Sigma = 1$	$bel_A = bel_B w_B + bel_C w_C$ $disb_A = disb_C w_B + disb_C w_C$	(III)
R-Arg	PR-Arg	↑	↑	$bel_A = bel_B w_B + bel_C w_C + [1 - (1 - bel_B)(1 - bel_C)]c_A$ $disb_A = disb_B w_B + disb_C w_C + disb_B disb_C c_A$	(IV)
	FR-Arg	1	0	$bel_A = 1 - (1 - bel_B)(1 - bel_C)$ $disb_A = disb_B disb_C$	(V)

Due to the limited space of this paper, the parameter formalization and the development process of assessment aggregation formulas are not presented. For more details and a general assessment model for N-sub-goal arguments, please refer to paper [19]. In Table 1, we directly provide the formulas to calculate $(bel_A, uncer_A, disb_A)$ according to the argument types.

3.3   Expert Judgment Extraction

While assessing an argument, a safety expert has to evaluate all the elements of this argument, i.e. statement, evidence, context, etc. In Fig. 4(a), a goal G1: *"Low-level requirements coverage is achieved"* is to be assessed. It is supported by the evidence S1: *"Low-level requirement coverage verification reports"*, which records the coverage verification of low-level requirements based on the contexts C1: *"Complete low-level requirements"* and C2: *"Structural coverage analysis (statement coverage, branch coverage, etc.) reports"*. We adopt an evaluation matrix as proposed by [7] to assess G1 by two criteria: the *decision* on the goal and the *confidence in the decision (dec, conf)*. In Fig. 4(b), there are 4 levels for decision scale from *"rejectable"* to *"acceptable"* and 6 levels for Confidence Scale from *"lack of confidence"* to *"for sure"*. We assume that, in both scales, the levels are evenly and linearly distributed. A solid dot represents the evaluation of this goal by an expert. Here, the expert accepts this goal with very high confidence. The decision *"acceptable"* indicates that the expert believes that all the low-level requirements were actually covered. Moreover, the *"very high confidence"* comes from relatively high coverage rate and thorough explanation of discrepancies in evidence S1.

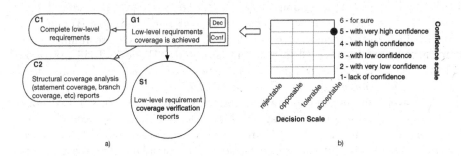

a)   b)

Fig. 4. An evaluation matrix for safety argument

In order to further assess the upper-level goals, we need to aggregate the expert's evaluation of sub-goals. As mentioned in the Sect. 3.1, the evaluation of the experts *(dec, conf)* will be transformed to *belief, uncertainty* and *disbelief*. In fact, this step is used to formalize the evaluation as a mass function in order to take advantage of the D-S Theory to combine uncertain information. This uncertainty theory offers a powerful tool to explicitly model and process information with uncertainty. We adopt the definition of *decision* and *confidence in the decision* of any claim A based on belief functions proposed in [7] to fit the input of the aggregation model (refer to Table 1). The modified definition is presented in Eqs. (2) and (3).

$$conf_A = bel_A + disb_A \qquad (2)$$

$$\begin{cases} dec_A = bel_A/(bel_A + disb_A), & bel_A + disb_A \neq 0 \\ dec_A = 0, & bel_A + disb_A = 0 \end{cases} \tag{3}$$

Due to the constrains of mass function of D-S Theory, we can deduce that $conf_A$, $dec_A \in [0, 1]$.

Once, the $(dec_A, conf_A)$ is obtained based on $(bel_A, uncer_A, disb_A)$, their values may not be exactly one of the values of 4 decision levels and 6 confidence levels. If so, these numbers should be rounded to find the nearest levels.

Furthermore, the inverse functions from $(dec, conf)_A$ to $(bel_A, uncer_A, disb_A)$ are given in the Eq. (4).

$$\begin{cases} bel_A = conf_A * dec_A \\ disb_A = conf_A * (1 - dec_A) \\ uncer_A = 1 - b_A - d_A \end{cases} \tag{4}$$

3.4 Application Example

In this subsection, we use a fragment of GSN argument shown in Fig. 5 as an example to present the use of the proposed safety case assessment framework. In this GSN model, it is assumed that *"G1: system is acceptably safe"* (claim A), if *"G2: Low-level requirements coverage is achieved "* (sub-goal B) and *"G3: High-level requirements coverage is achieved "* (sub-goal C) are fulfilled. The confidence in A is based on the assessment of sub-goals B and C. To illustrate the calculus, we provide the arbitrary values to assess B as *"opposable"* (weak reject) with *"very low confidence"* and C as *"acceptable"* with *"very high confidence"*. The low-level requirements coverage is verified through the structural coverage analysis based on functional testing; the high-level requirements coverage is also based on function testing. B and C are linked to each other, but they also cover two different aspects. Thus, they are considered as partial dependent arguments. We arbitrarily choose the values $c_A = 0.5$ and equal disjoint contributing weights $w_B = w_C = (1 - c_A)/2 = 0.25$. A possible approach is presented in Sect. 4 to extract the information about argument types and weights with the help of a survey.

Here follows the three-step process of the framework proposed in Sect. 3.1 to realize the assessment of confidence in A.

- Transforming the evaluation $(dec, conf)$ of B and C to $(bel, uncer, disb)$ using Eq. (4). $(bel_B, uncer_B, disb_B) = (0.066, 0.8, 0.134)$, $(bel_C, uncer_C, disb_C) = (0.8, 0.2, 0.0)$
- Aggregating the estimations of B and C with the aggregation formula of dependent argument (refer to (II) in Table 1). $(bel_A, uncer_A, disb_A) = (0.243, 0.657, 0.101)$
- Calculating the decision on A and the confidence in the decision $(dec_A, conf_A) = (0.707, 0.343)$. The level of decision and confidence in this decision are selected by the nearest value of the results. Thus, goal A is *"tolerable"*, *"with low confidence"*.

In brief, the framework can be regarded as a function f: $(dec_A, conf_A) = f[(dec_B, conf_B), (dec_C, conf_C)]$, where inputs are the evaluation of sub-goals B and C, the output is the assessment of the top goal A. More generally, this framework can be applied for a safety argument with multiple sub-goals and more hierarchical levels, thanks to the general version of aggregation formulas.

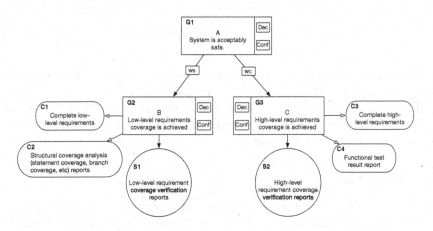

Fig. 5. A safety argument example to be estimated

4   A Survey for Expert Data Collection

To study the argument properties, such as the argument types and the sub-goal weights, we carried out a survey among experts in system safety domain.

4.1   Implementation of the Survey

In the questionnaire, four argument fragments are provided. These arguments includes Arg1 represented in Fig. 5 and Arg2–Arg4 in Fig. 6. They have the same form with an identical top goal A and two sub-goals B and C. For each argument, two pairs of estimation results of B and C (corresponding to Q1 and Q2 in Table 2) are initial information given to the respondents. Then, they are asked to make a decision on the top goals, that is, choosing an appropriate decision level among *rejectable (rej)*, *opposable (opp)*, *tolerable (tol)*, *acceptable (acc)*; and select their confidence level in this decision from *1-lack of confidence* to *6-for sure*. For better understanding of the assessment process, an introduction of the evaluation matrix is given at the beginning of the questionnaire; and explanations and assumptions of the 4 arguments are also provided. Furthermore, an extra question follows each argument asking respondents for their understanding degree of the argument. The degrees are "to great extent", "somewhat", "very little" and "not at all". An online version of this questionnaire is available [1].

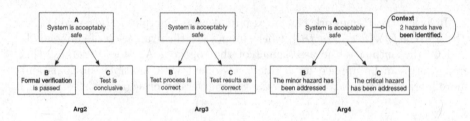

Fig. 6. Argument fragments questioned in the survey

35 experts answered this questionnaire, including: 18 system safety engineers, safety managers and other engineers of critical system fields, and 17 researchers and PhD candidates working in the system dependability domain. Due to no significant difference in the analysis results between the respondent's profiles, their answers are processed together.

4.2   Result Analysis

The case study aims to analyze the properties of the argument examples from the questionnaire responses, that is, to estimate the sub-goal weights and argument types implicitly considered by the experts. The collected data (*expert data*) are compared with the data calculated based on the assessment formulas introduced in Sect. 3 (*theoretical data*).

In Fig. 7, the theoretical data of dependent argument is shown as a cloud of dots derived from random trials of possible values of w_B and w_C. Note that the triangles will be explained later. Different shapes of clouds are due to the two pairs of inputs of B and C for questions Q1 (Fig. 7(a)) and Q2 (Fig. 7(b)). According to the process of the assessment framework, we calculate the values of $(dec_A, conf_A)$ from $(dec_B, conf_B)$ and $(dec_C, conf_C)$. Then we plot the values in the evaluation matrix. The solid dots represent the values with the constraint that $w_B > w_C$; whereas the crosses represent the values of $w_B \leq w_C$. In the figures, the "F" letters represent the output of a special case of dependent argument: *fully dependent argument*.

Then, in order to extract the consensus of experts, we filtered the data using the confidence intervals. Also, if the respondents chose "not at all" for the understanding of one argument, the answers for the corresponding two questions were removed. The expert data are presented with triangles in the evaluation matrix (Fig. 7). The size of the triangle indicates the number of respondents giving the same opinion.

Finally, the expert data are compared with the theoretical data clouds. Taking question Q1 of the argument Arg1 for example, we consider this argument as dependent argument, since there is some dependency between the two subgoals. Hence, in Fig. 7, the expert data are compared with framework output of dependent argument. Two large dots are matched with the distribution of dependent graphs. We assume that the argument type can be validated by the

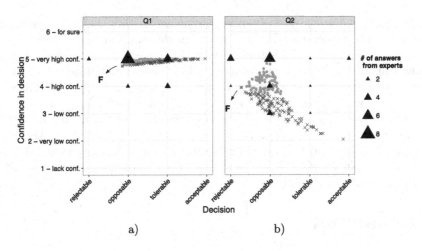

Fig. 7. Experts estimations of Argument 1 and theoretical data of dependent argument

degree of overlapping of these two sets of data. Thus, the percentage of the answers positioned in the cloud (matched answers) is calculated (see Table 2). Large percentages of overlapping for both of figures (a) and (b) confirm that the Arg1 is a dependent argument.

Furthermore, some weight information of B and C can be deduced. Looking at the biggest triangle in Fig. 7(a), it shows that 8 experts have given the *opposable* decision with *very high confidence* (denoted as *opp-5*). Compared with the theoretical data cloud, these 8 answers indicate that the argument can be either fully dependent argument with $w_B = w_C = 0$ or partial dependent argument with $w_B > w_C$.

Table 2. Validation of safety argument assessment approach

Arg.	Ques.	Initial values	Expert answer examples	Expected arg. types	Validated arg. types	Answer in cloud (%)	Weight info.
Arg1	Q1	B: opp-5 C: acc-5	A: opp-5, tol-5	PD-Arg.	PD-Arg.	65.0%	$w_B \geqq w_C$
	Q2	B: opp-5 C: acc-2	A: rej-5, opp-3,4,5			63.6%	-
Arg2	Q1	B: opp-5 C: acc-5	A: opp-5, tol-5	PR-Arg.	PR-Arg.	72.2%	$w_B \geqq w_C$
	Q2	B: opp-5 C: acc-2	A: opp-4,5			62.5%	$w_B > w_C$
Arg3	Q1	B: opp-5 C: acc-5	A: opp-5, tol-5	PD-Arg.	PD-Arg.	62.5%	$w_B \geqq w_C$
	Q2	B: opp-5 C: acc-2	A: rej-5, opp-5			58.3%	$w_B > w_C$
Arg4	Q1	B: opp-5 C: acc-5	A: tol-4,5	I-Arg.	PD-Arg.	57.7%	$w_B = w_C$
	Q2	B: opp-5 C: acc-2	A: opp-3, opp-5			77.8%	-

In Table 2, the analysis of the expert answers for 4 arguments is summed up. Some representative examples of the expert answers are given in this table. Comparing the "expected argument types" with "validated argument types",

Arg4 is considered as "partial dependent argument" rather than the "disparate argument". The percentages of the answers in the cloud are calculated for all the argument examples. These results show that experts have a certain degree of consensus on the type of the arguments based on our approach. Moreover, the experts' preference of weights for B and C are listed in the last column. "-" means that there is no clear opinion on the preference of weights.

A large percentage of the consensus answers matches the model output of the assessment framework proposed in this paper, which is a first validation of the framework. Furthermore, based on the above analysis of the survey data, we deduce the properties of the 4 argument examples including argument types and the disjoint contributing weights.

5   Related Work

Confidence assessment of safety case has been mainly addressed with two perspectives. The first one focuses on the identification of "defeaters" of an argument, and the construction of an additional argument dedicated to confidence [3,12]. Such approaches are mainly qualitative. A second trend is the development of quantitative approaches of confidence in argument. Indeed, excessive growth of argument leads it to make analysis for estimating confidence too complex; then quantitative tools might help analysts to estimate the confidence. To refer to some of them, we can cite [8], based on Bayesian Network, and [7,11] based on belief function theory. As presented in [10], many approaches are studied for quantitative assessment of safety argument confidence. In this last paper the authors study the flaws and counterarguments for each approaches, and conclude that whereas quantitative approaches for confidence assessment are of high interest, no method is currently fully applicable. Moreover, we argue that these quantitative approaches lack of practicability between assurance case and confidence assessment, or do not provide clear interpretation of confidence calculation parameters. Our framework over comes this flaw.

Compared to our approach, the paper [17] provides an expert judgment extraction of confidence and a propagation calculation based on belief theory in order to build a confidence case as proposed in [12]. Nevertheless they do not address inference type when aggregating information. They also do not study how the confidence level could be used by the analysts to make a decision regarding the safety case.

In [2], the authors mainly introduce four argument types and formulas to combine confidence regarding these types. They also use belief theory for calculation, and the result is provided with belief, disbelief and uncertainty estimation for each evidence of the safety case. Even if some types of argument are comparable with our proposal (e.g., their "Alternative" is near our "Redundant"), they do not provide any justification of the combining formulas, with a relative low intuitive interpretation of the parameters (which is a main drawback for potential users). Moreover, once calculation is performed, the results do not provide any justification for a decision regarding the acceptability of the safety case.

As already mentioned, we reuse a part of the approach presented in [7]. In this paper, the authors introduce a way to convert a decision on the acceptability of a statement in a safety case and its confidence, into belief theory parameters. We also use similar steps in our approach, from expert judgment extraction to calculation of a decision and its confidence in the top statement. Compared to our work, they did not use GSN for safety case modeling as we proposed; but the main difference is in the argument types and associated formulas. Indeed, they extended the work from [9] to propose 6 types of arguments. We found them too complex for an intuitive identification in a real safety case. Moreover, according to each of these types, several parameters are difficult to determine and interpret. Our objective is really to provide an efficient and pragmatic approach for analysts; thus we actually only propose 2 types of argument, and a direct application to GSN safety cases.

6   Conclusion

In this paper, an assessment framework has been put forward to support the safety argument assessment process. This 3-step framework only requires the evaluation results of the lowest-level claims; then it aggregates them to estimate the confidence in the top claim. The quantitative aggregation approach based on Dempster-Shafer theory was proposed in our previous work [19]. An evaluation matrix for extracting experts opinion is adopted [7] with the scales of decision and confidence in the decision. We define two main argument types: dependent and redundant arguments. By changing the weights of sub-goals, we also proposed to refine these types using the same formula. Meanwhile a possible approach to estimate argument properties is introduced. A survey was carried out to make a preliminary validation of our framework. We focus in this survey on validating the types of arguments, their aggregation models and the expert judgment extraction. 35 safety engineers and researchers in system dependable domain participated to this survey. We compared the questionnaire results with the theoretical output calculated by applying our assessment framework. This first experiment shows that our aggregation models are consistent with expert judgments. The framework makes practical the theoretical model in terms of the extraction of experts' opinion on the trustworthiness of sub-goals. However, while assessing an argument, this framework still requires the expert to determine the argument types and weights of sub-goals. A method to identify the argument types and weights for a given safety argument will be our future work.

References

1. Questionnaire for safety argument assessment research, January 2017. https://goo.gl/forms/V3vMnl59cTWA6Lws2
2. Ayoub, A., Chang, J., Sokolsky, O., Lee, I.: Assessing the overall sufficiency of safety arguments. In: 21st Safety-Critical Systems Symposium (SSS 2013), pp. 127–144 (2013)

3. Ayoub, A., Kim, B.G., Lee, I., Sokolsky, O.: A systematic approach to justifying sufficient confidence in software safety arguments. In: Ortmeier, F., Daniel, P. (eds.) SAFECOMP 2012. LNCS, vol. 7612, pp. 305–316. Springer, Heidelberg (2012). doi:10.1007/978-3-642-33678-2_26

4. Bishop, P., Bloomfield, R.: A methodology for safety case development. In: Redmill, F., Anderson, T. (eds.) Industrial Perspectives of Safety-Critical Systems, pp. 194–203. Springer, London (1998). doi:10.1007/978-1-4471-1534-2_14

5. Bloomfield, R., Littlewood, B., Wright, D.: Confidence: its role in dependability cases for risk assessment. In: 37th Annual IEEE/IFIP International Conference on Dependable Systems and Networks, DSN 2007, pp. 338–346. IEEE (2007)

6. Cyra, L., Gorski, J.: Supporting compliance with security standards by trust case templates. In: 2nd International Conference on Dependability of Computer Systems, DepCoS-RELCOMEX 2007, pp. 91–98. IEEE (2007)

7. Cyra, L., Gorski, J.: Support for argument structures review and assessment. Reliab. Eng. Syst. Saf. **96**(1), 26–37 (2011)

8. Denney, E., Pai, G., Habli, I.: Towards measurement of confidence in safety cases. In: 2011 International Symposium on Empirical Software Engineering and Measurement (ESEM), pp. 380–383. IEEE (2011)

9. Govier, T.: A Practical Study of Argument. Wadsworth, Cengage Learning, Belmont (2013)

10. Graydon, P.J., Holloway, C.M.: An investigation of proposed techniques for quantifying confidence in assurance arguments. Saf. Sci. **92**, 53–65 (2017)

11. Guiochet, J., Do Hoang, Q.A., Kaaniche, M.: A model for safety case confidence assessment. In: Koornneef, F., Gulijk, C. (eds.) SAFECOMP 2015. LNCS, vol. 9337, pp. 313–327. Springer, Cham (2015). doi:10.1007/978-3-319-24255-2_23

12. Hawkins, R., Kelly, T., Knight, J., Graydon, P.: A new approach to creating clear safety arguments. In: Dale, C., Anderson, T. (eds.) Advances in Systems Safety, pp. 3–23. Springer, London (2011). doi:10.1007/978-0-85729-133-2_1

13. ISO/IEC 15026–2: Systems and software engineering - systems and software assurance - part 2: Assurance case, 2011. International Organization for Standardization (ISO)/International Electrotechnical Commission (IEC)

14. Jøsang, A.: A logic for uncertain probabilities. Int. J. Uncertain. Fuzziness Knowl. Based Syst. **9**(03), 279–311 (2001)

15. Kelly, T.: Arguing safety - a systematic approach to safety case management. Ph.D. thesis, Department of Computer Science, University of York (1998)

16. Kelly, T., McDermid, J.: Safety case construction and reuse using patterns. In: Daniel, P. (ed.) Computer Safety, Reliability, and Security (SAFECOMP), pp. 55–69. Springer, London (1997). doi:10.1007/978-1-4471-0997-6_5

17. Nair, S., Walkinshaw, N., Kelly, T., de la Vara, J.L.: An evidential reasoning approach for assessing confidence in safety evidence. In: 2015 IEEE 26th International Symposium on Software Reliability Engineering (ISSRE), pp. 541–552, November 2015

18. Shafer, G.: A Mathematical Theory of Evidence, vol. 1. Princeton University Press, Princeton (1976)

19. Wang, R., Guiochet, J., Motet, G., Schön, W.: D-S theory for argument confidence assessment. In: Vejnarová, J., Kratochvíl, V. (eds.) BELIEF 2016. LNCS, vol. 9861, pp. 190–200. Springer, Cham (2016). doi:10.1007/978-3-319-45559-4_20

Safety Case Impact Assessment in Automotive Software Systems: An Improved Model-Based Approach

Sahar Kokaly[1]([⊠]), Rick Salay[2], Marsha Chechik[2], Mark Lawford[1], and Tom Maibaum[1]

[1] McMaster Centre for Software Certification,
McMaster University, Hamilton, Canada
{kokalys,lawford,maibaum}@mcmaster.ca
[2] Department of Computer Science, University of Toronto, Toronto, Canada
{rsalay,chechik}@cs.toronto.edu

Abstract. Like most systems, automotive software systems evolve due to many reasons including adding, removing or modifying features, fixing bugs, or improving system quality. In this context, safety cases, used to demonstrate that a system satisfies predefined safety requirements, often dictated by a standard such as ISO 26262, need to co-evolve. A necessary step is performing an impact assessment to identify how changes in the system affect the safety case. In previous work, we introduced a generic model-based impact assessment approach, that, while sound, was not particularly precise. In this work, we show how exploiting knowledge about system changes, the particular safety case language, and the standard can increase the precision of the impact assessment, reducing any unnecessary revision work required by a safety engineer. We present six precision improvement techniques illustrated on a GSN safety case used with ISO 26262.

1 Introduction

Safety engineers in various domains, including automotive, experience difficulties with safety case maintenance. As stated in [11], the main reason for this is that they do not have a systematic approach by which to examine the impact of change on a safety argument. The authors of [2] performed a study which suggested that engineers spend 50–100 h on Change Impact Assessment (CIA) per year on average. The second most commonly mentioned CIA challenge is related to information overload. The three most senior engineers in the study reported that obtaining a system understanding is hard due to the complexity of the systems. The sheer number of software artifacts involved makes traceability information highly complex. Based on the results of [2], determining how a change impacts the product source code seems to be less of a challenge than determining impact on non-code artifacts, e.g., requirements, specifications, and test cases. In [14,17], the authors further discuss the problem of CIA being a

© Springer International Publishing AG 2017
S. Tonetta et al. (Eds.): SAFECOMP 2017, LNCS 10488, pp. 69–85, 2017.
DOI: 10.1007/978-3-319-66266-4_5

challenge in safety-critical systems. Specifically, Leveson [14] mentions that inadequate CIA has been among the causes of accidents in the past. Thus, the current state of practice can clearly benefit from improved CIA techniques, especially to help perform safety assurance more cost-effectively.

In this paper, we build on our earlier work [13] which proposed using a model-based approach to perform impact assessment on an assurance case due to system changes. Our technique is applicable to assurance cases in general and ensures soundness, i.e., it does not miss any elements that are impacted. Yet, the approach is conservative. i.e., it can flag elements as impacted when they are not, resulting in "false positives". Using knowledge about the system models, the safety case language and the standard under consideration, the precision of our approach can be improved, thus reducing unnecessary effort by the safety engineer. The contributions of this paper are as follows: (1) we provide a model-based approach for impact assessment on GSN safety cases used with ISO 26262, and (2) we identify and describe six techniques for improving the precision of the impact assessment approach.

The rest of the paper is organized as follows: Sect. 2 introduces the power sliding door system used as a running example in the paper. Section 3 presents background material on ISO 26262. Section 4 describes how our model-based approach can be used for GSN safety cases linked to ISO 26262. Section 5 presents the techniques that can be used to improve the precision of our model-based impact assessment approach. Section 6 discusses related work, and Sect. 7 summarizes the paper and outlines problems for future work.

2   Running Example: Power Sliding Door (PSD) System

Consider an automotive subsystem that controls the behavior of a power sliding door in a car. The system has an `Actuator` that is triggered on demand by a `Driver Switch`. This example is presented in Part 10 of ISO 26262 [8]. Figure 1 shows the system models comprised of a Class Diagram (to model structure), a Sequence Diagram (to model behavior) and a relationship between them. This can be visualized at a high-level as the *megamodel* [16] in Fig. 4a, which includes other parts of the system such as results of model checking and testing. In practice, the system megamodel could include other system models, e.g., SysML representations, FMEA and FTA results.

The `Driver Switch` input is read by a dedicated Electronic Control Unit (ECU), referred to as `AC ECU` which powers the `Actuator` through a dedicated power line. The vehicle equipped with the item is also fitted with a control unit able to provide the vehicle speed, referred to as `VS ECU`. The system includes a safety element, namely, a `Redundant Switch`. Including this element ensures a higher level of integrity for the overall system.

The `VS ECU` provides the `AC ECU` with the vehicle speed. The `AC ECU` monitors the driver's requests, tests if the vehicle speed is less than or equal to 15 km/h, and if so, commands the `Actuator`. Thus, the sliding door can only be opened or closed if the vehicle speed is not higher than 15 km/h. The `Redundant Switch` is

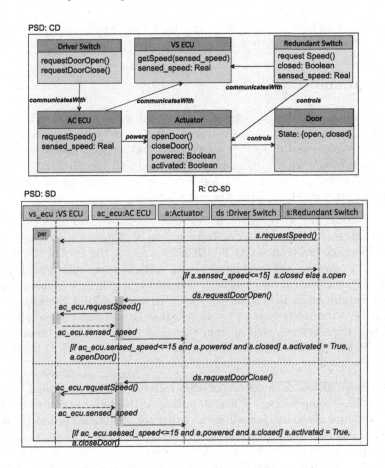

Fig. 1. Power sliding door class diagram-sequence diagram.

located on the power line between the AC ECU and the Actuator as a secondary safety control. It switches on if the speed is less than or equal to 15 km/h, and off whenever the speed is greater than 15 km/h. It does this regardless of the state of the power line (its power supply is independent). The Actuator operates only when it is powered.

Suppose that the PSD system changes such that the redundant switch is removed. In the new system, only the AC ECU checks the vehicle speed before commanding Actuator. Given a safety case for the original system (refer to Fig. 7 ignoring the annotations[1]), it is desirable to reuse as much as possible of its content in structuring a new safety case. An important prerequisite for this

---

[1] Note that the ASIL assignments are given in the example in Part 10 of ISO 262626, and we selected assignments for requirements B2 and B4 based on the possible ASIL C decompositions for redundancy as shown in Fig. 2 – ASIL decomposition schemes, in Part 9 of the standard.

is performing an assessment to identify the impact of the changes made in the system on the safety case components.

3   Background: ISO 26262

ISO 26262 is a standard that regulates functional safety of road vehicles. It recommends conducting a Hazard Analysis to identify and categorize hazardous events in the system and to specify safety goals and integrity levels related to the mitigation of the associated hazards. The standard has 10 parts, and we focus on one of them, "Product Development at the Software Level" (Part 6), and refer to Part 9 which explains Automotive Safety Integrity Levels (ASILs).

ASIL Allocation and Propagation. An ASIL refers to an abstract classification of inherent safety risk in an automotive system or elements of such a system. ASIL classifications are used within ISO 26262 to express the level of risk reduction required to prevent a specific hazard, with ASIL D representing the highest and ASIL A the lowest. If an element is assigned QM (Quality Management), it does not require safety management. The ASIL assessed for a given hazard is then assigned to the safety goal set to address that hazard and is then inherited by the safety requirements derived from that goal following ASIL propagation rules. The higher the ASIL, the more rigorous the application of ISO 26262 has to be. i.e., the more requirements need to be fulfilled.

ASIL Decomposition. The method of ASIL tailoring during the design process is called "ASIL decomposition". When allocating ASILs, benefit can be obtained from architectural decisions, including the existence of sufficiently independent architectural elements (as in the redundancy in the original PSD system). This offers the opportunity to implement safety requirements redundantly by these independent architectural elements, and to assign a potentially lower ASIL to these decomposed safety requirements[2].

Furthermore, ISO 26262 requires the production of over 100 work products, achieved via various requirements and methods used in the different phases of software development. For example, Sect. 9 of Part 6 of ISO 26262 discusses Software Unit Testing, and Sect. 9.5 outlines the required work products for it. One

Methods		ASIL			
		A	B	C	D
1a	Requirements-based test[a]	++	++	++	++
1b	Interface test	++	++	++	++
1c	Fault injection test[b]	+	+	+	++
1d	Resource usage test[c]	+	+	+	++
1e	Back-to-back comparison test between model and code, if applicable[d]	+	+	++	++

Fig. 2. Methods for software unit testing - ISO 26262 Part 6 (cropped for space).

---

[2] Refer to Fig. 2 in Part 9 of the standard for ASIL decomposition schemes.

of these work products is 9.5.1: Software Verification Plan which results from requirements 9.4.2–9.4.6 in the same section. Consider one of these requirements, 9.4.3, which describes which software testing methods can be used. These methods clearly link to ASILs. Specifically, Fig. 2, lists various methods for software unit testing and how they relate to the four ASILs. The degree of recommendation to use the corresponding method depends on the ASIL and is categorized as follows: "++" indicates that the method is highly recommended for the identified ASIL (we interpret this as "required"), "+" – that the method is recommended for the identified ASIL, and "o" – that the method has no recommendation for or against its usage for the identified ASIL. For example, methods 1a, 1b, 1e in Fig. 2 are required for unit testing for ASIL C. An increased ASIL D, now requires methods 1c and 1d which were only recommended for ASIL C.

4   GSN Safety Case Impact Assessment

In this section, we present our generic safety case impact assessment approach [13] specifically instantiated for GSN Safety Cases [10]. First, we define the GSN metamodel and the result of the impact assessment algorithm. Then, we describe the algorithm, which we name GSN-IA (GSN Impact Assessment), and the supporting model transformations. We have shown our algorithm to be sound [4] but do not replicate the argument due to space restrictions.

4.1   GSN and Annotation Models

Figure 3 gives a fragment of the GSN metamodel extended with state information. A Goal has a truth state and in this paper we assume that the truth state is two-valued truth (*true*, *false*) and that every goal represents a claim about the system for which the truth can be determined (e.g., claim expressed as a temporal logic statement). Thus, for the time being, we preclude more fine-grained measures of truth (e.g., degrees of confidence) and goals that have fuzzy truth conditions, and leave as future work. A Solution represents some kind of evidence about the system and has a validity state that indicates whether the evidence is applicable or it is "stale" and must be regenerated (e.g., old test results). A Strategy is used to decompose goals (conclusions) into subgoals (premises), and its validity state indicates whether the strategy is a valid one for connecting its premise goals to its conclusion. Finally, a Context element describes assumptions on the elements it connects to, and also has a validity state. We consider two ways that a change to the system can impact the elements of the safety case: (1) revise – the *content* of the element may have to be revised because it referred to a system element that has changed and the semantics of the content may have changed, and (2) recheck – the *state* of the element must be rechecked because it may have changed. For example, the goal "The power sliding door opens when the function DriverSwitch.RequestDoorOpen() is invoked and the vehicle speed is not greater than 15 km/h." (see the class diagram in Fig. 1)

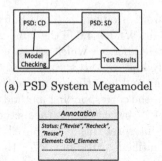

(a) PSD System Megamodel

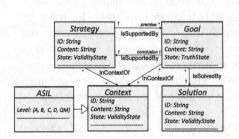

(b) Annotation Metamodel

Fig. 3. Fragment of GSN metamodel extended with validity states.

Fig. 4. PSD system megamodel and annotation metamodel.

must be revised if the function name is changed to `CommandDoorOpen()` since the goal now refers to an element that does not exist. However, if some aspect of the system that affects door opening functionality changes, then the goal must be rechecked because it may no longer hold. We assume that after a revision, a recheck must take place; thus, at most one of these impacts can apply to an element. If an element is not impacted by a system change we say that it can be reused and mark it as `reuse`.

The purpose of executing our impact assessment algorithm, GSN-IA, on a safety case is to determine the impact type for each safety case element and to "mark" the element accordingly. This marking is stored in a simple annotation model with the metamodel shown in Fig. 4b. Thus, an annotation model consists of an `Annotation` element for each GSN element that contains the marking as its `Status` attribute.

4.2   GSN-IA: GSN Impact Assessment Algorithm

Figure 5 shows the GSN-IA algorithm both in pseudocode and diagrammatically. The input to GSN-IA is the initial system model S and a safety case A connected by a traceability mapping R, the changed system S' and the delta D recording the changes between S and S'. Specifically, D is the triple $\langle C0a, C0d, C0m \rangle$ where of $C0a$ is the set of elements added in S', $C0d$ is the set of elements deleted from S and $C0m$ is the set of modified elements that appear in both S and S'. These are shown in the top part of the diagram. GSN-IA is parameterized by the model slicer $Slice_{Sys}$ used to determine how change impact propagates within the system model – that is, we consider this slicer to be given as an input to GSN-IA. Note that our approach readily applies not only to singleton models but also to more realistic cases where the system is described by a heterogeneous collection of related models as a megamodel. We have defined a sound slicing approach for this case [16]. The output of GSN-IA is the model K that annotates A to indicate which elements are marked for `revise`, `recheck` or `reuse`.

GSN-IA uses several *model transformations* described below. In line 1, the `Restrict` transformation extracts the subset R'_A of traceability links from R that are also valid for S'. Lines 2 and 3 use the model slicer Slice_{Sys} to expand the combined (using `Union`) set of changed elements in S and S', respectively, to all elements *potentially impacted* by the change. Then, in line 4, these potentially impacted elements are traced to A across the traceability relationships using the `Trace` transformation and combined to identify the subset of elements in A that must be rechecked. The subset of safety case elements for revision is identified in line 5 by tracing the deleted and modified elements of S to A. Note that the elements of A marked `revise` is a subset of those marked `recheck`. Only those that are directly traceable to changed elements of S may require revision; others only need to be rechecked. In lines 6 and 7, the appropriate GSN slicer Slice_{GSN_V} (Slice_{GSN_R}) is invoked to propagate each of the revise (recheck) subsets to dependent elements in A which are added to the recheck subset. Finally, line 8 invokes `CreateAnnotation` to construct the annotation model K from the identified subsets of A. The elements of the subset $C2_{\text{revise}}$ are marked `revise`; the remaining elements in the subset $C3_{\text{recheck2}}$ are marked `recheck`, and all other elements are marked `reuse`.

Algorithm: GSN-IA
Params: $\langle \text{Slice}_{Sys} \rangle$
Input: initial system model $S : Sys$, safety case $A : GSN$,
        traceability map R, changed system megamodel $S' : Sys$,
        delta $D = \langle C0a, C0d, C0m \rangle$
Output: Annotation K
  1: $R'_A \leftarrow \text{Restrict}(R, D)$
  2: $C1dm \leftarrow \text{Slice}_{Sys}(S, \text{Union}(C0d, C0m))$
  3: $C1am \leftarrow \text{Slice}_{Sys}(S', \text{Union}(C0a, C0m))$
  4: $C2_{\text{recheck}} \leftarrow \text{Union}(\text{Trace}(R, C1dm), \text{Trace}(R'_A, C1am))$
  5: $C2_{\text{revise}} \leftarrow \text{Trace}(R, C0d)$
  6: $C3_{\text{recheck1}} \leftarrow \text{Slice}_{GSN_V}(A, C2_{\text{revise}})$
  7: $C3_{\text{recheck2}} \leftarrow \text{Slice}_{GSN_R}(A, \text{Union}(C2_{\text{recheck}}, C3_{\text{recheck1}}))$
  8: $K \leftarrow \text{CreateAnnotation}(A, C3_{\text{recheck2}}, C2_{\text{revise}})$
  9: **return** K

Fig. 5. Algorithm for assessing impact of system changes on a GSN safety case.

Our Slice_{GSN_V} slicer uses the dependency rules in Table 1 adapted from the set of propagation rules described in [11] to identify elements to be marked for rechecking. For example, $\text{GSN}_{1.1}$ says that all goals and strategies linked to a goal G on either end of the `IsSupportedBy` relation are dependent on G (and are therefore marked "recheck"), if G is marked for revision. On the other hand, Slice_{GSN_R} only uses two dependency rules to identify elements to be marked for rechecking: (1) Conclusion goals depend on premise goals they are indirectly linked to by the same strategy, and (2) Goals depend on solutions they are linked to by the `IsSolvedBy` relation.

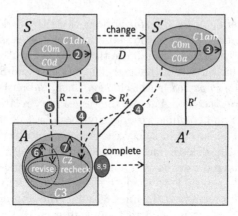

Fig. 6. Visualization of GSN-IA algorithm.

Table 1. Slice_{GSN_V} dependency rules.

Rule	Element	Dependent Element(s)
GSN_1	Goal G	1. All goals/strategies linked to G on either end of the `IsSupportedBy` relation.
		2. All solutions linked to G via the `IsSolvedBy` relation
GSN_2	Strategy S	All goals linked to S on either end of the `IsSupportedBy` relation
GSN_3	Context C	1. All goals, strategies and solutions A that introduce C as the context via the `InContextOf` relation
		2. All goals, strategies and solutions that inherit C as the context (i.e., all children of A)
GSN_4	Solution S	All goals related to S via the `IsSolvedBy` relation

While Slice_{GSN_V} only performs a one-step slice to find the revised elements' direct dependencies, Slice_{GSN_R} works by continuously expanding a subset of elements in a GSN model to include its dependent elements until no further expansion is possible.

4.3 Illustration: Power Sliding Door Example

In our PSD example, the change in the system is the removal of the redundant switch, so the delta D is $\langle \emptyset, (\text{RedundantSwitch}), \emptyset \rangle$. The change directly affects goals B3-6 shown in Fig. 7, which refer to the Redundant Switch, and are therefore marked as `revise` by GSN-IA. The change also affects solutions SN3-6 which would include information about the Redundant Switch. Goal B2 refers to the AC ECU which is traced to the Redundant Switch in the PSD Class Diagram. Slice_{Sys} would have detected that; therefore, B2 is marked `recheck`. Goal B1 does not link to any system components, so it does not appear in the result

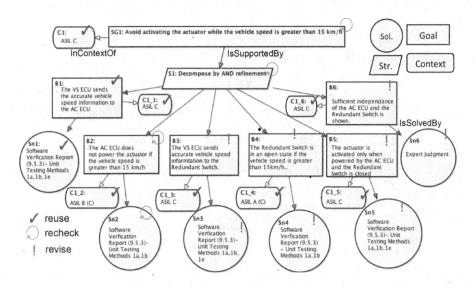

Fig. 7. An annotated GSN safety case for PSD system after running GSN-IA.

of Slice$_{Sys}$, and is therefore marked **reuse**. The remaining parts of the safety case elements are not traced directly to elements in the delta, but get marked using Slice$_{GSN_V}$ and Slice$_{GSN_R}$ described earlier. The result of GSN-IA is the annotation given on top of the original safety case and shown in Fig. 7.

5   A More Precise Impact Assessment

The algorithm GSN-IA, presented in in Sect. 4, is conservative, i.e., more elements are marked **recheck** and **revise** than potentially necessary to still be sound. In this section, we present six different techniques, T1-T6, aimed to improve the precision of GSN-IA. Together, they form a variant of GSN-IA, called GSN-IA-i (improved). The improvements in assigning annotation can be both at the level of safety case elements (goals, strategies, contexts and solutions), or finer, at the level of element identifiers. In order to validate GSN-IA-i, we use a metric $Cost_{IA}$ to compute the cost associated with revision and rechecking after impact assessment. The equation for $Cost_{IA}$ is shown in Fig. 8. For each technique, we describe the current state of GSN-IA, show how to improve the precision in each case (GSN-IA + Ti), present the prerequisites to ensure its soundness, and illustrate it on the PSD example. The techniques are summarized in Table 2.

$$Cost_{IA} = Cost_{Revise} + Cost_{Recheck}$$
$$= (Cost_{G_V} + Cost_{C_V} + Cost_{Sol_V} + Cost_{Str_V}) + (Cost_{G_R} + Cost_{C_R} + Cost_{Sol_R} + Cost_{Str_R})$$
$$= (\sum_{g \in G_V} K_V(1 + n(g)) + \sum_{c \in C_V} K_V(1 + n(c)) + \sum_{s \in Sol_V} K_V + \sum_{s \in Str_V} K_V) +$$
$$(\sum_{g \in G_R} K_R + \sum_{c \in C_R} K_R + \sum_{s \in Sol_R} K_R + \sum_{s \in Str_R} K_R)$$
$$= K_V(\sum_{g \in G_V}(1 + n(g)) + \sum_{c \in C_V}(1 + n(c)) + |Sol_V| + |Str_V|) + K_R(|G_R| + |C_R| + |Sol_R| + |Str_R|)$$
$$= K_V(\sum_{g \in G_V}(1 + n(g)) + \sum_{c \in C_V}(1 + n(c)) + |Sol_V| + |Str_V|) + K_R(|E_R|), \text{ where:}$$

- $Cost_{Revise}$ ($Cost_{Recheck}$): Cost of all revisions (rechecks).
- E_V (E_R): Number of total elements marked for revision (rechecking).
- G_V (G_R): Number of goals marked **revise** (**recheck**).
- C_V (C_R): Number of contexts marked **revise** (**recheck**).
- Str_V (Str_R): Number of strategies marked **revise** (**recheck**).
- Sol_V (Sol_R): Number of solutions marked for **revise** (**recheck**).
- $n(x)$: Number of identifiers in x marked for **revise**.
- K_V (K_R): Cost of performing a revision (a recheck).

Fig. 8. Cost equation for effort incurred after an impact assessment.

Table 2. GSN-IA + Ti techniques and improvements.

Technique	1	2	3–6
Improvement	$n(g) \downarrow, n(c) \downarrow$	$|G_V| \downarrow, |C_V| \downarrow$	$|E_R| \downarrow$

5.1   T1: Increasing the Granularity of Traceability Between the System and the Safety Case

GSN-IA: Trace links between the system and safety case provided to GSN-IA are assumed to link entire safety case elements to system elements. That is, if a change occurs in any of the linked system elements, the entire safety case element is marked for revision.

GSN-IA + T1: Trace links between the system and safety case connect *identifiers* in safety case elements to corresponding system elements. Annotations are then assigned to safety case element identifiers rather than to entire elements.

Improvement: With more fine-grained trace links, GSN-IA + T1 can identify which specific identifiers in a safety case element should be marked for revision, allowing the safety engineer to focus on revising only those parts instead of the entire element. This in turn decreases the number of unnecessary identifier revisions, i.e., $n(g)$ and $n(c)$, since only goals and context nodes are assumed to have identifiers traceable to the system, thus decreasing the overall cost.

Prerequisites: A safety case language that clearly distinguishes identifiers from other text, ensuring that the finer-grained trace links cover at least all the originally covered links in order to preserve soundness of the technique.

Example: In the PSD system, the goal B3 "The VS ECU sends accurate vehicle speed information to the Redundant Switch" can be traced to both VS ECU and Redundant Switch components. Currently, when either VS ECU or Redundant Switch changes, GSN-IA marks the entire goal `revise`. A more fine-grained traceability would link the identifier "VS ECU" to VS ECU in the system and the identifier "Redundant Switch" to the Redundant Switch in the system. Now, if Redundant Switch changes in the system but VS ECU does not, then only the identifier "Redundant Switch" in goal B3 needs to be marked for revision, while the rest of the goal can be reused.

Discussion: Traceability between the system and its safety case can be established at different levels of granularity. Formal safety case languages have clearly defined *identifiers*, thus they can easily be traced to the appropriate system elements. For example, the author of [12] defines a six-step approach for creating well-formed GSN goal structures that in turn aid in a finer-grained system traceability. For languages that only use natural language to describe goals, this fine grained traceability may not be feasible.

5.2   T2: Identifying Sensitivity of Safety Case to System Changes

GSN-IA: Any change to a system element will cause its associated element in the safety case to be marked for revision.

GSN-IA + T2: We mark the safety case element for revision only if it is required by the type of system change.

Improvement: Unnecessary revisions of safety case element are minimized by identifying cases where a system change should actually impact the element, and where it can be ignored. This in turn decreases the number of goal ($|G_V|$) and context ($|C_V|$) elements marked for revision, decreasing the overall cost.

Prerequisites: For each model type in the system megamodel, a sensitivity table that lists all element types of that model and the kinds of changes that they can undergo, and, for each trace link between the system and the safety case, the type of change the link is sensitive to. We assume that the *types* of changes that occur as part of the system evolution are captured with each of the corresponding changes in the *Delta* we are provided. Since the assignment of sensitivity to change is performed by the domain expert, we require these assignments to be correct to preservation of soundness.

Example: In the PSD System, the class Door in the Class Diagram model has an attribute *state*, which is an enumeration with possible values *open* and *closed*. Assume a goal such as "If the door state is open and the speed is greater than 15 km/h, the driver is notified.". Currently, if we add a new option to the door state (e.g., "stuck"), that is considered a change in the door state, which marks the goal for revision. However, such a change (an attribute enumeration extension) should not impact the goal which is only concerned with the door state being open. If we do not add that type of change in the sensitivity list of that particular trace link between system and goal, we are able to ignore it and allow the goal to be reused.

Discussion: In the example above, if the goal had been "If the door state is *not closed* and the speed is greater than 15 km/h, the driver is notified.", then the change should have impacted this goal, as "stuck" is considered "not closed". We assume that goals are structured in a way that specific states are identified; if they are not, T2 cannot be used. Interestingly, in such a case, the goal would have to be marked revise, which may allow detecting missing test cases or other evidence for the "stuck" state.

5.3   T3: Understanding Semantics of Strategies

GST-IA: Any truth valuation change of the premise goals of a strategy lead to rechecking the conclusion goal.

GSN-IA + T3: Here, we use semantic knowledge, i.e., which changes in truth values of the premises do not affect the truth value of the conclusion.

Improvement: We limit the unnecessary propagation of recheck annotations across the safety case, thus $|E_R|$ decreases, causing the overall cost to decrease.

Prerequisites: Semantics of the strategies connecting premise and conclusion goals. This applies to a fixed set of known strategies and not to strategies expressed in natural language. Soundness is preserved since we are using sound semantics of logical connectives to make decisions.

Example: Assume in the PSD system that SG1 was connected to its subgoals B1-B6 via an "OR" decomposition strategy (as opposed to an "AND"). Also assume that currently all of B1-B6 have *true* states. This means that SG1 is also evaluated to *true*. If the system changes so that B5-B6 are marked recheck, we don't need to mark SG1 recheck since, due to disjunction, it must still be *true*.

Discussion: Marking a premise of an "OR" strategy recheck (while other premises are marked reuse) can impact the overall confidence in the argument, as the premise can become *false* after the recheck is performed. We do not take confidence into account at this point and consider it future work.

5.4   T4: Decoupling Revision from Rechecking

GSN-IA: Forces a recheck every time an element is marked revise.

GSN-IA + T4: By knowing circumstances under which revising a goal will not impact its truth value, we require a recheck after a revision only when necessary.

Improvement: Eliminating unnecessary rechecks after revisions leads to possibly decreasing $|E_R|$ and, therefore, the overall cost.

Prerequisites: An extra column in the sensitivity table described in T2 that lists if a particular type of change affects the truth value of a goal. We require correctness of assignments of *changes* to their *effect on goal truth values* as well as completeness of trace links to ensure soundness of the approach.

Example: In the PSD system, changing the name of a system element such that it does not conflict with other names (e.g., Redundant Switch is renamed to Extra Switch) will cause the goals referring to that element (e.g., goal B3) to be marked for revision. However, since changing the name does not impact the truth state of the goal, rechecking can be skipped. Other examples include capitalization of names, spelling corrections or language translations, such that the renaming is done consistently in both the system and the safety case.

5.5 T5: Strengthened Solutions Do Not Impact Associated Goals

GSN-IA: If a piece of evidence that a solution points to changes, the goal supported by that solution is always marked `recheck`.

GSN-IA + T5: A change to a solution that strengthens it should not affect its support for associated goals.

Improvement: Understanding which changes in solutions do not necessitate a rechecking of associated goals can reduce the unnecessary goal rechecks. Thus, $|E_R|$ decreases causing the overall cost to decrease.

Prerequisites: A sensitivity table (similar to T2) that identifies, for each type of evidence, the types of changes it can undergo, and for each "isSupportedBy" link between a solution node pointing to this kind of evidence and a goal, whether or not it is sensitive to each kind of change. Assignments of *changes* to their *effect on goal truth values* need to be correct to guarantee soundness.

Example: Assume that B1 was "The VS ECU sends accurate vehicle speed information to the AC ECU *90% of the time*" and that it was linked to a solution with test cases which showed accuracy 90% of the time. If the system changes so that the test cases can now demonstrate accuracy 100% of the time, this does not affect goal B1, meaning that it should not be marked for rechecking.

5.6 T6: Exploiting Knowledge About ASIL Work-Product Dependencies and ASIL Propagation and Decomposition Rules

GSN-IA: Does not take into account how changes in the system impact ASILs.

GSN-IA + T6: Determine how ASILs should change due to system changes by using knowledge about ASIL work-product dependencies and ASIL propagation and decomposition rules.

Improvement: Increase in precision due to distinguishing between changes to the goals and changes to the ASILs, potentially decreasing the number of required goal rechecks. This decreases $|E_R|$, thereby decreasing the overall cost.

Prerequisites: Dependency tables from ISO 26262 Part 6 that describe the types of methods for each work product required to achieve certain ASILs, and

ASIL decomposition and propagation rules as presented in ISO 26262 (refer to Sect. 3). We assume the soundness of the tables and ASIL propagation and decomposition rules in order to guarantee soundness of our approach.

Example: We present two examples in the PSD system:

1. If method 1e (Back-to-back comparison test between models and code) used for unit testing as part of the Software Verification Report work product for goal B1 is deleted, the ASIL for B1 supported by Sn1 changes from ASIL C to ASIL B based on Table 1. This would in turn impact the ASIL on SG1, since the ASIL propagation rule no longer holds. In this case, claims B1 and SG1 themselves are not impacted, only their ASIL levels are.

2. With redundancy present in the PSD system, ASIL decomposition was used to allocate ASIL B to B2 and ASIL A to B4 (decomposed from ASIL C). B6 was added to demonstrate sufficient independence of the Redundant Switch element from the AC ECU as required by ASIL decomposition. When the system changes and the redundant switch is deleted, requirements B4 and B6 are marked for revision, causing the original decomposition rule to be impacted. B2 is only marked recheck, but its ASIL level will be marked for revision (from ASIL B to ASIL C) to respect ASIL propagation rules from SG1. The impact assessment now flags both C1_2 and Sn2 for revision. Ideally, the safety engineer will revise Sn2 to be strengthened (e.g., unit testing method 1e is added) to increase the ASIL on B2 to level C.

5.7   PSD Example Cost Comparison

Assume that the revision cost K_V is 2 units and the rechecking cost K_R is 1 unit[3]. On the PSD example, GSN-IA produced an annotation with 8 elements marked revise (4 goals, 4 solutions) and 4 marked recheck. Goals marked revise have the following number of identifiers: B3 has 3 (VS ECU, vehicle speed, Redundant Switch), and similarly, B4, B5 and B6 each respectively have 3, 6 and 2 identifiers. The cost incurred after GSN-IA is $2 \times ((1+3) + (1+3) + (1+6) + (1+2) + 4) + 1 \times (4) = 48$ units.

Using T1, changes to the redundant switch link only to the *Redundant Switch* identifier in goals B3-B6 (as opposed to the entire goals), dropping the number of revised elements in each of these goals to only 1 (as opposed to marking all the identifiers in the goal for revision). The cost after running GSN-IA + T1 is $2 \times ((1+1)+(1+1)+(1+1)+(1+1)+4)+1 \times (4) = 28$ units, representing a clear improvement. Due to space limitations, we do not demonstrate the application of the other techniques.

6   Related Work

Model-Based Approaches to Safety Case Management. Many methods for modeling safety cases have been proposed, including goal models and requirements models [3,6] and GSN [10]. The latter is arguably the most widely used

---

[3] In practice, $K_V > K_R$, since revision requires more effort than rechecking.

model-based approach to improving the structure safety arguments. Building on GSN, Habli et al. [7] examine how model-driven development can provide a basis for the systematic generation of functional safety requirements and demonstrates how an automotive safety case can be developed. Gallina [5] proposes a model-driven safety certification method to derive arguments as goal structures given in GSN from process models. The process is illustrated by generating arguments in the context of ISO 26262. We consider this category of work complimentary to ours; we do not focus on safety case construction but instead assume presence of a safety case and focus on assessing the impact of system changes on it.

Safety Case Maintenance. Kelly [11] presents a tool-supported process, based on GSN, that facilitates a systematic safety case impact assessment. The work by Li et al. [15] proposes an assessment process to specify typical steps in the safety case assessment. The authors develop a graphical safety case editor for assessing GSN-based safety case and use the Evidential Reasoning (ER) algorithm to assess the overall confidence in a safety case. Jaradat and Bate [9] present two techniques that use safety contracts to facilitate maintenance of safety cases. As far as we are aware, none of the approaches provide a structured model-based algorithm for impact assessment, or consider methods for improving its efficiency. In the context of safety case maintenance, Bandur and McDermid [1] present a formalization of a logical subset of GSN with the aim of revealing the conditions which must be true in order to guarantee the internal consistency of a safety argument. This provides a sound basis for understanding logical relationships between components of a safety case and thus to enhance impact assessment.

7   Conclusion

In this paper, we showed how using various sources of knowledge about the system changes, the particular safety case language and the safety standard can increase the precision of the previously proposed impact assessment technique [13], thus reducing the work required by the safety engineer. We presented six precision improvement techniques and illustrated our ideas using a GSN safety case used with ISO 26262. In the future, we aim to address the following problems:

Addressing Additions. Currently, our impact assessment approach addresses the effect of adding components in the system on the existing parts of the safety case. However, it currently cannot address how adding components can potentially require additions to the safety case. We plan to study this further and propose approaches for addressing this in the future.

Exploiting System Design Patterns. We would like to understand whether our approach can detect certain changes in the system design which change not the functionality of the system but its level of integrity. For example, consider the "redundancy pattern", where a component such as the redundant switch in our PSD example is added. We would like to study if it is possible to syntactically identify this case as a redundancy change by witnessing two paths to the actuator (one via the VS ECU and one via the redundant switch), and how this can be exploited for impact assessment.

Design Space Exploration. We believe that our approach can be used for impact assessment in general, and not just for safety case co-evolution due to system changes. One application for this is in design space exploration, to enable answering what-if questions about the impact of changes on safety cases. In this context, we would like to study the effect of changes, other than just system changes, on the safety case.

Constructing an Assurance Case for Change. Our impact assessment approach can guide the creation of a Change Argument: an argument for the changes made to the original safety case, providing evidence for such an argument. For example, our approach can support a `revise` marking in a safety case by linking the element to the appropriate counterparts in the system megamodel that caused this marking to be computed.

Confidence. We would like to augment our approach to handle a confidence model on top of safety cases. That is, we would like to assess the impact of changes not just on the safety case elements themselves but on the confidence level we assign them and on the safety case as a whole.

Tool Support and Validation. We are actively working on extending our model management framework MMINT [4] to include safety cases and model management operators for them (e.g., slice). We are also implementing our impact assessment approach using the workflow language defined in MMINT. We plan to incorporate the improvement techniques discussed in this paper and validate their effectiveness on a large scale industrial example.

Acknowledgements. This work is funded by Automotive Partnership Canada and NSERC in collaboration with General Motors.

References

1. Bandur, V., McDermid, J.: Informing assurance case review through a formal interpretation of GSN core logic. In: Proceedings of SafeComp 2015, pp. 3–14 (2015)
2. Borg, M., Vara, J.L., Wnuk, K.: Practitioners' perspectives on change impact analysis for safety-critical software – a preliminary analysis. In: Skavhaug, A., Guiochet, J., Schoitsch, E., Bitsch, F. (eds.) SAFECOMP 2016. LNCS, vol. 9923, pp. 346–358. Springer, Cham (2016). doi:10.1007/978-3-319-45480-1_28
3. Brunel, J., Cazin, J.: Formal verification of a safety argumentation and application to a complex UAV system. In: Ortmeier, F., Daniel, P. (eds.) SAFECOMP 2012. LNCS, vol. 7613, pp. 307–318. Springer, Heidelberg (2012). doi:10.1007/978-3-642-33675-1_27
4. Di Sandro, A., Salay, R., Famelis, M., Kokaly, S., Chechik, M.: MMINT: a graphical tool for interactive model management. In: Proceedings of MoDELS 2015 (Demo) (2015)
5. Gallina, B.: A model-driven safety certification method for process compliance. In: Proceedings of ISSRE 2014 Workshops, pp. 204–209. IEEE (2014)

6. Ghanavati, S., Amyot, D., Peyton, L.: A systematic review of goal-oriented requirements management frameworks for business process compliance. In: Proceedings
of RELAW 2011, pp. 25–34. IEEE (2011)

7. Habli, I., Ibarra, I., Rivett, R.S., Kelly, T.: Model-Based Assurance for Justifying
Automotive Functional Safety. Technical report, SAE (2010)

8. International Organization for Standardization: ISO 26262: Road Vehicles - Functional Safety, 1st version (2011)

9. Jaradat, O., Bate, I.: Systematic maintenance of safety cases to reduce
risk. In: Skavhaug, A., Guiochet, J., Schoitsch, E., Bitsch, F. (eds.) SAFE-
COMP 2016. LNCS, vol. 9923, pp. 17–29. Springer, Cham (2016). doi:10.1007/
978-3-319-45480-1_2

10. Kelly, T., Weaver, R.: the goal structuring notation - a safety argument notation.
In: Proceedings of DSN 2004 (2004)

11. Kelly, T.P., McDermid, J.A.: A systematic approach to safety case maintenance.
In: Felici, M., Kanoun, K. (eds.) SAFECOMP 1999. LNCS, vol. 1698, pp. 13–26.
Springer, Heidelberg (1999). doi:10.1007/3-540-48249-0_2

12. Kelly, T.: A Six-Step Method for the Development of Goal Structures. York Software Engineering, Flixborough (1997)

13. Kokaly, S., Salay, R., Cassano, V., Maibaum, T., Chechik, M.: A model management approach for assurance case reuse due to system evolution. In: Proceedings
of MoDELS 2016, pp. 196–206 (2016)

14. Leveson, N.: Engineering a Safer World: Systems Thinking Applied to Safety. MIT
Press, Cambridge (2011)

15. Li, Z.: A Systematic Approach and Tool Support for Assessing GSN-Based Safety
Case. Master's thesis, Technische Universiteit Eindhoven (2016)

16. Salay, R., Kokaly, S., Chechik, M., Maibaum, T.: Heterogeneous megamodel slicing
for model evolution. In: Proceedings of ME@MoDELS 2016, pp. 50–59 (2016)

17. de la Vara, J.L., Borg, M., Wnuk, K., Moonen, L.: An industrial survey of safety
evidence change impact analysis practice. IEEE TSE **42**(12), 1095–1117 (2016)

Formal Verification

Modeling Operator Behavior in the Safety Analysis of Collaborative Robotic Applications

Mehrnoosh Askarpour[1]([✉]), Dino Mandrioli[1], Matteo Rossi[1], and Federico Vicentini[2]

[1] DEIB, Politecnico di Milano, Milan, Italy
{mehrnoosh.askarpour,dino.mandrioli,matteo.rossi}@polimi.it
[2] CNR, ITIA, Milan, Italy
federico.vicentini@cnr.itia.it

Abstract. Human-Robot Collaboration is increasingly prominent in people's lives and in the industrial domain, for example in manufacturing applications. The close proximity and frequent physical contacts between humans and robots in such applications make guaranteeing suitable levels of safety for human operators of the utmost importance. Formal verification techniques can help in this regard through the exhaustive exploration of system models, which can identify unwanted situations early in the development process. This work extends our SAFER-HRC methodology with a rich non-deterministic formal model of operator behaviors, which captures the hazardous situations resulting from human errors. The model allows safety engineers to refine their designs until all plausible erroneous behaviors are considered and mitigated.

Keywords: Cognitive models · Formal verification · Task-analytic models · Human errors · Safety analysis · Human-robot collaboration

1 Introduction

Collaborative robot applications necessitate close proximity and possible physical contacts between operators and robots, due to the intrinsic nature of the activities they execute together. Thus, a central requirement in the design of this kind of applications is an assessment that identifies hazards and eliminates or mitigate risks. While informal assessment techniques such as HAZOP [28] might overlook some hazards; formal verification techniques are more reliable as they exhaustively check whether a system—modeled through a mathematical notation—satisfies required properties (e.g., safety properties), or has incompletenesses and inconsistencies [5]. However, modeling collaborative applications requires to consider the human behavior and its non-determinism caused by autonomous judgments and improvising actions [43].

In this paper we extend the SAFER-HRC methodology introduced in [3,4] for the assessment of the safety of Human-Robot Collaborative (HRC) applications, by improving the formal model of operators on which the methodology relies.

© Springer International Publishing AG 2017
S. Tonetta et al. (Eds.): SAFECOMP 2017, LNCS 10488, pp. 89–104, 2017.
DOI: 10.1007/978-3-319-66266-4_6

Unlike classic hazard identification approaches such as FTA [27] and FMECA [26] which cannot deal with unpredictable human behavior, the proposed model takes into account both normative human behavior and a number of possible deviations. Thus, previously unrecognized hazardous situations are detected.

Two common approaches to model human operators in system models are: (i) task-analytic models, which represent the observable manifestation of operators' behavior; and (ii) cognitive models, which instead describe the cognitive process behind the operator's observable behavior [11]. In the first approach tasks are represented as hierarchies of actions whose execution sequence is modeled by if-then logic rules, and the operator behavior is part of the overall model of the system. The latter techniques, instead, capture the knowledge used by the operator to execute the task. The human cognitive state is usually described by a set of variables that change with respect to the other elements in the system, following a set of logical production rules. Cognitive models, unlike task-analytic approach, highlight the erroneous behaviors of the operator—i.e., human activities that do not achieve their goals [39]—and provide clues about why such behavior arose, and flaws in the design that allow their occurrence [16]. These clues can be used to refine the system design to reduce the likelihood of operator errors. Pairing a hierarchical task model with a human cognitive architecture has been used to determine the role of operators in the system performance or failure [40]. Cognitive models can be integrated in a larger formal model and evaluated as a part of the system [8].

In [3,4] we formalized collaborative systems to verify the physical safety of human operators. We used a task-analytic approach that models collaborative systems in terms of three main modules—Operator, Robot and Layout—and breaks down tasks into atomic actions. In this work, we combine the previous model with a cognitive model capturing erroneous human behavior driven from the operator's perception of the environment and mental decisions. Thus, we can describe likely errors due to certain characteristics that are frequently found in human operators. To this end, the cognitive-driven reasons and phenotypes of errors are treated as black boxes, and their consequences leading to hazardous situations are analyzed in terms of human safety. The proposed methodology captures human errors and inspects harmful situations caused by those errors.

This paper is structured as follows: Sect. 2 discusses related works on the formalization of human behaviors, especially errors. Section 3 introduces SAFER-HRC and its extension with a model of operators' erroneous behaviors. Section 4 shows how the improved model helps detect new, previously unrecognized hazardous situations. Section 5 discusses some open issues and concludes.

2 Related Work on Human Behavior and Errors

Cognitive architectures such as SOAR [34], ACT-R [2,42], OCM [14,35] and PUM [45] have been widely-used to model the normative and erroneous human behavior. SOAR and ACT-R cannot be used in formal verification approaches since they lack a formal semantics, whereas OCM is known to be suitable only for designing air traffic control applications. PUM, instead, has been used in a wider range of applications [12,13,18,44], where the model of the operator includes a set of goals and a set of actions to achieve them. The operator's knowledge of how to execute actions is modeled as a set of rules. PUM models differentiate between mental and physical actions: first the operator decides to execute an action; then, the action eventually starts. PUM models can be used in different domains, such as Collaborative Robotics. Nevertheless they should be able to replicate human erroneous behavior, so that a verification process can detect the hazardous situations raised by them. Currently, model-based techniques that include human errors focus on interface devices and not physical collaboration and contacts [10]. For example, Physiograms [19] model interfaces of physical devices and [9,36] study the impacts of miscommunication in human-human collaboration while interacting with critical systems. [7,38] explore human deviation from correct instructions using ConcurTaskTrees [37]. [41] upgrades the SAL cognitive model with systematic errors taken from empirical data. Nevertheless, using data related to specific case studies can lead to the loss of generality. [17,19,33] are other examples that combine cognitive and formal models to capture erroneous human behaviors in interactions with devices.

No generally accepted classification of human errors is available. [43] divides errors into two main groups: location- and orientation-related. The former happen when an action is related to multiple locations, or if there are two actions which take place in different locations within the task. The latter happen, for example, when the operator needs to hold a workpiece while it is being screwdriven on a pallet: even if the location is correct, the action might not conclude due to the wrong orientation of the workpiece. [25], instead, classifies the simple phenotypes of human errors into: repetition of an action, reversing the order of actions, omission of actions, late actions, early actions, replacement of an action by another, insertion of an additional action from elsewhere in the task, and intrusion of an additional unrelated action. [22] manually introduces these phenotypes into task specifications, which suffers from many false negatives. The author identifies complex phenotypes created by the combination of simple ones: (i) undershooting, which occurs when an action stops too early; (ii) side tracking, where a segment of unrelated action is carried out, then the correct sequence is resumed; (iii) capturing, where an unrelated action sequence is carried out instead of the expected one; (iv) branching, where the wrong sequence of actions is chosen; (v) overshooting, where the action carries on past its correct end point by not recognizing its post-conditions. Complex phenotypes are combinations of simple ones, as shown in Fig. 1 (where "wrong place" refers to the action's temporal position in the execution sequence, not to a location in the layout). [16] proposes to include in the model strong enough design rules so that cognitively plausible erroneous behavior is not allowed, or is at least is unlikely. Further, authors in [15] propose a framework for reasoning about human-in-the-loop, to identify potential causes for human failure in human-automation interface applications. They have also explored the role of personal variables such as knowledge, experience, the ability to complete recommended actions (self-efficiency), effectiveness of those actions (response-efficiency) and operator trust in them.

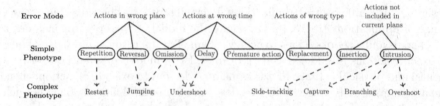

Fig. 1. A taxonomy of erroneous actions phenotypes, taken from [22]

To conclude this section, we remark that some works use probabilistic models to model human operators [20,23,32]. In this vein, [21] uses probability distributions to express human behavior, where distribution functions capture factors such as fatigue and proficiency. However, no validated data from live experiments with real users have been made available, and the article mentions that fictional data were used in order to simulate a distribution over erroneous human behavior. In this work, we do not use probabilistic models to capture human behaviors mainly for two reasons. The first one is a lack of data concerning realistic values for such probabilities. The second is that in our approach the operator model is part of a bigger one that is used to perform the safety analysis of systems. The main aim of the overall model is to identify hazardous situations (including those caused by human errors) and to define suitable Risk Reduction Measures (RRMs, see Sect. 3) to reduce their resulting risk. The goal is to eventually introduce relevant RRMs for every erroneous situation that the safety engineers deem relevant, regardless of their probability value. Nevertheless, once the causes of human errors are identified and categorized (as in Sect. 3), one could evaluate the corresponding probabilities of the different error causes. This can help refine the design by defining more efficient and relevant RRMs.

3   Operator Model

The SAFER-HRC methodology [3,4] hinges on a formal model of HRC applications that relies on a discrete notion of time, and on finite discretizations of the notion of space and of the scalar properties of systems—e.g., velocity. Let us first provide some background on the techniques on which the model is based.

Preliminaries. The SAFER-HRC formal model is expressed through the TRIO metric temporal logic, which features an underlying linear temporal structure and a quantitative notion of time [24]. TRIO formulae are built out of the usual first-order connectives, operators, and quantifiers, as well as a single basic modal operator, called Dist, that implicitly relates the *current time*, to another time instant: given a time-dependent formula ϕ and a (arithmetic) term t indicating a time distance (either positive or negative), formula $\text{Dist}(\phi, t)$ specifies that ϕ holds at exactly t time units from the current one. While TRIO can exploit both discrete and dense time domains, in this work we assume the standard

Table 1. List of derived TRIO operators

Operator	Definition	Meaning
$\text{Futr}(\phi, d)$	$d > 0 \wedge \text{Dist}(\phi, d)$	ϕ occurs exactly at d time units in the future
$\text{Past}(\phi, d)$	$d > 0 \wedge \text{Dist}(\phi, -d)$	ϕ occurred exactly at d time units in the past
$\text{AlwF}(\phi)$	$\forall t(t > 0 \Rightarrow \text{Dist}(\phi, t))$	ϕ holds always in the future
$\text{Until}(\phi, \psi)$	$\exists t(\text{Futr}(\psi, t) \wedge \forall t'(0 < t' < t \Rightarrow \text{Dist}(\phi, t')))$	ϕ will hold until ψ occurs
$\text{SomF}(\phi)$	$\exists t(t > 0 \wedge \text{Dist}(\phi, t))$	ϕ occurs sometimes in the future
$\text{SomP}(\phi)$	$\exists t(t > 0 \wedge \text{Dist}(\phi, -t))$	ϕ occurred sometimes in the past

model of the nonnegative integers $\mathbb{N}$ as discrete time domain. TRIO defines a number of *derived* temporal operators from the basic Dist, through propositional composition and first-order logic quantification. Table 1 defines some of the most significant ones, including those used in this work. The satisfiability of TRIO formulae is in general undecidable. SAFER-HRC uses a decidable subset of the language, which can be handled by automated verification tools, such as the Zot bounded satisfiability checker [1]. Zot is used to check the model of the system against desired safety properties. If the property is not satisfied, Zot provides a counterexample witnessing a system execution that violates the property.

Basic Model. The proposed model for HRC applications includes three main modules: operator (O), robot (R), and layout (L). ISO15066 [31] contains biomechanical studies that divide the human body into 26 sections according to their pain tolerance and being injury prone. In consistency to this standard, O describes all of the identified body sections, the relative constraints concerning their movements, and their position and velocity at each time instant. R divides robots into their components (arms and end-effectors), and captures the velocity, position and force of each part at each time instant. The values for velocity and force range over the quantized set $\{none, low, mid, high\}$. These values will later be used to calculate the risk value of the system. The layout L of the workspace is partitioned into a finite number of regions, each with a defined shape, material and an attribute stating the presence of obstacles $(\{occluded, clear, free, warning\})$. At each time instant, the position of each element of R and O corresponds to the region in which it is located.

SAFER-HRC aims to identify hazardous situations—as described in [29]—by providing their formalization, compute a quantized risk $(\in \{0, 1, 2\})$, and define corresponding Risk Reduction Measures (RRMs) in conformance with [30]. Each HRC task is broken down into a set of elementary actions, which are the smallest possible functional units and are executed either by operators (the performer of the action is the operator: $a_{i, actor} = op$) or by robots (the performer is the robot: $a_{i, actor} = ro$). Each action is associated with a pair $\langle preC, postC \rangle$ of pre- and post-conditions, which are formalized through logical constraints capturing the action's temporal relations with other actions (e.g., precedence). In each instant, the state of an action is described by one of the following atomic formulae:

- $a_{i,sts}$ =ns (not started): state in which not all pre-conditions are true, yet.
- $a_{i,sts}$ =wt (waiting): a state of human actions only, in which all pre-conditions are true, but the action has not yet started. It allows for the introduction of delays or hesitations in human actions.
- $a_{i,sts}$ = exe (executing): running state, triggered by the validity of all pre-conditions.
- $a_{i,sts}$ =sfex (safe executing): special running state, triggered by the activation of at least one RRM. This means that there are currently detected hazards in the system but their consequences are being mitigated by RRMs without interrupting the execution of the action.
- $a_{i,sts}$ = hd (hold): exception state, entered upon an explicit suspension of execution due to a request from the operator. When the state is active, the execution is momentarily paused, although some RRMs may be enabled.
- $a_{i,sts}$ = dn (done): regular termination state, triggered by the validity of all post-conditions.
- $a_{i,sts}$ = exit: whenever the desired safety properties are violated in any state value, the action quits (together with all other actions). The transition may be triggered by situations (e.g., hazards and risks) detected in other actions.

The proposed model also includes the formalization of two recognized types of physical hazards, according to [31]: (i) Transient (Tr) ones, which are fast, impact-like contacts, where body parts are hit and then recoil because of the kinetic energy transferred to the body; and (ii) Quasi-static (Qs) ones, which are sustained contacts of body parts against a constraining object with continuous energy flow from the robot. SAFER-HRC introduces two types of RRMs to treat the detected hazards: Speed and Separation Monitoring (SSM) and Power and Force Limitation (PFL) to avoid physical contacts or limit their consequences, respectively. The former type maintains the robot speed constantly low when the robot works at a distance less than a predefined threshold from the operator; the latter type, instead, limits the value of the robot force.

The original version of the O module focused more on modeling the normative and expected behavior of the operator. In this paper, our aim is to model the operator behavior more realistically, and to capture also situations such as unintended behavior—errors or misuses. The operator model has been extended by including reasonably predictable human errors, to detect hazards that they cause which have been overlooked in the basic model.

Extended Operator Model: Formal Cognitive Model. We now present an extension of module O of the model proposed in [3]. The new model allows for the generation of traces that include human errors and encompasses functional and behavioral human modeling. Since the model is used to generate errors and to analyse the effects of errors on human safety, it focuses on the consequences of human errors rather than their causes. We explain below how phenotypes of

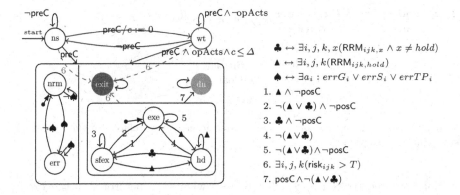

Fig. 2. Parallel composition of execution and erroneous state of each action

erroneous human behavior are taken into account, but we leave the study of genotypes for future work. The model relies on the following assumptions.

(i) Operator actions are fully non-deterministic and are rationally possible to be taken by the operator as their pre-conditions turn true. Every action has a timeout Δ within which the operator needs to decide whether to start the execution of the action after its pre-conditions hold.

(ii) Each action has a corresponding preceding mental decision $opActs_i$, which works as its trigger. When $opActs_i$ becomes true, it means that in the next instant the operator starts executing action a_i. An action which is waiting starts executing right after when the operator makes her mental decision to start acting. Each action has also a corresponding mental decision about stopping (ending, pausing) its execution, captured by predicate $opStops_i$. These two predicates capture the perception of the operator from processing the state of her environment, and the decisions (starting/stopping) she will make according to those perceptions. The decision of the operator to start and end an action is due to what she may see, touch or feel. Instead of modeling each of these causes separately, we model the decision itself directly.

(iii) Additional states for operator actions are introduced describing if the execution state is normative (nrm) or erroneous (err). Figure 2 shows the state-chart capturing the evolution of a single action, which can be in one of the possible execution states {exe, sfex, hd, exit} **and** at the same time in one of {err, nrm}.

(iv) The number of possible human errors is bounded, to avoid making the model too complex and also to avoid generating a lot of false positive situations.

Formalizing Human Errors. Given the classification of [43] and the phenotypes introduced in [25], we categorize human errors in three main types:

1. Time-related errors ($errTP$), which occur when the operator does not follow the correct temporal ordering of actions. Eventually these errors lead to an instance of one of the phenotypes introduced in Fig. 1.

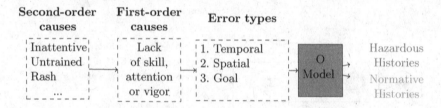

Fig. 3. Types of error that occur due to first-order causes related to the operator's state during execution

2. Space-related errors ($errS$), that happen when the operator is in the wrong L region or places the instruments in the wrong regions.
3. Goal-related errors ($errG$), that arise when the operator is in the right spot to execute an action and starts the execution with no time-related error, but she does not follow instructions correctly and the action is performed poorly. This happens more frequently when the operator is untrained and unskillful.

An error can appear due to two different layers of motives: first-order and second-order causes. Errors originate directly from first-order causes, which are the lack of at least one of the following factors: skill (knowledge + experience + trust in design), attention or vigor. First-order causes themselves originate from the state of the operator, who can be fatigued, inattentive, unaware of the instructions, rash, etc. The goal of this work is to enrich the list of detected hazards, and to this end considering only first-order causes is enough. Second-order causes, on the other hand, are less relevant during the process of identifying new instances of hazardous situations and assessing their corresponding risks. The relations between errors and their first- and second-order causes are shown in Fig. 3. In the rest of this section we illustrate how the formal model takes human errors into account and represents the situations that can arise because of them. In fact, human errors must be formalized and included in the model to systematically generate and verify them during application of the SAFER-HRC methodology.

1. Time-related Errors happen when the operator manipulates the expected temporal order of actions and creates an unwanted situation.

$$errTP_i \Leftrightarrow Repetition_i \vee Omission_i \vee Late_i \vee Early_i \vee Intrusion_i \qquad (1)$$

Our proposed model formalizes each phenotype introduced in [25] and listed in Fig. 1 through the formulae below. Implicitly, since we are dealing with operator errors, constraint $a_{i,actor} = $op is assumed in all the following formulae.

The model captured in module O does not force the operator to start another action or remain idle after executing an action. Consider for example the case (see Sect. 4) where the operator should prepare the jigs and fixtures before the robot starts moving towards the pallet. If the operator repeats the preparation for other jigs or continues to play with jigs after they are already in place, there could be a collision between the operator's hand and the robot end-effector. The formula below formalizes an erroneous **repetition** of an action i by stating that this occurs when the action is currently done and either it was just completed without the operator acknowledging this (i.e., $\mathrm{Past}(\neg a_{i,sts} = \mathrm{dn} \wedge \neg opStops_i, 1)$ holds), or the operator decides to perform it again (i.e., $opActs_i$ holds).

$$Repetition_i \Leftrightarrow a_{i,sts} = \mathrm{dn} \wedge (\mathrm{Past}(a_{i,sts} \neq \mathrm{dn} \wedge \neg opStops_i, 1) \vee opActs_i) \qquad (2)$$

The cases of **reversed** and **replaced** actions in the temporal model are actually covered by the formalization of early/late actions presented below. To allow for the wrong sequencing of operator actions, the corresponding pre-conditions are looser than those for actions executed by robots. In fact, whereas the pre-condition for a robot action typically includes a list of other actions that must have been completed, this does not occur for operator actions, which can be executed as soon as the operator is in the right area and has the required tools.

An action a_i is **omitted** if the operator never executes it, thus predicate $opActs_i$ is never true ($\mathrm{AlwF}(\neg opActs_i)$ holds). Consequently, the status of a_i will always remain ns or wt in the future (i.e., $\mathrm{AlwF}(a_{i,sts} = \mathrm{wt} \vee a_{i,sts} = \mathrm{ns})$ holds), which prevents the execution of robot actions whose pre-conditions require the termination of a_i. Subformula $\mathrm{SomP}(\mathrm{Lasted}(a_{i,sts} = \mathrm{wt}, \Delta))$ states that for action i to be considered omitted it must have previously been in the waiting state for at least Δ time units—otherwise it might simply be the case that not enough time has been given the operator to start it.

$$Omission_i \Leftrightarrow \mathrm{AlwF}(\neg opActs_i \wedge (a_{i,sts} = \mathrm{wt} \vee a_{i,sts} = \mathrm{ns})) \wedge$$
$$\mathrm{SomP}(\mathrm{Lasted}(a_{i,sts} = \mathrm{wt}, \Delta)) \qquad (3)$$

An action i is **delayed** (i.e., predicate $Late_i$ holds) if the operator starts executing it (i.e., $opActs_i$ holds), and the timeout Δ to start the action after it was enabled has already expired sometimes in the past.

$$Late_i \Leftrightarrow opActs_i \wedge \mathrm{SomP}(\mathrm{Lasted}(a_{i,sts} = \mathrm{wt}, \Delta)) \qquad (4)$$

Action i is **prematurely executed** (i.e., $Early_i$ holds) when its preconditions are not yet satisfied (it is still "not started"), but the operator has already decided to execute it ($opActs_i$ holds). In fact, the operator's act does not change the status of a_i, which remains "not started".

$$Early_i \Leftrightarrow a_{i,sts} = \mathrm{ns} \wedge \mathrm{Past}(opActs_i, 1) \qquad (5)$$

Intrusion and **insertion** errors occur when the operator confuses the task to be executed with another one. Both these situations are captured by predicate $Intrusion_i$, which is formalized by the formula below. More precisely, if T is the task being executed, $Intrusion_i$ holds when there is an action of T that is in the waiting state, but the operator starts executing an action j that is not in T:

$$Intrusion_i \Leftrightarrow a_{i,sts} = \mathrm{wt} \wedge \exists j \notin T : \mathrm{Past}(opActs_j, 1) \qquad (6)$$

2. Space-related errors are raised due to movements of the operator in the layout which are not over-constrained in the model. An action is prone to space-related errors when the operator violates its location-base requirements during its execution (i.e., $safeL_i$ is false while the action is executing), or if the action goes into a "hold" state without the operator having asked to stop the action (i.e., $opStops_i$ is false, which means that the holding state has been entered for reasons related to the behavior of the operator). Examples of operator behaviors that lead to such situations are: leaving her required position or safe spot, getting closer to robot than the distance indicated in the instructions, approaching the robot when an alarm signals to stay away.

$$errS_i \Rightarrow \left(\neg safeL_i \wedge (a_{i,sts} = \text{exe} \vee a_{i,sts} = \text{sfex})\right) \vee$$
$$\left(a_{i,sts} = \text{hd} \wedge (\text{Past}(a_{i,sts} \neq \text{hd} \wedge \neg opStops_i), 1)\right) \tag{7}$$

3. Goal-related Errors deal with actions which are not executed consistently with the instructions of the task. For example if the operator does not place the fixtures properly or tightens the part on the pallet while screw-driving. The presence of goal-related errors.is represented by predicate $errG_i$, which is non-deterministically assigned values during the exploration of the system traces. Notice that, in practice, goal-related errors can be detected, for example, through the use of cameras installed in the work-cell; hence, predicate $errG_i$ can be seen as capturing the information provided by such cameras.

The addition of the formalization of these phenotypes to the model allows us to check whether there are hazardous situations that cannot be mitigated by currently introduced RRMs, thus if the base model failed to capture hazards that arise due to human errors. As mentioned in Sect. 3, the model introduces constraints on the number of human errors during execution of a task. In fact, it is reasonable that an operator does not make too many errors during a single execution of an application; on the other hand, this number can be configured in the model, although the higher the number, the greater the complexity of the model and the required analysis time. The following formula—which has been simplified for the sake of brevity, and where $past(count_i, 1)$ is the function returning the value of $count_i$ at the previous instant—describes the increment of the counter of errors made during action i:

$$count_i = \text{past}(count_i, 1) + 1 \Leftrightarrow (errG_i \wedge \text{Past}(\neg errG_i, 1)) \vee (errS_i \wedge \text{Past}(\neg errS_i, 1))$$
$$\vee (errTP_i \wedge \text{Past}(\neg errTP_i, 1)) \tag{8}$$

The total counter $count$ is simply the sum of all $count_i$, and we impose that it never exceeds a (configurable) threshold N: $\text{AlwF}(count \leq N)$. Notice that, in a similar vein, in the formal model we impose a constraint that $errG_i$ cannot occur more often than every 5 time units.

The next section shows how experiments carried out with the enhanced model can highlight hazardous cases that originate from human errors.

4   Case Study

The case study on which we applied the enhanced SAFER-HRC methodology features a hybrid human-robot assembly task in the preparation of a machine tool pallet—i.e., setting jigs and mounting/dismounting workpieces into fixtures before/after machining. In Flexible Manufacturing Systems, load/unload stations are the only parts handled manually in a largely automatic procedure. A collaborative robot, capable of relocating inside the production plant, can be used for a number of tasks—e.g., carrying containers with workpieces or finished items, supporting workpieces during assembly. The overall goal of the HRC application is to provide all services that improve the ergonomics of manual operations, release the operators from repetitive/heavy/dull tasks, provide quantitative logs of operations, reduce errors. The operator can choose to achieve the task in different ways: either she performs the actions related to the pick-and-place subtask while the robot screw-drives (alternative V1), or vice-versa (alternative V2). The work-cell layout $\mathcal{L}$ is divided according to a polar grid, partitioning the angular range of the robot shoulder joint and the outreach of the manipulator from its base (see Fig. 4).

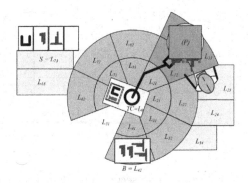

Fig. 4. Top-view representation of the discretized layout

Formal verification was carried out through the Zot [1] tool, which exhaustively explores the state-space of traces of the model up to a bounded length [24]. All verification experiments were performed using the bvzot plugin [6] on a 2.6 GHz Intel® core™ i5 machine. The bounded search depth for Zot was set to 30, and the verification execution was a matter of few seconds. We verified that the risk does not exceed a desired threshold (2, in this case), unless there is a RRM which mitigates it right at the next time instant. The property is captured by the following formula:

$$\forall i, j, k \left(\text{Alw}\left((\text{risk}_{ijk} < 2) \ \lor \ (\text{risk}_{ijk} = 2 \land \exists y(\text{RRM}_{ijk,y}) \land \text{Futr}(\text{risk}_{ijk} < 2, 1))\right)\right) \tag{9}$$

Given the extensions introduced in the operator model, we aim to guarantee that the property is verified also when human errors are systematically considered at design time. In particular, we observed new hazardous situations that the old model was not able to capture or mitigate. Here we report on a pair of them: the first one describes a new quasi-static hazard instance that persists even though

Table 2. Output of the verification tool: state of the model at each time instant

(a) Risk Analysis Table: hazards present (Hzds), location of the occurrence (L_k), moving and direction of operator and robot parts (end-effector, first and second links), relative speed, force and separations and current risk value

```
+--+---------+-----------+-----+--+---------+----------+----+----+-----+-----+-----+----+
|t |Executing|   Hzds    |L_k|Se| Still/Move| Direction | v | f | Sep | Sep | Sep |Risk|
|  |         |           |     |  |          |(Reach/Leave)|   |   |(ee,op)|(R1,op)|(R2,op)|    |
+--+---------+-----------+-----+--+---------+----------+----+----+-----+-----+-----+----+
|  | actn-V  |           |     |  |Op-EE-R2-R1| EE-R2-R1 |   |    |     |     |     |    |
|  |   ...   |1.Qs of Waist| 2 |4 |          |          |   |    |     |     |     |    |
|15|         | area by R1|     |  |          |          |   |    |     |     |     |    |
|  |  8 - 1  |           |     |  | m -m -s -m| l -l -l |high|high| close | close | close | 2 |
|  |         |2.Qs of Arm| 2 |4 |          |          |   |    |     |     |     |    |
|  |   ...   | area by R1|     |  |          |          |   |    |     |     |     |    |
+--+---------+-----------+-----+--+---------+----------+----+----+-----+-----+-----+----+

+--+---------+-----------+-----+--+---------+----------+----+----+-----+-----+-----+----+
|t |Executing|   Hzds    |L_k|Se| Still/Move| Direction | v | f | Sep | Sep | Sep |Risk|
|  |         |           |     |  |          |(Reach/Leave)|   |   |(ee,op)|(R1,op)|(R2,op)|    |
+--+---------+-----------+-----+--+---------+----------+----+----+-----+-----+-----+----+
|  | actn-V  |           |     |  |Op-EE-R2-R1| EE-R2-R1 |   |    |     |     |     |    |
|  |   ...   |1.Qs of Arm| 1 |3 |          |          |   |    |     |     |     |    |
|16|         | area by R1|     |  |          |          |   |    |     |     |     |    |
|  |  8 - 1  |           |     |  | s -m -m -m| r -r -r |high|low | close | close | close | 2 |
|  |         |2.Qs of Waist| 1 |3 |          |          |   |    |     |     |     |    |
|  |   ...   | area by R2|     |  |          |          |   |    |     |     |     |    |
+--+---------+-----------+-----+--+---------+----------+----+----+-----+-----+-----+----+
```

(b) Error Detection Table

```
+--+-------+------+--------------+----------+------------------+----+----+
| t|Actn-V | status|Erroneous State| error type|       Hzds       |Risk|RRMs|
+--+-------+------+--------------+----------+------------------+----+----+
|  |       |      |              |S - G - TP |                  |    |    |
|  |  ...  | ...  |     ...      |   ...     |Qs of Arm area by R1|   | 3 |
|15|7 - 1  | done |     err      |0 , 0 , (re)|Qs of Waist area by R1| 2 | 6 |
|  |8 - 1  | exrm |     norm     |0 , 0 , (-) |                  |    |    |
|  |  ...  |      |              |   ...     |                  |    |    |
+--+-------+------+--------------+----------+------------------+----+----+

+--+-------+------+--------------+----------+------------------+----+----+
| t|Actn-V | status|Erroneous State| error type|       Hzds       |Risk|RRMs|
+--+-------+------+--------------+----------+------------------+----+----+
|  |       |      |              |S - G - TP |                  |    |    |
|  |  ...  | ...  |     ...      |   ...     |Qs of Arm area by R1|   | 3 |
|16|7 - 1  | done |     err      |0 , 0 , (re)|Qs of Waist area by R2| 2 | 6 |
|  |8 - 1  | exrm |     norm     |0 , 0 , (-) |                  |    |    |
|  |  ...  |      |              |   ...     |                  |    |    |
+--+-------+------+--------------+----------+------------------+----+----+
```

RRMs are active in the system. The second one demonstrates a situation for which there is not actually a reasonable RRM that can fully mitigate it.

Persistent Hazard. Table 2 shows an example of the output of the Zot formal verification. Table 2(a) is used by safety analyzers to examine the risk level at each time instant. In this example, the chosen alternative is V1 and actions from V2 are considered as Intrusion errors. The table shoes that there are two time instants in a row with risk value equal to two, which violates the desired safety property. Table 2(b) shows where human errors happen; in particular, it shows that, although there are active RRMs at times 14 and 15, the risk level is still 2 and the error present is $Repetition_7$. Thus, we associate a stronger RRM to the hazard "Qs on Arm area by R1", which not only limits the relative force—which was enough in absence of human errors—but also the relative velocity value.

Unreasonably Uncommon Behavior. The formal model presented in this paper has not been designed to directly address irrational human behaviors or intentional misuses. Nevertheless, it is able to detect some situations that can be classified as "unreasonably uncommon", as they should be very unlikely to occur. For example, consider the case of an operator that purposely throws

Table 3. New hazardous situations detected by the tool (a) Situation where the operator is rapidly closing on the robot, which is still (b) Error cause: the operator is mistakenly executing an action belonging to another task, which requires her to move where the robot is (**in** refers to intrusion error)

(a) Situation where the operator is rapidly closing on the robot, which is still

t	Executing	Hzds	L_k	Se	Still/Move	Direction (Reach/Leave)	v	f	Sep (ee,op)	Sep (R1,op)	Sep (R2,op)	Risk
	actn-V				Op-EE-R2-R1	EE-R2-R1						
5	–		–	–								0
					m –s –s –s	r –r –r.	high	mid	close	close	close	

(b) Error cause: the operator is mistakenly executing an action belonging to another task, which requires her to move where the robot is (**in** refers to intrusion error)

t	Actn-V	status	Erroneous State	error type	Hzds	Risk	RRMs
				S – G – TP			
	1 – 1	done	norm	0 , 0 , (–)			
5	2 – 1	done	err	0 , 0 , (re)		0	
	3 – 1	wt	err	0 , 0 , (in)			
	...	...	...	...			

herself under the robot sharp end-effector. Defining a RRM for this case can be considered useless, because a determined operator would still not follow it. The experiment of Table 3 shows a case where the operator is unexpectedly moving towards the robot. The reason could be intentional harm—caused by an instance of $errG$— or that the operator is doing something wrong that leads to an unwanted situation—presence of instances of $errTP$, $errS$ or $errG$. However, no hazard has been identified by the tool because we kept very unlikely scenarios out of the model when formalizing hazards and risks (essentially, the risk for these kinds of situations is considered low), and in any other case a still robot in the homing position (L_0) is not considered a source of harm and danger. In fact, the situation in this case has been detected by perusing a trace produced by the Zot tool in "simulation mode", that did not highlight a high risk.

5 Discussion and Conclusion

In this work, the SAFER-HRC methodology is extended to capture and consider also the erroneous behavior of human operators. Using the improved model, we re-checked desired safety properties of previously analyzed HRC applications; the new checks highlighted some instances of hazards that had been overlooked in previous runs of the methodology due to a lack of precise human modeling.

The improved accuracy of the model opens the possibility to refine previously-introduced RRMs in order to provide a trade-off between safety and efficiency. Previously, very general RRMs had to be introduced, such as "reduce speed down to a certain value", or "reduce applied force down to zero". However, the newly introduced details concerning the reasons behind and the exact configuration of hazards allow us to define more specific and hazard-dependent RRMs and avoid the use of over-conservative RRMs when a less strict RRM can provide safety.

As a future step, we plan to associate probability distributions with relations between hazards and human errors to see how errors can increase the occurrence of hazards. In this way we might be able to provide more efficient treatments for hazards without compromising the functionality of the system. We are also concluding a prototype tool—a plug-in for Papyrus Eclipse Environment—which resolves the difficulty of dealing with logic formulae to model the applications for safety experts. The tool automatically transforms UML diagrams to Logical formulae and invokes Zot to verify the safety property so that the design and verification of HRC application is made easier, faster and more automated.

Acknowledgment. We thank the anonymous reviewers for their comments and suggestions, which helped us improve the paper.

References

1. The Zot bounded satisfiability checker. http://github.com/fm-polimi/zot
2. Anderson, J.R.: ACT: a simple theory of complex cognition. Am. Psychol. **51**, 355–365 (1996)
3. Askarpour, M.: Risk assessment in collaborative robotics. In: Proceedings of FM-DS (2016)
4. Askarpour, M., Mandrioli, D., Rossi, M., Vicentini, F.: SAFER-HRC: safety analysis through formal verification in human-robot collaboration. In: Skavhaug, A., Guiochet, J., Bitsch, F. (eds.) SAFECOMP 2016. LNCS, vol. 9922, pp. 283–295. Springer, Cham (2016). doi:10.1007/978-3-319-45477-1_22
5. Baier, C., Katoen, J.P.: Principles of Model Checking (2008)
6. Baresi, L., Pourhashem Kallehbasti, M.M., Rossi, M.: Efficient scalable verification of LTL specifications. In: Proceedings of ICSE (2015)
7. Basnyat, S., Palanque, P.: A task pattern approach to incorporate user deviation in task models. In: Proceedings of ADVISES (2005)
8. Bolton, M.L.: Automatic validation and failure diagnosis of human-device interfaces using task analytic models and model checking. Comput. Math. Organ. Theory **19**, 288–312 (2013)
9. Bolton, M.L.: Model checking human-human communication protocols using task models and miscommunication generation. J. Aerospace Inf. Syst. **12**, 476–489 (2015)
10. Bolton, M.L., Bass, E.J., Siminiceanu, R.I.: Generating phenotypical erroneous human behavior to evaluate human-automation interaction using model checking. Int. J. Hum.-Comput. Stud. **70**(11), 888–906 (2012)
11. Bolton, M.L., Bass, E.J., Siminiceanu, R.I.: Using formal verification to evaluate human-automation interaction: a review. IEEE Trans. SMC Syst. **43**(3), 488–503 (2013)
12. Butterworth, R., Blandford, A., Duke, D.: The role of formal proof in modelling interactive behaviour. In: Markopoulos, P., Johnson, P. (eds.) Proceedings of DSV-IS, pp. 87–101. Springer, Vienna (1998). doi:10.1007/978-3-7091-3693-5_7
13. Butterworth, R., Blandford, A., Duke, D.: Demonstrating the cognitive plausibility of interactive system specifications. Form. Asp. Comp. **12**, 237–259 (2000)
14. Cerone, A., Lindsay, P.A., Connelly, S.: Formal analysis of human-computer interaction using model-checking. In: Proceedings of SEFM (2005)

15. Cranor, L.F.: A framework for reasoning about the human in the loop. In: Proceedings of UPSEC (2008)
16. Curzon, P., Blandford, A.: From a formal user model to design rules. In: Forbrig, P., Limbourg, Q., Vanderdonckt, J., Urban, B. (eds.) DSV-IS 2002. LNCS, vol. 2545, pp. 1–15. Springer, Heidelberg (2002). doi:10.1007/3-540-36235-5_1
17. Curzon, P., Blandford, A.: Formally justifying user-centred design rules: a case study on post-completion errors. In: Boiten, E.A., Derrick, J., Smith, G. (eds.) IFM 2004. LNCS, vol. 2999, pp. 461–480. Springer, Heidelberg (2004). doi:10.1007/978-3-540-24756-2_25
18. Curzon, P., Rukšėnas, R., Blandford, A.: An approach to formal verification of human-computer interaction. Form. Asp. Comput. 19(4), 513–550 (2007)
19. Dix, A.J., Ghazali, M., Gill, S., Hare, J., Ramduny-Ellis, D.: Physigrams: modelling devices for natural interaction. Form. Asp. Comput. 21, 613 (2009)
20. Feng, L., Humphrey, L., Lee, I., Topcu, U.: Human-interpretable diagnostic information for robotic planning systems. In: Proceedings of IROS (2016)
21. Feng, L., Wiltsche, C., Humphrey, L., Topcu, U.: Synthesis of human-in-the-loop control protocols for autonomous systems. IEEE T-ASE 13(2), 450–462 (2016)
22. Fields, R.E.: Analysis of erroneous actions in the design of critical systems. Ph.D. thesis, University of York (2001)
23. Fu, J., Topcu, U.: Synthesis of joint control and active sensing strategies under temporal logic constraints. IEEE Trans. Automat. Contr. (2016)
24. Furia, C.A., Mandrioli, D., Morzenti, A., Rossi, M.: Modeling Time in Computing (2012)
25. Hollnagel, E.: Cognitive reliability and error analysis method (CREAM) (1998)
26. International Electrotechnical Commission: IEC 60812: 2006: Analysis techniques for system reliability - Procedure for failure mode and effects analysis
27. International Electrotechnical Commission: IEC 60812: 2006: Fault tree analysis
28. International Electrotechnical Commission: IEC 61882: Hazard and operability studies (HAZOP studies) - Application guides
29. International Standard Organisation: ISO12100: 2010, Safety of machinery - General principles for design - Risk assessment and risk reduction
30. International Standard Organisation: ISO14121-2: 2007, Safety of machinery - Risk assessment - Part 2
31. International Standard Organisation: ISO/TS15066: 2015, Robots and robotic devices - Collaborative robots
32. Junges, S., Jansen, N., Katoen, J., Topcu, U.: Probabilistic model checking for complex cognitive tasks - A case study in human-robot interaction. CoRR (2016)
33. Kim, N., Rothrock, L., Joo, J., Wysk, R.A.: An affordance-based formalism for modeling human-involvement in complex systems for prospective control. In: Proceedings of WSC (2010)
34. Laird, J.E.: The Soar Cognitive Architecture. MIT Press, Cambridge (2012)
35. Lindsay, P.A., Connelly, S.: Modelling erroneous operator behaviours for an air-traffic control task. In: Proceedings of AUIC (2002)
36. Pan, D., Bolton, M.L.: Properties for formally assessing the performance level of human-human collaborative procedures with miscommunications and erroneous human behavior. Int. J. Ind. Ergonom. (2016)
37. Paterno, F., Mancini, C., Meniconi, S.: ConcurTaskTrees: a diagrammatic notation for specifying task models. In: Howard, S., Hammond, J., Lindgaard, G. (eds.) INTERACT 1997. IFIP AICT, pp. 362–369. Springer, Boston, MA (1997). doi:10.1007/978-0-387-35175-9_58

38. Paternò, F., Santoro, C.: Preventing user errors by systematic analysis of deviations from the system task model. Int. J. Hum.-Comput. Stud. **56**, 225–245 (2002)
39. Reason, J.: Human Error. Cambridge University Press, Cambridge (1990)
40. Ritter, F.E., Rooy, D.V., Amant, R.S., Simpson, K.: Providing user models direct access to interfaces: an exploratory study of a simple interface with implications for HRI and HCI. IEEE Trans. SMC Syst. (2006)
41. Ruksenas, R., Back, J., Curzon, P., Blandford, A.: Verification-guided modelling of salience and cognitive load. Form. Asp. Comput. **21**, 541 (2009)
42. Salvucci, D.D., Lee, F.J.: Simple cognitive modeling in a complex cognitive architecture. In: Proceedings of CHI (2003)
43. Shin, D., Wysk, R.A., Rothrock, L.: Formal model of human material-handling tasks for control of manufacturing systems. IEEE Trans. SMC Syst. **36**(4), 685–696 (2006)
44. Werther, B., Schnieder, E.: Formal cognitive resource model: modeling of human behavior in complex work environments. In: Proceedings of CIMCA-IAWTIC (2005)
45. Young, R.M., Green, T.R.G., Simon, T.J.: Programmable user models for predictive evaluation of interface designs. In: Proceedings of CHI (1989)

Development and Verification of a Flight Stack for a High-Altitude Glider in Ada/SPARK 2014

Martin Becker[✉], Emanuel Regnath, and Samarjit Chakraborty

Chair of Real-Time Computer Systems,
Technical University of Munich, 80333 Munich, Germany
becker@rcs.ei.tum.de

Abstract. SPARK 2014 is a modern programming language and a new state-of-the-art tool set for development and verification of high-integrity software. In this paper, we explore the capabilities and limitations of its latest version in the context of building a flight stack for a high-altitude unmanned glider. Towards that, we deliberately applied static analysis early and continuously during implementation, to give verification the possibility to steer the software design. In this process we have identified several limitations and pitfalls of software design and verification in SPARK, for which we give workarounds and protective actions to avoid them. Finally, we give design recommendations that have proven effective for verification, and summarize our experiences with this new language.

Keywords: Ada/SPARK · Formal verification · Limitations · Rules

1 Introduction

The system under consideration is a novel kind of weather balloon which is actively controlled, and thus requires verification to ensure it is working properly in public airspace. As any normal weather balloon, the system climbs up to the stratosphere (beyond an altitude of 10 km), while logging weather data such as temperature, pressure, NO_2-levels and so on. Eventually the balloon bursts, and the sensors would be falling back to the ground with a parachute, drifting away with prevailing wind conditions. However, our system is different from this point onwards: the sensors are placed in a light-weight glider aircraft which is attached to the balloon. At a defined target altitude, the glider separates itself from the balloon, stabilizes its attitude and performs a controlled descent back to the take-off location, thus, bringing the sensors back home. In this paper we focus on the development and formal verification of the glider's onboard software.

The requirements for such a system are challenging already because of the extreme environmental conditions; temperatures range from 30 °C down to −50 °C, winds may exceed 100 kph, and GPS devices may yield vastly different output in those altitudes due to decreasing precision and the wind conditions.

The source code for this project is available at github.com/tum-ei-rcs/StratoX.

© Springer International Publishing AG 2017
S. Tonetta et al. (Eds.): SAFECOMP 2017, LNCS 10488, pp. 105–116, 2017.
DOI: 10.1007/978-3-319-66266-4_7

The combination of those extreme values is likely to trigger corner cases in the software, and thus should be covered by means of extensive testing or by analysis.

We use this opportunity of a safety-critical, yet hardly testable system to explore the new state-of-the art verification tools of Ada/SPARK 2014 [7], especially to identify limitations, pitfalls and applicability in practice. To experience this new SPARK release to its full extent, we applied a *co-verification* approach. That is, we did not perform verification on a finished product, but instead in parallel to the software development (the specific strategy is not of relevance for this paper, but only the effect that this enabled us to identify code features that pose challenges in verification, and find workarounds for them). The implementation could therefore be shaped by verification needs. Moreover, since the high-altitude glider was a research project, we allowed ourselves to modify the initial software design to ease verification when needed.

2   Verification in Ada/SPARK

SPARK 2014 is a major redesign of the original SPARK language, which was intended for formal verification. SPARK 2014 now adopts Ada 2012 syntax, and covers a large subset of Ada. As a result, the GNAT Ada compiler can build an executable from SPARK 2014 source code, and even compile a program which mixes both languages. Compared to Ada, the most important exclusions are pointers (called *access*), aliasing and allocators, as well as a ban of exception handling. As a consequence, SPARK programs first and foremost must be shown to be free of run-time exceptions (called *AoRTE* - absence of run-time errors), which constitutes the main verification task.

The SPARK language – for the rest of this paper we refer to SPARK 2014 simply as SPARK – is built on functional contracts and data flow contracts. Subprograms (procedures and functions) can be annotated with pre- and postconditions, as well as with data dependencies. GNATprove, the (only) static analyzer for SPARK 2014, aims to prove subprograms in a modular way, by analyzing each of them individually. The effects of callees are summarized by their post-condition when the calling subprogram is analyzed, and the precondition of the callee is imposing a proof obligation on the caller, i.e., the need to verify that the caller respects the callee's precondition. Further proof obligations arise from each language-defined check that is executed on the target, such as overflow checks, index checks, and so on. If all proofs are successful, then the program is working according to its contracts and no exceptions will be raised during execution, i.e., AoRTE is established.

Internally, GNATprove [7] builds on the Why3 platform [6], which performs deductive verification on the proof obligations to generate verification conditions (VCs), and then passes them to a theorem solver of user's choice, e.g., cvc4, alt-ergo or z3. Note that there exists also a tool for abstract interpretation, which is, however, not discussed here.

2.1   The GNAT Dimensionality Checking System

We also want to introduce a feature that is not part of the SPARK language itself, but an implementation-defined extension of the GNAT compiler, and thus available for SPARK programs. Since Ada 2012, the GNAT compiler offers a dimension system for numeric types through implementation-defined aspects [9]. The dimension system can consist of up to seven base dimensions, and physical quantities are declared as subtypes, annotated with the exponents of each dimension. Expressions using such variables are statically analyzed by the compiler for their dimensional consistency. Furthermore, the dimensioned variables contribute to readability and documentation of the code. Inconsistencies such as the following are found (dividend and divisor are switched in the calculation of rate):

```
1  angle : Angle_Type  := 20.0 * Degree;
2  dt    : Time_Type   := 100.0 * Milli * Second;
3  rate  : Angular_Velocity_Type := dt / angle; -- compiler error
```

Note that scaling prefixes like Milli can be used, and that common conversions, such as between Degree and Radian in line 1, can be governed in a similar way.

In our project, we specified a unit system with the dimensions *length*, *mass*, *time*, *temperature*, *current*, and *angle*. Adding angle as dimension provides better protection against assignments of dimensionless types, as proposed in [11].

3   Initial System Design and Verification Goals

Target Hardware. We have chosen the "Pixhawk" autopilot [8]. It comprises two ARM processors; one Cortex-M4F (STM32F427) acting as flight control computer, and one Cortex-M3 co-processor handling the servo outputs. We implemented our flight stack on the Cortex-M4 from the ground up, thus completely replacing the original PX4/NuttX firmware that is installed when shipped.

Board Support, Hardware Abstraction Layer & Run-Time System. We are hiding the specific target from the application layer by means of a board support package (not to be confused with an Ada package). This package contains an hardware abstraction layer (HAL) and a run-time system (RTS). The RTS is implementing basic functionality such as tasking and memory management. The HAL is our extension of AdaCore's Drivers Library [1], and the RTS is our port of the Ada RTS for the STM32F409 target. Specifically, we have ported the Ravenscar Small Footprint variant [3], which restricts Ada's and SPARK's tasking facilities to a deterministic and analyzable subset, but meanwhile forbids exception handling, which anyway is not permitted in SPARK.

Separating Tasks by Criticality. Separating tasks has been one goal, since multi-threading is supported in SPARK. In particular, 1. termination of low-critical tasks shall not cause termination of high-critical tasks, 2. higher-criticality tasks shall not be blocked by lower-critical tasks and, 3. adverse effects such as deadlocks, priority inversion and race conditions must not occur.

We partitioned our glider software into two tasks (further concurrency arises from interrupt service routines):

1. The *Flight-Critical Task* includes all execution flows required to keep the glider in a controlled and navigating flight, thus including sensor reads and actuator writes. It is time-critical for control reasons. High-criticality.
2. The *Mission-Critical Task* includes all execution flows that are of relevance for recording and logging of weather data to an SD card. Low-priority task, only allowed to run when the flight-critical task is idle. Low-criticality.

The latter task requires localization data from the former one, to annotate the recorded weather data before writing it to the SD card. Additionally, it takes over the role of a flight logger, saving data from the flight-critical task that might be of interest for a post-flight analysis. The interface between these two tasks would therefore be a protected object with a message queue that must be able to hold different types of messages.

Verification Goals. First and foremost, AoRTE shall be established for all SPARK parts, since exceptions would result in task termination. Additionally, the application shall make use of as many contracts and checks as possible, and perform all of its computations using dimension-checked types. Last but not least, a few functional high-level requirements related to the homing functionality have been encoded in contracts. Overall, the focus of verification was the application, not the BSP. The BSP has been written in SPARK only as far as necessary to support proofs in the application. The rationale was that the RTS was assumed to be well tested, and the HAL was expected to be hardly verifiable due to direct hardware access involving pointers and restricted types.

4   Problems and Workarounds

In this section, we describe the perils and difficulties that we identified during verification of SPARK programs. We use the following nomenclature:

- **False Positive.** Denotes a failing check (failed VC) in static analysis which would not fail in any execution on the target, i.e., a false alarm.
- **False Negative.** Denotes a successful check (discharged VC) in static analysis which would fail in at least one execution on the target, i.e., a missed failure.

4.1   How to Miss Errors

There are a few situations in which static analysis can miss run-time exceptions, which in a SPARK program inevitably ends in abnormal program termination. Before we show these unwanted situations, we have to point out one important property of a deductive verification approach: Proofs build on each other. Consider the following example (results of static analysis given in comments):

```
1  a := X / Z; -- medium: division check might fail
2  b := Y / Z; -- info: division check proved
```

The analyzer reports that the check in line 2 cannot fail, although it suffers from the same defect as line 1. However, when the run-time check at line 1 fails, then line 2 cannot be reached with the offending value of z, therefore line 2 is not a False Negative, unless exceptions have been wrongfully disabled.

Mistake 1: Suppressing False Positives. When a developer comes to the conclusion that the analyzer has generated a False Positive (e.g., due to insufficient knowledge on something that is relevant for a proof), then it might be justified to suppress the failing property. However, we experienced cases where this has generated False Negatives which where hiding (critical) failures. Consider the following code related to the GPS:

```
1  function toInt32 (b : Byte_Array) return Int_32 with Pre => b'Length= 4;
2  procedure Read_From_Device (d : out Byte_Array) is begin
3     d := (others => 0); -- False Positive
4     pragma Annotate (GNATprove, False_Positive,"length check might fail",
          ...);
5  end Read_From_Device;
6
7  procedure Poll_GPS is
8     buf     : Byte_Array (0..91) := (others => 0);
9     alt_mm  : Int_32;
10 begin
11    Read_From_Device (buf);
12    alt_mm := toInt32(buf(60..64)); -- False Negative, guaranteed exception
13 end Poll_GPS;
```

Static analysis found that the initialization of the array d in line 3 could fail, but this is not possible in this context, and thus a False Positive[1]. The developer was therefore suppressing this warning with an annotation pragma. However, because proofs build on each other, a severe defect in line 12 was missed. The array slice has an off-by-one error which *guaranteed* failing the precondition check of toInt32. The reason for this False Negative is that everything after the initialization of d became virtually *unreachable* and that all following VCs consequently have been discharged. In general, a False Positive may exclude some or all execution paths for its following statements, and thus hide (critical) failure. We therefore recommend to avoid suppressing False Positives, and either leave them visible for the developer as warning signs, or even better, rewrite the code in a prover-friendly manner following the tips in Sect. 5.1.

Mistake 2: Inconsistent Contracts. Function contracts act as barriers for propagating proof results (besides inlined functions), that is, the result of a VC in one subprogram cannot affect the result of another in a different subprogram. However, these barriers can be broken when function contracts are inconsistent, producing False Negatives by our definition. One way to obtain inconsistent contracts, is writing a postcondition which itself contains a failing VC (line 2):

---

[1] This particular case has been fixed in recent versions of GNATprove.

```
 1 | function f1 (X : Integer) return Integer
 2 |    with Post => f1'Result = X + 1 is -- overflow check might fail
 3 | begin
 4 |    return X;
 5 | end f1;
 6 |
 7 | procedure Caller is
 8 |    X : Integer := Integer'Last;
 9 | begin
10 |    X := X + 1; -- overflow check proved.
11 |    X := f1(X);
12 | end Caller;
```

Clearly, an overflow must happen at line 10, resulting in an exception. The analyzer, however, proves absence of overflows in `Caller`. The reason is that in the Why3 backend, the postcondition of `f1` is used as an axiom in the analysis of `Caller`. The resulting theory for `Caller` is an inconsistent axiom set, from which (*principle of explosion*) anything can be proven, including that false VCs are true. In such circumstances, the solver may also produce a *spurious* counterexample.

In the example above, the developer gets a warning for the inconsistent postcondition and can correct for it, thus keep barriers intact and ensure that the proofs in the caller are not influenced. However, if we change line 4 to `return X+1`, then the failing VC is now indicated in the body of `f1`, and – since the proofs build on each other – the postcondition is verified and a defect easily missed. Therefore, failing VCs within callees may also refute proofs in the caller (in contrast to execution semantics) and have to be taken into account. Indeed, the textual report of GNATprove (with flag `--assumptions`) indicates that AoRTE in `Caller` depends on both the body and the postcondition of `f1`, and therefore the reports have to be studied with great care to judge the verification output. Finally, note that the same principle applies for assertions and loop invariants.

Mistake 3: Forgetting the RTS. Despite proven AoRTE, one procedure which rotates the frame of reference of the gyroscope measurements was sporadically triggering an exception after a floating-point multiplication. The situation was eventually captured in the debugger as follows:

```
 1 | -- angle = 0.00429, vector (Z) = -2.023e-38
 2 | result(Y) := Sin (angle) * vector(Z);
 3 | -- result(Y) = -8.68468736e-41 => Exception
```

Variable `result` was holding a *subnormal* floating-point number, roughly speaking, an "underflow". GNATprove models floating-point computations according to IEEE-754, which requires support for subnormals on the target processor. Our processor's FPU indeed implements subnormals, but the RTS, part of which describes floating-point capabilities of the target processor, was incorrectly indicating the opposite[2]. As a result, the language-defined float validity check occasionally failed (in our case when the glider was resting level and motionless at the ground for a longer period of time). Therefore, the RTS must be carefully configured and checked manually for discrepancies, otherwise proofs can be refuted since static analysis works with an incorrect premise.

---

[2] This also has been fixed in recent versions of the embedded ARM RTS.

Mistake 4: Bad Patterns. *Saturation* may seem like an effective workaround to ensure overflows, index checks and so on cannot fail, but it usually hides bigger flaws. Consider the following example, also from the GPS protocol parser:

```
subtype Lat_Type is Angle_Type range -90.0 * Degree .. 90.0 * Degree;
Lat : Lat_Type := Dim_Type (toInt32 (data_rx(28..31))) * 1.0e-7 * Degree;
```

The four raw bytes in `data_rx` come from the GPS device and represent a scaled float, which could in principle carry a value exceeding the latitude range of $[-90, 90]$ Degree. To protect against this sort of error, it is tempting to implement a function (even a generic) of the form `if X > Lat_Type'Last then X := Lat_Type'Last else...` that limits the value to the available range, and apply it to all places where checks could be failing. However, we found that almost every case where saturation was applied, was masking a boundary case that needs to be addressed. In this example, we needed handling for a GPS that yields faulty values. In general, such cases usually indicate a missing software requirement.

4.2   Design Limitations

We now describe some cases where the current version of the SPARK 2014 *language* – not the static analysis tool – imposes limitations.

Access Types. The missing support for pointers in SPARK becomes a problem in low-level drivers, where they are used frequently. One workaround is to hide those in a package body that is not in SPARK mode, and only provide a SPARK specification. Naturally, the body cannot be verified, but at least its subprograms can be called from SPARK subprograms. Sometimes it is not possible to hide access types, in particular when packages use them as interface between each other. This is the case for our SD card driver, which is interfaced by an implementation of the FAT filesystem through access types. Both are separate packages, but the former one exports restricted types and access types which are used by the FAT package, thus requiring that wide parts of the FAT package are written in Ada instead of SPARK. As a consequence, access types are sometimes demanding to form larger monolithic packages, here to combine SD card driver and FAT filesystem into one (possibly nested) package.

Polymorphism. While being available in SPARK, applications of polymorphism are limited as a result of the access type restriction. Our message queue between flight-critical and mission-critical task was planned to hold messages of a polymorphic type. However, without access types the only option to handover messages would be to take a deep copy and store it in the queue. However, the queue itself is realized with an array and can hold only objects of the same type. This means a copy would also be an upcast to the base type. This, in turn, would loose the components specific to the derived type, and therefore render polymorphism useless. As a workaround, we used mutable variant records.

Interfaces. Closely related to polymorphism, we intended to implement sensors as polymorphic types. That is, specify an abstract sensor interface that must be overridden by each sensor implementation. Towards that, we declared an abstract tagged type with abstract primitive methods denoting the interface that a specific sensor must implement. However, when we override the method for a sensor implementation, such as the IMU, SPARK requires specifying the global dependencies of the overriding IMU implementation as class-wide global dependencies of the abstract method (SPARK RM 6.1.6). This happens even without an explicit `Global` aspect. As workaround, we decided to avoid polymorphism and used simple inheritance without overriding methods.

Dimensioned Types. Using the GNAT dimensionality checking system in SPARK, had revealed two missing features. Firstly, in the current stable version of the GNAT compiler, it is not possible to specify general operations on dimensioned types that are resolved to specific dimensions during compilation. For example, we could not write a generic time integrator function for the PID controller that multiplies any dimensioned type with a time value and returns the corresponding unit type. Therefore, we reverted to dimensionless and unconstrained floats within the generic PID controller implementation. Secondly, it is not possible to declare vectors and matrices with mixed subtypes, which would be necessary to retain the dimensionality information throughout vector calculations (e.g., in the Kalman Filter). As a consequence, we either have split vectors into their components, or reverted to dimensionless and unconstrained floats. As a result of these workarounds, numerous overflow checks related to PID control and Kalman Filter could not be proven (which explains more than 70% of our failed floating-point VCs).

4.3   Solver Weaknesses

We now summarize some frequent problems introduced by the current state of the tooling.

The `'Position` attribute of a record allows evaluating the position of a component in that record. However, GNATprove has no precise information about this position, and therefore proofs building on that might fail.

Another feature that is used in driver code, are *unions*, which provide different views on the same data. GNATprove does not know about the overlay and may generate False Positives for initialization, as well as for proofs which build on the relation between views.

We had several False Positives related to possibly uninitialized variables. SPARK follows a strict data initialization policy. Every (strict) output of a subprogram must be initialized. In the current version, GNATprove only considers initialization of arrays as complete when done in a single statement. This generates warnings when an array is initialized in multiple steps, e.g., through loops, which we have suppressed.

5   Results

In general, verification of SPARK 2014 programs is accessible and mostly automatic. Figure 1 shows the results of our launch release. As it can be seen, we

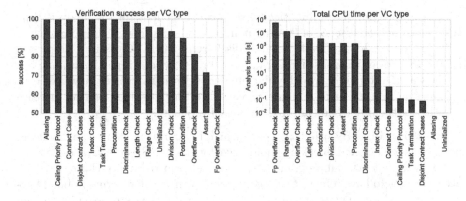

Fig. 1. Statistics on Verification Conditions (VCs) by type.

could not prove all properties during the time of this project (three months). The non-proven checks have largely been identified as "fixable", following our design recommendations given below.

The complexity of our flight stack and verification progress are summarized in Table 1. It can be seen that our focus on the application part is reflected in the SPARK coverage that we have achieved (82% of all bodies in SPARK, and even 99% of all specifications), but also that considerably more work has to be done for the BSP (currently only verified by testing). In particular, the HAL (off-chip device drivers, bus configuration, etc.) is the largest part and thus needs a higher SPARK coverage. However, we should add that 43% of the HAL is consisting of specifications generated from CMSIS-SVD files, which do not contain any subprograms, but only definitions of peripheral addresses and record definitions to access them, and therefore mostly cannot be covered in SPARK. Last but not least, a completely verified RTS would be desirable, as well.

Table 1. Metrics and verification statistics of our Flight Stack.

Metric	Application	Board Support Package		All
		HAL	RTS	
Lines of code (GNATmetric)	6,750	32,903	15,769	55,422
Number of packages	49	100	121	270
Cyclomatic complexity	2.03	2.67	2.64	2.53
SPARK body/spec	81.9/99.4 %	15.5/23.5 %	8.6/11.8 %	30.0/38.5 %
Number of VCs	3,214	765	2	3,981
VCs proven	88.1 %	92.5 %	100 %	88.8 %
Analysis time[a]	–	–	–	19 min

[a]Intel Xeon E5-2680 Octa-Core with 16 GB RAM, timeout = 120 s, steps = inf.

Floats are expensive. Statistically, we have spent most of the analysis time (65%) for proving absence of floating-point overflows, although these amount to only 21% of all VCs. This is because discharging such VCs is in average one magnitude slower than discharging most other VC types. In particular, one has to allow a high step limit (roughly the number of decisions a solver may take, e.g., deciding on a literal) and a high timeout. Note that at some point an increase of either of them does not improve the result anymore.

Multi-threading. By using the Ravenscar RTS, our goals related to deadlock, priority inversion and blocking, hold true by design. Several race conditions and non-thread-safe subprograms have been identified by GNATprove, which otherwise would have refuted task separation. To ensure that termination of low-criticality tasks cannot terminate the flight-critical task, we provided a custom implementation for GNAT's last chance handler (outside of the SPARK language and therefore not being analyzed) which reads the priority of the failing task and acts accordingly: If the priority is lower than that of the flight-critical task (i.e., the mission-critical task had an exception), then we prevent a system reset by sending the low-priority task into an infinite null loop (thus keeping it busy executing nops, and keeping the flight-critical task alive). If the flight-critical task is failing, then our handler allows a system reset. Multi-threading is therefore easy to implement, poses no verification problems, and can effectively separate tasks by their criticality.

High-Level Behavioral Contracts. Related to the homing functionality we proved high-level properties with the help of ghost functions, although this is beyond the main purpose of SPARK contracts. For example, we could prove the overall behavior in case of loosing the GPS fix, or missing home coordinates.

5.1 Design Recommendations

The following constructs and strategies have been found amenable to verification:

1. Split long expressions into multiple statements → discharges more VCs.
2. Limit ranges of data types, especially floats → better analysis of overflows.
3. Avoid saturation → uncovers missing error handling and requirements.
4. Avoid interfaces → annotations for data flows break concept of abstraction.
5. Emulate polymorphic objects that must be copied with mutable variant records.
6. Separation of tasks by criticality using a custom last chance handler → abnormal termination of a low-criticality task does not cause termination of high-criticality tasks.

6 Related Work

Only a small number of experience reports about SPARK 2014 have been published before. A look back at (old) SPARK's history and its success, as well as an initial picture of SPARK 2014 is given by Chapman and Schanda in [4]. We can report that the mentioned difficulties with floating-point numbers are solved in SPARK 2014, and that the goal to make verification more accessible, has been reached. A small case study with SPARK 2014 is presented in [10], but at that point multi-threading (Ravenscar) was not yet supported, and floating point numbers have been skipped in the proof. We can add to the conclusion given there, that both are easily verified in "real-world" code, although float proofs require more (computational and mental) effort. Larger case studies are summarized by Dross et al. in [5], with whom we share the opinion of minor usability issues, and that some small amount of developer training is required. Finally, SPARK 2014 with Ravenscar has recently been announced to be used in the Lunar IceCube [2] satellite, a successor of the successful CubeSat project that was implemented in SPARK 2005. It will be a message-centric software, conceptually similar to NASA's cFE/CFS, but fully verified and striving to become an open source platform for spacecraft software. In contrast to all the above publications, this paper is not focused on the application or case studies, but pointing out typical sources of errors in SPARK programs, which a developer has to know in order to get correct verification results.

7   Conclusion

Although the verification of SPARK 2014 programs is very close to execution semantics and therefore mostly intuitive, we believe that developers still need some basic training to avoid common mistakes as described in this paper, which otherwise could lead to a false confidence in the software being developed. Overall, the language forces developers to address boundary cases of a system explicitly, which eventually helps understanding the system better, and usually reveals missing requirements for boundary cases. As a downside, SPARK 2014 programs are often longer than (approximately) equivalent Ada programs, since in the latter case a general exception handler can be installed to handle all pathological cases at once, without differentiating them. Furthermore, static analysis is ready to replace unit tests, but integration tests have still been found necessary.

Regarding the shortcomings of the GNAT dimensionality system, we can report that as a consequence of our experiments, a solution for generic operations on dimensioned has been found and will be part of future GNAT releases.

Our remaining criticism to SPARK 2014 and its tools is as follows: next to some minor tooling enhancements to avoid the mistakes mentioned earlier and adding some more knowledge to the analyzer, it is necessary to support object-oriented features in a better way. All in all, SPARK 2014 raises the bar for formal verification and its tools, but developers still have to be aware of limitations.

Acknowledgements. Thanks to the SPARK 2014 development and support team of AdaCore for their guidance and insights.

References

1. AdaCore: Ada Drivers Library (2015). https://github.com/AdaCore
2. Brandon, C., Chapin, P.: The use of SPARK in a complex spacecraft. In: HILT (2016)
3. Burns, A.: The ravenscar profile. ACM SIGAda Ada Lett. **19**(4), 49–52 (1999)
4. Chapman, R., Schanda, F.: Are we there yet? 20 years of industrial theorem proving with SPARK. In: Klein, G., Gamboa, R. (eds.) ITP 2014. LNCS, vol. 8558, pp. 17–26. Springer, Cham (2014). doi:10.1007/978-3-319-08970-6_2
5. Dross, C., Efstathopoulos, P., Lesens, D., Mentr, D., Mentré, D., Moy, Y.: Rail, space, security: three case studies for SPARK 2014. In: ERTS2 2014, pp. 1–10 (2014)
6. Filliâtre, J.C., Paskevich, A.: Why3: Where Programs Meet Provers (2013)
7. Hoang, D., Moy, Y., Wallenburg, A., Chapman, R.: SPARK 2014 and GNATprove. Int. J. Softw. Tools Technol. Transf. **17**(6), 695–707 (2015)
8. Meier, L., Tanskanen, P., Fraundorfer, F., Pollefeys, M.: PIXHAWK: a system for autonomous flight using onboard computer vision. In: ICRA, pp. 2992–2997 (2011)
9. Schonberg, E., Pucci, V.: Implementation of a simple dimensionality checking system in Ada 2012. In: HILT 2012, pp. 35–42. ACM, New York (2012)
10. Trojanek, P., Eder, K.: Verification and testing of mobile robot navigation algorithms: a case study in SPARK. In: IROS 2014, pp. 1489–1494 (2014)
11. Xiang, J., Knight, J., Sullivan, K.: Real-world types and their application. In: Koornneef, F., Gulijk, C. (eds.) SAFECOMP 2015. LNCS, vol. 9337, pp. 471–484. Springer, Cham (2015). doi:10.1007/978-3-319-24255-2_34

A Simplex Architecture for Hybrid Systems Using Barrier Certificates

Junxing Yang[1]([✉]), Md. Ariful Islam[2], Abhishek Murthy[3], Scott A. Smolka[1], and Scott D. Stoller[1]

[1] Department of Computer Science, Stony Brook University, Stony Brook, USA
junyang@cs.stonybrook.edu
[2] Department of Computer Science, Carnegie Mellon University, Pittsburgh, USA
[3] Philips Lighting Research North America, Cambridge, USA

Abstract. This paper shows how to use Barrier Certificates (BaCs) to design Simplex Architectures for hybrid systems. The Simplex architecture entails switching control of a plant over to a provably safe Baseline Controller when a safety violation is imminent under the control of an unverified Advanced Controller. A key step of determining the switching condition is identifying a *recoverable region*, where the Baseline Controller guarantees recovery and keeps the plant invariably safe. BaCs, which are Lyapunov-like proofs of safety, are used to identify a recoverable region. At each time step, the switching logic samples the state of the plant and uses bounded-time reachability analysis to conservatively check whether any states outside the zero-level set of the BaCs, which therefore might be non-recoverable, are reachable in one decision period under control of the Advanced Controller. If so, failover is initiated.

Our approach of using BaCs to identify recoverable states is computationally cheaper and potentially more accurate (less conservative) than existing approaches based on state-space exploration. We apply our technique to two hybrid systems: a water tank pump and a stop-sign-obeying controller for a car.

Keywords: Simplex architecture · Hybrid systems · Barrier certificates · Reachability · Switching logic

1 Introduction

The Simplex Architecture [20], illustrated in Fig. 1, traditionally consists of two versions of a controller, called the *advanced controller* (AC) and *baseline controller* (BC), and a physical *plant* (P). The advanced controller is designed for maximum performance and is in control of the plant under nominal operating conditions. However, certification that the advanced controller keeps the plant state within a prescribed safety region (i.e., region of safe operation) may be infeasible, due to its complexity or adaptiveness, or because an accurate model of it is unavailable for analysis. In contrast, the baseline controller is certified to maintain safety of the plant. When the plant is under control of AC, a *decision*

© Springer International Publishing AG 2017
S. Tonetta et al. (Eds.): SAFECOMP 2017, LNCS 10488, pp. 117–131, 2017.
DOI: 10.1007/978-3-319-66266-4_8

module (*DM*) periodically, with decision period Δt, monitors the state of the plant and switches the control of the plant to the baseline controller if the plant is in imminent danger (i.e., within the next decision period) of entering a state that might lead to a safety violation.

The switching condition used in the decision module is determined as follows. A state of the plant is *recoverable* if BC can take over from that state (due to a switch) and keep the plant invariably safe; in other words, the composition of P and BC, denoted $P \times BC$, when started from a recoverable state, will always remain within the safety region. An unbounded time horizon is used in the definition of recoverable states because, in general, we have no bound on how long BC needs to take corrective actions and overcome the plant's momentum (in a general sense, not limited to physical motion) toward unsafe states.

A state is *switching* if the plant, under control of AC, may enter an unrecoverable state during the next decision period, i.e., within time Δt. This definition reflects the discrete-time nature of DM. The switching condition simply checks whether the current state is switching.

Note that switching states are a subset of recoverable states which are a subset of safe states.

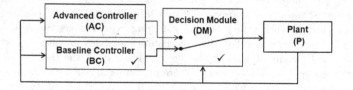

Fig. 1. The two-controller simplex architecture.

The earliest methodology for computing switching conditions is based on Lyapunov stability theory and reduces the problem to solving linear matrix inequalities (LMIs) [4]. The method applies to plants with linear time-invariant dynamics and a linear baseline controller [19]. This approach is computationally efficient but limited in applicability. More general approaches were later developed [2,3], based on state-space exploration, also called state-space *reachability*. Several reachability algorithms for hybrid systems have been developed, e.g., [1,6,7,21].

There are many reachability algorithms, varying in the shape of the regions (e.g., boxes or regions bounded by polynomials), whether the partitioning of the state space into regions is pre-determined or adaptive, etc.

Methods based on reachability are attractive for their broad applicability: they can handle nonlinear hybrid systems. A *hybrid system* is a system with both discrete and continuous variables and with multiple modes, each with a different dynamics (for the continuous variables). However, they face several issues. The main issue is the high computational cost associated with their reachability analysis, especially for high-dimensional systems, since the number of explored regions tends to grow exponentially with the dimensionality. While reachability algorithms are improving, the computational cost, in time or memory, remains prohibitive in many cases.

Accuracy is also an issue. Reachability algorithms generally compute an over-approximation of the reachable states. The amount of over-approximation is generally larger for non-linear systems, and it tends to increase over time (i.e., proportional to the time horizon of the reachability calculation). Reachability computations with an unbounded time horizon (as when identifying recoverable states) can in theory converge (i.e., reach a fixed-point) when the set of reachable states lies within a bounded region of the state space. In practice, however, the ever-increasing "looseness" of the over-approximation often causes the reachability computation to diverge even in those cases. Even if it converges, a loose over-approximation of reachability makes the computation of recoverable states conservative, i.e., many recoverable states will not be recognized as such, causing unnecessary switches to BC.

A third issue is the required expertise and manual effort. Reachability algorithms typically have several numerical parameters that indirectly control the cost and accuracy of the computation. While there are general guidelines and heuristics for choosing initial parameter values, detailed understanding of the reachability algorithm and the hybrid system, and considerable experimentation, are often needed to tune the parameters in order to obtain acceptably accurate results in reasonable time, when this is possible.

This paper presents an alternative approach to computing recoverable states, based on *barrier certificates* [16,17], a methodology developed for safety verification of hybrid systems. Specifically, we observe that the 0-level set of a barrier certificate for $P \times BC$ separates recoverable and unrecoverable states. We still use reachability to compute switching states. This combination of techniques— namely, using barrier certificates to compute recoverable states, and reachability to compute switching states, instead of using reachability for both—is advantageous, because the issues with reachability algorithms are much more severe when computing recoverable states, due to the unbounded time horizon, than when computing switching states, which involves a short time horizon.

Our approach is mostly automatic for a class of systems that includes some nonlinear hybrid systems. For these systems, the problem of computing a barrier certificate can be reduced to solving a sum-of-squares (SOS) optimization problem [16,17], which can be solved by semidefinite programming solvers. We use SOSTOOLS [14], a MATLAB toolbox for solving SOS optimization problems; we also experimented with Spotless (https://github.com/spot-toolbox). SOS-TOOLS can handle hybrid systems in which the differential equations, guards, and invariants are defined by polynomial expressions such that the minimum and maximum degrees of each polynomial are even. SOSTOOLS does require some expertise and manual effort to choose suitable parameter values.

To increase assurance in the correctness of barrier certificates computed by SOSTOOLS, we use Z3 (https://github.com/Z3Prover/z3/wiki), a state-of-the-art satisfiability modulo theories (SMT) solver, to verify their correctness. This ensures that bugs or limitations of numerical accuracy in SOSTOOLS cannot compromise the soundness of our results.

We apply our approach to two hybrid systems as case studies. A water tank system that controls the flow of water via a valve into a tank is modeled using a three-mode hybrid automaton with one continuous variable. The next case study describes a stop-sign-obeying controller for a car as a hybrid automaton with three-modes and two continuous variables. The implementation aspects of computing the barrier certificates are discussed and the switching logics are illustrated for the two case studies.

The rest of the paper is organized as follows. Section 2 provides background knowledge on Hybrid Systems and Barrier Certificates. Section 3 presents our approach to computing the switching logic using BaCs and bounded-time reachability. Section 4 considers our SOS characterization of BaCs. Sections 5 describes our two case studies. Section 6 discusses related work. Section 7 offers our concluding remarks and directions for future work.

2   Background

From the discussion above, we can see that the two central issues for designing the Simplex Architecture are: (1) **Identifying the Safety Region**, which results in a proof of safety of $P \times BC$, and (2) **Deriving the recoverable region and the switching boundaries**, which defines the switching logic implemented by the DM.

In this paper, we model $P \times BC$ as a hybrid system, denoted by H_B. This formalism allows us to model both the continuous-time evolution and the discrete-time instantaneous changes in the behavior of the plant under the BC's control. We formally define a hybrid system as follows.

Definition 1. *A Hybrid System $H = (\mathcal{X}, L, X_0, I, F, T)$ is a six-tuple [16]:*

- $\mathcal{X} \subseteq \mathbb{R}^n$ *is the continuous state space.*
- *L is a finite set of modes, also known as locations. The overall state space of the system is $X = L \times \mathcal{X}$ and a state of the system is denoted by $(l, \mathbf{x}) \in L \times \mathcal{X}$.*
- *$X_0 \subseteq X$ is a set of initial states.*
- *$I : L \to 2^{\mathcal{X}}$ is the invariant, which assigns to each location l an invariant set $I(l) \subseteq \mathcal{X}$ that contains all possible continuous states while in mode l.*
- *$F : X \to 2^{\mathbb{R}^n}$ is a set of vector fields. F assigns to each $(l, \mathbf{x})$ a set $F(l, \mathbf{x}) \subseteq \mathbb{R}^n$ that constrains the evolution of the continuous state as $\dot{\mathbf{x}} \in F(l, \mathbf{x})$.*
- *$T \subseteq X \times X$ is a relation that captures the discrete transitions between two modes. A transition $((l', \mathbf{x}'), (l, \mathbf{x}))$ indicates that the system can undergo a discrete (instantaneous) transition from the state $(l', \mathbf{x}')$ to the state $(l, \mathbf{x})$.*

Discrete mode-transitions occur instantaneously in time. We define *Guards* and *Reset maps* for mode-transitions as follows. $\text{Guard}(l', l) = \{\mathbf{x}' \in \mathcal{X} : ((l', \mathbf{x}'), (l, \mathbf{x})) \in T \text{ for some } \mathbf{x} \in \mathcal{X}\}$ and $\text{Reset}(l', l) : \mathbf{x}' \mapsto \{\mathbf{x} \in \mathcal{X} : ((l', \mathbf{x}'), (l, \mathbf{x})) \in T\}$, whose domain is $\text{Guard}(l', l)$.

As per [16], for computational purposes, the uncertainty in the continuous flows, defined by F, is the result of exogenous disturbance inputs such that:

$$F(l, \mathbf{x}) = \{\dot{\mathbf{x}} \in \mathbb{R}^n : \dot{\mathbf{x}} = f_l(\mathbf{x}, d) \text{ for some } d \in D(l)\}$$

where f_l is a vector field that governs the flow of the system in location l and d is a vector of disturbance inputs that take the value in the set $D(l) \subset \mathbb{R}^m$.

Trajectories or *behaviors* of H start from some initial state $(l_0, \mathbf{x}_0) \in X_0$ and evolve in continuous time as per the dynamics defined by F until the invariant, defined by I, is violated and/or a guard is enabled resulting in an instantaneous mode switch. Trajectories are obtained by concatenating the continuous evolutions and the instantaneous discrete-time jumps between the modes.

Given a set of unsafe states $X_u \subseteq X$, H is said to be *safe* if all its trajectories avoid entering X_u. We define a mapping for mode-specific unsafe states as Unsafe$(l) = \{\mathbf{x} \in \mathcal{X} : (l, \mathbf{x}) \in X_u\}$. We also define model-specific initial states as Init$(l) = \{\mathbf{x} \in \mathcal{X} : (l, \mathbf{x}) \in X_0\}$.

It is assumed that the description of the hybrid system given above is well-posed. For example, $(l, \mathbf{x}) \in X_u$ and $(l, \mathbf{x}) \in X_0$ automatically implies that $\mathbf{x} \in I(l)$, and $((l', \mathbf{x}'), (l, \mathbf{x})) \in T$ implies that $\mathbf{x}' \in I(l')$ and $\mathbf{x} \in I(l)$.

Given a set of unsafe states X_u, the safety of a hybrid system H can be proved by computing *Barrier Certificates* (BaCs) [16]. BaCs are functions that capture the following safety requirements of a hybrid system: (1) the continuous-time evolutions within the modes must ensure that the states remain safe and (2) a mode-transition $((l', \mathbf{x}'), (l, \mathbf{x}))$ from the mode l' to l must reset a safe state $(l', \mathbf{x}') \notin$ Unsafe(l') to a safe state $(l, \mathbf{x}) \notin$ Unsafe(l). Next, we introduce the formal definition of BaCs from [16].

Definition 2. *Let the hybrid system $H = (\mathcal{X}, L, X_0, I, F, T)$, the unsafe set X_u and some fixed non-negative constants $\sigma_{(l,l')}$, for all $(l, l') \in L \times L$, be given. A BaC is a collection of functions $B_l(\mathbf{x})$, for all $l \in L$, that are differentiable with respect to its argument and satisfy:*

$$B_l(\mathbf{x}) > 0 \quad \forall \mathbf{x} \in Unsafe(l) \tag{1}$$

$$B_l(\mathbf{x}) \leq 0 \quad \forall \mathbf{x} \in Init(l) \tag{2}$$

$$\frac{\partial B_l}{\partial \mathbf{x}}(\mathbf{x}).f_l(\mathbf{x}, d) \leq 0 \quad \forall (\mathbf{x}, d) \in I(l) \times D(l) \tag{3}$$

$$B_l(\mathbf{x}) - \sigma_{(l',l)} B_{l'}(\mathbf{x}') \leq 0 \quad \forall (\mathbf{x}, \mathbf{x}') \in \mathcal{X}^2 \text{ such that}$$
$$\mathbf{x}' \in Guard(l', l) \text{ and } \mathbf{x} \in Reset(l', l)(\mathbf{x}') \tag{4}$$

Theorem 3 and Proposition 2 of [16] ensure that the existence of BaC, as defined above, proves the safety of H. Initial states are assumed to be safe (Eqs. 1 and 2). Equation 3 dictates that the value of the BaC cannot increase along the continuous evolution of any trajectory within a mode. Finally Eq. 4 ensures that the discrete mode transitions reset safe states to safe states. Equations 1–4 ensure that a trajectory that starts out in an initial state, and thus with a BaC value ≤ 0, can never obtain a BaC-value of > 0. Thus the zero level sets of the functions, $B_l(\mathbf{x}) = 0$, create a "barrier" between Unsafe(l) and the safe states of the mode.

3   Switching Logic

Let P be the physical plant, AC the advanced controller, BC the baseline controller, and H_B the hybrid system modeling the composition of P and BC. We use the following notations: $\mathbf{x}_{AC}(T)$ denotes the the state of the plant under control of the AC, $\mathbf{u}_{AC}(T)$ is the control input provided by the AC, and T is the discrete time. Let M be the number of modes in H_B.

Safety of P under the BC can be established by computing a BaC $\{B_1(\mathbf{x}), B_2(\mathbf{x}), ..., B_M(\mathbf{x})\}$ for H_B. The implementation aspects of computing the BaC are deferred to Sect. 4. Given a mode l of H_B, Recov(l) denotes the intersection of the interior of the zero-level set of $B_l(x)$ and $I(l)$. Note that the sets of states Recov(l) contain the initial states and are recoverable under AC.

We make the following assumptions.

1. DM samples $\mathbf{x}_{AC}(T)$ and $\mathbf{u}_{AC}(T)$ every Δt units of time.
2. The AC also works in discrete time: $\mathbf{u}_{AC}(T)$ is updated at time $(T + \Delta t)$.

The assumptions made by the switching logic are not restrictive. Knowledge of the control input allows the switching logic to become less conservative, as discussed later in the section. The assumptions can also be relaxed by assuming conservative bounds on the plant dynamics under the AC's control. The system models also assume reliable hardware, since Simplex is not intended to tolerate hardware failures.

Reachability computation is a key element of the switching logic. $Reach_{\leq \Delta t}(\mathbf{x}_{AC}(T), \mathbf{u}_{AC}(T))$ denotes the set of plant states reachable under the control input $\mathbf{u}_{AC}(T)$ in the time interval $[T, T + \Delta t]$. $Reach_{= \Delta t}(\mathbf{x}_{AC}(T), \mathbf{u}_{AC}(T))$ is the set of plant states that are reachable under the control input $\mathbf{u}_{AC}(T)$ at time $t = T + \Delta t$.

Algorithm 1. DM's Switching Logic

---

1 Obtain the sample $(\mathbf{x}_{AC}(T), \mathbf{u}_{AC}(T))$;
2 Compute $Reach_{\leq \Delta t}(\mathbf{x}_{AC}(T), \mathbf{u}_{AC}(T))$ and $Reach_{= \Delta t}(\mathbf{x}_{AC}(T), \mathbf{u}_{AC}(T))$;
3 $safety = (Reach_{\leq \Delta t}(\mathbf{x}_{AC}(T), \mathbf{u}_{AC}(T)) \cap X_u == \emptyset)$;
4 $recoverability = Reach_{= \Delta t}(\mathbf{x}_{AC}(T), \mathbf{u}_{AC}(T)) \subseteq (\bigcup_{l=1}^{M} Recov(l))$;
5 **if** $safety \wedge recoverability$ **then**
6 $\quad |\quad$ Continue with AC;
7 **else**
8 $\quad |\quad$ Switch to BC;
9 **end**

Algorithm 1 outlines the switching logic. Step 2 involves two on-the-fly reachability computations. For scalability, the reach-set computation time must be less than or equal to Δt. The online reach-set computation algorithm of [5] can handle fairly large hybrid systems. The dimension of the largest system considered for online reachability in [5] is 30. Alternatively, we can use the real-time reachability algorithm from [9]. When online reachability computation is not scalable, we can employ a combination of offline and online strategies. In the offline step, the state and input spaces are partitioned into finite regions and reach-sets for the partitions, computed apriori, are stored in a table. At run-time, given the state and the control input, the reach set of the corresponding partition is applied.

To compute the set intersections in steps 3 and 4, we can employ standard polyhedral libraries, like *PolyLib* [10]. Non-convex zero-level sets of BaCs may need to be over-approximated as convex sets to enable set intersection. When *safety* and *recoverability* evaluate to True, the plant is guaranteed to be (i) safe in $[T, T + \Delta t]$ and (ii) recoverable at $T + \Delta t$.

Next, we sketch a proof of the safety of P under the switching logic.

Lemma 1. *P remains safe during time* $t \in [T, T + \Delta t]$, *i.e.* $\forall t \in [T, T + \Delta t]$: $\mathbf{x}_{AC}(t) \notin X_u$.

Proof. The proof is based on the observation that after obtaining the sample $(\mathbf{x}_{AC}(T), \mathbf{u}_{AC}(T))$, the switching logic ensures that AC does not drive P into unsafe states: if $Reach_{\leq \Delta t}(\mathbf{x}_{AC}(T), \mathbf{u}_{AC}(T))$ has a non-zero intersection with the unsafe states, then in step 3, *safety* will become False, resulting in a failover being performed in step 8. Note that $\mathbf{u}_{AC}(T)$ does not change in $[T, T + \Delta t]$ under Assumption 2. □

Lemma 2. *Every state sample* $\mathbf{x}_{AC}(T)$ *seen by the switching logic in step 1 of the algorithm is recoverable.*

Proof. The proof is based on induction. As the base case, we know that the initial states are recoverable. Consider the sample $\mathbf{x}_{AC}(T)$ and assume that it is recoverable. The set of all possible samples $\mathbf{x}_{AC}(T + \Delta t)$ is contained in $Reach_{= \Delta t}(\mathbf{x}_{AC}(T), \mathbf{u}_{AC}(T))$. If any of these reachable states lies outside the union of the *Recov(.)* sets of all of the modes of H_B, then it may be potentially non-recoverable. If such a state is reachable, then a failover will be triggered as *recoverability* will become False in step 4. Thus every state sample $\mathbf{x}_{AC}(T)$ seen in step 1 will be recoverable. □

Theorem 1. *The switching logic of the Simplex architecture defined in Algorithm 1 keeps P invariably safe.*

Proof. At every time step T, the switching logic ensures that P remains safe over the finite time horizon of length Δt as per Lemma 1. Additionally, it follows from Lemma 2 that the switching logic ensures that the next state sample $\mathbf{x}_{AC}(T+\Delta t)$ remains recoverable, and therefore safe. If the next state sample is potentially non-recoverable, indicated by *recoverability* becoming False in step 4, then the failover that is executed in step 8 ensures the plant remains safe under BC.

Thus, the switching logic ensures that P remains invariably safe. □

Algorithm 1 combines the offline computation of the BaCs with the online reachability computation at step 2 to guarantee the safety of the plant. The set intersection and the union operations involved in computing *safety* and *recoverability* in steps 2 and 3 must also be performed online, and add to the computational cost of performing on-the-fly reachability analysis.

Online reachability computations may be avoided by conservatively precomputing the sets for different partitions of the state space. The state space may be partitioned into different equivalence classes that reach the same sets of states in time up to, and at $T + \Delta t$ for conservative assumptions of the AC's inputs. Despite being computationally efficient, such a switching logic is prone to being overly conservative by not allowing the AC to operate over the largest possible region in the state space.

The switching logic in Algorithm 1 ensures that the operating region of the AC is maximized if the computation of the reachable sets is exact and the recoverable regions of the modes, obtained by intersecting the interior of the zero-level sets with the mode invariants, is maximal. This is often desired as the AC is intended to deliver better performance and/or serve mission-critical purposes.

4   Computing BaCs for Hybrid Systems

Let the hybrid system H and the descriptions of all the sets $I(l)$, $D(l)$, $Init(l)$, $Unsafe(l)$, $Guard(l', l)$, and $Reset(l', l)(x')$ be given along with some nonnegative constants $\sigma_{l',l}$, for each $l \in L$ and $(l, l') \in L^2, l \neq l'$. The search for a BaC for H can be cast as an instance of SOS optimization as follows. Find values of the coefficients which make the expressions

$$- B_l(x) - \sigma_{Init(l)}^T(x) g_{Init(l)}(x) \tag{5}$$

$$B_l(x) - \epsilon - \sigma_{Unsafe(l)}^T(x) g_{Unsafe(l)}(x) \tag{6}$$

$$- \frac{\partial B_l}{\partial x}(x) f_l(x, d) - \sigma_I(l)^T(x, d) g_{I(l)}(x) - \sigma_{D(l)}^T(x, d) g_{D(l)}(d) \tag{7}$$

$$- B_l(x) + \sigma_{l,l'} B_{l'}(x') - \sigma_{Guard(l,l')}^T(x, x') g_{Guard(l,l')}(x - \\ \sigma_{Reset(l,l')}^T(x, x') g_{Reset(l,l')}(x, x') \tag{8}$$

and the entries of $\sigma_{Init(l)}, \sigma_{Unsafe(l)}, \sigma_I(l) \sigma_{D(l)}, \sigma_{Guard(l,l')}, \sigma_{Reset(l,l')}$ sum of squares, for each $l \in L$ and $(l, l') \in L^2, l \neq l'$. See [16] for further details on computing BaCs for hybrid systems, e.g., the definitions of $g_{Init(l)}$ and $g_{Unsafe(l)}$, etc. Such SOS optimization programs can be solved using SOSTOOLS [16,17]. SOS optimization and SOSTOOLS itself have been applied to large systems, e.g., an industry-level hybrid system with 10-dimensional state in [8].

SOSTOOLS may run into numerical issues or provide incorrect solutions for some inputs as reported in [12,13]. We can overcome these issues by validating the BaCs using satisfiability modulo theory solvers, like Z3. Validation entails casting the negation of the assertion: for all relevant states, Eqs. 5–8 are non-negative. That is, Z3 looks for a state that makes any of these equations negative. The domain of SMT formulae depends upon the mode or mode-pair under consideration. SOSTOOLS is re-parameterized if Z3 reports unsoundness of the solutions.

5   Case Studies

5.1   Case Study 1: Simple Water Tank System

We consider a simple water tank system adopted from [15], where a controller seeks to keep the water level x in a tank between a certain range. Figure 2a shows the hybrid automaton of the composition H_B. In mode *on*, the water tank is filled by a pump that increases the water level ($x' = 1$). The pump can be turned off when $x \geq 7$, and must be turned off when $x > 9$. More water pours in ($x := x + 1$) when the pump is shutting down.

In mode *off*, the pump is off and the valve is closed, but water leaks slowly ($x' = -0.1$). We assume that the valve must be opened completely (mode *open*) before reactivating the pump. The valve can be turned on when $x < 5$, and must be turned on when $x < 3$. In mode *open*, water drains quickly, and the system closes the valve and turns on the pump when $1 \leq x \leq 2$.

We assume that the disturbance in the continuous evolution is 0. The system is not asymptotically stable as the value of x varies within a certain range without reaching an equilibrium point. Its behavior is also nondeterministic.

Due to the fact that SOSTOOLS requires the minimum and maximum degrees of an SOS to be even, we made several changes to the original model of [15]. In particular, we modified the degrees of the invariants and guards to meet this requirement without affecting the behavior of the system.

BaCs and Switching Logic. Note that the zero-level sets of BaCs separate an unsafe region from all system trajectories. Thus, we need to have margins between the unsafe region and the system trajectories. The unsafe region of the system is $X_u = \{x | x \leq 0\} \cup \{x | x \geq 11\}$. We compute the barrier certificates for the initial states $x_0 \in [1, 9]$. Since in each location l, x can only take a value within the invariant $I(l)$ of l, BaCs only need to satisfy Eqs. 5–8 in the invariant set $I(l)$ [16]. We take the intersection of X_u and $I(l)$ as the unsafe region for mode l. The runtimes needed to compute the BaCs using SOSTOOLS and to

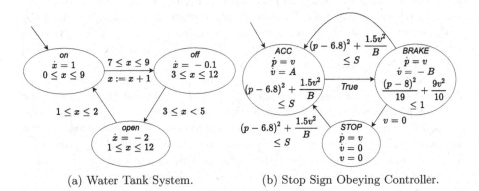

(a) Water Tank System.   (b) Stop Sign Obeying Controller.

Fig. 2. Hybrid automata of the composition H_B for the two case studies.

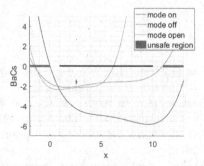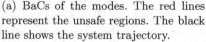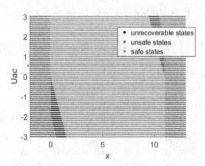

(a) BaCs of the modes. The red lines represent the unsafe regions. The black line shows the system trajectory.

(b) Safe, unsafe and unrecoverable states with $\Delta t = 0.5$ under different control inputs $\mathbf{u}_{AC}$.

Fig. 3. BaCs of the system and snapshot of the switching logic at run-time. (Color figure online)

validate them on Z3 are 1.142 s and 0.206 s, respectively, on an Intel Core i7-4770 CPU @ 3.4 GHz with 16 GB RAM.

Figure 3a shows the resulting BaCs. The zero-level set of the BaCs for modes *on*, *off*, and *open* is $\{x = 0.0384\}$, $\{x = 10.9709\}$, and $\{x = 6.2624\}$, respectively. Note that we only consider the zero-level set within the invariant of the mode. The recoverable regions are $\text{Recov}(on) = [0.0384, 9]$, $\text{Recov}(off) = [3, 10.9709]$, and $\text{Recov}(open) = [1, 6.2624]$. The figure shows that the intersection of the interior of the zero-level set and the invariant of each mode separates the unsafe region from all system trajectories. The validation of the BaCs using Z3 proves that they satisfy all of the conditions. We obtain the recoverable region of the system as $\bigcup_{l=1}^{M} \text{Recov}(l) = [0.0384, 10.9709]$.

As an instance of the Simplex architecture, the water tank system could be controlled by an advanced controller with a more complex control objective. At any given time, the decision module in the Simplex architecture decides whether or not to switch to BC based on Algorithm 1. Figure 3b illustrates a snap-shot of the switching logic at time T across the state space. For illustration purposes, we discretize the state space and apply the switching logic for each discrete state with the corresponding control input $\mathbf{u}_{AC}$. Note that the control input is applied to the water level, i.e., $\dot{x} = \mathbf{u}_{AC}$. We have $x(T + \Delta t) = x(T) + \mathbf{u}_{AC} \cdot \Delta t$.

To check the *safety* condition in Algorithm 1, it is sufficient to check if the intersection of the line segment from $x(T)$ to $x(T + \Delta t)$ and the unsafe region X_u is empty. A red dot is used in Fig. 3b to represent unsafe states that do not satisfy the *safety* condition. To check the *recoverability* condition, we use the recoverable region computed above and check if $x(T + \Delta t) \in \bigcup_{l=1}^{M} \text{Recov}(l)$. A black dot is used to represent the unrecoverable states that do not satisfy the *recoverability* condition. We switch to BC if the current state is unsafe or unrecoverable. If the current state satisfies both *safety* and *recoverability*, shown as a green dot, we continue with the AC. Note that if $\mathbf{u}_{AC} < 0$, then the smaller

$\mathbf{u}_{AC}$ is, the larger lower bound we have for the safe states. Also, when $\mathbf{u}_{AC} > 0$, the larger $\mathbf{u}_{AC}$ is, the smaller upper bound we have for the safe states.

5.2 Case Study 2: Stop-Sign-Obeying Controller

Our second case study is a stop-sign-obeying controller of a car that chooses when to begin decelerating so that it stops at or before a stop sign [18]. Figure 2b shows the corresponding hybrid automaton H_B. The system of stop-sign obeying controller has 2 variables with second order derivatives and quadratic functions as guards and invariants.

The state variables p and v denote the position and velocity of the car, respectively and S denotes the position of the stop sign. In mode ACC, the car accelerates with a constant rate A. It can stay in the mode as long as the invariant is satisfied, or switch nondeterministically to mode $BRAKE$. In mode $BRAKE$, the car decelerates with a constant rate $-B$. It can switch nondeterministically to mode ACC if the guard condition is satisfied. It also switches to mode $STOP$ if $v = 0$. In mode $STOP$, the velocity and the acceleration are both 0. We assume that the disturbance in the continuous evolution is 0.

Note that, due to the practical limitation of SOSTOOLS, also mentioned in Sect. 5.1, we slightly modify some guards and invariants of stop-sign-obeying controller. The original model can be found in [18].

BaCs and Switching Logic. To compute BaCs, we consider ACC as the initial mode and $\{(p,v)|(p-6)^2 + v^2 \geq 1\}$ as the initial set. We choose $A = 1$, $B = 0.5$ and $S = 11.3$. To compute feasible BaCs, we consider the stop sign is at $p = S - d$ during the computation, where d is some non-negative offset. This allows us to maintain a safe margin $(d > 0)$ between the unsafe region and all possible system trajectories. Using a simple binary search, we find $d = 1.3$ as the smallest possible value in the interval $[0, 2]$, a reasonable safety margin in this case. We set $\sigma_{l,l'} = 0$ for all $(l, l') \in L^2$ in Eq. 8. We validate the resulting BaCs on Z3 as discussed in Sect. 4. The runtimes to compute the BaCs using SOSTOOLS and to validate them on Z3 are 1.497 s and 0.295s, respectively, on an Intel Core i7-4770 CPU @ 3.4 GHz with 16 GB RAM.

In Fig. 4a, the solid curves represent zero-level sets of the computed BaCs, whereas the regions with dashed boundary are the corresponding mode invariants. The dashed red ellipse and pink rectangular region represent the initial and unsafe states, respectively. The figure shows that the intersection of the interior of zero-level set of the BaC for any mode and its mode invariant does not intersect with the unsafe region. This ensures that the union of all the intersections of interior of zero-level set of BaC with its corresponding mode invariant, denoted as $\bigcup_{l=1}^{M} \text{Recov}(l)$, can be used as the recoverable sets in the switching logic.

Figure 4 illustrates a snap-shot of switching logic at run-time t across the state-space in stop-sign-obeying controller in three different cases. For the illustration purpose, we consider a discrete state-space. For each discrete state, we apply the decision logic by computing both $Reach_{\leq \Delta t}(\mathbf{x}_{AC}(t), \mathbf{u}_{AC}(t))$ and

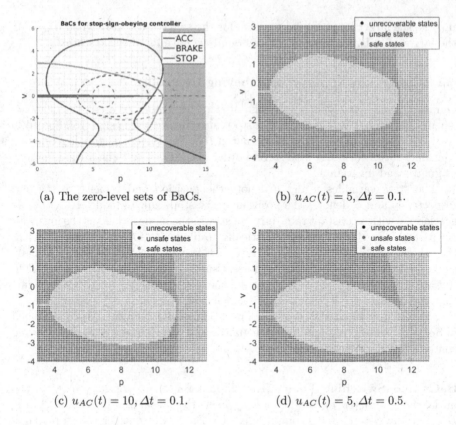

(a) The zero-level sets of BaCs.   (b) $u_{AC}(t) = 5, \Delta t = 0.1$.

(c) $u_{AC}(t) = 10, \Delta t = 0.1$.   (d) $u_{AC}(t) = 5, \Delta t = 0.5$.

Fig. 4. (a) Illustration of BaCs. (b)–(d) Online switching decision at time t in stop-sign-obeying controller across the state-space for a given $\mathbf{u}_{AC}(t)$ of AC and Δt.

$Reach_{=\Delta t}(\mathbf{x}_{AC}(t), \mathbf{u}_{AC}(t))$, where $\mathbf{x}_{AC} = [p, v]^T$ and $\mathbf{u}_{AC}(t)$ is some acceleration input provided by AC at t, i.e., $v' = \mathbf{u}_{AC}(t)$. For $\mathbf{x}(t + \Delta t) = [p(t + \Delta t), v(t + \Delta t)]^T$, we have $v(t + \Delta t) = v(t) + \mathbf{u}_{AC}(t)\Delta t$ and $p(t + \Delta t) = p(t) + v(t)\Delta t + \frac{1}{2}\mathbf{u}_{AC}(t)\Delta t^2$. To check the *safety* condition in Algorithm 1, we check if the intersection of the enclosure from $\mathbf{x}(t)$ to $\mathbf{x}(t + \Delta t)$ (which can be over-approximated with a rectangle) and the unsafe region X_u is empty. To check the *recoverability* condition, we use the recoverable region computed above and check if $\mathbf{x}(t + \Delta t) \in \bigcup_{l=1}^{M} \text{Recov}(l)$. If $\mathbf{x}_{AC}(t)$ satisfies both *safety* and *recoverability* condition of Algorithm 1, we call it a safe state (green dot) and continue with AC. But if it only satisfies the *safety* condition, we call the state as unrecoverable (black dot) and switch to BC. The states represented as red dots do not satisfy any condition, i.e., it is either unsafe or will go to unsafe region within Δt. Among the subfigures of Fig. 4, we either vary $\mathbf{u}_{AC}(t)$ or Δt. Note that we assume some arbitrary values for $\mathbf{u}_{AC}(t)$ for all cases that AC may provide during run-time.

6   Related Work

Our BaC-based approach is similar to the combination of offline and online strategies in [9], but there are some key differences. The authors use the following switching logic. The AC controls the plant if it is well within the largest ellipsoidal safe sublevel set of the Lyapunov function that establishes the safety of the BC. If the plant is near the boundary of the ellipsoid, the AC retains control if reachability analysis shows that (i) the plant will remain safe under the control of the BC over a finite horizon and (ii) the BC can guarantee to bring the plant back into the ellipsoid, thus guaranteeing recoverability, at the end of the finite horizon. The logic is designed to maximize the AC's operating region. Moreover, the plant is allowed to leave the ellipsoid as long as it is guaranteed to be recoverable at the end of the finite horizon. Our Algorithm 1 also achieves this objective. The recoverability test in step 4 checks if all the states reachable under the AC's control at the end of Δt are recoverable. In other words, the plant is allowed to cross the zero-level sets of the barrier certificates if it is guaranteed to return into at least one of the zero-level sets at the end of Δt.

Additionally, [9] relies on LMI, which is primarily intended for stability analysis of linear systems; nonlinear systems must be linearized for analysis. BaCs, on the other hand, inherently encode the notion of safety for hybrid automata and other nonlinear systems. Our approach enables us to go beyond simple single-mode systems, like the inverted pendulum model of [9], and design Simplex architectures for multi-mode hybrid systems. Specifically, we detail the relationship between the reach-sets and the BaC-based recoverable regions.

We also make a simplifying assumption: the decision module can observe the control input produced by the AC, and that the control input does not change during the decision period, which is the same as the control period. This assumption eliminates the need to abstract AC as a hybrid automaton.

The concept of Simplex is closely related to Run-Time Assurance (RTA). BaCs were proposed for RTA of hybrid systems in [11], but the switching logic was not described in detail. Moreover, the details of computing BaCs and case studies were not presented. In [3], reachability analysis on hybrid systems is applied to produce a decision module that guarantees safety, which is completely offline with assumptions about the maximum derivative of the states. By contrast, our online computation assumes that the current control input is known.

In [22], compositional barrier functions are used to guarantee the simultaneous satisfaction of composed objectives. They rely on a single controller and an optimization-based approach to correct the controller in a minimally invasive fashion when violations of safety are imminent. This approach is limited by the single controller, and consequently less flexible compared to Simplex.

7   Conclusions and Future Work

We presented a Barrier-Certificates-based two-controller Simple Architecture for hybrid systems. In addition to establishing safety of the plant under the baseline controller, the zero-level sets of the BaCs also yield recoverable regions, where the safety is guaranteed for infinite time. The switching logic of the architecture, which samples the state of the plant under the advanced controller periodically in discrete time, uses on-the-fly reachability computations to ensure that (i) the plant remains safe between successive samples and (ii) every sample is recoverable. Two case studies, a water-tank system and a stop-sign-obeying controller, were presented to illustrate the implementation aspects of our approach.

We plan to extend our work along several directions. We will pursue the computation of barrier certificates that guarantee optimal switching, which ensures that the operating region of the advanced controller is maximized. Our approach will be applied to more complicated systems with nonlinearities and exogenous inputs. Finally, we will extend our approach to compositions of barrier certificates that simultaneously satisfy multiple composed safety constraints.

Acknowledgments. Author Abhishek Murthy contributed to this research as part of his doctoral studies at Stony Book University. This work is supported in part by AFOSR Grant FA9550-14-1-0261, NSF Grants IIS-1447549, CNS-1421893, CNS-1446832, CNS-1445770, CNS-1445770, and CCF-1414078, and ONR Grant N00014-15-1-2208. Any opinions, findings, and conclusions or recommendations expressed in this material are those of the author(s) and do not necessarily reflect the views of these organizations.

References

1. Asarin, E., Dang, T., Girard, A.: Reachability analysis of nonlinear systems using conservative approximation. In: Maler, O., Pnueli, A. (eds.) HSCC 2003. LNCS, vol. 2623, pp. 20–35. Springer, Heidelberg (2003). doi:10.1007/3-540-36580-X_5
2. Bak, S.: Verifiable COTS-Based Cyber-Physical Systems. Ph.D. thesis, University of Illinois at Urbana-Champaign (2013)
3. Bak, S., Manamcheri, K., Mitra, S., Caccamo, M.: Sandboxing controllers for cyber-physical systems. In: Proceedings of the 2011 IEEE/ACM International Conference on Cyber-Physical Systems, ICCPS, pp. 3–12. IEEE Computer Society (2011)
4. Boyd, S.P., El Ghaoui, L., Feron, E., Balakrishnan, V.: Linear Matrix Inequalities in System and Control Theory, vol. 15. SIAM, Philadelphia (1994)
5. Chen, X., Sankaranarayanan, S.: Decomposed reachability analysis for nonlinear systems. In: Real-Time Systems Symposium (RTSS), pp. 13–24. IEEE (2016)
6. Chutinan, A., Krogh, B.H.: Computational techniques for hybrid system verification. IEEE Trans. Autom. Control **48**(1), 64–75 (2003)
7. Dang, T., Maler, O.: Reachability analysis via face lifting. In: Henzinger, T.A., Sastry, S. (eds.) HSCC 1998. LNCS, vol. 1386, pp. 96–109. Springer, Heidelberg (1998). doi:10.1007/3-540-64358-3_34
8. Glavaski, S., Papachristodoulou, A., Ariyur, K.: Safety verification of controlled advanced life support system using barrier certificates. In: Morari, M., Thiele, L. (eds.) HSCC 2005. LNCS, vol. 3414, pp. 306–321. Springer, Heidelberg (2005). doi:10.1007/978-3-540-31954-2_20
9. Johnson, T.T., Bak, S., Caccamo, M., Sha, L.: Real-time reachability for verified simplex design. ACM Trans. Embed. Comput. Syst. (TECS) **15**(2), 26 (2016)
10. Loechner, V.: Polylib: A library for manipulating parameterized polyhedra (1999)

11. Murthy, A., Bartocci, E., Zadok, E., Stoller, S., Smolka, S., Grosu, R.: Simplex architecture for run time assurance of hybrid systems. In: Safe and Secure Systems and Software Symposium (S5) (2012)
12. Murthy, A., Islam, M.A., Smolka, S.A., Grosu, R.: Computing bisimulation functions using SOS optimization and δ-decidability over the reals. In: Proceedings of the 18th International Conference on Hybrid Systems: Computation and Control, pp. 78–87. ACM, New York (2015)
13. Murthy, A., Islam, M.A., Smolka, S.A., Grosu, R.: Computing compositional proofs of input-to-output stability using sos optimization and δ-decidability. Nonlinear Anal. Hybrid Syst. **23**, 272–286 (2017)
14. Papachristodoulou, A., Anderson, J., Valmorbida, G., Prajna, S., Seiler, P., Parrilo, P.A.: SOSTOOLS: Sum of squares optimization toolbox for MATLAB (2013)
15. Platzer, A.: Logical Analysis of Hybrid Systems: Proving Theorems for Complex Dynamics. Springer, Heidelberg (2010)
16. Prajna, S., Jadbabaie, A.: Safety verification of hybrid systems using barrier certificates. In: Alur, R., Pappas, G.J. (eds.) HSCC 2004. LNCS, vol. 2993, pp. 477–492. Springer, Heidelberg (2004). doi:10.1007/978-3-540-24743-2_32
17. Prajna, S., Jadbabaie, A., Pappas, G.J.: A framework for worst-case and stochastic safety verification using barrier certificates. IEEE Trans. Autom. Control **52**(8), 1415–1429 (2007)
18. Quesel, J.D., Mitsch, S., Loos, S., Aréchiga, N., Platzer, A.: How to model and prove hybrid systems with keymaera: a tutorial on safety. Int. J. Softw. Tools Technol. Transf. **18**(1), 67–91 (2016)
19. Seto, D., Sha, L.: An engineering method for safety region development. Technical Report CMU/SEI-99-TR-018, Software Engineering Institute (1999)
20. Sha, L.: Using simplicity to control complexity. IEEE Softw. **18**(4), 20–28 (2001)
21. Tomlin, C.J., Mitchell, I., Bayen, A.M., Oishi, M.: Computational techniques for the verification of hybrid systems. Proc. IEEE **91**(7), 986–1001 (2003)
22. Wang, L., Ames, A.D., Egerstedt, M.: Multi-objective compositions for collision-free connectivity maintenance in teams of mobile robots. CoRR abs/1608.06887 (2016)

Autonomous Systems

A Conceptual Safety Supervisor Definition and Evaluation Framework for Autonomous Systems

Patrik Feth[✉], Daniel Schneider, and Rasmus Adler

Fraunhofer Institute for Experimental Software Engineering, Kaiserslautern, Germany
{patrik.feth,daniel.schneider,rasmus.adler}@iese.fraunhofer.de

Abstract. The verification and validation (V&V) of autonomous systems is a complex and difficult task, especially when artificial intelligence is used to achieve autonomy. However, without proper V&V, sufficient evidence to argue safety is not attainable. We propose in this work the use of a Safety Supervisor (SSV) to circumvent this issue. However, the design of an adequate SSV is a challenge in itself. To assist in this task, we present a conceptual framework and a corresponding metamodel, which are motivated and justified by existing work in the field. The conceptual framework supports the alignment of future research in the field of runtime safety monitoring. Our vision is for the different parts of the framework to be filled with exchangeable solutions so that a concrete SSV can be derived systematically and efficiently, and that new solutions can be embedded in it and get evaluated against existing approaches. To exemplify our vision, we present an SSV that is based on the ISO 22839 standard for forward collision mitigation.

1 Introduction

Ever since software has been used to control machines, its role in this task has expanded continuously. In order to fulfill the ever-increasing number of functional and non-functional requirements, software is becoming more and more complex. Currently we are witnessing that the requirement to act autonomously is gaining importance. We consider autonomy not as the capability to act without direct operator commands but as the capability to act without a predefined behavior specification. To fulfill this need in cases where complex environment perception and complex decision making are necessary, techniques known from artificial intelligence, such as neural networks, are being introduced as part of classical control systems. This brings a new class of complexity into these potentially safety-critical systems: *hard to analyze* can become *not analyzable*. Even bigger than the complexity problem is the problem of autonomy. While most established safety engineering techniques consider deviations from the intended functionality, the creation of this intended functionality is now the systems responsibility and can thus become an additional safety threat. For these reasons, most established V&V techniques, methods, and tools are not applicable for AI-controlled

S. Tonetta et al. (Eds.): SAFECOMP 2017, LNCS 10488, pp. 135–148, 2017.
DOI: 10.1007/978-3-319-66266-4_9

systems. Still, we need to gain confidence in their safety if they are to be used in a real environment.

An approach for addressing the complexity problem that is already established fairly well is runtime verification [21]. Runtime verification is a means for continuously verifying properties during runtime. This is in contrast to verifying them once and for all at development time already, which might be infeasible or even impossible in some cases. The system is steered into a safe state before or after a violation of the properties happens. In its essence, runtime verification is concerned with the correctness, i.e., the correct implementation of a given specification, of the system. By shifting the verification of properties to runtime, runtime verification addresses the problem that the increasing complexity of the system makes high coverage testing and analysis infeasible. Yet these runtime verification approaches still need a precise specification that is checked at runtime. However, autonomy realized with the help of AI techniques is explicitly used to eliminate the need for a precise specification of the system behavior in every possible situation. Thus, classical runtime verification is not sufficient to guarantee the safety of autonomous systems, and an additional runtime monitoring approach is needed that focuses on safety as the absence of unreasonable risk. We are using the term *Safety Supervisor* (SSV) for this class of monitoring approaches. The term *Supervisor* emphasizes that the SSV has the final say about the control of the system.

Safety engineering for traditional systems, as with the ISO 26262 [9], is usually concerned with functional safety. Functional safety considers malfunctions as deviations from a defined intention, usually the operator input. It is the system's responsibility to follow this input as closely as possible even in the presence of random, unavoidable hardware failures. Because of that, a safety analysis, e.g. a Fault Tree Analysis, may look a lot like a reliability analysis. We argue that for the new class of autonomously acting systems, systematic achievement of a safe system behavior is increasingly becoming the focus of core system development, e.g. by including a Safety Supervisor in the system architecture. This is not covered by existing safety standards. The current discussion on the topic *safety of the intended functionality* is a symptom of this development. As the necessary safety supervisory systems are highly complex and can influence the system behavior significantly, we see great potential in the use of a Safety Supervisor Definition and Evaluation Framework (SSV DEF).

A definition and evaluation framework on the level of functional abstraction can be used to support early design decisions for the development of an SSV. From an engineering perspective, the framework can be used to conduct what-if analyses, comparing different meaningful combinations of available solutions to arrive at an evidence-based decision about which algorithms to choose for the further development of a safety monitor. From a research perspective, the framework can be used to guide and support future research in the field. New solutions can be embedded in it and can be evaluated against existing approaches. The contribution of this paper is a well-founded conceptual framework aimed at guiding our future development of the definition and evaluation framework.

The SSV DEF will be instantiated for the automotive domain in our future work, but the conceptual framework is domain-independent and can also be instantiated for other domains, such as industry automation. As a further contribution, we will give an overview of recent work regarding the elements of our conceptual framework.

This paper is structured as follows: In Sect. 2, we present our conceptual framework for the definition of an SSV. The explanations of the different elements of the framework contain pointers to relevant related work in this area and thus to design alternatives that can be considered when implementing a Safety Supervisor. To illustrate the individual elements, we give an example of a platoon driving system. Simulation results underline the benefit of analyzing design alternatives early in the design process. Section 3 provides evidence for the validity of our framework by analyzing existing runtime safety monitoring approaches. Section 4 concludes the paper.

2   Conceptual Framework

Figure 1 presents our conceptual definition framework by means of a metamodel for the safety supervision of autonomous systems and thus the main contribution of this work. The metamodel can be seen as a template that assists in creating a concrete SSV as an instantiation of this model. The parts that form the *Safety World Model* are motivated and justified by the related work analysis presented later on. In addition to this, we see the necessity for a *Risk Reduction Strategy* to decide which behavior shall be triggered if the current situation is too critical. The *Safety Argumentation* explains the role of the Safety Supervisor in guaranteeing system safety. In previous versions of the metamodel, we focused more on the observability problem, i.e., on mapping internal variables in the individual models to monitored and controlled variables of the system. We stepped back from such a model as we see the observability problem as a problem closer related to the implementation phase, and we decided to shift our focus to the functional design phase. The main challenge that we see for this phase of the development is how to choose the right models and algorithms to create a functionally effective supervisor. The SSV DEF in intended to assist in this step. The outcome is a functional specification of the Safety Supervisor containing evidence regarding effectiveness. How the variables in the algorithms are mapped to observable variables and how the SSV is implemented is dealt with in the subsequent development steps. One future goal of our approach is the development of proper tool support for creating an SSV specification in order to move from a conceptual framework to a library-like Safety Supervisor Definition and Evaluation Framework, which will additionally assist in the creation of evidences that can be used in safety argumentation. In the following, we will go through the individual elements of the metamodel and explain their role in the context of the SSV. For each of the elements that form the SSV, we give an initial set of design considerations and point to related work in this field. To develop a concrete example for the instantiation of the metamodel, we use a forward collision avoidance system for truck platooning.

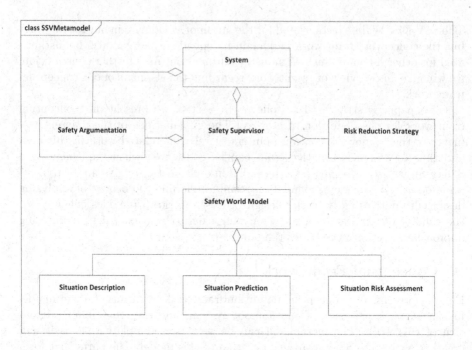

Fig. 1. SSV Metamodel: A conceptual framework for the definition of a Safety Supervisor

2.1 Metamodel Elements

System. The Safety Supervisor is part of an autonomously acting system that uses complex control algorithms in a safe case and is interrupted and overruled by the SSV in a potentially unsafe case. This is in accordance with the SIM-PLEX architecture introduced in [24]. We are considering a system specified on the functional architecture level, for example using Simulink models. In the SIMPLEX architecture, an SSV should be simple. Being too simple might end up being too conservative and thus producing many false alerts. As a solution to this issue, we consider a layered SSV design that contains very simple behavior in a core layer and more complex behavior in an outer layer. This can be supported by a definition framework by assigning costs to design alternatives. Such a layered architecture additionally supports the fail-operational behavior required for such a safety-critical component as the SSV. Detailed thoughts on how to model an adaptive system with fail-operational behavior can be found in [2]. We see potential in including this methodology in our SSV DEF.

In our example, we are supervising a control algorithm for platoon driving. In platoon driving, two or more trucks are driving directly behind each other and only the leading truck is operated by a human driver. The motivation behind platooning is to relief drivers from the burden of driving, to save fuel due to optimal driving distance, and, last but not least, ideally to be safer than driving in manual mode. The latter might be achieved based on the fact that response times are generally faster for machines and, maybe even more importantly, they are known factors and not subject to fluctuations as is the case for human response times. Even for such a rather simple system, let alone for fully autonomous driving, formal verification to prove that the distance between two trucks is always more than 0 m is not possible. Also, testing each and every possible truck combination and every scenario on every possible track does not appear to be feasible or would require the possible situation space to be limited significantly. Consequently, monitoring in the form of an SSV makes sense for such a platoon driving system.

Safety Supervisor. The safety supervisor is the core component of the framework and responsible for performing the actual monitoring. To this end, it utilizes the other entities of the framework; hence it is the central element of the metamodel. Based on the information from the Safety World Model (explained later), the SSV assesses the safety of the current situation. If this results in the decision to initiate a countermeasure, a suitable one is selected automatically from the set of Risk Reduction Strategies.

In the platoon driving system, we install a Safety Supervisor that is responsible for avoiding forward collisions. The ISO 22839 standard for *Intelligent transport systems - Forward vehicle collision mitigation systems - Operation, performance and verification requirements* [10] defines *forward collision* as a collision between a vehicle (subject vehicle) and the vehicle in front of this vehicle that is driving in the same direction (target vehicle). As the platoon driving system shall only be used on highways and changing lanes is not considered as part of the functionality, it makes sense to focus on such forward collision accidents for the Safety Supervisor.

Safety World Model. This element is a container for the information needed to assess the safety and thus the risk of a situation. The output is a decision about whether the normal control algorithm is allowed to control the system further or whether some countermeasures are needed to steer the system into a safer state. Setting this into context of the SIMPLEX architecture [24], the Safety World Model is a special form of *Decision Logic* focusing on safety. The Safety World Model is composed of an internal representation of the current environment – the Situation Description – an understanding of how this situation may evolve in the future – the Situation Prediction – and an assessment of the risk of this situation – the Situation Risk Assessment. These elements have been identified in the related work study. An approach that covers the full spectrum of elements is presented in [23]. The three elements that build the Safety World Model are dependent on each other. Only the state of those elements that are part of the Situation Description can be predicted, and any quantification of the risk of a situation highly depends on the available knowledge about the current and possible future situations.

For the platoon driving example the elements of the Safety World Model will be presented together after the Situation Risk Assessment element, as in the

ISO standard the metrics used for the Situation Risk Assessment are the most explicitly represented element.

Situation Description. The highly dynamic environment in which autonomous systems act needs to be modeled explicitly by a Situation Description. The first decision for such a model regards which elements of the environment to consider. For the automotive use case, alternatives include considering all elements in the same lane, all elements in the same lane and in the adjacent lane, or all elements within a certain radius. For other domains, other alternatives are possible. After that decision, it needs to be decided which attributes of the elements to consider, starting with the size, speed, or acceleration of the elements and proceeding to more complex attributes, such as the value of an element or its probability of existence. The final decision regarding which elements and which attributes to consider must take into account that the Situation Description needs to contain as much information about the environment as needed by the other elements of the Safety Supervisor. Related work on the topic can be found in [8, 11, 12] or [15].

Situation Prediction. The methods used for Situation Risk Assessment evaluate a situation according to potential future harm. Predictions need to be made covering the entire period from the point in time where the evaluation is performed to the point in time where the harm might happen. Thus, the Situation Risk Assessment is inherently based on prediction models. Lefvre et al. provide a more detailed insight on this dependence in [17]. We demand that these prediction models need to be made explicit. The models can only address elements and attributes that are represented in the Situation Description and describe how the attributes will evolve in the future. For the supervised system, the future development can be based on the intended behavior of the AI system, if known. For other elements in the Situation Description, the observed attributes might influence the predictions. For example, if an element is classified as a child, the prediction will differ from elements that are classified as trained traffic participants. Potentially, a multitude of prediction models is possible, from non-probabilistic and simple constant velocity/acceleration models via non-probabilistic model-based prediction models to probabilistic models that may be arbitrarily complex. A good trade-off between overcomplicated and oversimplified prediction models needs to be found. Overcomplicated models might show a set of possible future situations that could be too large to handle, while oversimplified models might not consider important future situations at all. Wiest et al. propose a framework for probabilistic maneuver prediction in [30]. In this framework, the prediction models are created with machine learning methods. They show the application of this approach for the creation of a Situation Prediction for an intersection. We find this approach very promising and see additional potential in using comparable approaches for Situation Risk Assessment with the use of data mining techniques from recorded vehicle data.

Situation Risk Assessment. The assessment of the risk of a situation can be done qualitatively, as in [18], or quantitatively, as in [28]. If done quantitatively, special safety metrics are needed. These metrics rate a situation regarding its criticality, i.e., the risk that it may result in a harmful situation. A risk assessment is needed to separate the situation space that the system might encounter in a safe space, where the complex control algorithm is allowed to operate, and a potentially unsafe space, where actions by the Safety Supervisor are needed to keep accidents from happening. The space of possible metrics is limited by the attributes considered in the Situation Description and the prediction models in the Situation Prediction. The *time to critical collision probability* metric used in [23] requires a probabilistic Situation Prediction while a simple *time to collision* metric is not compatible with such a probabilistic model but works with a constant relative velocity model. These strong dependencies among the elements of the Safety World Model further motivate the use of an SSV DEF.

The ISO 22839 standard uses two time-to-collision metrics and gives two equations for the calculation of the metrics based on different assumptions. Equation 1 is used to calculate the *time to collision*, which is defined in the standard as *time that it will take a subject vehicle to collide with the target vehicle assuming the relative velocity remains constant.* Thus, the constant relative velocity prediction is made explicit. Implicit is the prediction that both vehicles stay on the collision course. Equation 2 is used to calculate the *enhanced time to collision*, which is defined in the standard as *time that it will take a subject vehicle to collide with the target vehicle assuming the relative acceleration between the subject vehicle and the target vehicle remains constant.* Again, the collision course assumption is implicit.

$$- \frac{x_c}{v_r} \tag{1}$$

$$\frac{-(v_{TV} - v_{SV}) - \sqrt{(v_{TV} - v_{SV})^2 - 2 * (a_{TV} - a_{SV}) * x_c}}{a_{TV} - a_{SV}} \tag{2}$$

x_c is defined as the distance; v_r as the relative velocity ($v_{TV} - v_{SV}$); v_{TV} as the velocity of the target vehicle, i.e., the leading truck; v_{SV} as the velocity of the subject vehicle, i.e., the following truck; a_{SV} and a_{TV} as the respective acceleration.

These time-to-collision metrics can be calculated using a very simple Situation Description that exists of one fixed trajectory on which the subject vehicle travels and a potential target vehicle that travels in front of it in the same direction on the same trajectory with a certain distance, velocity, and acceleration. This model already allows the calculation of the time-to-collision metric using the Eqs. 1 and 2. The simplicity of this Situation Description directly shows the limits of the SSV that we are instantiating for the platoon driving system. Static objects, vehicles in other lanes, or any other vehicles besides the subject and target vehicles are not considered in the representation of the environment. Consequently, no criticality metric refers to these elements and they are not considered in the risk assessment of the current situation.

By applying the ISO 22839 standard, we are using two prediction models for the Situation Prediction. The first is a constant-relative-velocity model used for the calculation in Eq. 1 and the second is a constant-relative-acceleration model used for the calculation in Eq. 2. In both prediction models, it is assumed that the vehicles keep on traveling along the same trajectory.

Risk Reduction Strategy. The Safety Supervisor uses the Safety World Model to determine whether to become active. Once the decision to become active has been made, the SSV needs to select a behavior that will lead to a less critical situation. The knowledge needed to select the right behavior strategy is encapsulated in the Risk Reduction Strategy element. Also, different solutions are possible in this field. The strategies can be derived by solving an optimization problem regarding the Safety World Model and considering the control capabilities given to the Safety Supervisor. Thoughts on this can be found in [4]. Alternatively, the set of strategies can be fixed as proposed in [26]. Considering the selection of an adequate behavior as an optimization problem might be a promising solution, but adds complexity to the SSV. Following the idea of a layered Safety Supervisor presented above, such complex behavior can be considered on an outer layer that is only used if resources are available, while in other cases a simpler Risk Reduction Strategy is used.

In the ISO 22830 standard, strategies are recommended based on the value of the time-to-collision metrics. For rather high values, the standard recommends a driver warning while for low values, the system shall actively perform a braking maneuver. The definition of the exact thresholds is left to the producer of the system. However, an SSV DEF could also assist in this step.

Safety Argumentation. It is hard to design a compelling safety argumentation for an autonomous system, in particular when AI algorithms are involved. Actions towards this goal can be found in [25]. It is an interesting and highly important, but still open question which role a Safety Supervisor can play in an overall safety concept for autonomous systems. Especially in the domain of autonomous vehicles, we can see that modern cars already contain systems such as collision avoidance systems that override the input of the human driver to avoid or mitigate the consequences of a collision in very critical situations. These systems act as a Safety Supervisor for the human driver and we expect high reuse of such systems for the supervision of autonomous vehicles. Nevertheless, the functionality of such existing avoidance and mitigation systems needs to be placed into the context of a compelling safety argumentation for autonomous systems. Related to the element of Safety Argumentation is the production of evidences. After specifying the behavior of an SSV, we need to gain trust in the correct implementation of this specification but also in its effectiveness for making the system safe. Testing in the context of autonomous systems has been considered a big challenge in the literature [13] and is one of the reasons why we use monitoring at runtime in the first place. Thus, great care is necessary to assure that the developed supervisor components can be tested and analyzed.

Still, execution in a controlled environment is necessary before the release. As argued in [29], this can only be done efficiently with the right methodological and tool support. We see early multi-domain simulation in the form of virtual validation as one of the key enablers for this [6].

For the platoon driving system, we derived the high-level safety goal *Driving performed by the system is acceptably safe*. From this safety goal, three sub-goals are derived: *System is not performing situation-specific unsafe behavior*, *The driver is performing the driving activity if the system is not capable to do it sufficiently safe* and *System is not producing a situation of unreasonable risk*. The first goal leads to a description of what *safe driving* means. Thoughts on this part of an overall safety concept for autonomous vehicles can be found in our earlier work [1]. The second goal refers to a safe operator-in-the-loop concept and is a crucial part for systems up to automation level three of the SAE standard [22]. A methodology for deriving safe operator-in-the-loop concepts is currently being developed by the authors in parallel to this work. The last sub-goal is attached to the SSV. At the early functional abstraction level, evidence for the fulfillment of these goals needs to be created with the help of simulation. More thoughts on this and thus on the evaluation part of the SSV DEF will be presented in the following subsection.

2.2   Simulation Results

The narrative description of the instantiation of the Safety Supervisor meta-model given in the previous subsection was translated into an executable Simulink model. The resulting system with the SSV in place was used for the simulation.

The results of the simulation of a specific scenario can be seen in Fig. 2. The executed scenario is represented by the given acceleration of the leader truck drawn on the right Y-axis. The platoon driving system shall adequately adapt the acceleration of the following truck to this. The optimization goal is to minimize the distance while avoiding forward collisions. Without the Safety Supervisor in place, the system performs well regarding the first optimization goal, but regarding freedom from collision, a violation occurs at the end of the simulated scenario. The SSV, which uses the enhanced time-to-collision metric as in Eq. 2, avoids this collision. As a drawback, the distance increases to an unacceptable value as the SSV destabilizes the control algorithm. Using the time-to-collision metric as in Eq. 1 shows good performance regarding both collision avoidance and minimization of the distance between the trucks.

On the one hand, this simulation result provides evidence that the use of an SSV can be beneficial for the safety of an autonomously acting system. More important than this is the fact that it illustrates the need to analyze the design alternatives of a Safety Supervisor component as early in the development process as possible. Great care needs to be taken to maintain both safe and adequate behavior of the overall system. Different design options exist for the definition of a Safety Supervisor, as has been shown by pointing to related work for the elements of the metamodel. It cannot be expected that any of these

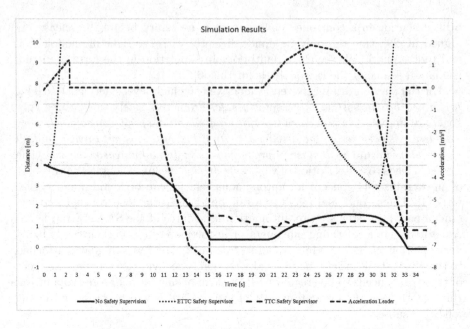

Fig. 2. Simulation results of the platoon driving system

approaches will be superior in all cases, but careful selection needs to take place. Such a selection can be made on a more stable basis if evidence created by an evaluation framework exists. In order to perform an appropriate evaluation and produce sufficient evidence, more powerful simulation tools and more reasoning about the safety argumentation are needed. As an important part of a future SSV DEF we see an evaluation platform capable of delivering results regarding the effectiveness of a particular design decision. As we are focusing on the functional, i.e., the algorithmic level, we can abstract from details such as sensor effects. This favors simulation solutions such as Pelops for automotive [7] or FERAL as a more general solution [14] over solutions such as V-REP [20], which focuses on a detailed physical simulation of the system. The question remains what to simulate in such a tool. For autonomous vehicles, this question is currently being investigated in the Pegasus project [19]. As part of this project, different OEMs are cooperating to build a database with relevant driving situations that shall be successfully executed by an autonomous vehicle to increase trust in its safe behavior. As part of our future work, an appropriate simulator has to be chosen and needs to be integrated with a meaningful set of scenarios in the SSV definition framework.

3   Related Work

An analysis of related work on supervisors that are concerned with safety led to the observation that these approaches share common aspects that are represented in the metamodel presented above. Safety Supervisor approaches can be found, for example, in [10,18,23,28,31]. Of these approaches, only [18] considers safety monitoring at runtime in general. The other approaches are instantiations of the concept for the automotive domain, i.e., active safety systems for collision avoidance. All approaches need models to assess the current safety of the system. We refer to this collection of models as the *Safety World Model*. How this Safety World Model is built differs among the solutions, but patterns can be found that helped us to derive our conceptual framework. We claim that a complete Safety World Model needs models for *Situation Description*, *Situation Prediction*, and *Situation Risk Assessment*. This is also in accordance with Situation Awareness Theory [5]. In this theory, it takes three steps to create situation awareness: Perception, Comprehension, and Projection. The Safety World Model in the metamodel is our equivalent of Situation Awareness with a focus on safety. Thus, the three elements of the Safety World Model map to the three steps: Situation Description enables Perception, Situation Prediction allows Projection, and Situation Risk Assessment is our special form of Comprehension for safety. Furthermore, we will demonstrate how the three elements are represented in the related work listed above.

In [18], the authors explicitly model the possible state space that the system can encounter with the values of observable variables. They present a methodology for deriving properties that clearly classify the situation space into safe states, warning states, and catastrophic states. In their work, the Situation Description is done via the variables and value ranges. Situation Predictions are paths leading from one state to another. In this prediction, they are not probabilistic but are concerned with the reachability of critical states. In addition, the risk of situations or states is not quantified but qualitatively assessed by assigning it to either the safe, the warning, or the catastrophic class of states. In [28], the authors propose a *Safety Decision Unit* to safeguard a truck platooning scenario. In this decision unit, they quantify the risk of the current situation using different metrics such as the *Break Threat Number* or the *worst-case impact speed* (Situation Risk Assessment). Implicitly, they limit the analysis of the current situation to the truck driving in front of the next vehicle in the truck platoon (Situation Description). The prediction made from this situation is a worst-case prediction where at any point in time it is assumed that the leading truck may initiate maximum braking. Under the prerequisite that the leading truck communicates its environmental perception, they propose a method for a more precise calculation of the probability of a braking maneuver by the leading truck. This can help to reduce the false positives created by the supervisory component by lowering the criticality of certain situations (Situation Prediction). The Safety Supervisor approach presented in [23] and its implementation presented in [31] motivated parts of the Safety World Model presented above. In their work, the authors describe the current situation by assigning probabilities for maneuvers to all vehicles in the driving scene. Based on these maneuvers, they then determine probabilities for trajectories and quantify the situation's risk with an extension of the time-to-collision metric called *Time-to-Critical-Collision Probability*. Thus, the three elements of the Safety World Model are explicitly represented in this solution. Another example was given when we instantiated the metamodel with a forward collision avoidance system for a truck platooning system following the ISO 22839 standard [10] in the previous section.

Thus, we can see patterns in what is needed to determine the risk of a current situation, i.e., the elements of which a Safety World Model consists. Additionally, a Safety Supervisor needs a Risk Reduction Strategy, which is also part of the presented safety monitoring approaches. In their work [16], Kurd et al. present GSN-based argumentation on how dynamic risk management assures the safety of a system. We see our Safety Supervisor as a component realizing dynamic risk management, and we further see the need to create proper safety argumentation that sets the SSV in relation to the supervised system and argues how the safety of the overall system is achieved. As for the safety criticality of the supervisor component, we see this as a necessary and natural part of the development that shall be supported by an SSV DEF through the production of evidences.

4   Conclusion

We see that monitoring at runtime will become necessary to create trust in the safety of autonomously acting systems. In this work, we have presented a conceptual framework by means of a metamodel to define a component for safety monitoring – a Safety Supervisor (SSV) – as an instantiation of the metamodel. The central part of the metamodel – the Safety World Model – has been developed by deriving patterns in an analysis of related work on existing Safety Supervisor solutions. The Safety Supervisor Definition and Evaluation Framework (SSV DEF) shall assist in conducting what-if analyses in the design of a concrete supervisor component. To be able to validate design alternatives in a cost-efficient way, we are focusing on the functional behavior of the supervisor and on the development of a functional specification of the SSV in order to validate its conceptual feasibility and to evaluate design alternatives through simulation. Furthermore, the conceptual framework can assist in guiding future research in the field and putting existing work into context. We demonstrated the complexity of the definition of an SSV by highlighting an initial set of design alternatives of those components that form the SSV. We exemplified the instantiation of the metamodel by defining a supervisor for a platoon driving system and used simulation results to demonstrate the methodological need to assess the design alternatives early in the SSV development process. To pave the way for enriching the framework with predefined functionality, we introduced related work in the specific areas of interest. Following this path will lead from a conceptual framework to a library-like definition framework for the functionality of a Safety Supervisor for autonomous systems. We see great potential in such an approach as it allows considering different design alternatives for a safety monitoring system based on evidences early in the development process. As the concrete instantiations of the metamodel elements will naturally be highly domain-specific, we will focus on the automotive domain and thus on autonomous vehicles in future work. The conceptual framework presented in this work, however, is domain-independent and can be implemented for other domains as well.

Another promising direction, staying on the conceptual level, is to consider the elements of the metamodel not as being static but rather as elements that can adapt during runtime. Turning the individual models into models-at-runtime allows the supervisor to adapt to changes in the environment and learn from experience. Such an open and adaptive SSV can be embedded into existing conceptual frameworks for the safety assurance of open adaptive systems [27].

We also see great potential in the use of an SSV in the development of autonomous vehicles that follow an end-to-end deep learning approach, as demonstrated in [3]. In the learning process, a well-defined SSV can supervise the learning and guarantee that, regardless of the precise learning objectives, no unsafe behavior is learned.

Acknowledgments. The work presented in this paper was created in context of the *Dependability Engineering Innovation for CPS - DEIS* Project, which is funded by the European Commission.

References

1. Adler, R., Feth, P., Schneider, D.: Safety engineering for autonomous vehicles. In: Workshop on Safety and Security of Intelligent Vehicles (2016)
2. Adler, R., Schaefer, I., Schule, T.: Model-based development of an adaptive vehicle stability control system. Modellbasierte Entwicklung von eingebetteten Fahrzeugfunktionen (2008)
3. Bojarski, M., Testa, D.D., Dworakowski, D., Firner, B., Flepp, B., Goyal, P., Jackel, L.D., Monfort, M., Muller, U., Zhang, J., Zhang, X., Zhao, J., Zieba, K.: End to end learning for self-driving cars (2016)
4. Eidehall, A.: Multi-target threat assessment for automotive applications. In: IEEE International Conference on Intelligent Transportation Systems (2011)
5. Endsley, M.R.: Toward a theory of situation awareness in dynamic systems. Hum. Fact. J. Hum. Fact. Ergon. Soc. **37**(1), 32–64 (1995)
6. Feth, P., Bauer, T., Kuhn, T.: Virtual validation of cyber physical systems. In: Software Engineering & Management (2015)
7. FKA: Pelops. http://www.fka.de/pdf/pelops_whitepaper.pdf
8. Hornung, A., Wurm, K.M., Bennewitz, M., Stachniss, C., Burgard, W.: An efficient probabilistic 3D mapping framework based on octrees. Auton. Robot. **34**(3), 189–206 (2013)
9. ISO: 26262: Road vehicles - functional safety (2009)
10. ISO: 22839: Intelligent transport systems - forward vehicle collision mitigation systems - operation, performance, and verification requirements (2013)
11. Johansson, R., Nilsson, J.: The need for an environment perception block to address all asil levels simultaneously. In: IEEE Intelligent Vehicles Symposium (2016)
12. Jungnickel, R., Kohler, M., Korf, F.: Efficient automotive grid maps using a sensor ray based refinement process. In: IEEE Intelligent Vehicles Symposium (2016)
13. Koopman, P., Wagner, M.: Challenges in autonomous vehicle testing and validation. SAE Int. J. Transp. Saf. **4**(1), 15–24 (2016)
14. Kuhn, T., Forster, T., Braun, T., Gotzhein, R.: FERAL - framework for simulator coupling on requirements and architecture level. In: IEEE/ACM International Conference on Formal Methods and Models for Codesign (MEMOCODE) (2013)

15. Kuhnt, F., Pfeiffer, M., Zimmer, P., Zimmerer, D., Gomer, J.M., Kaiser, V., Kohlhaas, R., Zollner, M.J.: Robust environment perception for the audi autonomous driving cup. In: IEEE International Conference on Intelligent Transportation Systems (2016)

16. Kurd, Z., Kelly, T., McDermid, J., Calinescu, R., Kwiatkowska, M.: Establishing a framework for dynamic risk management in 'intelligent' aero-egine control. In: International Conference on Computer Safety, Reliability and Security (2009)

17. Lefèvre, S., Vasquez, D., Laugier, C.: A survey on motion prediction and risk assessment for intelligent vehicles. ROBOMECH J. 1, 1 (2014)

18. Mekki-Mokhtar, A., Blanquart, J.P., Guiochet, J., Powell, D., Roy, M.: Safety trigger conditions for critical autonomous systems. In: IEEE Pacific Rim International Symposium on Dependable Computing (2012)

19. Pegasus: Pegasus research project (2017). http://www.pegasus-projekt.info/en/

20. Rohmer, E., Surya, P.N.S., Freese, M.: V-REP: a versatile and scalable robot simulation framework. In: IEEE/RSJ International Conference on Intelligent Robots and Systems (2013)

21. Rushby, J.: Runtime certification. In: Leucker, M. (ed.) RV 2008. LNCS, vol. 5289, pp. 21–35. Springer, Heidelberg (2008). doi:10.1007/978-3-540-89247-2_2

22. SAE: J3016: Taxonomy and definitions for terms related to driving automation systems for on-road motor vehicles (2016)

23. Schreier, M., Willert, V., Adamy, J.: Bayesian, maneuver-based, long-term trajectory prediction and criticality assessment for driver assistance systems. In: IEEE Intelligent Vehicles Symposium (2014)

24. Sha, L.: Using simplicity to control complexity. IEEE Softw. 18(4), 20–28 (2001)

25. Stolte, T., Bagisch, G., Maurer, M.: Safety goals and functional safety requirements for actuation systems of automated vehicles. In: IEEE International Conference on Intelligent Transportation Systems (2016)

26. Tamke, A., Dang, T., Breuel, G.: A flexible method for criticality assessment in driver assistance systems. In: IEEE Intelligent Vehicles Symposium (2011)

27. Trapp, M., Schneider, D.: Safety assurance of open adaptive systems – a survey. In: Bencomo, N., France, R., Cheng, B.H.C., Aßmann, U. (eds.) Models@run.time. LNCS, vol. 8378, pp. 279–318. Springer, Cham (2014). doi:10.1007/978-3-319-08915-7_11

28. van Nunen, E., Tzempetzis, D., Koudijs, G., Nijmeijer, H., van den Brand, M.: Towards a safety mechanism for platooning. In: IEEE Intelligent Vehicles Symposium (2016)

29. Wachenfeld, W., Winner, H.: The release of autonomous vehicles. In: Maurer, M., Gerdes, C.J., Lenz, B., Winner, H. (eds.) Autonomous Driving. Springer, Heidelberg (2015). doi:10.1007/978-3-662-48847-8_21

30. Wiest, J., Karg, M., Kunz, F., Reuter, S., Kreßel, U., Dietmayer, K.: A probabilisitc maneuver prediction framework for self-learning vehicles with application to intersections. In: IEEE Intelligent Vehicles Symposium (2015)

31. Winner, H., Lotz, F., Bauer, E., Konigorski, U., Schreier, M., Adamy, J., Pfromm, M., Bruder, R., Lueke, S., Cieler, S.: PRORETA 3: comprehensive driver assistance by safety corridor and cooperative automation. In: Winner, H., Hakuli, S., Lotz, F., Singer, C. (eds.) Handbook of Driver Assistance Systems. Springer, Cham (2016). doi:10.1007/978-3-319-09840-1_19-1

A Strategy for Assessing Safe Use of Sensors in Autonomous Road Vehicles

Rolf Johansson[1,2(✉)], Samieh Alissa[3], Staffan Bengtsson[4], Carl Bergenhem[5], Olof Bridal[6], Anders Cassel[7], De-Jiu Chen[8], Martin Gassilewski[4], Jonas Nilsson[2], Anders Sandberg[9], Stig Ursing[3], Fredrik Warg[1], and Anders Werneman[5]

[1] RISE, Boras, Sweden
rolf.johansson@zenuity.com
[2] Zenuity, Gothenburg, Sweden
[3] Semcon, Gothenburg, Sweden
[4] Volvo Car Corporation, Gothenburg, Sweden
[5] Qamcom Research & Technology, Gothenburg, Sweden
[6] Volvo Group Trucks Technology, Gothenburg, Sweden
[7] Autoliv, Linköping, Sweden
[8] KTH, Stockholm, Sweden
[9] Delphi E&S, Gothenburg, Sweden

Abstract. When arguing safety for an autonomous road vehicle it is considered very hard to show that the sensing capability is sufficient for all possible scenarios that might occur. Already for today's manually driven road vehicles equipped with advanced driver assistance systems (ADAS), it is far from trivial how to argue that the sensor systems are sufficiently capable of enabling a safe behavior. In this paper, we argue that the transition from ADAS to automated driving systems (ADS) enables new solution patterns for the safety argumentation dependent on the sensor systems. A key factor is that the ADS itself can compensate for a lower sensor capability, by for example lowering the speed or increasing the distances. The proposed design strategy allocates safety requirements on the sensors to determine their own capability. This capability is then to be balanced by the tactical decisions of the ADS equipped road vehicle.

Keywords: ISO 26262 · Automated driving systems · Systematic system design faults · Sensor systems · Tactical decisions

1 Introduction

There is an increasing expectation for autonomous road vehicles to become available in a not too distant future, and there are many initiatives in the automotive industry aiming for such a development. One of the largest challenges is to come up with a safety case arguing that the automated drive system (ADS) feature is sufficiently safe, and has equal or better driving capability than the human driver it replaces. This is a difficult task, especially when it comes to the environment sensing capability. In order to claim that the verification and validation is sufficient, i.e. that the sensors of an ADS always have the capability implied by the task of ADS operation, all relevant scenarios, potential

© Springer International Publishing AG 2017
S. Tonetta et al. (Eds.): SAFECOMP 2017, LNCS 10488, pp. 149–161, 2017.
DOI: 10.1007/978-3-319-66266-4_10

failure modes and corresponding hazards must be covered by relevant test cases. As the number of possible scenarios an ADS-equipped vehicle needs to handle is very large, it is hard to show that the set of test cases provide sufficient evidence that the vehicle will be able to act safely.

As a starting point when realizing an ADS feature, the functionality, limitations and system boundaries must be defined. Given this definition, the task of showing that the sensors will provide the information needed for the vehicle to behave sufficiently safe implies three challenges. The first is to identify the use scenarios, potential failure modes of the ADS feature, and carry out a hazard analysis and risk assessment. In the functional safety standard for road vehicles, ISO 26262, the result is a number of safety goals (top level safety requirements) each with an integrity level ranging from ASIL A (lowest) to ASIL D (highest), where higher integrity levels require higher confidence in the absence of failures. The second implication is the difficulty to reach the coverage of the argumentation required by the higher ASIL levels. The third is the implicit implication, begging the question if it is at all reasonable to provide the sensor capability necessary to reach the last part of the probability tail needed show coverage for the higher ASILs. One typical safety goal for an ADS might be to control the vehicle in such a way as to avoid collision with a vulnerable road user with a velocity that could cause a specific harm. In order to argue that this safety goal is satisfied, we need to show that the ADS has sufficient capability of the sensors that the vehicle can react in time to avoid a collision; under various drive scenarios, road and weather conditions. Achieving such a capability level can be both very difficult and very costly, but if we cannot argue that the ADS vehicle will fulfill this safety goal to the required ASIL level, we cannot introduce this vehicle on the market. Based on the reasoning above, a number of key questions need to be addressed for an ADS function:

- How to select a limited number of drive scenarios, carry out hazard analysis, define safety goals and be able to argue completeness.
- How to define sufficient sensing capability to sense the surroundings and drive scenarios in various conditions.
- How to define sufficient level of sensing redundancy given the limitations in technology and cost.

In this paper, we argue that these challenges are solvable. ADS-equipped vehicles need to perform tactical decisions [1, 2], such as e.g. when to perform a lane change, preferred ego speed and preferred distance to vehicles in front. Therefore, we propose to allocate safety requirements on tactical decisions such that the safety goals can more easily be shown to be fulfilled. Instead of solving a statically defined sensing task, the sensors need to report what they can promise, and the tactical decisions can be adjusted by the ADS accordingly. In the example safety goal above regarding avoiding collision with vulnerable road users, the maximum safe speed of the vehicle will depend on the current ability of the sensors to detect vulnerable road users with enough confidence regarding the required ASIL. This means that we get on the one hand a framework for how to argue that the chosen sensors can have sufficiently specific test cases for showing completeness with respect to the safety requirements. On the other hand we get a pattern where we do not need to introduce unnecessarily expensive sensing solutions just to meet the very last part of the probability tail for higher ASILs.

The rest of the paper is organized as follows: Related work is discussed in Sect. 2, our solution is explained in detail in Sect. 3, and finally some conclusions and future work is provided in Sect. 4.

2 Related Work

Terminology and definitions in this paper aims to conform to taxonomy and definitions made in SAE J3016 [3]. This standard provides a taxonomy describing the full range of levels of driving automation in on-road motor vehicles and includes functional definitions for advanced levels of driving automation and related terms and definitions.

2.1 Standards Addressing Sensor Performance

PAS 21448 - SOTIF[1] (Safety of the Intended Function) [4] is an ISO TC 22/SC 32/WG 8 initiative that proposes "guidance on the design, verification and validation measures applicable to avoid malfunctioning behavior in a system in the absence of faults, resulting from technological and system definition shortcomings". Hence, PAS 21448 claims that this (safety violations in a system without failure) is outside the scope of ISO 26262, and that this issue therefore requires additional guidance.

PAS 21448 proposes a process that aims to improve the nominal function specification to avoid or handle hazardous behavior due to the nominal function or technical limitations in the implementation. To ensure that the intended function is sufficiently safe PAS 21448 proposes a process to define and improve the function definition to reduce to an acceptable level the risk of:

- residual risk of the intended function, through analysis.
- unintended behavior in known situations through verification
- residual unknown situations that could cause unintended behavior, through validation of verification situations.

The updated intended function can be used as an input to the process of ensuring that functional safety is achieved using ISO26262. Although applicable to ADS, SOTIF is primarily focused on ADAS (Advanced Driver Assistance Systems) functions; that rely on environmental sensors such as camera and radar.

Another approach to addressing sensor performance is considered by IEC TC44 in the committee draft[2] "IEC 62998 CD – Safety-related sensors used for protection of person" [5], which aims to be complementary to the functional safety standards IEC 61508 [6], IEC 62061 [7] and ISO 13849 [8]. As opposed to PAS 21448, 62998 CD

---

[1] The SOTIF PAS is in working draft phase and is available for internal review as of Q1 2017. Hence the statements below are subject to change based on the outcome of the development process of the PAS.

[2] Since this description is based on a committee draft, the content is subject to change.

does not claim that safety violations due to the sensor system making hazardous decisions about the environment is outside the scope of the corresponding functional safety standard. Instead this draft provides guidance on how the safety-related sensors can achieve the integrity levels determined by the HA&RA performed in the main standard, when a sensor is used as a safety-related subsystem. The draft considers necessary performance, which static (e.g. environmental conditions or reliability) and dynamic (sensor readings and associated confidence) information must be available, and how to validate the sensors for enabling their use as part of a safety-related control system. The run-time confidence information can be used by the control system, to adapt the operation to the current capabilities of the sensors. The draft also gives guidelines on sensor fusion, and the separation of safety-related and automation-related information, where the latter is information needed for non-safety critical detection requirements.

2.2 Aerospace

Automation in the aviation world (Aviation Automation Systems (AAS)) plays a pivotal role nowadays. Its presence on board airplanes is pervasive and highly useful in improving the pilots' performance and to enhance safety. When developing safety critical system in aerospace, MIL-STD-882 [9] shall be used. This standard uses a prescriptive process that details the steps that shall be taken. The methods employed in this standard are qualitative, quantitative, or both. The development process based on MIL-STD-882 is iterative in nature. The process begins with concept design and derives an initial set of safety requirements. During design development, if any changes are made, and the modified design must be reassessed to meet safety objectives. This may create new design requirements. These in turn may necessitate further design changes. The safety assessment process ends with verification that the design meets safety requirements and regulatory standards.

In general, AAS is not designed to be responsible completely for safe operation of the aircraft. This implies that if the AAS fails, the pilot has responsibility e.g. to safely land the airplane. This is a similar relation as between the human driver and ADAS functions. The vehicle environment (ADAS and ADS), on other hand, is less cooperative than the environment in the air; meaning that Air Traffic Control (ATC) plays an important role to maintain safety, e.g. ensure the adequate separation of the airspace. Airplanes do not need to "stay on the road"; as long as they are at normal flying altitude there are no obstacles to avoid, no lane to follow, hardly any flying objects to avoid. Since an airplane operates in three dimensions it is less likely that two randomly flying objects will collide. A minor collision avoidance effort is required for the airplane, e.g. a simple radar based avoidance algorithm. The number of scenarios and tactical decisions in AAS are relatively low and the tactical decisions are the responsibility of pilot and the ATC in controlled airspace. If something happens, the human pilot usually has in the order of minutes to react. In a vehicle (ADAS and ADS), the reaction time for the driver is in the order of seconds. This leads to high requirements on the human driver (ADAS) or ADS. Further, due to the shorter time-frame any sensing may have lower precision. This is mainly a challenge for ADS since with ADAS, omission of function is generally not an issue.

In contrast to AAS and ADAS (which assume human operator(s) e.g. ATC, pilot or driver), ADS have low controllability. A challenge in ADS is to automate behavior planning on a tactical level. This has different challenges related to the complexity of real world traffic situations. Based on the above, we argue that ADS are more complex than AAS or ADAS. Table 1 gives an overview of the comparison between AAS, ADAS and ADS.

Table 1. Comparison between AAS, ADAS and ADS.

	AAS	ADAS	ADS
Environment	Cooperative	Not necessarily cooperative	Not necessarily cooperative
Sensing precision	High	Low	Low
Controllability level	High	High	Low
Scenarios number	Low	High	Low
Tactical decisions number	Low	Low	High
Failure severity	Catastrophic	Normal	Severe

2.3 ISO 26262 Safety Requirement Refinement

The specification of requirements at different levels (Safety Goals (SG), Functional Safety Concept (FSC)/Functional Safety Requirements (FSR), Technical Safety Concept (TSC)/Technical Safety Requirements (TSR)) are described in the ISO 26262 standard. The definitions of SG, FSC and FSR are:

- SG is a top-level safety requirement as a result of a hazard analysis and risk assessment
- FSR is specification of implementation-independent safety behavior, or implementation-independent safety measure, including its safety-related attributes.
- FSC specification of the functional safety requirements, with associated information, their allocation to architectural elements, and their interaction necessary to achieve the safety goals

The flow and sequence of the safety requirement development is illustrated in the Fig. 1 below.

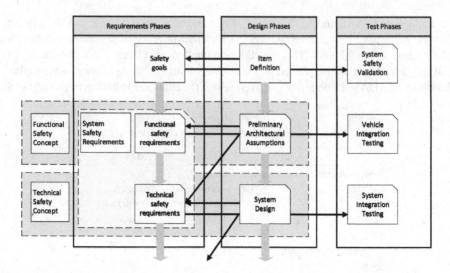

Fig. 1. Safety requirements, design and test flow. Excerpt from ISO 26262

A critical factor for achieving a safe ADS is a proper division of responsibility between sensors and sensor fusion blocks. In a sensor fusion system a significant effort has to be put into evaluating the redundancy needed to take into account in order to get a balanced and efficient design fulfilling all safety requirements. This is necessary when for example evaluating operational capabilities (redundancy and degradation concepts). Effort is put into identifying a methodology bridging the discrete domain of ASIL and the continuous domain of probabilities.

Different Sensors have different efficiency in interpreting different objects, and are even further differentiated with environmental conditions (rain, snow, dust). Radar for instance may show absence of objects (soft tissue) even when there is an object present, but if it shows presence of an object it is very accurate.

The "distance" between two requirement levels e.g. SG (Safety Goal) and FSRs (Functional Safety Requirement), or any other adjacent requirements levels, is denoted the Semantic Gap, see Fig. 2 (left) above. The concept phase of ISO 26262 describes how SGs are determined from the results of the HA&RA (Hazard Analysis and Risk Assessment). SGs are refined into FSRs, which implies that the SGs can be interpreted as top-level safety requirements in a layered requirement hierarchy. An SG is a high-level description of an objective on vehicle level, and the refinement of the SGs into an FSC (Functional Safety Concept, i.e. a set of FSRs allocated to architectural elements) may need a substantial amount of assumptions, domain knowledge and other input. If no or only weak arguments for the refinement of SGs to FSC exist, then verification to argue correctness and completeness is at best difficult.

A requirement (the upper level of two adjacent requirement levels) is refined into a composition of lower level requirements and rationale, known as satisfaction arguments. The satisfaction arguments shall be collected for the composition, see Fig. 2 (right). This bridge of information should "fill" the semantic gap. Satisfaction arguments may be e.g. assumptions, domain knowledge, design patterns. This is essential in almost every

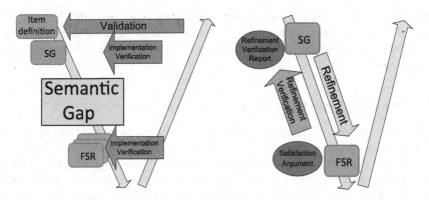

Fig. 2. The semantic gap (left) & activities between adjacent requirement levels (right)

nontrivial refinement. The rationale justifies the "refinement path taken" through the semantic gap and improves to traceability. This is further discussed in [10].

Filling the semantic gap is particular challenging with systems that use sensor fusions due to the incomplete and overlapping redundancy that different sensors may have. To prove the correctness of the refinement, the satisfaction argument must document the overlaps and gaps between sensors. To attain this knowledge deep understanding needs to be collected with e.g. field tests and simulation of sensor properties.

3   Arguing Safety for an ADS

The safety analysis procedure, as defined by the ISO26262, is to define the Item (i.e. the overall system providing a specific vehicle-level function), carry out a hazard analysis and risk assessment (HA&RA) of the Item's potential failure modes, assess the risk, and define associated safety goals with appropriate ASIL values. A safety goal expresses the goal of preventing or avoiding a hazardous event, i.e. a combination of a specific failure mode and a situation in which this failure mode may be hazardous. Each hazardous event shall be covered by a safety goal. The task of performing hazard analysis for an ADS and make sure the set of safety goals is complete and correct, taking into account all driving scenarios the function is designed for, is a big challenge in itself. This is still subject to research and not addressed in this paper, but initial attempts have been made [11] and it is reasonable to expect more guidance for this task in the future. In the section below we assume that safety goals have been identified, discuss what kind of safety requirements that might be allocated to the sensors, and how to argue that we can get evidence that all such safety requirements are met at all times under all conditions. As an example, we present some safety goals that might be hard to show that they are always fulfilled.

The functional safety concept (FSC), including functional safety requirements (FSRs), is derived from the safety goals, typically based on function analysis of the Item, evaluation of suitable architectural design patterns and other system design factors. FSRs are typically allocated to sensors, control system and actuators. The arguing we propose is illustrated by one typical architectural pattern for the functional safety concept, and it is then further described what is needed from the different blocks of that architecture. Note that the general argumentation in this paper is not limited to the architectural choice of the example.

3.1 Some Safety Goals for an ADS

In an ADS-equipped vehicle, the responsibility of driving is moved from the human driver to an ADS. In order to replace the driver, the ADS must be able to sense the surroundings (road objects, road conditions, weather conditions), control the vehicle behavior, assess any risks that lie ahead and make appropriate decisions. It must be at least equally capable as the human at operating the vehicle without causing any accidents and, as far as reasonable, mitigate dangerous situations caused by other road users. The phrase "Avoid collision" in our example safety goals below shall be interpreted with this definition in mind. Introducing the ADS function, means that we need to analyze and specify the functional capability maneuvering the vehicle equal to an experienced driver, taking in to account potential hazards caused by the limitations of the ADS and its ability in sensing the surroundings. The resulting safety goals needs to be specific and shall express what shall be avoided, e.g. a condition or functional limit, which could cause a hazard. For instance, it is difficult to assign a fair ASIL to a very general safety goal like 'never collide'. The severity of collisions with different objects and at different impact speeds varies. Hence, we need to refine the safety goal on avoiding collisions into a number of specific ones. In this paper, we do not discuss further how to best elicit a set of safety goals, we merely use a few examples to illustrate the reasoning needed to show the safety goals we have are fulfilled. Here we chose a set of safety goals, for the ADS, addressing the importance not to collide with another vehicle in front.

SG I.   Avoid collision with a higher impact speed than 65 km/h with a vehicle being on the road in front, ASIL D

SG II.   Avoid collision with a higher impact speed than 40 km/h with a vehicle being on the road in front, ASIL C

SG III. Avoid collision with a higher impact speed than 25 km/h with a vehicle being on the road in front, ASIL B

SG IV.   Avoid collision with a higher impact speed than 15 km/h with a vehicle being on the road in front, ASIL A

The difference between the safety goals in this example comes from the severity factors of the HA&RA. The numbers used are just examples, and could of course be determined differently. The important thing is that different impact speeds and collisions with different object types will result in different ASIL values.

3.2 Generic Architectural Pattern for ADS

On a very generic high level we could derive safety requirements on the sensors from the safety goals based on a conceptual architecture like the one in Fig. 3 below.

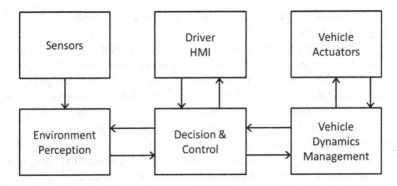

Fig. 3. Conceptual architecture for ADS

When defining the functional safety concept it is critical to show that all safety goals are completely and correctly refined into functional safety requirements allocated to the elements of the FSC architecture. This means that the division of responsibility between the Environment Perception block and the Decision & Control block must support the fulfilment of all the safety goals.

We assume that the Environment Perception block has a functional requirement: "The Environment Perception block shall detect vehicles in front of the subject vehicle".

What is needed as output from the Environment Perception block depends on the needed input to the Decision & Control block to fulfill its duties. Let us for now assume that the Decision & Control block would be satisfied if the Environment Perception block always could fulfill the following functional safety requirements, still just addressing the four safety goals in the example above:

FSR I.   No omission of detected vehicles in front up to a distance of 30 m, ASIL D
FSR II.   No omission of detected vehicles in front up to a distance of 40 m, ASIL C
FSR III. No omission of detected vehicles in front up to a distance of 50 m, ASIL B
FSR IV.   No omission of detected vehicles in front up to a distance of 60 m, ASIL A

Note that these functional safety requirements might be needed to show that the safety goals are completely and correctly refined. They are requirements that need to be fulfilled regardless of what set of sensors that are chosen in the detailed implementation. In further refinement into a technical safety concept, it is important to show that these FSR always are fulfilled. As discussed above in the paragraph on ISO26262 refinement, each refinement step needs a convincing argumentation.

Assuming that the above set of functional safety requirements are identified as applicable for the aggregated and fused sensor information employed in the realization of the Environment Perception block above, we need to argue that the chosen sensors made explicit on lower levels, can provide evidence to always and under all applicable conditions fulfill these functional safety requirements. If we choose a set of sensors for which we cannot show compliance with all these FSRs, we will not be able to fulfill the refinement verification step. And we could hence regard such a design candidate as introducing a design fault: the E/E functionality will not fulfill all safety goals. This is not due to the presence of random hardware faults, but rather due to systematic faults in the system design process.

A way to describe the challenge of showing that the sensors of an ADS have been tested enough to show capabilities of all applicable scenarios according to its operational design domain, ODD, [3] is to say that we need to address all system design failures for the sensor blocks. Of course, we still have to show that the contributions from random hardware faults and from systematic hardware and software faults are restricted according to the ASIL levels, but we also need to obtain sufficient confidence that systematic system design faults are avoided. This is nothing new for sensors. It is the same problem whenever we choose to implement a given architectural element with a specific component. If we for example chose a CPU with insufficient processing power for the tasks allocated to it, this is to be regarded as a systematic system design fault.

To summarize the big challenge for sensor systems for ADS, it is to show sufficient confidence in the avoidance of systematic design faults, such as selecting sensors that do not meet the required capabilities according to the ODD, and hence violate the functional safety requirements. In order to argue for such freedom of systematic design faults, we need evidence covering all ODD applicable scenarios and environmental situations. To collect such a large set of evidence is very hard, and it is also very hard to argue that the set of performed test cases etc, is complete with respect to this purpose.

3.3   Decision Hierarchy

One task that is characteristic for an ADS equipped vehicle is the need to perform tactical decisions, which in this example, is part of the Decision & Control block (Fig. 3). Examples of those are what target speed to aim for, what distance to aim for to the vehicles in front, what lane to choose, whether to perform an overtake, etc. Such tasks are generally left to the driver for manually driven vehicles, even when having ADAS functionality. ADAS is in general focusing on operational decisions. For an adaptive cruise control (ACC) it might be expected from the driver to choose a target speed and some preferred distance to vehicle in front. Then the ACC in the operational decisions determines what vehicle speed this implies in the actual situation, taking care of how fast the vehicles in front are driving etc.

Returning to the example safety goals above, they can be more easily shown to be fulfilled if we introduce requirements on the tactical decisions. Let us for example assume four FSRs to be allocated to the Decision & Control block:

FSR V.   Vehicle speed request shall be limited to a vehicle speed implying a maximal impact speed of 65 km/h in any vehicle objects on road, ASIL D

FSR VI.   Vehicle speed request shall be limited to a vehicle speed implying a maximal impact speed of 40 km/h in any vehicle objects on road, ASIL C

FSR VII.   Vehicle speed request shall be limited to a vehicle speed implying a maximal impact speed of 25 km/h in any vehicle objects on road, ASIL B

FSR VIII.   Vehicle speed request shall be limited to a vehicle speed implying a maximal impact speed of 15 km/h in any vehicle objects on road, ASIL A

This is functional safety requirement expression based on the four safety goals. But we also say that we can give the full responsibility to the tactical decision to what is considered safe in the current situation. Instead of giving an absolute static task to the Environment Perception block, we now say that if the Environment Perception block reports what it can promise, we can then compensate for this by means of the tactical decisions.

Assume the Decision & Control block has a functional requirement: "The Decision & Control block shall output world coordinates identifying where there is a higher/lower risk of a hazard".

Given that we have the above FSRs on the Decision & Control block, we can revise the FSRs for the Environment Perception block to:

FSR I.   No omission of detected vehicles in front inside the stated coordinates, ASIL D
FSR II.   No omission of detected vehicles in front inside the stated coordinates, ASIL C
FSR III.   No omission of detected vehicles in front inside the stated coordinates, ASIL B
FSR IV.   No omission of detected vehicles in front inside the stated coordinates, ASIL A

At a first glance this might look like redundant requirements, but this is not the case. What it says is that the Environment Perception block needs to state inside what boundaries that each of the ASIL attributes apply. Instead of giving static horizon distance requirements as in the example above (30 m ASILD, 40 m ASILC, 50 m ASILB, 60 m ASILA), we ask the block to dynamically determine the borders for each ASIL with respect to systematic design fault.

On the one hand we give a possibility for the sensor system to cut the assumed very high extra cost for the probability tail for higher ASIL, but on the other hand we ask it to determine itself what the ASIL capability is. What we say is that we can handle temporary reductions of sensor capabilities as long as the system is continuously aware of the current sensor capability. If we can determine the capability limit in run time, we can by the tactical decision assure to avoid systematic design faults.

3.4 Dynamic ASIL Capability Maps

Above we list four different FSRs to be allocated to an Environment Perception block all formulated as: 'No omission of detected vehicles in front of ego vehicle inside the stated coordinates' with different ASIL values. This implies that for each of these requirements the EP block is expected to provide a map of the boundaries that apply for the respective ASIL value. Collecting such map data into one map showing information of the integrity of claiming absence of a certain object type can look like what is depicted in Fig. 4 below. The white area in this map, closest to the vehicle, is where the perception block can provide the highest confidence (ASILD) that there is no object of the specified kind. The black area in the map, most far away from the vehicle, shows that this is beyond the high-integrity sensing horizon. There might be object here; at least there is no possibility for the Environment Perception block to claim the absence of the actual object.

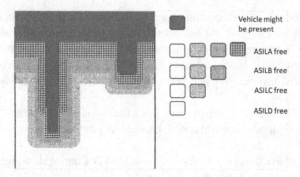

Fig. 4. Example map w.r.t. claiming absence of object of type vehicle. The ego vehicle is in the bottom of this figure

For each type of object this kind of dynamic ASIL capability map is provided by the Environment Perception block. Furthermore there is also one such map telling the ASIL level of claiming the presence of each object kind.

By defining statically in design time exactly what object types to consider, the task for the Environment Perception block is to provide all the dynamic ASIL capability maps for claiming the absence and presence respectively of each object type. Then the Decision & Control block, by means of tactical decision, can make sure that no systematic design fault w.r.t. sensor capability will violate any safety requirement.

It is beyond the scope of this article to show in detail how an Environment Perception block in run-time can produce such maps showing the ASIL-limits of absence of each object category. The message from this paper is that by formulating the safety requirements for an Environment Perception block in this way, it is possible to argue safety by asking the tactical decisions to find a safe alternative for any set of maps. A detailed strategy how to construct these maps is subject to current research. However, basic means will be design-time information from each sensor based on extensive test under various conditions, geographical data and sensing of environmental conditions showing what conditions that the sensors are (not) facing, and run-time analysis of how the different (redundant) sensors in the Environment Perception block are more or less consistent in their observations.

4   Conclusions

This paper outlines a strategy that enables and supports the argumentation in a safety case that the ADS is sufficiently safe, despite the difficulty to show sufficiently safe environmental sensing capability. A key factor in such a safety case is to argue that at all instances the vehicle will balance the sensing capability with the tactical decisions. The higher sensor capability, the higher performance (e.g. vehicle speed on the road) can be shown safe.

We argue that the ADS may need different sensor capabilities depending on the driving conditions and the chosen style of driving. If the sensors in order to enable safety for the vehicle are required to have a capability higher than they actually have, we denote this systematic design fault. This means that when performing a refinement of safety requirements, we have not allocated such safety requirements on all blocks (for example a sensor block), that can be shown to be fulfilled at all conditions.

Instead of allocating a static set of safety requirements on the sensors w.r.t. systematic design faults, we propose to formulate the safety requirements in terms of dynamic ASIL capability maps. This means that for each type of object, the sensing systems are required to provide a map showing the limit for each ASIL confidence level. If such maps can be provided to the block in charge of tactical decisions, the overall ADS including both sensors and tactical decisions can be argued to behave safely at all times.

Acknowledgements. The research has been supported by the Swedish government agency for innovation systems (VINNOVA) in the ESPLANADE project (ref 2016-04268).

References

1. Sukthankar, R.: Situation awareness for tactical driving. Ph.D. thesis, Robotics Institute, Carnegie Mellon University, USA, January 1997
2. Diem, T.X.P., Pasquier, M.: From operational to tactical driving: a hybrid learning approach for autonomous vehicles. In: 2008 10th International Conference on Control, Automation, Robotics and Vision, Hanoi, Vietnam, December 2008
3. SAE International: SAE J3016: Taxonomy and Definitions for Terms Related to Driving Automation Systems for on-Road Motor Vehicle (2016)
4. ISO/AWI PAS 21448 Road vehicles – Safety of the intended functionality
5. IEC 62998 CD – Safety-related sensors used for protection of person
6. IEC 61508: Functional safety of electrical/electronic/programmable electronic safety-related systems. The International Electrotechnical Commission (2010)
7. IEC 62061: Safety of machinery – Functional safety of safety-related electrical, electronic and programmable electronic control systems. Ed. 1.2. The International Electrotechnical Commission (2015)
8. ISO 13849: Safety of machinery – Safety-related parts of control systems. International Organization for Standardization (2015)
9. MIL-STD882(E): Department of Defense Standard Practice, System Safety, May 2012
10. Bergenhem, C., Johansson, R., Söderberg, A., Nilsson, J., Tryggvesson, J., et al.: How to reach complete safety requirement refinement for autonomous vehicles. Matthieu Roy, CARS 2015 - Critical Automotive applications: Robustness & Safety, Paris, France, September 2015
11. Warg, F., Gassilewski, M., Tryggvesson, J., Izosimov, V., Werneman, A., Johansson, R.: Defining autonomous functions using iterative hazard analysis and requirements refinement. In: Skavhaug, A., Guiochet, J., Schoitsch, E., Bitsch, F. (eds.) SAFECOMP 2016. LNCS, vol. 9923, pp. 286–297. Springer, Cham (2016). doi:10.1007/978-3-319-45480-1_23

Modeling the Safety Architecture
of UAS Flight Operations

Ewen Denney, Ganesh Pai[✉], and Iain Whiteside

SGT/NASA Ames Research Center, Moffett Field, CA 94035, USA
{ewen.denney,ganesh.pai,iain.whiteside}@nasa.gov

Abstract. We develop a notion of safety architecture, based on an extension to bow tie diagrams, to characterize the overall scope of the mitigation measures undertaken to provide safety assurance in the context of unmanned aircraft systems. We use a formal semantics as a basis for implementation in our assurance case tool, AdvoCATE. We also describe the functionality that a safety architecture affords to support both the related safety analysis and subsequent development activities. We motivate the need for a safety architecture through an example based upon a real safety case, whilst also illustrating its application and utility. Additionally, we discuss its role, when combined with structured arguments, in providing a more comprehensive basis for the associated safety case.

Keywords: Argument structures · Bow tie models · Safety architecture · Safety case · Safety system · Unmanned aircraft systems

1 Introduction

Layered or barrier models of safety, as embodied by *bow tie diagram* (BTD), have been used in civil aviation for operational safety risk management [1,2]. The emphasis in this approach is, largely, on maintaining an established safety baseline during operations, and integrating the safety management system (SMS) [3]. BTDs are now also being adopted in the context of regulatory acceptance and operational approval of unmanned aircraft systems (UAS)—our main application domain for this paper—being recommended as the basis for the associated safety case [4,5].

We have also recently used them in our process for creating real UAS safety cases [6], as part of NASA's UAS traffic management (UTM) effort [7]. Based on that experience, our observation is that the operational focus of BTDs, whilst essential, is insufficient to fully address the different facets of the safety case that must be provided: for example, the assurance concerns pertaining to the changes that may be needed, such as introducing a new technical system that implements a pre-existing safety function, or a new safety function altogether. In this paper, our goal is to provide a more comprehensive basis for a UAS safety case. Our approach is, broadly, to integrate BTDs into our process for safety case/argument development [8].

© Springer International Publishing AG 2017
S. Tonetta et al. (Eds.): SAFECOMP 2017, LNCS 10488, pp. 162–178, 2017.
DOI: 10.1007/978-3-319-66266-4_11

We have previously explored combining safety assurance arguments with BTDs as a common framework that supports both operational safety assurance [9], as well as pre-operational assurance concerns, such as type design compliance and airworthiness [10]. In the current paper, we build upon our earlier work, although our focus is on extending BTDs in the following ways:

(a) identified hazards can be associated with one or more BTDs, each of which can themselves share different admissible BTD elements (described in Sect. 2). To our knowledge, traditionally there is no representation or means for viewing the full scope of safety concerns. We define a notion of *safety architecture* (SA) to capture this "big picture" of the scope of safety (described in more detail in Sect. 4).

(b) there is a notion of *chaining* BTDs[1] that is loosely related to the above idea of SA. However, so far as we are aware, there is a lack of compatibility rules. As we will see subsequently (Sect. 3.3), arbitrarily combining certain legitimate BTDs can produce some structures that we may want to reconcile or rule out. Hence, we define structural properties to maintain internal consistency across the whole assemblage of BTDs.

(c) we introduce a new notion of bow tie *views* to support specific activities of the safety analysis, assurance, and the subsequent development processes, e.g., risk assessment, specifying barrier functionality, etc. The idea is, in part, to enable BTD use during the pre-operational stages of safety assurance, as well as to facilitate reuse.

(d) there is a lack of support for integrating BTDs and assurance arguments within a common safety case.[2] We formalize BTDs and the safety architecture as first-class notions within our toolset, AdvoCATE [12], so as to associate assurance arguments and various elements of the safety architecture.

To the best of our knowledge, none of the commercial BTD tools currently available offer a capability to create SAs, BTD views, or to check their properties.

2   Methodology

Safety risk assessment with the aim of developing a UAS safety case starts with the concept of operations (CONOPS), which describes the intended mission, and the system usage, boundaries, and characteristics. Per NASA program safety requirements [13], we undertake a scenario-based hazard identification to create *hazard risk statements* (HRS). That is, we elaborate the activities, conditions, or entities that pose a potential for harm, specifying the relevant operational context and system state. Then we identify the potential worst-case consequences, after which we undertake a hazard analysis. Traditionally, this is documented

---

[1] For example, see http://www.cgerisk.com/knowledge-base/risk-assessment/chaining-bowties/.

[2] We are aware of only one other tool that supports both BTDs and argument structures [11].

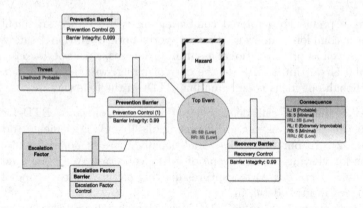

Fig. 1. Simple BTD structure and elements, as implemented in AdvoCATE.

in the form of hazard tables, augmented here with BTDs that we incrementally develop, in parallel with the hazard analysis.

Each HRS can be mapped to the *hazard*, and the so-called *top event* and *consequence* elements of a BTD (Fig. 1). From a bow tie perspective, note that hazards capture operational contexts, whereas top events reflect loss of control system states that, if unmitigated, lead to harm. This is compatible with, but subtly different from, hazards as traditionally specified. The events/situations that precede the scenario described by the HRS, traditionally considered as *hazard causes*, correspond to the *threats* leading to a top event in a BTD (Fig. 1).

In general, a top event can have a plurality of threats and consequences, although Fig. 1 only illustrates a single threat and consequence for the top event. Intuitively, multiple threats and consequences connected to a single central top event can be seen to resemble a bow tie, giving the structure its name. Also note that a BTD can be viewed as a combination of a fault tree (FT) and an event tree (ET). For example, in one representation, (*a*) the left half of a BTD is the FT (rotated right), so that the top event of the BTD is also the top event of the FT, and (*b*) the right half of the BTD is the ET so that the top event of the BTD is the *initiating event* of the ET. Other mappings are also feasible [14].

During hazard analysis, we identify pre-existing risk mitigation measures, after which we undertake a risk analysis and assessment towards developing new mitigations. This process iterates until the risk assessment indicates that an acceptable level of safety risk—established on the basis of NASA standards or guidelines, or as per the applicable *Federal Aviation Regulations* (FARs)—will be attained. The collection of mitigation measures, in turn, represent the prevention and/or recovery *barriers* in a BTD (Fig. 1), which will effect risk reduction upon proper implementation. Depending on the level of detail to which we develop the mitigations, we can refine the barriers on a specific path into their constituent *controls*.[3] Further, we can include the *escalation factors* (EFs) which

---

[3] The term *barrier* is often used interchangeably with *control* in bow tie literature, although we will distinguish them here.

are, effectively, a second level of threats that can compromise barriers. In turn, EFs can be managed by deploying *escalation factor barriers* (EFBs) that are, themselves, identified during a (preliminary or functional) hazard analysis, or through lower-level safety activities.

One of the key outcomes from this process are related BTDs corresponding to the different HRS. Collectively, they give the scope of UAS mission safety, whilst specifying the measures for safety risk mitigation and management. We can see this as a coherent and high-level picture of the overall *safety architecture*, which elaborates how safety is *designed in*, and maintained during operations. As we will describe subsequently, this provides a convenient basis for risk assessment, also serving as the interface to address specific assurance concerns. Indeed, the safety architecture together with assurance arguments comprise two key components of a UAS safety case. Although the focus of this paper is on the former, in brief, we apply our methodology for assurance argument development [8] to produce the latter at the level of individual BTDs, as well as for specific bow tie elements, e.g., barriers.

3   Illustrative Example

3.1   Preliminary BTD

In a safety case that we recently developed [6], the CONOPS involves beyond visual line of sight (BVLOS) operations with multiple small UAS, within a defined operating range (OR). The OR is a volume of airspace that includes sparsely populated and minimally built-up areas on the surface, as well as conventionally piloted air traffic (i.e., aircraft with onboard human pilots) within the surrounding airspace. We undertake a hazard analysis on this CONOPS creating BTDs in parallel.

Figure 2 (made using our tool AdvoCATE) shows a fragment of the preliminary BTD for an identified hazard: *airborne unmanned aircraft (UAs) operating BVLOS within the OR*. An associated top event is *airborne conflict from a loss of separation*. There are other top events (not shown here), such as *deterioration of separation from the terrain*. A credible worst-case consequence for the identified hazard is a *midair collision (MAC) between a UA and a non-cooperative manned aircraft*. One of the main causes leading to the top event is an airborne intrusion into the OR, which we have shown in Fig. 2 as the threat '*non-cooperative aircraft intrudes into the OR when UAs are airborne*'.

Through the hazard analysis, we identify pre-existing mitigations deployed in the current airspace system that we can use to reduce risk, e.g., pilot actions, such as *see-and-avoid* (as shown in Fig. 2 to the immediate right of the top event). We also develop new mitigation measures, e.g., invoking a flight abort capability that grounds a UA, thereby precluding a near midair collision (NMAC) (shown to the immediate left of the top event in Fig. 2). Figure 2 also shows some of the identified EFs and corresponding EFBs for the identified barriers. For instance, *loss of voice communication capability* is an EF which, if unchecked, will preclude communication during emergencies, either with air traffic control (ATC), or with

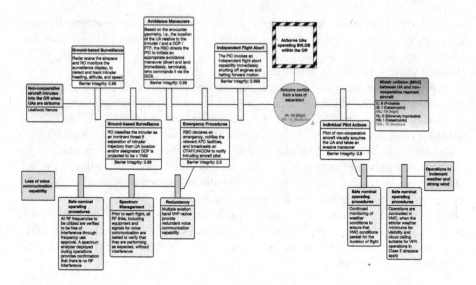

Fig. 2. Fragment of a preliminary BTD for the running example, showing the top event (airborne conflict/near midair collision), an identified threat (intrusion into the OR), and a worst-case consequence (midair collision), together with specific risk mitigation controls, EFs, and EFBs. The specific barriers to which the controls belong have also been given.

other pilots operating in the vicinity. EFBs that contribute to minimizing the associated risk include *redundancy* in the aviation radios used, and *spectrum management* to address potential radio frequency (RF) interference.

In general, the BTDs so created can be interpreted as follows: barriers/controls to the left of the top event represent preventative mitigation measures, while those to the right of the top event are recovery measures to prevent the consequence from occurring.

Also, the visual ordering of barriers/controls corresponds loosely to the temporal order in which they may be invoked, so that they prevent the events preceding them. Thus, events given after a barrier indicate event occurrence after a barrier has been breached. However, the diagrams (intentionally) abstract from the exact ordering and organization of barriers. Indeed, barriers/controls may operate sequentially, in parallel, in a continuous, or a demand mode, etc.

We assume that threats are independently occurring events, i.e., there is a likelihood of simultaneous occurrence and, therefore, they are not disjoint. Consequences can be disjoint events. With this interpretation, threats, top events and consequences can be ascribed an *initial* and a *residual risk level*, computed as a combination of their (initial/residual) *likelihoods* of occurrence and *severity*. Barriers and controls are each ascribed a measure of *integrity*, that corresponds to the likelihood that barriers are breached in a dangerous manner. We use these parameters in safety risk assessment.

3.2   Safety Architecture

We can now expand the scope of the preliminary BTD (*a*) to discover opportunities to proactively manage hazards by considering precursors to the identified threats, or (*b*) when the controls used may not suffice in terms of their effectiveness.

For example, we can assess the identified threat of Fig. 2 further, by considering it as a top event in a different BTD. Within AdvoCATE, this would create a new, partially developed BTD, where the (erstwhile) threat is now designated as a top event, the top event of Fig. 2 is its consequence, and all the barriers in between the two are retained. Then, we repeat hazard analysis to identify additional threats, mitigating barriers, EFs, and EFBs as appropriate.

Thus, applying our methodology, we incrementally develop BTDs for the different top events for each identified hazard, giving the details of the relevant operational risk scenarios for the CONOPS, and the applicable safety mitigations. The resulting collection of BTDs comprises the SA for the system, and the overall structure can be seen to characterize the total scope of safety. There is a subtle difference, however, since the SA makes no distinction between top, threat, and consequence events. They are simply events. It is only when we focus on an individual event as the top event of a bow tie that the distinction arises in the resulting BTD.

In our implementation, AdvoCATE automatically assembles the SA in the background as the BTDs are being created. If required, however, the SA can be directly edited and AdvoCATE maintains consistency with the constituent BTDs. Figure 3 shows a fragment of a (partially developed) SA for our running example. Intuitively, this structure can be considered as a *composition* of related BTDs [9]. As such, we do not distinguish top events from threats or consequences, simply considering event chains and the measures that stop the temporal progression of the associated events. The shaded box to the bottom right shows the part of the SA that corresponds to the BTD fragment shown in Fig. 2; the paths

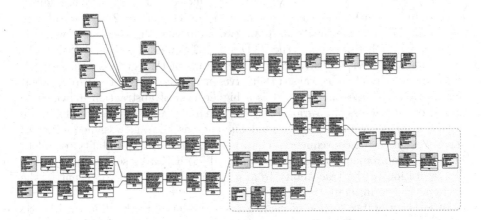

Fig. 3. Fragment of a partially developed safety architecture (SA) (shown zoomed out).

to its left are the events (threats) and controls resulting from further developing the threat identified in Fig. 2, as described earlier in this section.

3.3   Views

When deploying a system that is to be integrated with or without changes to an existing, wider system in which it will be situated, implicit or explicit choices may be required—even during the early stages of development—that affect the SA and, in turn, system safety, e.g., choosing a specific type or number of surveillance sensors, or using specific equipment onboard the airborne system, etc.

The provision of different *views* of the overall SA can well support the associated trade-offs as well as other insights that can be used to refine the SA. Moreover, together with risk assessment, views can aid in providing early assurance that the required safety targets can be met. In turn, that can be used to drive subsequent development stages, e.g., by developing a high-level requirements specification for particular barrier functions. Next, we describe some of the views that we have found useful.

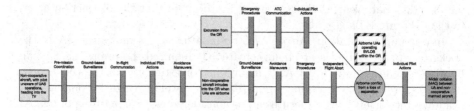

Fig. 4. Barrier-centric view for the running example.

The *barrier-centric view* of the SA shows a BTD with only the barriers shown, abstracting away the details of the specific constituent controls. Figure 4 is an example, which includes and expands on the BTD of Fig. 2 (not considering the EF or EFBs). Specifically, it shows two additional threats, one of which is obtained by further developing the BTD of Fig. 2 as described earlier (Sect. 3.2).

Although this view abstracts from the details of the controls being used it is useful in a number of ways: (*1*) it gives a simple basis for a rapid, albeit qualitative, risk assessment; (*2*) it is a higher-level of abstraction at which to apportion risk across the various barriers, given a *safety target*—specified by a regulator, or determined using a guideline such as [5]—and assigned either to the top event or the consequence. That, in turn, provides a reliability (or safety integrity) requirement for barrier design; and (*3*) it can be seen as a graphical representation of the traceability from a specific hazard and top event to the barriers used to mitigate their risk.

Another useful collection of views are *slices* relative to the different bow tie elements. For example, a slice focusing on a specific (prevention) barrier gathers

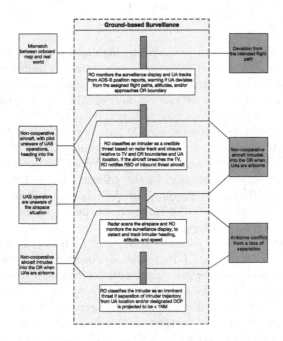

Fig. 5. Slice view of the *ground-based surveillance* barrier.

all the constituent controls, the threats (or top events) being mitigated and the top events (or consequences) that may result if the barrier is breached.

Figure 5 shows an example of such a slice across the SA of Fig. 3, focusing on the *ground-based surveillance* barrier. From the perspective of developing and implementing a barrier function, this slice view can be thought of as a system level specification of the required barrier functionality. Moreover, this view presents all the safety concerns being addressed for a specific barrier, and can be useful in communicating to the regulator what a new component of the overall safety system—in this case, ground-based surveillance—is intending to address. Here, note that since the SA of Fig. 3 is partially developed, the barrier slice only shows those controls that have, thus far, been mapped to the barrier, along with the appropriate events being managed. As the SA is developed to completion, AdvoCATE automatically updates the view.

Similarly, a slice focusing on a specific threat can present all the resulting top events and their related barriers. Effectively, that slice is the event chain beginning from a single threat event, across the entire system. Such a view could be useful to focus safety discussions on specific high priority threats presenting all the safety assets available, and how they are organized to manage those threats. A related slice focusing on a consequence shows all the top events leading to a particular consequence/chain of consequences, the associated recovery barriers, and their organization. Thus, we can define other such slices that focus on the different elements (or combination of elements) of the SA, including EFs and EFBs.

3.4 Properties

Whilst creating the SA, it can be useful to highlight potential inconsistencies, and to check that certain[4] well-formedness properties are maintained.

For instance, in incrementally building up the SA, there can be legitimate paths that bypass or *short circuit* controls/barriers [15]. That is, when some controls/barriers on a path are breached, (different) controls (of either the same or different barriers) subsequently used on that path are ineffective. Such structures can result when the composition attempts to reconcile different paths between the same pair of bow tie elements, such that there is at least one path with no other elements between the pair. In the general case, either an intervening independent control/barrier is required on the (short circuiting as well as the short circuited) paths to correct the violation, or there are missing threats in at least one of the BTDs comprising the SA.

Likewise, if there are two paths t—$\mathbf{b}$—c_1 and t—$\mathbf{b}$—c_2, in different BTDs, where t is a threat (or top event), $\mathbf{b}$ represents a collection of barriers (or controls) and c_1, c_2 are different intermediate/top events (or consequences), then there is a potential inconsistency in the overall safety architecture, if there are different outcomes for a common threat t and identical breaches of $\mathbf{b}$. Such a situation may arise if there are missing barriers (or events) on the two paths. In some circumstances, though, we may want to allow both structures: e.g., when c_1 and c_2 are, in fact, on the same causal chain but the respective BTDs are being applied at different levels of abstraction.

Additional properties that can be checked include structural constraints such as the conditions under which controls can be repeated (e.g., same path, different threats, for a threat and an EF, etc.). In the implementation in our assurance case tool, AdvoCATE, note that we enforce some properties by construction, e.g., loop-freedom and consistency of event ordering, whereas others are permitted with warnings.

4 Formalization

Section 3 gave a worked example illustrating some of the functionality that Advo-CATE supports for BTDs and SAs. We now give the formalization underlying our implementation. First, we note that the structures we want to define are parametrized over underlying sets of events, controls, and barriers.

Definition 1 (Safety Signature). *A safety signature, Σ, is a tuple $\langle E, C, B, bar \rangle$, where E, C, and B are disjoint sets of events, controls, and barriers, respectively, and $bar : C \rightarrow B$ associates each control with a unique barrier.*

We will henceforth assume the existence of a common safety signature for all definitions. Before defining BTDs formally, we introduce the notion of *controlled event structure* (CES), representing the totality of all events associated with a

---

[4] E.g., Properties whose violations could translate into weaknesses in the risk analysis and, as a consequence, in the implemented safety system.

hazard and their associated barriers and controls. In a sense to be made precise later, a collection of inter-related BTDs specifies this structure. In fact, Fig. 3 shows a CES for one hazard.

Definition 2 (Controlled Event Structure). *A controlled event structure (CES) is a tuple $\langle N, \rightarrow, l, esc \rangle$ where N is a set of nodes disjoint from the underlying safety signature, $\langle N, \rightarrow \rangle$ is a DAG representing temporal ordering of events, l_x, $x \in \{t, d, c\}$ is a family of labeling functions such that $l_d : E \cup B \cup C \rightarrow$ string gives descriptions and $l_t : N \rightarrow E \cup B$ gives node types. Writing N_e for $\{n \in N \mid l_t(n) \in E\}$ and similarly for N_b, we specify $l_c : N_b \rightarrow \mathcal{P}(C)$ such that if $c \in l_c(n_b)$ then $bar(c) = l_t(n_b)$, and $esc : N_b \rightarrow \mathcal{P}(N_e)$ such that if $n_e \in esc(n_b)$ then $n_e \rightarrow^* n_b$.*

Let $CES(\Sigma)$ denote the collection of CESs over signature Σ. Nodes of a CES represent specific events or barriers (and their associated controls) in the safety system. The same barriers can occur in multiple locations, though each may have different controls (and, as we will see later, can have different integrities). We refer to each such location as a *barrier instance* and likewise for controls.

In contrast to BTDs, which are intended to represent (eventually) well-designed safety systems, a CES models a more general underlying set of events, with a partially developed safety system, possibly without controls yet in place. To facilitate more detailed modeling of a partially developed safety system, we also allow multiple intermediate events between controls, allow events to have multiple successors (i.e., consequences) and predecessors (i.e., causes), so that paths can split and rejoin, and allow empty barriers (for when a particular barrier function is known to be required, before we have chosen or developed its constituent controls).

The interpretation of an escalation branch is that the barriers on the path between the escalation e and barrier b represent escalation factor barriers. Note that the definition allows n-ary escalations, that is, escalations of escalation factor barriers, and so on, though in practice a single level of escalation is typical.

Next, we assign integrity and initial likelihood values to the elements of a CES.

Definition 3 (Initial Risk Assignment). *An initial risk assignment for a CES consists of mappings $int_b : N_b \rightarrow$ num and $int_c : N_b \times C \rightarrow$ num, giving integrities of barrier and control instances, respectively, and $lik : N_e \rightarrow$ num giving the initial likelihood of event instances.*

We allow separate instances of controls and barriers to have distinct integrities because it is feasible for controls and barriers to have different effectiveness against different threats. Moreover, separate barrier instances can be implemented with different controls. In general, we do not require any consistency between risk assignments for different hazards, since the context is different.

Initial likelihood need only be specified for *global* threats, that is, those that do not have any preceding events. We derive the residual likelihood for all other events (working rightwards). We also assign severity to global consequences (i.e., those that are rightmost), and derive severity on all other events (working leftwards—the simplest approach is to set the severity of an event to be the maximum severity of its immediate successors). The integrity of a barrier is, in principle, derived from its constituent controls. This should be computed via a *risk model*, such as fault trees, possibly implemented via an external tool. Currently, in our tool, we simply provide the integrities of barriers directly and will not consider this further here.

We can now define a safety architecture (SA) as a set of mutually consistent CESs.

Definition 4 (Safety Architecture). *Given safety signature, Σ, a safety architecture, $\langle H, l_h, ces \rangle$ consists of a set of hazards, H, hazard descriptions, $l_h : H \to string$, and a mapping ces : $H \to CES(\Sigma)$, which for each hazard, h, returns a controlled event structure such that the CESs are mutually temporally consistent, i.e., for hazards h_1, $h_2 \in H$, if $e \to_1^* e'$ then $e' \not\to_2^* e$.*

Though we require mutual consistency for event ordering (in effect, that the combined relation on events is a DAG), we do not require similar consistency for controls between different CES since they represent different contexts in which controls can be used in different ways. This definition of SA is slightly more permissive than an earlier one given in [9], but is more convenient for implementation and, as we will show below, is essentially equivalent. We now define a BTD as a specific sub-structure of a CES.

Definition 5 (Bow Tie Diagram). *A bow tie diagram, B, is a CES such that: (1) there is a designated event, t_p, called the top event; (2) there exists at least one threat, i.e., an event, t such that $t \to^* t_p$, and one consequence, $t_p \to^* c$; and (3) for all events e in B, $e \to^* t_p$ or $t_p \to^* e$, (i.e., all threats lead to a top event, all consequences follow from top events, and all escalations lead to a control that leads to the top event).*

In contrast to the classical notion of BTD, here we permit arbitrary breadth BTDs with intermediate events and arbitrary depth escalations. Moreover, since we allow arbitrary event chains, paths can split and rejoin. A "good" BTD, however, will satisfy additional properties. For example, it is *free of short circuits* (Sect. 3.4) if $e \to c \to e' \to c'$ implies $e \not\to c'$. A stronger property that may be enforced is that no barrier can have multiple outputs. We say that a BTD is *maximal* relative to a safety architecture if it includes all events before or after its top event, and *well-controlled* if it has controls between all events. Similar structural conditions that can be indicative of poor design can also be checked.

Next, we show that a CES can be factorized into a set of mutually consistent BTDs which, in combination, give the original CES. To simplify matters, we only consider BTDs relative to a common parent structure, so they can be combined simply by merging. We also assume the existence of initial risk assignments. For shared threats, we must assume that the initial likelihood is the same. Likewise, for severity levels of shared consequences. We need to take care with residual likelihoods since they can differ depending on whether they are computed over paths in a single BTD or the overall CES. However, since those values are derived, we can ignore them when considering the factorization and combination of BTDs.

Theorem 1 (Bow Tie Factorization). *A CES is equivalent to a set of mutually consistent BTDs for distinct top events.*

Proof. Define an ordering on events: $e_1 \leq e_2 \iff \forall e . e_1 \leftrightarrow^* e \Rightarrow e_2 \leftrightarrow^* e$, where $\leftrightarrow^*$ means comparable (either $\rightarrow^*$ or $\leftarrow^*$). Intuitively, e_2 subsumes the set of potential threats and consequences of e_1. It can be seen that $\leq$ is a partial order, so we can talk of maximal elements. Say that maximal events in $\leq$ are *central*. Define a relation, R, on central events, by saying that t_1 and t_2 are *co-central* if they are $=$ relative to $\leq$. Equivalently, $t_1 \, R \, t_2 \iff t_1 \leftrightarrow^* t_2$ and for all events, e, that are not between t_1 and t_2, if $e \rightarrow^* t_1$ then $e \rightarrow^* t_2$ and if $t_1 \rightarrow^* e$ then $t_2 \rightarrow^* e$. Since R is an equivalence relation on central events (and a partial equivalence on all events), we can create the partition of central events in the CES by R. Next, choose one member of each partition, and generate the maximal BTD from it. This gives us a set of BTDs. They cover the CES, and can overlap, but are disjoint for central events (and top events, in particular). Since they are sub-dags of the CES they are mutually consistent. $\qquad\square$

Thus, a safety architecture can be thought of, equivalently, as a collection of (mutually consistent) BTDs for each hazard.

5   Supporting the Safety Case

Recalling the CONOPS for our running example (Sect. 2), the safety case is concerned with providing assurance that flight operations can be safely conducted, i.e., that a level of safety can be met that is equivalent to the prevailing safety target with respect to MACs, and that an acceptable level of risk is posed to the population on the ground. Additionally the safety case is required to show that a ground-based detect and avoid capability—comprising radar, transponders, surveillance displays, along with a suite of avoidance maneuvers, and crew functions—can be safely used in lieu of visual observers, the prevailing means of compliance with certain FARs.

Next, we describe the role played by the combination of the SA and argumentation in providing a more comprehensive basis for the safety case. We also discuss the utility of using an SA and its views, and the tool support we have leveraged.

5.1   Assurance of Risk Reduction

We establish that the SA achieves an acceptable residual risk level for the consequence(s), using (*1*) barrier integrity, given as nearest order of magnitude estimates based upon data where available and/or conservative assumptions as appropriate; (*2*) the (initial) likelihood of occurrence of the threats; (*3*) the (initial) severity of the worst-case consequence; and (*4*) a *risk model*, based on the barrier-centric view, that combines the above.

Unless using barriers whose specific function is to substantially reduce consequence severity (e.g., frangible airframes), the residual severity for the worst-case consequence is the same as its initial severity. Thus, to assess the magnitude of risk reduction we compute the (residual) likelihood of the consequence(s). We omit the details of the mathematical specification used to implement this capability in AdvoCATE. In brief, however, first we compute top event occurrence likelihood from the initial likelihoods of occurrence of the identified threats, and barrier integrities. Then we compute the likelihood that the consequence in question occurs given the occurrence of the specific top event shown in the view. In either case, the probability of an event (excepting those without any preceding events) is the probability of the disjunction over all paths leading to that event, which we compute using the *inclusion-exclusion principle*. That, in turn, relies on the computation of path probabilities, which is determined for a path as the joint probability that all the events on that path (including barrier breach events) occur. Here, a key assumption is that barrier breaches occur independently.

The safety target against which we compare the residual likelihood is based upon a qualitative risk acceptance matrix [16], i.e., a risk classification. For example, for a midair collision (MAC) consequence (which has a *catastrophic* severity), the safety target is set as at least *extremely improbable*. For other consequences that have different severities, the risk classification, likewise, provides the corresponding safety targets.

5.2   Relationship to Structured Arguments

Whilst safety assurance using risk assessment based on views of the SA can be very useful, it trades off accuracy for simplicity, at the cost of greater uncertainty in the estimate. Although we can usefully improve model accuracy—e.g., considering the specific controls, EFs, EFBs, and by using formalisms such as Bayesian networks, or dynamic event/fault trees [14]—that, itself, can present substantial challenges in quantification and validation [17]. An acceptable compromise is to combine the SA with structured assurance arguments that substantiate specific safety-related assertions, to (qualitatively) offset risk assessment uncertainty. Moreover, argument structures are well suited to supply the rationale why the safety objectives and requirements for changes to a safety baseline—e.g., as derived through a top-down, risk-based approach using BTDs [3]—have been met.

In general, we can associate a number of assurance arguments, each addressing a specific assurance concern, either with a *specific* BTD (or a view), *multiple elements* of a BTD, or *multiple* BTDs. For instance, we can augment the risk assessment based on the barrier-centric view, as described earlier, with an argument that (*1*) not only marshals detailed rationale and evidence substantiating how the barriers (especially those whose integrities are unknown or difficult to quantify) contribute to risk reduction, but also (*2*) include a rigorous justification of related assurance concerns such as barrier (failure) independence, sufficiency of the identified threats and event chains, mitigation of common-cause failure modes, etc. Similarly, we can associate arguments with specific barriers [6] (and/or their constituent controls), whose top-level claims address the appropriate barrier-specific assurance concerns, e.g., provision of the required safety functions, fitness for purpose, achievement of a specific level of safety integrity, etc. At a mission level, assurance arguments straddle the collection of BTDs, justifying why the overall SA enables safety in operation.

5.3   Utility and Tool Support

The SA provides an integrated and consistent view on the full scope of the applicable safety concerns. The barrier-centric view (Sect. 3.3) supplies the core rationale for how the SA reduces risk: defense-in-depth through independent, loosely-coupled, layers (barriers) of protection. This view also gives a basis for a risk assessment, towards providing assurance of safety during operations. These facets constitute the core value addition provided by the extensions described in this paper, over other approaches.

Additionally, combining assurance arguments and a SA affords a common framework to provide (*i*) the pre-operational assurance required for regulatory acceptance of both potential changes to an existing safety system, and the introduction of new safety functions; as well as (*ii*) operational safety assurance.

In practice, the tool support that is currently commercially available for creating barrier models[5] largely permits creating only a disconnected collection of BTDs. To the best of our knowledge, they neither support the creation of an SA as we have described it, nor do they provide view-based abstraction. In other words, none of the commercial tools provide the extensions we have developed in this paper. Consequently, there is a need for implementing the associated functionality for it to be useful in practice. The formalization we have described in Sect. 4 underpins the implementation of BTDs, SAs, views, and the support for risk assessment, in our toolset AdvoCATE. The models for these notions, implemented using the Eclipse Modeling Framework [21], closely follow the formalization we have described.

6   Concluding Remarks

We have described novel extensions to BTDs supporting view-based risk assessment and its integration into an argument-based safety case methodology. We have applied this methodology (including BTD-based risk assessment) in the context of creating, managing, and updating real safety cases required for regulatory approval to conduct BVLOS UAS operations, as part of NASA's UTM effort.

For instance, in the safety case that provided the running example for this paper, we used views of the underlying SA to communicate to the aviation regulator how safety risk reduction would be achieved during UAS operations.

---

[5] For example, BowTieXP: http://www.cgerisk.com/, BowTie Pro: http://www.bowtiepro.com/, RiskView: http://www.meercat.com.au/, THESIS BowTie: http://www.abs-group.com/, etc..

That, in turn, proved to be one of the linchpins of the safety case that contributed to its acceptance and, subsequently, a successful grant of operational flight approval. Our efforts have leveraged our tool, AdvoCATE [12], making full use of its functionality to construct and analyze both BTDs and assurance arguments, including checking properties, creating views, and seamlessly linking and navigating between the two. Our implementation is based on a formal semantics that admits the construction of arbitrary event structures to guide an incremental, interactive development of a well-designed safety architecture.

As mentioned earlier (Sect. 1), BTDs are used both in civil aviation and for safety assurance of UAS, although existing tools do not implement the functionality we have described here. Moreover, with the exception of one tool that does support argument development [11], so far as we are aware, no other tool provides a common framework to integrate BTDs with assurance arguments for (UAS) safety case development.

Our notion of SA is compatible with classical safety control architectures (i.e., 1oo1, 1oo2, etc.), which represent implementation-level organizations of (largely hardware-based) safety instrumentation and typically exist at a lower-level of abstraction. The work that is, perhaps, most closely related to ours reconciles early architectural knowledge of a system—modeled using AADL—with traditional safety analysis [18]. The focus, however, is on (safety) system design and pre-operational assurance. Our notion of SA is, again, compatible with this work, but conceptually at a higher-level of abstraction. A key point of difference is that our notion retains an operational relevance and, thus, links to the underlying SMS [1].

Our ongoing work is investigating the relationship between argument structures and BTDs both from (a) the perspective of formal mappings that can be used to generate one from the other, and (b) how they best complement each other in a safety case. For example, one possibility is to associate argument patterns with generic controls, composing patterns to form an *argument architecture* [9,19], analogously to how we combine barriers/controls to form the safety architecture. Then, instantiating the argument patterns, based on the context in which the controls are used, will generate the associated assurance argument.

We plan to further develop view generation, leveraging prior work on *queries* [20]. Additionally, we plan to investigate various levels of integration of more detailed quantitative risk analysis models [14], to be able to verify barrier integrity requirements prior to deployment, and to update the risk assessment during operations, based on safety performance monitoring. Eventually, we want to provide capabilities for risk apportionment and deriving the related safety requirements. More broadly, we envision tighter integration into a model-based systems engineering process, with tool support for linking to, and maintaining consistency across, all the safety artifacts relevant for through-life safety assurance.

Acknowledgements. This work was funded by the Safe Autonomous Systems Operations (SASO) project under the Airspace Operations and Safety Program of the NASA Aeronautics Research Mission Directorate.

References

1. FAA Air Traffic Organization: Transforming Risk Management: Understanding the Challenges of Safety Risk Measurement, December 2016. https://go.usa.gov/xXxea

2. UK Civil Aviation Authority: Bowtie Risk Assessment Models (2015). http://www.caa.co.uk/Safety-Initiatives-and-Resources/Working-with-industry/Bowtie/

3. Acfield, A.P., Weaver, R.A.: Integrating safety management through the bowtie concept: a move away from the safety case focus. In: Australian System Safety Conference, pp. 3–12, May 2012

4. Clothier, R.A., Williams, B.P., Fulton, N.L.: Structuring the safety case for unmanned aircraft system operations in non-segregated airspace. Saf. Sci. **79**, 213–228 (2015)

5. Joint Authorities for Rulemaking of Unmanned Systems: JARUS Guidelines on Specific Operations Risk Assessment (SORA) (External Consultation Draft), August 2016

6. Denney, E., Pai, G.: Safety considerations for UAS ground-based detect and avoid. In: 35th IEEE/AIAA Digital Avionics Systems Conference, pp. 1–10, September 2016

7. Prevot, T., Rios, J., Kopardekar, P., Robinson III, J., Johnson, M., Jung, J.: UAS Traffic Management (UTM) concept of operations to safely enable low altitude fight operations. In: 16th AIAA Aviation Technology, Integration, and Operations Conference, AIAA-2016-3292, June 2016

8. Denney, E., Pai, G.: A methodology for the development of assurance arguments for unmanned aircraft systems. In: 33rd International System Safety Conference, August 2015

9. Denney, E., Pai, G.: Architecting a safety case for UAS flight operations. In: 34th International System Safety Conference, August 2016

10. Denney, E., Pai, G.: Argument-based airworthiness assurance of small UAS. In: 34th IEEE/AIAA Digital Avionics Systems Conference, pp. 5E4-1–5E4-17, September 2015

11. Adelard LLP: Assurance and Safety Case Environment. http://www.adelard.com/asce/

12. Denney, E., Pai, G., Pohl, J.: AdvoCATE: an assurance case automation toolset. In: Ortmeier, F., Daniel, P. (eds.) SAFECOMP 2012. LNCS, vol. 7613, pp. 8–21. Springer, Heidelberg (2012). doi:10.1007/978-3-642-33675-1_2

13. NASA Office of Safety and Mission Assurance: NASA General Safety Program Requirements. NPR 8715.3C (2008)

14. Dugan, J., Pai, G., Xu, H.: Combining software quality analysis with dynamic event/fault trees for high assurance systems engineering. In: 10th IEEE High Assurance Systems Engineering Symposium, pp. 245–255, November 2007

15. Duijm, N.J.: Safety-barrier diagrams as a safety management tool. Reliab. Eng. Syst. Saf. **94**(2), 332–341 (2009)

16. FAA Air Traffic Organization: Safety Management System Manual version 4.0, May 2014

17. Brooker, P.: Air Traffic Management Accident Risk. Part 1: The Limits of Realistic Modelling. Saf. Sci. **44**(5), 419–450 (2006)

18. Feiler, P., Gluch, D., Mcgregor, J.: An Architecture-led Safety Analysis Method. In: 8th European Congress on Embedded Real Time Software and Systems, January 2016

19. Denney, E., Pai, G.: Composition of safety argument patterns. In: Skavhaug, A., Guiochet, J., Bitsch, F. (eds.) SAFECOMP 2016. LNCS, vol. 9922, pp. 51–63. Springer, Cham (2016). doi:10.1007/978-3-319-45477-1_5
20. Denney, E., Naylor, D., Pai, G.: Querying safety cases. In: Bondavalli, A., Di Giandomenico, F. (eds.) SAFECOMP 2014. LNCS, vol. 8666, pp. 294–309. Springer, Cham (2014). doi:10.1007/978-3-319-10506-2_20
21. Steinberg, D., Budinsky, F., Paternostro, M., Merks, E.: EMF: Eclipse Modeling Framework 2.0, 2nd edn. Addison-Wesley Professional, Reading (2009)

Generic Management of Availability in Fail-Operational Automotive Systems

Philipp Schleiss[1(✉)], Christian Drabek[1], Gereon Weiss[1], and Bernhard Bauer[2]

[1] Fraunhofer ESK, Munich, Germany
{philipp.schleiss,christian.drabek,gereon.weiss}@esk.fraunhofer.de
[2] Department of Computer Science, University of Augsburg, Augsburg, Germany
bernhard.bauer@esk.fraunhofer.de

Abstract. The availability of functionality is a crucial aspect of mission- and safety-critical systems. This is for instance demonstrated by the pursuit to automate road transportation. Here, the driver is not obligated to be part of the control loop, thereby requiring the underlying system to remain operational even after a critical component failure. Advances in the field of mixed-criticality research have allowed to address this topic of fail-operational system behaviour more efficiently. For instance, general purpose computing platforms may relinquish the need for dedicated backup units, as their purpose can be redefined at runtime. Based on this, a deterministic and resource-efficient reconfiguration mechanism is developed, in order to address safety concerns with respect to availability in a generic manner. To find a configuration for this mechanism that can ensure all availability-related safety properties, a design-time method to automatically generate schedules for different modes of operations from declaratively defined requirements is established. To cope with the inherent computational complexity, heuristics are developed to effectively narrow the problem space. Subsequently, this method's applicability and scalability are respectively evaluated qualitatively within an automotive case study and quantitatively by means of a tool performance analysis.

1 Introduction

Within the automotive domain, the demand for highly available systems is increasing through the vision of automated driving. As a driver is not required to constantly be part of the control loop in an automated vehicle, the underlying control system must be capable of compensating for all safety-relevant failures. With respect to availability, a system can either account for failure-induced reduction of computational capacity by means of over-provisioning, for instance with dedicated hardware and triple redundant architectures, or alternatively resort to a form of *graceful degradation* [8]. Within the transportation domain the need for *fail-operational behaviour* has traditionally been solved through dedicated redundancy in form of federated architectures [1], as most prominently seen in the triple-triple redundant architecture of modern *Fly-by-Wire* systems [16]. In contrast, the latter option of graceful degradation is of special interest in

© Springer International Publishing AG 2017
S. Tonetta et al. (Eds.): SAFECOMP 2017, LNCS 10488, pp. 179–194, 2017.
DOI: 10.1007/978-3-319-66266-4_12

the cost-sensitive automotive industry in order to limit the required amount of spare computing resources. Here, automated vehicles may only require a limited set of functionality for a short period of time until the vehicle can be safely halted.

With respect to availability, general purpose computing platforms pose as a promising solution to limit the amount of required hardware, as there purpose can be redefined at runtime. The foundation for such reconfiguration schemes was laid in mixed-criticality research by allowing a platform to host multiple independent functions, as for instance demonstrated by the *Integrated Modular Avionics (IMA)* in the aviation domain [15]. Despite this, reconfiguration generally competes with the principles of safety-critical systems, which require an operation free of unpredictable interference. This is for instance seen in the functional safety standard ISO 26262 [7] of the automotive domain, which is restrictive with respect to reconfiguration. Therefore, the question arises how availability can be ensured through reconfiguration schemes in order to benefit from the resource saving potential of integrated architectures and graceful degradation while at least maintaining the current level of safety.

Consequently, this work develops a generic *monitoring and reconfiguration service (MRS)* to ensure the availability of multiple independent functions during runtime based on the notion of a *Safety-Element-out-of-Context*. As guaranteeing deterministic behaviour is imperative within the safety domain, this service is designed in a static manner, thereby only utilising *mitigation plans* that were previously verified. From a design perspective, the need to manage failure modes further increases the effort of developing already complex automotive systems. As such, this work further focuses on a method to define reconfiguration behaviour declaratively and automatically calculate configurations for all managed modes of operation. For this, a system model is developed, which is then enriched with scheduling information through the use of a novel set of heuristics and mixed-integer linear programme (MILP) techniques. This additional scheduling information poses as an extension of the system's interface description to guarantee the required real-time behaviour when implemented correctly on each control unit, thus providing the basis for a compositional system integration.

In detail, Sect. 2 introduces this monitoring and reconfiguration service, followed by a method for synthesising schedules of fail-operational systems in Sect. 3. Section 4 analyses applicability in an automotive case study and evaluates the performance quantitatively before concluding in Sect. 5.

2   Fail-Operational Safety Mechanism

2.1   Monitoring and Reconfiguration Service (MRS)

In the following, a *monitoring and reconfiguration service (MRS)* is developed in order to provide a safety mechanism that can generically ensure the availability of multiple independent functions within a set of distributed control units during runtime. For this, a synchronously operating MRS instance is deployed onto each control unit participating in the management of failure modes. The period of the software-based MRS is in turn based on the failover times of the managed functionality, which describe the maximal amount of time a functionality can remain unavailable. These figures are typically determined during a *Hazard and Risk Analysis*. Further, the MRS itself consists of a reporting and an evaluating task that are respectively responsible for informing all other control units about the current state of the hosted applications in form of a heart-beat, and evaluating all received heart-beats to trigger a reconfiguration. Based on this heart-beat information, each control unit can determine the status of the complete system. More precisely, the state of all applications in the system is concatenated to one lookup key for use in a reconfiguration database, which is deployed on each control unit. Based on this key, a lookup occurs that either results in the control unit remaining in the current state or alternatively performing a reconfiguration based on the predetermined *mitigation plan*. A mitigation plan includes a new schedule for all application instances hosted on the respective control unit. Through this decentralised architecture it is possible to conduct reconfiguration involving multiple control units without the need for a central coordinating unit.

2.2   Hardware Architecture

As each control unit expects to receive a heart-beat from each other control unit within each period, the missing of a heart-heat is interpreted as the failure of a control unit. From a hardware-perspective, additional guarantees with respect to reliable communication links between control units are however necessary in order to deduct the failure of a control unit from a missing heart-beat. Moreover, control units utilising this reconfiguration scheme must be equipped with strong diagnostic capabilities to perform fail-silent behaviour in case of unrecoverable local faults, thereby ensuring the fail-operational properties of the entire system (see Fig. 1). To provide fail-operational behaviour between control units in a cost-efficient manner, a *1-out-of-2 safety architecture with diagnostics (1oo2D)* was deployed on basis of previous research [11]. Here, each unit is equipped with strong diagnostic capabilities in form of lock-stepping mechanisms and additional

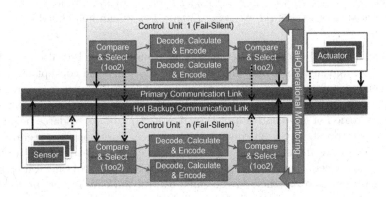

Fig. 1. 1oo2D architecture

monitoring elements, such as hardware watchdogs. In addition, the use of diverse hardware platforms and bus systems further limits the potential occurrence of faults originating from a common cause.

3   Method for Reconfiguration Planning

3.1   System Model

In order to configure the previously described monitoring and reconfiguration service, an automated design process is used to generate mitigation plans for all managed failure modes. Hereby special focus is laid on the declarative nature of the approach. This allows system designers to only specify availability requirements without the need to manually determine a schedule for each failure mode and without needing to ensure that all failover times are met. For this, a minimal system model is derived under consideration of distributed topologies, operating modes, hierarchical resources access patterns, and preemption. This model is later formalised and used as part of a reconfiguration planning approach based on the advances in constraint-based system synthesis [3].

Jobs, Tasks and Compositions. In this work, a *task* is defined as the use of exactly one resource during a specific time interval, which is in turn bounded by a task- and resource-specific *worst case execution time* (WCET), as seen in the software architecture of a simplified automated driving use case depicted in Fig. 2. Tasks in turn are logically grouped to *task composition*, to allow for an abstraction of the system (e.g. *Steer-by-Wire*). As such, multiple instantiation of a specific type of composition or task are required to provide functionality redundantly (e.g. *Wheel Tick* tasks), which are each responsible for one specific wheel of a vehicle. Moreover, a task consists of a sequence of *jobs*, each representing a specific invocation of a task. To ensure the periodic execution of a task's jobs, each task can be annotated with a period (cf. *Steering* or *Highway Pilot*). In additional, other real-time constraints, such as the maximal age of processed data (cf. *Trajectory Planning* or *Steering Engine 1*) or synchronous executions between jobs of two tasks (cf. *Steering Engine 1 & 2*) can be defined.

Resources. A *resource* can represent a control unit or bus, but also any other type of resource such as a hardware controller. For this, the concept of hierarchical dependencies between resources is introduced. For instance, a control unit can pose as a top-level resource without dependencies to other resources, whereas a memory region of this control unit is seen as a subordinate resource belonging to the superordinate top-level control unit resource. Based on this, hierarchical dependency between tasks are used to, for instance, describe that a subordinate task can only access the memory region of that specific control unit if its superordinate task is also assigned to the same control unit. Moreover, interleaved access patterns are possible, allowing multiple tasks to cooperatively share a resource through preemption. Despite this, some activities, such as accessing a

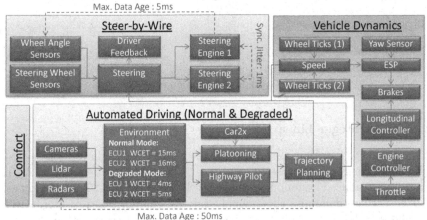

Fig. 2. Example software architecture

critical memory structure, must remain atomic to prevent data corruption and indeterministic behaviour. In such cases, a resource is deemed non-preemptable.

Graceful Degradation and Modes. As it is often not desirable to completely eliminate functionality in overload conditions [4], a more fine-grained consideration of required functionality in each system mode is needed. Despite this, current mixed-criticality research often only applies a rigid model of HI and LO criticality levels. Further, computational peaks and variable workloads are often simply classified into hard and soft real-time requirements, thus squandering the potential for resource-efficient designs. Consequently, a generalised taxonomy was developed in [10] to classify resource access in the dimensions of quantity of resources and frequency of occurrence. To incorporate these previous research results, the developed system model captures such fine-grained information on resource requirements by allowing compositions to be assigned to *system modes* and sorted by their importance (e.g. the *Comfort* is less important than *Steer-by-Wire* in Fig. 3). These system modes are defined for the entire (sub-)system, including hardware component failures or environmental changes. In contrast, functionality can be modelled as multiple distinct modes of a composition that are only allowed to be admitted under mutual exclusion in order to address functionality that can degrade internally (e.g. Normal & Degraded Mode for *Automated Driving* in Fig. 3) or exhibit variable workloads. Moreover, tasks can be annotated with different *scheduling modes* to account for application-specific data consistency requirements of standby tasks. For instance, a *cold-standby* task will only be assigned to a resource and thus only attain an internal state after being scheduled, whereas a *hot-standby* task will exhibit similar scheduling demands as an active task as only the task's external effects will be suppressed.

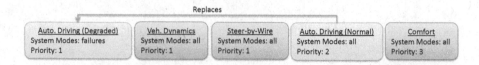

Fig. 3. Graceful degradation example

3.2   Mixed-Integer Linear Programme

Motivated by the fact that mixed-integer linear programmes have been successfully utilised for real-time system synthesis [13], a MILP representation of the
previously introduced system model was developed. This MILP formulation can
either be used to maximise the amount of active compositions or alternatively
find valid schedules for a predetermined set of required compositions for each
system mode. Due to the extensive nature of the derived MILP (22 constraints
in total), this work focuses on the most distinctive and less straight-forward
equations. All variables and constants are summarised in Table 1.

Target Function. In favour of limiting the wasteful deployment of processing
resources, it is desirable to achieve a high level of resource utilisation. For this, a
global view of the system is inevitable to always find an optimal configuration.
As such, this problem is formulated with the intention of maximising the amount
of compositions that can be successfully scheduled on a given set of resources (1).
The admission of a composition $c \in C$ to the system's configuration is encoded
in a binary variable u_c by setting $u_c = 1$.

$$\max \sum_{c}^{C} u_c \tag{1}$$

Graceful Degradation. To account for the possibility of insufficient resources,
compositions may be assigned priorities to define a hierarchical ordering of their
importance. Therefore, a composition may only be admitted if all compositions
of a higher priority C_c^+ are also included in the schedule. All compositions of
lower priority are defined as C_c^-. To enforce these restrictions, u_c shall only
take a true value when all $u_{c'}$ for $c' \in C_c^+$ are also true. Therefore, u_c is to
be multiplied with the cardinality of C_c^+ to prevent an unwanted admission of
composition c (cf. Fig. 3):

$$\bigvee_{c}^{C} u_c |C_c^+| \leq \sum_{c'}^{C_c^+} u_{c'} \tag{2}$$

Tasks to Resources Mapping. To represent the smallest schedulable entities,
each composition is broken down into tasks $t \in T$ which must be mapped to

a single resource r out of a task-dependent set of resources R_t. The binary variable $a_{tr} = 1$ indicates that a task is permanently assigned to a certain resource. During implementation a substantial performance penalty was noticed when formulating this constraint in form of an inequation ($<= 1$), Therefore, an additional virtual resource, on which jobs can be executed with infinite speed, is introduced, thus extending the set R_t with the virtual resources to R_t^+. This allows every task to always be assigned to exactly one resource (3).

$$\bigvee_c^C \bigvee_t^{T_c} \sum_r^{R_t^+} a_{tr} = 1 \tag{3}$$

Mutual Exclusion. To account for the degradation within a functionality, it must be ensured that the same functionality is not simultaneously provided by multiple compositions. Therefore, the composition providing normal functionality can disable tasks of its degraded compositions (e.g. Normal Mode is preferable over Degraded Mode for *Automated Driving* in Fig. 3). All tasks in c that are disabled by a composition $c' \in C_c^-$ are contained in the set $T_{cc'}^D$. The Eq. 4 allows a number of tasks in the composition c to be disabled, if c' is enabled. However, it does not specify which tasks. As only tasks replaced by tasks from other compositions may be disabled, the a_{tr} variable of each disabled task must be forced to zero (5). Moreover, to ensure that either all or none of the tasks within a composition are admitted, the sum of all respective binary variables a_{tr} must either be equal to the amount $|g|$ of tasks within that composition or zero.

$$\bigvee_c^C \sum_t^{T_c} \sum_r^{R_t} a_{tr} = |T_c|u_c - \sum_{c'}^{C_c^-} |T_{cc'}^D|u_{c'} \tag{4}$$

$$\bigvee_c^C \bigvee_{c'}^{C_c^-} \sum_t^{T_{cc'}^D} \sum_r^{R_t} a_{tr} = |T_{cc'}^D|u_c - |T_{cc'}^D|u_{c'} \tag{5}$$

Unified Timeline. During the implementation of this work, an up to 10-fold performance benefit was attained by conceptually partitioning all resources along one sequential timeline Z (see Fig. 4). For this, the concept of a *hyper-period* is utilised. It is defined as the least common multiple of all occurring periods, thus describing the shortest time frame after which a schedule may be repeated in a symmetric manner. Based on this, the minimal length of the unified timeline Z could be determined by multiplying the system's hyper-period H with the number of resources and adding the largest deadline. This addition of $max(Deadline)$ is required to account for jobs that start within the last period of a hyper-period and potential only end after the start of the next hyper-period.

Order of Execution and Preemption. To determine if a job j is activated after a job j' has ended, the activation time of j is represented by a real variable

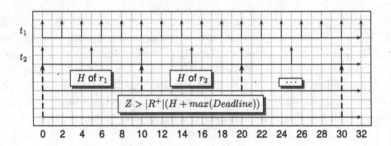

Fig. 4. Hyper-periods in a unified timeline

s_j, whereas the time of completion of j' is defined through the real variable e'_j. For each period of a task t, the start-time of a respective job $j \in J_t$ is bounded by a constant start-offset P_j^S and end-offset P_j^E. With respect to the unified timeline, the resource-specific offset must be subtracted in order to attain the actual time value (6). The jitter of start- and end-times between a task's periods can also be bounded through this definition. In addition, the order of execution between tasks is encoded in the binary variables $b_{jj'}$ (see Fig. 5). To force the variable $b_{jj'}$ to only be zero if e'_j lies before s_j, $b_{jj'}$ is multiplied with a constant that is larger than any other variable. As such, only a positive difference of $s_j - e_{j'}$ leads to $b_{jj'} = 0$ (7).

$$\bigvee_t^T \bigvee_j^{J'_t} P_j^S \leq s_j - \sum_r^{R_t} Z_r a_{tr} \leq P_j^E \tag{6}$$

$$\bigvee_t^T \bigvee_j^{J_t} \bigvee_{t'}^{T \setminus t} \bigvee_{j'}^{J_{t'}} 0 \leq s_j - e_{j'} + b_{jj'} Z \leq Z \tag{7}$$

An overlap free schedule is defined as the start of an execution occurring after another job's execution ends. In this case, exactly one variable in the set $(b_{jj'}, b_{j'j})$ must be true, as all other cases lead to logical contradictions or execution overlaps (see Fig. 5). If an overlapping resource access is allowed for a specific resource, one job can preempt another job. Through setting $b_{jj'} + b_{j'j} = 1$ such inter-job preemption can be selectively prohibited, for instance, to prevent negatively influencing WCETs through cache invalidation effects.

Execution Times. When assigning a task t exclusive control over a resource, the largest possible time that can elapse between its activation s_j and completion e_j is defined as a task's resource-specific WCET W_{tr}. In addition, tasks operating on shared resources must also account for the preemption-incurred prolongation of their jobs' execution times by considering the overhead of every context switch. The total time delay of a job j by any potentially preempting job $j' \in J_j^P$ and the therewith connected temporal overhead is represented by a variable $i_{jj'}$. In all, the maximal distance between s_j and e_j is defined through the task's resource-dependent WCET and the sum of all interferences (8). As a job's execution

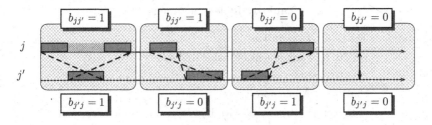

Fig. 5. Execution overlaps

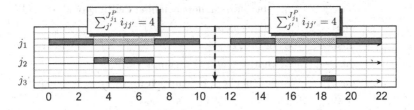

Fig. 6. Cascading preemption

may only lie entirely before, within, or after another job's execution window, interruption $i_{jj'}$ caused by each job j' can be added together to obtain the total time of preemption for job j, as depicted in Fig. 6.

$$\overset{T}{\underset{t}{\forall}} \overset{J_t}{\underset{j}{\forall}} e_j - s_j = \overset{R_t}{\underset{r}{\sum}} a_{tr} W_{tr} + \overset{J_j^P}{\underset{j'}{\sum}} i_{jj'} \tag{8}$$

The non-negative preemption time $i_{jj'}$ of a task's job j by another job $j' \in J_{t'}$ is defined by the resource-dependent WCET $W_{t'r}$ of the preempting job and is further influenced by effects related to the used resource, such as activation jitters, or storing and loading of registers, which are all accounted for with a worst-case constant overhead O_r. As O_r is only resource-dependant, it must be chosen large enough to account for the worst performing task allocated on r. In cases where this constant overhead is however too pessimistic, as for instance seen in caching strategies, a set of finer constraints can be utilised instead of the simplified model of cascading preemptions (see Fig. 6). Moreover, preemption may be completely prohibited for a task or only permitted at predefined points. When formulating this constraint, a one sided bound on $i_{jj'}$ is sufficient, as the target function indirectly minimises $i_{jj'}$. In consequence, every overlap $i_{jj'}$ will diverge to its minimum in case of resource restrictions. Through this, the introduction of another binary variable is circumvented. Equation 9 provides a lower bound for the preemption time $i_{jj'}$:

$$\overset{T}{\underset{t}{\forall}} \overset{J_t}{\underset{j}{\forall}} \overset{J_j^P \subset J_{t'}}{\underset{j'}{\forall}} \overset{R_t}{\underset{r}{\forall}} a_{t'r} W_{t'r} + a_{tr} O_r + b_{j'j} Z + b_{jj'} Z - 2Z \leq i_{jj'} \tag{9}$$

Table 1. Table of notations

Notation	Type	Description
a_{tr}	var $\{0,1\}$	Assignment of task t to resource r ($a_{tr} = 1$)
$b_{jj'}$	var $\{0,1\}$	Start of job j is before end of j' ($b_{jj'} = 1$)
C	const set	All compositions
C_c^+/C_c^-	const set	Composition with higher/lower importance than composition c
e_j	var $\mathbb{R}$	End of job j
H	const $\mathbb{R}$	Hyper-period (smallest common multiple of all periods)
$i_{jj'}$	var $\mathbb{R}$	Time that j is preempted by j'
J_t	const set	Jobs of task t
J_j^P	const set	Jobs that potentially preempt job j
O_r	const $\mathbb{R}$	Task-independent preemption overhead of resource r
P_j^S & P_j^E	const $\mathbb{R}$	Begin and end of job j's period
R_t	const set	Potential regular resources of task t
R_t^+	const set	As R_t with additional virtual resource
s_j	var $\mathbb{R}$	Start of job j
T	const set	All tasks
$T_{cc'}^D$	const set	Tasks in c that can be replaced through tasks from c'
u_c	var $\{0,1\}$	Composition c is admitted to system schedule ($u_c = 1$)
W_{tr}	const $\mathbb{R}$	Raw WCET of task t on resource r
Z_r	const $\mathbb{R}$	Offset of resource r on unified timeline Z

3.3 Heuristics

Through the NP-hard nature of this optimisation problem, scalability becomes an important concern. As general MILP solving techniques cannot fully exploit problem-specific characteristics, heuristics pose as a promising solution for extending the scope of systems that can be successfully synthesised [6]. The following paragraphs describe three strategies (S1–S3) which aim at limiting the problem space while trying to only minimally impair the solution space.

S1: Resource Assignment. To decrease the problem's complexity, tasks may be pre-assigned to a certain resource in cases where multiple potential resource allocations exist. For this, tasks are ordered by the ratio between their WCET and potential window of resource access (*WCET-window ratio*). Thereby, tasks with small WCETs and large access windows are first assigned to resources. The assignment process aims at balancing tasks fairly by selecting the resource with the least utilisation. This process repeats until either the *WCET-window ratio* or the resource utilisation grow above their respective threshold.

S2: Grouping of Tasks. Moreover, multiple tasks may be combined into a single task whenever their periods are identical. This strategy requires all tasks grouped within the newly created task to be assigned to the same resource.

S3: Sequential Resource Access Windows. To eliminate further binary MILP variables, potentially conflicting executions can be resolved through sequentialisation. Here, each job's earliest start and latest end time is determined by analysing the system's data flow graph. Thereafter, the heuristic sequentialises conflicts of jobs with similar WCETs, as these jobs are unlikely to benefit from mutual preemption. In contrast, the enforcement of a sequential execution pattern on jobs with strongly varying WCETs would remove opportunities for preemption. The pairs of tasks are then sorted based on how much each job's execution window must be narrowed to allow a sequential execution (cf. Fig. 7). This sum is then weighted by the potential changes in ratios between WCETs and execution windows, in order to find conflicts that barely overlap or alternatively exhibit large WCET-window ratios. The respective earliest start and latest end times of the best job pair are then narrowed by balancing the remaining ratio between WCETs and potential execution windows. The process is repeated until no pair can be sequentialised without falling below a threshold based on the WCET-window ratio.

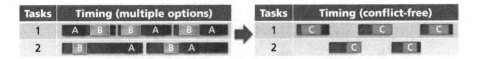

Fig. 7. S3 heuristic for sequential resource access (red: resource access windows) (Color figure online)

4 Evaluation

To determine the value of this method, its applicability in the automotive domain and scalability are of interest, as these factors are crucial for ensuring a successful transfer of this prototypical concept into future systems throughout the industry. As such, the applicability will be evaluated qualitatively by performing an assessment based on criteria that was identified as relevant during the implementation of a full-scale e-vehicle with a fail-operational *Steer-by-Wire* system. With respect to scalability, the solving performance of the MILP- and heuristic-based system synthesis approach is analysed quantitatively for different synthetic workloads to determine its practical limits with respect to realistic future system sizes.

4.1 Automotive Case Study

Within the SafeAdapt [12] research project an electric prototype vehicle was developed that aims at integrating multiple critical functionalities, such as Steer- and Brake-by-Wire compositions, onto a shared control infrastructure based on a 1oo2D safety architecture (cf. Sect. 2.2). Here two diverse hardware platforms were utilised on basis of an AURIX safety controller and two ARM MCUs with software-based lock-stepping mechanism, which are interconnected by a time-trigger redundant ethernet backbone.

To illustrate the granularity of a typical data flow, the *Steer-by-Wire (SbW)* system is described. With this functionality, two independent timing chains exist to respectively adjust the angle of the front wheels with a redundant pair of steering rack engines in accordance to the steering wheel angle and further provide information to the driver with respect to the road surface conditions in form of vibrations. Focusing on the steering engine control loop, both engines must be readjusted periodically, actuate synchronously within a certain time margin, and only apply control signals originating from recently sampled sensor data. In addition, each of the steering wheel and steering angle position sensors is individually modelled as three tasks: one for polling the sensor, one for placing it in a designated buffer of a network chip, and one for the network controller's transmission of the queued data (cf. Fig. 8).

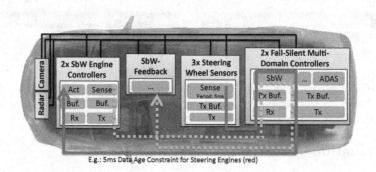

E.g.: 5ms Data Age Constraint for Steering Engines (red)

Fig. 8. Steer-by-Wire architecture

4.2 Assessment of Applicability

To determine the applicability of the proposed method within the automotive domain, a non-exhaustive set of criteria was identified as relevant through experience gained from the previously described e-vehicle project. Based on these criteria, the method's applicability is evaluated in the following:

Tool-interoperability. The generic and minimal nature of the developed system model promotes the binding of different domain specific modelling concepts. As an example, the vehicle's hardware architecture, data flow, modes of operation, availability requirements, and timing characteristics were modelled in the ARXML exchange format of the predominant AUTOSAR standard [2] and subsequently transformed into the domain-independent system model (cf. Sect. 3). The results of the configuration planning process were then again automatically added to the ARXML format, thus providing a seamless integration into existing tool chains.

Stability. Extensions, changes, and fixes for individual applications are common within the life-cycle of a vehicle. To not adversely affect other functionalities, it is common practice to maintain a stable schedule for all bus systems. With respect to the developed synthesis method, such stability can be easily achieved by statically pre-defining the schedule for all applications that must remain stable. Hence, only a new schedule for the remaining applications must be found, thus guaranteeing future interoperability and the ability to only partially update an already existing system.

Standardisation. As automotive system architectures are often based on components from multiple independent vendors, it is crucial to standardise any service that requires interoperability across control units. As such, the MRS (cf. Sect. 2.1) was integrated as a basic AUTOSAR service with a uniform communication protocol as part of an already standardised software architecture in order to showcase the feasibly of a future standardisation.

Reusability. Through the design of the runtime reconfiguration mechanism based on the concept of a *Safety-Element-out-of-Context*, the required reconfiguration logic had to only be implemented once instead of individually for each functionality, thus substantially reducing the development, verification, and validation effort.

Runtime overhead. With respect to runtime overhead, the generic runtime mechanism showed WCETs of less than $100\,\mu s$ and was executed in 5 ms periods in order to always meet the strictest failover times of 10 ms. Moreover, the excepted overhead remains close to constant with an increasing amount of managed functionalities. This is attributed to the fact that the execution and usage of bus systems only occurs once per period for all functionalities as compared to each functionality utilising an individual monitoring mechanism and communication slot. In addition, mechanisms for ensuring the data consistency of standby tasks more dominantly influences resource usage. Here different concepts reaching from *cold-standby* over *warm-standby* (e.g. cyclic data updates) to *hot-standby* implementation exist, depending on the task-specific requirements of the individual compositions (cf. Sect. 3.1).

4.3   Scalability and Tool Performance

Setup. To experimentally evaluate how this approach scales, the total amount of jobs, the number of interconnections, the degree of potentially overlapping executions, and the system's total utilisation were identified as factors that are likely to influence the solving time. During non-exhaustive tests, the system's utilisation was identified as the most interesting factor, as an increased utilisation already lead to monotonously growing and strongly diverging solving times at around 500 jobs. In contrast, the degree of potentially overlapping executions and the amount of interconnections showed less divergent performance differences. As such, the further evaluation focuses on determining the performance effects of different levels of utilisation with an without the use of heuristics while increasing the amount of jobs. For this, the other influencing factors are kept at a constant ratio in relation to the amount of jobs in order to enable an isolated evaluation of the utilisation parameter. The measurements are performed with the Gurobi optimisation software (version 6.0.3) [5] on an Intel Xeon E5-2660 CPU (2.2 Ghz) with 8 cores by synthetically scaling the previous automotive example.

Performance Evaluation. Based on these synthesised workloads, 10 test sets were extracted with four predefined average resource utilisations (20%, 40%, 60%, 80%). As seen in the experimental results in Fig. 9(a), performance generally deteriorates with increased utilisation. Further, the strategies S1 to assign tasks to a fixed resource, S3 to sequentialise potentially conflicting resource utilisations, and the combination of both strategies were applied to the 80% utilisation test set, representing a typically used utilisation limit within the automotive industry. The strategy S2 for grouping tasks was not analysed in isolation, as its performance is directly dependent on the amount of tasks with identical periods. Moreover, non-exhaustive tests were conducted to experimentally determine an acceptable parametrisation of the heuristics. As seen in Fig. 9(b), the point at which the performance deteriorates could be substantially postponed through the use of heuristics, allowing a system with 80% utilisation and 1000 jobs to be synthesised in around ten minutes. Most notably, the combination of resource assignment and sequential resource access heuristics exhibits the largest benefit, thus proving a promising opportunity to design more complex systems.

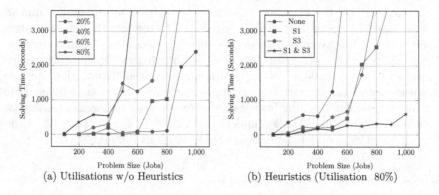

(a) Utilisations w/o Heuristics   (b) Heuristics (Utilisation 80%)

Fig. 9. Performance evaluation

4.4   Discussion

Based on the experience collected in the automotive case study, the proposed combination of a safety mechanism for generically ensuring availability and a system synthesis process poses as a viable option for designing automated vehicles in a more cost- and resource-efficient manner. Regardless, special rigour must be applied during the design of a generic availability management component, as an incorrect implementation could adversely affect multiple independent functionalities. This concern is however mitigated by the simplicity of the runtime mechanism, which is implemented on basis of a formally provable state machine. In addition, all calculated mitigation plans can be verified through an simple process by comparing the time-driven schedules of each operating mode against the formalised availability and timing requirements. This already ensures the correctness of the mitigation plans and further fosters manual quality improvements, such as jitter optimisations, by allowing an automated verification of any modification. Moreover, typically occurring timing issues during system integration can be mitigated through the early enrichment of the system's interface description with detailed timing requirements. This enables a compositional integration in which the correct timing behaviour is ensured during system integration even though each control unit was designed individually. Hereby, each control unit must however adhere to its predetermined temporal interface description. In addition, this reduced development effort can be utilised to create larger variant diversity and customised products that would otherwise be deemed infeasible.

In light of the solving performance, it seems reasonable to presume that automated schedule synthesis is a feasible method for substantially reducing development effort. In addition, the long development-cycles of safety-critical systems can even make solving times of multiple days an acceptable option. Regardless, the future use of project specific knowledge as well as the creation of more sophisticated heuristics is likely to substantially increase the method's performance and allow the synthesis of systems with higher complexity. Similarly, an alternative implementation based on saturated module theory concepts, which have proven to be useful for similar problems [14] and even outperform MILP approaches [9], could further increase performance.

5   Conclusion

In pursuit of designing fail-operational systems in a cost-efficient manner, this work exploits a monitoring and reconfiguration service that is utilised as a generic safety mechanism for ensuring availability of independent functionalities. Based on this, an accompanying synthesis process for automatically generating mitigation plans in form of schedules for all anticipated operational modes of a system was researched and implemented. The method's applicability was then demonstrated successfully on basis of experiences gained during the development of a real e-vehicle. Moreover, the performance of the synthesis was significantly increased by applying heuristic strategies, thus ensuring its applicability with respect to the more complex systems of future vehicles.

Acknowledgment. The research leading to these results has partially received funding from the European Commission within the Seventh Framework Programme as part of the SafeAdapt project (grant agreement 608945) and from the Bavarian Ministry of Economic Affairs and Media, Energy and Technology.

References

1. Di Natale, M., Sangiovanni-Vincentelli, A.: Moving from federated to integrated architectures in automotive: the role of standards, methods and tools. Proc. IEEE **98**(4), 603–620 (2010)
2. Durisic, D., Staron, M., Tichy, M., Hansson, J.: Evolution of long-term industrial meta-models. In: 40th EUROMICRO Conference on Software Engineering and Advanced Applications, pp. 141–148 (2014)
3. Gorcitz, R., Kofman, E., Carle, T., Potop-Butucaru, D., Simone, R.: On the scalability of constraint solving for static/off-line real-time scheduling. In: Sankaranarayanan, S., Vicario, E. (eds.) FORMATS 2015. LNCS, vol. 9268, pp. 108–123. Springer, Cham (2015). doi:10.1007/978-3-319-22975-1_8
4. Graydon, P., Bate, I.: Safety assurance driven problem formulation for mixed-criticality scheduling. In: Proceedings of 1st International Workshop on Mixed Criticality Systems (WMC), pp. 19–24 (2013)
5. Gurobi Optimizer Reference Manual (2017). http://www.gurobi.com
6. Hamann, A., Ernst, R.: TDMA time slot and turn optimization with evolutionary search techniques. In: Proceedings of Conference on Design, Automation and Test in Europe (DATE), pp. 312–317 (2005)
7. ISO 26262: Road Vehicles - Functional Safety (2011)
8. Kanekawa, N.: Dynamic autonomous redundancy management strategy for balanced graceful degradation. In: Proceedings of IEEE Workshop on Fault-Tolerant Parallel and Distributed Systems, pp. 18–23 (1994)
9. Kothmayr, T., Kemper, A., Scholz, A., Heuer, J.: Synthesizing Schedules through Heuristics for Hard Real-Time Workflows. In: IEEE International Conference on Industrial Technology (ICIT), pp. 1937–1944 (2015)
10. Lin, C., Kaldewey, T., Povzner, A., Brandt, S.A.: Diverse soft real-time processing in an integrated system. In: Proceedings of 27th IEEE Real-Time Systems Symposium (RTSS), pp. 369–378 (2006)
11. Ruiz, A., Juez, G., Schleiss, P., Weiss, G.: A safe generic adaptation mechanism for smart cars. In: Proceedings of 26th IEEE International Symposium on Software Reliability Engineering (ISSRE) (2015)
12. SafeAdapt Project. http://www.safeadapt.eu
13. Sagstetter, F., Andalam, S., Waszecki, P., Lukasiewycz, M., Stähle, H., Chakraborty, S., Knoll, A.: Schedule integration framework for time-triggered automotive architectures. In: 51st ACM/EDAC/IEEE Design Automation Conference (DAC), pp. 1–6 (2014)
14. Steiner, W.: An evaluation of SMT-based schedule synthesis for time-triggered multi-hop networks. In: 31st IEEE Real-Time Systems Symposium, pp. 375–384 (2010)
15. Windsor, J., Deredempt, M.H., De-Ferluc, R.: Integrated modular avionics for spacecraft. In: Proceedings of 30th IEEE/AIAA Digital Avionics Systems Conference (DASC), pp. 1–16 (8A6) (2011)
16. Yeh, Y.C.: Triple-triple redundant 777 primary flight computer. In: Proceedings of IEEE Aerospace Applications Conference, vol. 1, pp. 293–307 (1996)

Static Analysis and Testing

Benchmarking Static Code Analyzers

Jörg Herter[1], Daniel Kästner[1(✉)], Christoph Mallon[1], and Reinhard Wilhelm[2]

[1] AbsInt GmbH, Science Park 1, 66123 Saarbrücken, Germany
kaestner@absint.com
[2] Saarland University, Saarland Informatics Campus, Saarbrücken, Germany

Abstract. We show that a widely used benchmark set for the comparison of static analysis tools exhibits an impressive number of weaknesses, and that the internationally accepted quantitative evaluation metrics may lead to useless results. The weaknesses in the benchmark set were identified by applying a sound static analysis to the programs in this set and carefully interpreting the results. We propose how to deal with weaknesses of the quantitative metrics and how to improve such benchmarks and the evaluation process, in particular for *external* evaluations, in which an ideally neutral institution does the evaluation, whose results potential clients can trust.

1 Introduction

Some years ago static analysis meant manual review of programs. Nowadays, automatic static analysis tools are gaining popularity in software development as they offer a tremendous increase in productivity by automatically checking the code under a wide range of criteria. They come in several flavors. Many software development projects are developed according to coding guidelines, such as MISRA C, aiming at a programming style that improves clarity and reduces the risk of introducing bugs. For safety-critical software projects obeying to such coding guidelines is strongly recommended by all current safety standards. Compliance checking by static analysis tools has become common practice.

However, to prevent critical programming errors, checking coding guidelines is not enough. This is recognized by the MISRA C norm by a particular rule which recommends deeper analysis: "Minimization of run-time failures shall be ensured by the use of at least one of (a) static analysis tools/techniques; (b) dynamic analysis tools/techniques; (c) explicit coding of checks to handle run-time faults." (MISRA C:2004, rule 21.1). Current safety norms require demonstrating the absence of runtime errors or data races, e.g. DO-178B/C, ISO-26262, EN-50128, IEC-61508. Semantics-based static analysis has become the predominant technology to detect runtime errors and data races.

Thus it is not surprising that there is a variety of different static analysis tools on the market. Comparing them and choosing the best fitting tool is a challenging task. The first problem is that the term static analysis is used for a wide range of techniques that are conceptually very different. They all have in common that they compute their results just from the program code, without

© Springer International Publishing AG 2017
S. Tonetta et al. (Eds.): SAFECOMP 2017, LNCS 10488, pp. 197–212, 2017.
DOI: 10.1007/978-3-319-66266-4_13

actually executing the program under analysis. They can be categorized in three main groups:

Syntax Checkers. They are limited to investigating the program syntax. Most of the algorithmically checkable MISRA C rules can be checked at a purely syntactic level, e.g. in MISRA C:2012, 78 of the 143 rules are classified as decidable, which in this context implies being checkable at a syntactic level.

Unsound Semantic Analyzers. They report semantic errors in the program, such as runtime errors (division by zero, arithmetic overflows or buffer overflows) and data races. They can report false positives (spurious alarms where there are no true defects) and false negatives (a true defect for which they produce no alarm). Examples are Klocwork [18], CodeSonar [6], Polyspace Bug Finder [10], and Coverity [21].

Sound Semantic Analyzers. They are mostly based on abstract interpretation, a formal method for program analysis, which provides a mathematically rigorous way to prove the absence of defects without potential false negatives: no defect is missed (from the class of defects under consideration). They can report semantic errors in the program, including runtime errors and data races, and can be used to prove functional assertions, e.g. that output values will always be in an expected range. False positives, i.e. spurious alarms without true defect, can still occur. Examples are Astrée [7,12], Polyspace Code Prover [4,11], and AdaCore CodePeer [2].

The difference between these approaches can be illustrated at the example of division by 0. In the expression $x/0$ the division by zero can be detected syntactically, but not in the expression a/b. When an *unsound* analyzer does not report a division by zero in a/b it might still happen in scenarios not taken into account by the analyzer. When a *sound* analyzer does not report a division by zero in a/b, this is a proof that b can never be 0.

Benchmarks for static analysis tools provide a basis for comparing different tools. They should (at least) precisely define which defects are investigated, weigh the severity of different defects, be aware of the analysis depth (i.e. syntactic vs. unsound semantic vs. sound semantic), and determine false positive and false negative rates.

This article builds on the publication by Shiraishi et al. [19] which proposes benchmark suites for common types of code defects as well as evaluation criteria for tool selection. We critically review their benchmark suites and the proposed evaluation criteria and formulate explicit guidelines for designing and evaluating such benchmarks. We apply those guidelines to the test cases in [19] to increase their usefulness and propose improvements to the evaluation process.

2   Related Work

Shiraishi et al. [19] proposes benchmark suites of code defects aiming at safety defects and suggests evaluation criteria tailored to static analysis tools. In addition to true/false positive rates, Shiraishi et al. propose advanced evaluation criteria derived from the two primary evaluation criteria. They suggest to include a cost measurement to determine the cost efficiency of the tools evaluated. Shiraishi's benchmark suite had a significant impact in industry.

Lu et al. collected representative bug benchmarks in their benchmark suite BugBench [8]. They require a benchmark to be representative, diverse, portable, accessible, and fair, for selecting suitable test cases for their benchmark suite and propose several evaluation metrics to rate the effectiveness of bug detection tools. They also propose additional criteria to measure usability (reliance on manual effort and hardware, reporting and ease of investigating findings) and further overhead (time for setting up and running the analysis, time and costs for training) [8]. In contrast to their rather generic selection criteria we aim at giving strict, easy-to-follow guidelines on how to design new test cases or rate existing ones.

The Juliet benchmark sets [15] and the Secure Coding Validation Suite [20] propose test cases aiming largely at covering security issues. Due to the interdependence between safety and security many tests in those suites are also related to safety properties.

3   Rating Static Analysis Tools

The two most important metrics for evaluating a static code analyzer usually are:

- Rate of true positives R_TP, i.e., percentage of intended, true defects reported. Let P be the number of intended, true defects in the code and TP be the number of intended, true defects recognized by the tool, then $R\_TP = TP/P * 100$.
- Rate of false positives (false alarms) R_FP. The false alarm rate is defined with respect to defect-free entities, e.g. expressions, statements, or test cases. Let FP be the number of false positives, and N be the number of defect-free entities, then $R\_FP = FP/N * 100$.

Both criteria are listed in [19] as the two primary evaluation criteria. In [8], they are listed as the functional metrics used to rate the effectiveness of a bug detection tool.

Caveats

At a first glance this is straightforward, but actually these numbers are not only hard to obtain, but they also have to be interpreted in context.

The analyzer might report unintended, true defects, i.e., defects not counted by P above. A tool correctly identifying non-intended defects will actually be penalized by increasing its false-positive rate! Even comparing the number of findings per line might be inconclusive since different tools might report the same defect in different ways, or there might be some leeway in choosing the place to report it (e.g. position of macro definition vs. position of macro usage for some MISRA rules). The solution proposed by [19] is to just consider findings for defects expected to be present/absent at specific code places in the test cases, and completely ignore other findings. In general all relevant findings have to be manually inspected to aggregate the correct number of false positives and false negatives.

Another aspect to be considered is that the false alarm rate is meaningless when the true positive rate is not taken into account. Otherwise, a tool which does not report any defect might rank first because its false alarm rate is 0. On the other hand, when comparing sound tools, the rate of true positives of a covered defect type must always be 100%. In this case the primary metrics is the false-positive rate.

Remedies

A company evaluating a set of tools will in their own interest be aware of the shortcomings of the quantitative metrics. However, both external evaluators and the tool providers themselves should always report the false-positive and the false-negative rates together to avoid the pitfall described above. In the case of unintended errors, they should correct the number P above.

An additional helpful metrics is the False Discovery Rate FDR, defined as $FDR = FP/(FP + TP)$, with FP denoting the number of false positives and TP the number of true positives. The advantage is that the numbers are clearly defined and can be easily derived from the findings of the tool.

A given evaluation criterion relies on given properties of the test cases used. So far, no exhaustive, commonly agreed-on design guidelines have been proposed to ensure high quality test cases and, in consequence, to ensure the evaluation criteria to be determined in a well-founded way.

4   Criteria for Benchmarks

To close this gap we propose a set of design guidelines for test cases to provide a basis for quantitatively measuring the performance of static code analyzers. Our work is focused on benchmarks targeting analyzers for detecting runtime errors in C code, but the guidelines presented also apply to other types of static analysis tools.

Test Cases Shall be Free of Unintended Defects. All test cases shall be free of unintended defects. One single test cases may, however, contain several defects, e.g., to allow the evaluated tool to demonstrate that defects may not hide other defects. It might also be desirable to evaluate how tools continue their analysis after detecting a defect which also requires more than one defect in a test case. All defects need to be documented such that the intended analysis output is clear.

As suggested by [15], this criterion largely excludes real-life applications (natural code in the terms of [15]) where it is in practice too time-consuming to judge whether or not all defects have been located. Adherence to the proposed criterion may also lead to test cases being simpler than natural code.

Even for small, artificial test cases, test suites often fail to satisfy this criterion. For the Juliet benchmarks, the documentation states that "many uncommented incidental flaws remain in the test cases so users should not draw any conclusions about tool reports of non-target flaw types without investigating the reported result fully". Section VII elaborates on our findings how the test cases of [19] adhere to this criterion.

Defect Types Shall be Appropriately Weighted. Different defect types may be more or less severe. Consider C where a distinction is often made between undefined behavior (e.g., invalid pointer access), unspecified behavior (e.g., bitfield alignment), bad coding style (e.g., integral type names instead of typedefs that indicate size and signedness), and inappropriate code, which may indicate a logical error (e.g., unreachable code or infinite loops). While undefined behavior should always be detected and be fixed, suspicious-looking code may be just bad style that does work as intended but never leads to a bug.

In consequence defect types shall be weighted accordingly and penalize undetected undefined behavior more than a situation in which bad coding style is not reported.

Defect Types Shall be Commonly Accepted. The defect types covered by the provided test cases shall be commonly accepted as defects. We propose to restrict test cases to defects that are either (a) real runtime errors or (b) violating industry-wide accepted coding rules. For example, code violating MISRA C rules [13,14] may be considered a commonly-accepted defect as MISRA adherence is widely enforced in the automotive sector. A company-specific coding rule that will never provoke a runtime error, but is deemed to indicate a logical bug, shall not be considered commonly accepted.

In addition, a benchmark set aiming at a particular type of industry should cover the defect types relevant and only contain code typical for that industrial domain.

Test Cases Shall Not Rely on Inappropriate Code. No test case shall rely on a precise analysis of code commonly deemed inappropriate for the target industry. For example, recursive function calls are deemed inappropriate for safety-critical code. This is not only commonly accepted in aerospace and automotive industry, but across industry sectors as evidenced by the MISRA rule set where recursion would violate rules 16.2 (MISRA C:2004) and 17.2 (MISRA C:2012), respectively. In consequence, test cases shall avoid recursive function calls unless such calls themselves are the code defect whose detection rate is being tested.

Test Cases Shall Document All Assumptions. Test cases shall not rely on implicit assumptions, e.g., about the size of data types, and the definition of derived types and constants (e.g., value of INT_MAX, or definition of wchar_t). If there are test cases that specifically aim at 16-bit vs. 32-bit machines this should be clearly documented. Similar requirements apply to the behavior of library functions. As an example if there are test cases which implicitly assume that malloc() never returns a null pointer, this should be clearly documented.

5   Pitfalls of Test Suites

We would like to note that even the best designed benchmark suite is prone to several pitfalls. This section discusses our basic concerns even with well-designed benchmark suites and recommends remedies.

5.1   Applicability

Benchmarking results generated by a third party potentially involving a large set of analysis tools might be misleading. First, there is often a considerable delay between running the benchmarks and publishing the results so that at the time of publication the behavior of the tools might have changed. Also the benchmark suite itself might have changed. Furthermore, the performance of a static analyzer in terms of analysis precision and resource requirements (analysis time, CPU and memory requirements) strongly depends on the application under analysis. In consequence, the performance of such a tool on a given benchmark set may be very different from its performance on real industry code.

Recommendation: Evaluation results should clearly show the version of the tools and of the benchmarks. Benchmark suites may only be an additional, we propose first, step to evaluate a static analyzer. But benchmark suites should not replace an evaluation phase in which the evaluated static analyzer is used on the company's real code.

5.2   Explicit Adaption to Test Cases

Once a benchmark suite is widely accepted, there is the risk that tool vendors adapt their tools explicitly to the benchmark applications.

Unsound code analyzers are especially prone to such adaptations. Their heuristics that decide whether or not a code fragment is likely defective can often easily be adapted to known test cases in order to improve the analysis results on these test cases. However, this may cause the rate of correct decisions made by these heuristics on real applications to deteriorate and in the worst case lead to more real defects staying undetected.

Sound tools must not miss a true defect, but still they might be tuned to improve the false alarm rate on a specific benchmark – which might increase the analysis time of real applications.

5.3   Comparison of Sound to Unsound Tools

If a benchmark is used to compare different static analysis tools, care should be taken when comparing sound to unsound tools.

Recommendation: In case sound and unsound tools are considered, a good strategy is first to benchmark the sound tools against one another, the unsound tools against one another, and only then compare tools from different groups.

This separation is reasonable because of the different designs of the two tool classes: one is designed never to miss a real code defect and hence, must report every code location that cannot be shown to be free of defects. The second class can freely decide which potential code defects to present to the user, but cannot guarantee the absence of defects. For all of them the false positive rate mirrors the accuracy of the findings, but the preconditions are different for sound and unsound tools.

5.4 Execution and Evaluation

The Juliet suite for C/C++ [15] consists of 61,387 test cases that cover 1,617 flaw types which again cover 118 CWE entries [9]. Each test case targets exactly one type of flaw and is either intended to contain the targeted flaw or be free of the targeted flaw. Although, small artificial test cases are used instead of natural code in order to avoid unintended flaws, unrelated flaws may be incidentally present. Hence, Juliet's user guide advises to just consider reports for the marked code location targeting the intended flaw and ignore additional reports that may or may not report true, but unintended flaws.

Given the number of test cases it is obvious that a completely automatic execution of the analysis and a completely automatic evaluation of the results is strongly desirable. However, due to unintended flaws the benchmark results may not be reliable, so at least in case of unexpected findings, the issues have to be manually investigated.

Recommendation: Well-defined test cases enable automatic result assessment.

Further hurdles to an automatic evaluation of the findings reported is leeway in the reporting of a defect, and leeway in the code place for reporting a defect.

As an example when a C expression enclosed in parentheses may cause a runtime error, a tool may choose to report it at the opening parenthesis, at the closing parenthesis, or for the precise extent of the expression (i.e. for all characters belonging to the expression). If there is an alarm about a potential defect, say an overflow, one tool may choose to distinguish between overflow and underflow while another subsumes both cases under one category 'overflow'.

Finally there might be subtle tool configuration issues, e.g., regarding sizes of data types, alignment restrictions, automatic variable initialization, handling of volatile variables, etc.

Recommendation: All involved tools need to be carefully configured so that they work under the same assumptions. The configuration should be documented in the evaluation results.

6   Remarks on the ITC Benchmark Set

In the past years, the test suites for benchmarking static analysis tools proposed by Shiraishi et al. [19] (also known as ITC benchmark) were often utilized in industry to measure the performance of tools. We choose to contribute to the C benchmarks of the ITC benchmark suite as (a) in the safety-critical area, the ITC benchmarks belong to the benchmarks most often encountered, (b) C (C99) is the predominant implementation language for safety-critical systems.

In the following we will discuss whether and how the C benchmark suites of ITC meet the criteria and design guidelines proposed in this paper.

Adherence to *Test Cases Shall be Free of Unintended Defects*. Other wise tools reporting these defects will be penalized by a higher false-positive rate. Our analysis found 442 issues with the test cases that are presumably unintended. Hence, roughly 37% of the 1,188 analyzed test cases are affected. A detailed list of our findings is given in Sect. 7.

Adherence to *Defect Types Shall be Appropriately Weighted*. The error types covered by the ITC benchmark are only implicitly weighted by the numbers of test cases per error type.

Adherence to *Defect Types Shall be Commonly Accepted*. In the ITC suites there are several defect types that do not exhibit undefined nor unspecified behavior nor are they, to the best of our knowledge, discouraged by any coding guidelines.

Adherence to *Test Cases Shall Not Rely on Inappropriate Code*. We have found two test cases relying on interpreting recursive function calls. Furthermore, dynamic memory allocation is frequently used in the test cases. Both, recursion and dynamic memory management, are commonly deemed inappropriate for safety-critical code [13,14,17]. Furthermore, there are 48 goto statements in the test cases. Rules prohibiting the use of `goto`, `setjmp`, and `longjmp` are also very common [13,14,17] and test cases should in consequence avoid such constructs.

The test cases aiming at concurrency defects rely on POSIX Threads (Pthreads). In the relevant industries, typically more restricted concurrency models are applied. Therefore, to satisfy the demand for industry-relevant and industry-specific test cases, the test cases using pthread functionality should be reimplemented using the OSEK/AUTOSAR library functions (to target the automotive sector) and ARINC (to target the avionics sector), respectively.

7   Contributions to the ITC Benchmarks

The ITC Benchmarks consist of 51 flaw types for C and one flaw type for C++. The 51 C-related flaw types are grouped into 9 classes of flaw types (pointer-related defects, numerical defects, dynamic memory defects, inappropriate code, etc.). Each flaw type has several test cases covering different variations of the targeted flaw. The number of variations per flaw type ranges from 1 (e.g. for types useless assignment and live lock) to 54 (for type static buffer overrun), implicitly weighting the importance of the flaw. Each such test case exists in a version with and without the intended flaw. In total, there are 638 test cases with intended C flaws and 638 intended to be free of the targeted flaws. In total, 44 of test cases (totaling 88 versions) target concurrency flaws.

For the purpose of this article we used the sound static analyzer Astrée [1] to detect both intended and unintended code defects in the test cases, including runtime errors and concurrency-related errors like data races, deadlocks, etc. Since Astrée is sound another goal was to prove the absence of errors in the code parts marked as defect-free. In case of unintended errors in the test cases we corrected the code aiming at minimal changes of the code. Consider for example test case shown in Fig. 1:

```
/*
 * Types of defects: Underflow
 * Complexity: int  underflow at    An array of element values
 */        /
void data_underflow_012 ()
{
    int min = -2147483647;
    int dlist[4] = {0, 1, -2, -1};
    int ret;
    ret = min - dlist[2]; /*Tool should detect this line as error*/
            sink = ret;
}
```

Fig. 1. Example of flawed test case

There is no underflow present at the marked location as the result is -2147483647 (value of min) $+ 2$ (minus the -2 stored at index 2 of array dlist) which is -2147483645. This is still greater than the smallest int value (-2147483648). The minimal fix to make this test case work is to change the operator from minus ($-$) to plus ($+$), i.e., compute the value of ret as $-2147483647 + (-2)$ which yields -2147483649 and hence underflows the data type.

Following this approach, we identified and corrected the following types of test case defects.

7.1 Wrong Error Markers

The test cases contain markers in which line the intended error is located and, consequently, which line shall be reported by the evaluated analyzer. These markers are at incorrect locations in 48 test cases. We moved the markers to the correct locations.

Consider for example the test case shown in Fig. 2: The underrun occurs in the array access within the for loop once i evaluates to -1. However, the error marker is placed at the header of the loop.

```
void dynamic_buffer_underrun_031()
{
  int i;
  char* ptr1=(char*) calloc(12, sizeof(char));
  char a[12],*ptr2 = a;
  if(ptr1!=((void*)0))
  {
    ptr1[11]='\0';
    for(i=10;i>=-1;i--) /*Tool should detect
                              this line as error*/
                       /*ERROR:Buffer Underrun*/
    {
      ptr1[i]='a';
    }
    memcpy(ptr2,ptr1,12);
    free(ptr1);
  }
}
```

Fig. 2. Test case with wrong error marker

7.2 Missing Error Markers

Some test cases do not contain (non-)error markers. Consequently, there is no hint to the user of the benchmarks for which location a report is to be expected. In such cases, we added markers at the location where the code defect manifests or no false alarm should be reported. We encountered this issue 2 times.

7.3 Unreachable Error Locations

In 8 test cases, the intentional code defects are actually unreachable. Static analyzers may therefore choose to simply mark these locations unreachable without further attempts to interpret the code and report the desired error type.

Consider the example from Fig. 3: In the code from which the test case is invoked the variable func_pointer_018_global_set is written two times: it is set to 0 at initialization and later set to 1. Consequently, it can never take the value 10, so the error location can never be reached during program execution.

```
void wrong_arguments_func_pointer_018_func_004(
              wrong_arguments_func_pointer_018_s_001 st,
              wrong_arguments_func_pointer_018_s_001* st1)
{
  if (func_pointer_018_global_set == 10)
  {
    wrong_arguments_func_pointer_018_fptr1_gbl =
          (void (*)(char*))wrong_arguments_func_pointer_018_func_002;
    wrong_arguments_func_pointer_018_fptr1_gbl((char*)st1);/*Tool should
                                     detect this line as error*/
                     /*ERROR:Wrong arguments passed to a function pointer*/
  }
  else
  {
    wrong_arguments_func_pointer_018_fptr2_gbl =
                        wrong_arguments_func_pointer_018_func_003;
    wrong_arguments_func_pointer_018_fptr2_gbl(&st,1);
  }
}
```

Fig. 3. Test case with unreachable error location

7.4   Hidden Error Locations

Similar to the previous category, there are test cases where the intended error is preceded by an unintended, definitely occurring error. This may provoke analyzers to report the unintended error and stop the analysis for the context in which the error occurs. This may cause the test case never to be reached. From the analyzer perspective, this is a valid approach in cases of severe errors, e.g., due to undefined behaviors in C. As an example a write access via an illegal pointer might cause the program to crash with segmentation fault, it may corrupt data and cause erratic program behavior, and the compiler might even change the program code. In such cases no reasonable assumptions can be made about what happens after the defect occurred, so the analyzer may chose not to continue the analysis in the context exhibiting the code defect. In such test cases, we removed the unintended error.

Consider for example the test case from Fig. 4: As loc1 is always −1 when reaching the assignment `doubleptr[loc1][loc2]='T'`; the behavior at that point is undefined. Hence, there is no reasonable continuation possible, so it makes sense for an analyzer to stop at this point after reporting the detected code defect. In total, we identified 14 such cases.

```
void dynamic_buffer_underrun_035()
{
 int i,loc1=0,loc2=0;
 char** doubleptr=(char**) malloc(10* sizeof(char*));

 for (i=0;i<10;i++)
 doubleptr[i]=(char*) malloc(10*sizeof(char));

 if (loc1==0)
 loc1--;

 doubleptr[loc1][loc2]='T';

 if(loc2==0)
 loc2--;

 doubleptr[0][loc2]='T'; /*Tool should detect this line as error*/
 for (i=0;i<10;i++)
 {
  free(doubleptr[i]);
 }
 free(doubleptr);
}
```

Fig. 4. Test case with hidden error locations

7.5   Error-Free Code Marked as Erroneous

In some cases marked, intended to-be-erroneous code is indeed legal, valid code. We modified the code to provoke code defects fitting existing comments and the overall aim of the respective test suite. We found 15 test cases in which valid code has been considered invalid.

7.6　Erroneous Code Marked as Error-Free

Conversely, we found 3 test cases which are documented to be free of a certain defect, but actually contain an error of the covered error type at the marked location.

Consider for example the test case from Fig. 5. As Z is not a character of the string stored at s.buf at the marked location, variable len will eventually be −1 and cause an array underrun. Note that the check to prevent this in the example is only executed after the critical access.

```
typedef struct {
  char buf[10];
  char buf1[10];
  char buf2[10];
  char buf3[10];
  char buf4[10];
  char buf5[10];
  char buf6[10];
} st_underrun_002_s_001;

void st_underrun_002_func_001(st_underrun_002_s_001 s)
{

  int len = strlen(s.buf) - 1;
  for (;s.buf[len] != 'Z';len--) /*Tool should not detect this line as error*/
                                 /* No Stack Under RUN error */
  {
    if ( len < 0 )
    break;
  }
}

void st_underrun_002 ()
{
  st_underrun_002_s_001 s;
  strcpy(s.buf,"STRING");
  st_underrun_002_func_001(s);
}
```

Fig. 5. Test case with erroneous code marked as error-free

7.7　Valid Code that May Lead to Invalid Uses

Similar to the category *Error-free code marked as erroneous*, there are test cases which do not contain errors, but construct objects that may be used in a way that constitutes undefined or generally erroneous behavior. However, the test cases do not contain any subsequent use of the objects. In all such cases, we added a subsequent use that provokes an error. We counted 8 such test cases.

Consider the example in Fig. 6: First, the marked statement does not contain any code defect. There is also no use of foo which might falsely assume that foo points to a \0-terminated string which seems to be what the test case aims at. Inserting e.g. a call strln(foo) before free(foo) would lead to the desired flaw.

```
/*
 * Types of defects: Deletion of a data structure sentinel
 * Complexity: Not leaving a place for '\0' which is the
 * terminator for the string.
 */

void deletion_of_data_structure_sentinel_001()
{
 char* foo;
 int counter;
 foo=calloc(10,sizeof(char));
 for(counter=0;counter<10;counter++)
 {
   foo[counter]='a'; /*Tool should detect this line as error*/
                /*ERROR:Deletion of a data structure sentinel*/
 }
 free(foo);
}
```

Fig. 6. Test case with missing error trigger

7.8 Erroneous Code Labeled with an Incorrect Error Type

In further cases, the marked code does not exhibit the documented code defect or is correctly marked as being free of a documented defect, but there is nonetheless an unintended defect at that location. We found 8 such issues.

Consider for example the test case from Fig. 7: Consider the statement highlighted red and labeled as intentionally overflowing. Presumably due to a copy and paste error, the data structure accessed at this location is not initialized at all. There is, however, the definition of the structure visible. Hence, while there is no overflow as indicated, there is nonetheless a true code defect: dereferencing a null pointer.

7.9 Mismatch Between Documentation and Source Code

We refrained from a deeper analysis of source code documentation, but restricted our analysis of the benchmark files to the actual C code. For the purpose of completeness, we nonetheless note that source code comments are in many cases misleading or plainly incorrect.

7.10 Wrong Assumptions About Language and Libraries

The test cases made some assumptions about the behavior of the standard C library as well as properties of data types.

For example, 14 test cases require the benchmarked tool to report invocations of free() as a code defect when called with a null pointer as parameter. However, the C standard explicitly states: "If ptr is a null pointer, no action occurs" (7.20.3.2 ISO/IEC 9899:1999). Therefore calling free() with a null pointer parameter is perfectly legal. This behavior also is reflected in the clib model of Astrée. To "successfully" evaluate these test cases we temporarily changed the Astrée

```
typedef struct {
  int a;
  int b;
  int c;
} littlemem_st_008_s_001;

littlemem_st_008_s_001 *littlemem_st_008_s_001_gbl_str;

char littlemem_st_008_gbl_buf[10];

void littlemem_st_008_func_001 ()
{
  littlemem_st_008_s_001_gbl_str =
         (littlemem_st_008_s_001 *)littlemem_st_008_gbl_buf;
}

void littlemem_st_008_func_002 (int flag)
{
  int i=0;
  while(i<2)
  {
    if(flag == 10)
    {
      ;
    }
    else if(flag == 1)
    {
      littlemem_st_007_s_001_gbl_str->c = 1; /*Tool should
      detect this line as error*//*ERROR:Little Memory or Overflow*/
    }
      i++;
  }
}

void littlemem_st_008 ()
{
  littlemem_st_008_func_001();
  littlemem_st_008_func_002(1);
}
```

Fig. 7. Excerpt H

clib to report null pointers passed to `free()`, after which all "defects" were reported as expected. However, that means that in order to successfully pass these tests a more restricted semantics has to be chosen than prescribed by the C standard.

Furthermore, implicit assumptions about `malloc` and `calloc` have been made. In many (but not all!) test cases it is assumed that dynamic memory allocation will not fail, i.e., will not return a null pointer. As a sound analyzer must not make such an assumption, this leads to justified reports about subsequent usage of potential null pointers that the benchmark falsely classifies as false alarms.

There are also implicit assumptions about the application binary interface. For the 19 test cases (totaling to 38 versions) of flaw type data_lost to work as intended, the data type `char` needs to be signed.

In total, we investigated 1,188 test cases and found 442 issues that were presumably unintended. We applied 106 code modifications to the ITC test cases in order to remove unintended errors and other mistakes preventing the test cases from working as intended. We incorporated observed implicit assumptions into the analysis model to make 280 test cases work as intended. These 280 test cases sum up as follows: There were 214 unintended potential runtime errors (92 in the test cases with errors and 122 in the test cases without errors) due to implicitly assuming that memory allocations will always be successful and another 14 test cases per benchmark group (with and without errors) relied on wrong assumptions on `free()`; assumptions about the application binary interface prevented 38 test cases from working as intended. Additionally, 56 of the 58 test cases related to the `pow()` library function did not work as intended for various reasons (from misuse of the bitwise XOR operator to code not matching the test case documentation).

Our corrected versions of the test cases are publicly available at https://github.com/AbsInt/itc-benchmarks.

8   Evaluation Processes

Ideally, an external evaluation will be performed by a neutral institution, as happens in many Verification Challenges [3,5,16]. This institution would be responsible for a fair process and a clear publication of the results.

9   Conclusion

Static analysis tools to check coding guidelines and detect code defects are widely used in industry. Commonly available industry benchmarks designed for the purpose of evaluating such tools play an important role in order to get a first measurable rating of the available tools.

In this article we have summarized recent approaches to rate static analyzers and discussed considerations to be taken into account when applying the two primary tool evaluation criteria, the true positive rate and the false positive rate. Our primary goal is to support establishing a commonly accepted set of benchmark suites to objectively rate static analysis tools. To this end we have discussed general design principles for test cases to ensure valid and meaningful benchmark results. We have summarized common traps and pitfalls when applying benchmarks, and have critically reviewed the ITC benchmark suites with respect to our design principles. We have encountered flaws in 37% of the ITC test cases, have fixed all issues detected, and made the improved version of the ITC benchmarks publicly available.

Acknowledgment. The work presented in this paper is supported by the European ITEA3 project ASSUME.

References

1. AbsInt Angewandte Informatik GmbH: Astrée. http://www.astree.de
2. AdaCore: CodePeer. http://www.adacore.com/codepeer

3. DARPA - Defense Advanced Research Projects Agency: Space/Time Analysis for Cybersecurity (STAC). http://www.darpa.mil/program/space-time-analysis-for-cybersecurity
4. Deutsch, A.: Static verification of dynamic properties. In: ACM SIGAda 2003 Conference (2003)
5. ETAPS/TAPAS: Competition on Software Verification (SV-COMP). http://sv-comp.sosy-lab.org/2017/
6. GrammaTech: CodeSonar. http://www.grammatech.com/products/codesonar
7. Kästner, D., Miné, A., Mauborgne, L., Rival, X., Feret, J., Cousot, P., Schmidt, A., Hille, H., Wilhelm, S., Ferdinand, C.: Finding all potential runtime errors and data races in automotive software. In: SAE World Congress 2017. SAE International (2017)
8. Lu, S., Li, Z., Qin, F., Tan, L., Zhou, P., Zhou, Y.: BugBench: benchmarks for evaluating bug detection tools. In: Workshop on the Evaluation of Software Defect Detection Tools (2005)
9. Martin, R., Christey, S., Jarzombek, J.: The case for common flaw enumeration. In: NIST Workshop on Software Security Assurance Tools, Techniques, and Methods, Long Beach, California, USA, November 2015. http://cwe.mitre.org/documents/case_for_cwes.pdf
10. Mathworks: Polyspace Bug Finder. http://www.mathworks.com/products/polyspace-bug-finder.html
11. Mathworks: Polyspace Code Prover. http://www.mathworks.com/products/polyspace-code-prover.html
12. Miné, A., Mauborgne, L., Rival, X., Feret, J., Cousot, P., Kästner, D., Wilhelm, S., Ferdinand, C.: Taking static analysis to the next level: proving the absence of run-time errors and data races with Astrée. In: Embedded Real Time Software and Systems Congress ERTS^2 (2016)
13. MISRA-C:2004 - Guidelines for the use of the C language in critical systems (2004)
14. MISRA-C:2012 - Guidelines for the use of the C language in critical systems (2013)
15. NIST - National Institute of Standards and Technology: Juliet Suite for C/C++. http://samate.nist.gov/SRD/view.php?tsID=86
16. NIST - National Institute of Standards and Technology: SAMATE - Software Assurance Metrics And Tool Evaluation. http://samate.nist.gov/Main_Page.html
17. Holzmann, G.J.: The power of 10: rules for developing safety-critical code. Computer 39(6), 95–97 (2006). NASA/JPL Laboratory for Reliable Software. http://dx.doi.org/10.1109/MC.2006.212
18. Rogue Wave Software: Klocwork^{TM}. http://www.klocwork.com
19. Shiraishi, S., Mohan, V., Marimuthu, H.: Test suites for benchmarks of static analysis tools. In: 2015 IEEE International Symposium on Software Reliability Engineering Workshops, ISSRE Workshops, Gaithersburg, MD, USA, pp. 12–15, 2–5 November 2015. http://dx.doi.org/10.1109/ISSREW.2015.7392027
20. Software Engineering Institute, Carnegie Mellon University: CERT Secure Coding Validation Suite. http://www.cert.org/secure-coding/tools/validation-suite.cfm
21. Synopsys: Coverity. http://www.synopsys.com/software-integrity/products/static-code-analysis.html

Automatic Estimation of Verified Floating-Point Round-Off Errors via Static Analysis

Mariano Moscato[1]([⊠]), Laura Titolo[1]([⊠]), Aaron Dutle[2], and César A. Muñoz[2]

[1] National Institute of Aerospace, Hampton, VA, USA
{mariano.moscato,laura.titolo}@nianet.org
[2] NASA Langley Research Center, Hampton, VA, USA
{aaron.m.dutle,cesar.a.munoz}@nasa.gov

Abstract. This paper introduces a static analysis technique for computing formally verified round-off error bounds of floating-point functional expressions. The technique is based on a denotational semantics that computes a symbolic estimation of floating-point round-off errors along with a proof certificate that ensures its correctness. The symbolic estimation can be evaluated on concrete inputs using rigorous enclosure methods to produce formally verified numerical error bounds. The proposed technique is implemented in the prototype research tool PRECiSA (Program Round-off Error Certifier via Static Analysis) and used in the verification of floating-point programs of interest to NASA.

1 Introduction

Floating-point arithmetic is the most commonly used representation of real arithmetic in computer programs. One significant problem of floating-point arithmetic is the presence of round-off errors that can make a numerical computation significantly different from the actual real arithmetic computation. These errors are especially problematic in safety-critical applications such as aerospace and avionics software, where even small computation errors can lead to catastrophic consequences. Having a correct and externally verifiable estimation of how close a computed result is to the ideal real number computation is fundamental to the safety analysis of such systems.

This paper presents a modular static analysis technique for computing *provably sound* over-approximations of floating-point round-off errors. Given a set of functions over floating-point values, symbolic upper bounds on the round-off error of these functions are automatically computed by using a denotational semantics framework. Additionally, proof certificates assuring the correctness of such bounds are also generated. The main features of the proposed technique are: (1) automatic generation of proof certificates that provide an externally verifiable guarantee that the computed error estimations are correct; (2) modularity and reusability, due to being defined by a compositional denotational semantics that symbolically models the accumulation of floating point round-off errors in functional expressions; (3) correctly handling of conditional expressions, i.e., the *stable test hypothesis* is not assumed in conditional if-then-else expressions where

© Springer International Publishing AG 2017
S. Tonetta et al. (Eds.): SAFECOMP 2017, LNCS 10488, pp. 213–229, 2017.
DOI: 10.1007/978-3-319-66266-4_14

the logical value of the condition is compromised by round-off errors; (4) extensibility, i.e., new floating-point operations can be integrated into the denotational semantic framework assuming they satisfy some basic properties; and (5) computation of accurate round-off errors via a generic branch-and-bound algorithm that supports several rigorous enclosure methods, e.g., interval arithmetic, affine arithmetic [1], and Bernstein polynomials [2].

The static analysis presented in this paper has been implemented in a prototype tool called PRECiSA (Program Round-off Error Certifier via Static Analysis). The current implementation of PRECiSA uses SRI's Prototype Verification System (PVS) [3], but the theoretical framework presented in this paper can be implemented in any modern interactive proof assistant. PRECiSA accepts as input a program composed of a set of functional floating-point expressions. The output of the tool is a PVS theory that consists of a set of lemmas stating accumulated round-off error estimations for each function in the program. These lemmas are equipped with PVS proof scripts that *automatically* discharge them. When numerical values for the input variables appearing in the program are provided, PRECiSA also generates PVS lemmas stating concrete numerical bounds on the round-off errors, along with corresponding proof scripts to discharge them without user intervention. PRECiSA is publicly available under NASA's Open Source Agreement[1] and can be used, without installation, through a web interface[2].

The paper is organized as follows. A formalization of floating-point round-off errors is presented in Sect. 2. This formalization enables the generation of proof certificates and the computation of provably correct bounds. In Sect. 3, a compositional denotational semantics modeling the accumulation of floating-point round-off errors is defined. This semantics is the core of the proposed analysis and it computes a symbolic over-approximation of the round-off error of a given function, along with a proof certificate ensuring its correctness. PRECiSA, an implementation of the proposed analysis, is presented in Sect. 4. This implementation is illustrated with an example taken from a verification effort at NASA. Experimental results and comparison to similar tools are shown in Sect. 5. Related work is discussed in Sect. 6.

2   Formalization of Floating-Point Round-Off Errors

The NASA PVS Library[3] includes two formalizations of floating-point numbers: a hardware-level model of the IEEE-854 floating-point standard [4] and high-level model of the IEEE-754 standard [5]. These formalizations are related by functions that translate from one representation into the other. In the high-level model, a *floating-point number*, or simply a *float*, is defined as a pair of integers (m, e), where m is called the *significant* and e the *exponent* of the float. A conversion function $\mathbf{R} : \mathbb{F} \mapsto \mathbb{R}$ is defined to refer to the real number represented

---

[1] https://github.com/nasa/PRECiSA.

[2] http://precisa.nianet.org.

[3] https://shemesh.larc.nasa.gov/fm/ftp/larc/PVS-library.

by a given float, i.e., $\mathbf{R}((m, \mathbf{e})) = m \cdot \beta^{\mathbf{e}}$, where $\beta \in \mathbb{N}$ is called the *base* or *radix* of the system. IEEE-754 *formats*, e.g., binary single and double precisions, can be defined in this formalization by instantiating specific theory parameters. As this representation is redundant, notions about normality and canonicity are also defined (see [5] for details). By abuse of notation, $\tilde{v}$ will be used to represent a floating-point number in $\mathbb{F}$ and its real value $\mathbf{R}(\tilde{v})$.

Since not every real number can be exactly represented by a float, a notion of representation error is defined as follows. Let $\tilde{v}$ be a floating-point number that represents a real number r, the difference $|\tilde{v} - r|$ is called the *round-off error* (or *rounding error*) of $\tilde{v}$ with respect to r. The *closest* floating-point to r, denoted $\mathbf{F}(r)$, is defined as a floating-point number for which the round-off error with respect to r is minimal. In cases where this float is not unique, the IEEE-754 standard defines several *rounding modes* such as the *round-ties-to-even* mode, where the float with even significand is chosen, and the *round-ties-to-away* mode, where the float with the greater absolute value is chosen.

The *unit in the last place* (*ulp*) is a measure of the precision of a floating-point number $\tilde{v}$ as a representation of a real number. It can be defined as $\mathsf{ulp}(\tilde{v}) = \beta^{\mathbf{e}_{\tilde{v}}}$, where $\mathbf{e}_{\tilde{v}}$ is the exponent of the canonical form of $\tilde{v}$. Note that the canonical form of a given float depends on the format being used (single precision, double precision, etc.). Then, the ulp also depends on the format. The ulp of a floating point can be used as a bound of the round-off error since, as shown in [5], if $\tilde{v}$ is the closest representation of some real r, the two numbers are apart from each other for no more than half of the ulp of $\tilde{v}$. The ulp of a real number is defined as the ulp of the canonical form of its closest floating-point representation, i.e., $\mathsf{ulp}(r) = \mathsf{ulp}(\mathbf{F}(r))$. Then, the previous bound can be stated as follows [6].

$$|\tilde{v} - r| \leq \tfrac{1}{2}\mathsf{ulp}(r). \tag{1}$$

The work presented in this paper extends the high-level model with a formalization of round-off errors of floating-point expressions $\widetilde{\mathsf{op}}(\tilde{v}_1, \ldots, \tilde{v}_n)$ with respect to a real-valued expression $\mathsf{op}(r_1, \ldots, r_n)$, where $\widetilde{\mathsf{op}}$ is a floating-point operator representing a real-valued operator op and $\tilde{v}_i$ is a floating-point value representing a real value r_i, for $1 \leq i \leq n$. For that purpose, it is necessary to consider: (a) the error introduced by the application of $\widetilde{\mathsf{op}}$ versus op and (b) the propagation of the errors carried out by the arguments, i.e., the difference between $\tilde{v}_i$ and r_i, for $1 \leq i \leq n$, in the application. In the case of arithmetic operators, the IEEE-754 standard states that every operation should be performed as if it would be calculated with infinite precision and then rounded to the nearest floating-point value. Then, from Formula (1), the application of an n-ary floating-point operator $\widetilde{\mathsf{op}}$ to the floating-point values $\tilde{v}_1, \ldots, \tilde{v}_n$ must fulfill the following condition.

$$|\widetilde{\mathsf{op}}(\tilde{v}_i)_{i=1}^n - \mathsf{op}(\tilde{v}_i)_{i=1}^n| \leq \tfrac{1}{2}\mathsf{ulp}(\mathsf{op}(\tilde{v}_i)_{i=1}^n), \tag{2}$$

where the notation $f(x_i)_{i=1}^n$ is used to represent $f(x_1, \ldots, x_n)$.

To estimate how the errors of the arguments are propagated to the result of the application of the operator, it is necessary to bound the difference between the application of the real operator on real values and the application of the same operator on the floating-point arguments. The expression $\epsilon_{op}(e_i)_{i=1}^n$ is used to represent such difference, where each e_i is a bound of the round-off error carried by every floating point $\tilde{v}_i$ representing a real value r_i, i.e., $|\tilde{v}_i - r_i| \leq e_i$. Therefore, $\epsilon_{op}(e_i)_{i=1}^n$ satisfies the following condition.

$$|op(\tilde{v}_i)_{i=1}^n - op(r_i)_{i=1}^n| \leq \epsilon_{op}(e_i)_{i=1}^n. \tag{3}$$

The following bound of the round-off error between the floating-point expression and the real-valued counterpart follows from Formula (2), Formula (3), the triangle inequality, and the fact that ulp is monotonically increasing on non-negative inputs [5].

$$|\widetilde{op}(\tilde{v}_i)_{i=1}^n - op(r_i)_{i=1}^n| \leq \varepsilon_{\widetilde{op}}(r_i, e_i)_{i=1}^n, \tag{4}$$

where $\varepsilon_{\widetilde{op}}(r_i, e_i)_{i=1}^n = \epsilon_{op}(e_i)_{i=1}^n + \frac{1}{2}\,ulp(v(r_i, e_i)_{i=1}^n)$ and $v(r_i, e_i)_{i=1}^n$ is a real-valued expression that satisfies $|op(\tilde{v}_i)_{i=1}^n| \leq v(r_i, e_i)_{i=1}^n$.

Additional restrictions on the variables in Formula (4) are needed when the operators are not total. For example, when dealing with the division operation, it is necessary to guarantee that the second argument of both the floating-point operator and the real-valued operator is not zero. The expressions $\eta_{op}(r_i)_{i=1}^n$ and $\eta_{\widetilde{op}}(\tilde{v}_i)_{i=1}^n$ will be used to represent any such conditions on the arguments of the operators.

In this work, the operators $\widetilde{op}$ and op in Formula (4) are generic. They can be instantiated with any floating point operation and its real counterpart as long as Formula (4) holds for all $\tilde{v}_1, \ldots, \tilde{v}_n \in \mathbb{F}$, $r_i, \ldots, r_n \in \mathbb{R}$, $e_1, \ldots, e_n \in \mathbb{R}_{\geq 0}$, when $|\tilde{v}_i - r_i| \leq e_i$ with $1 \leq i \leq n$, $\eta_{op}(r_i)_{i=1}^n$, and $\eta_{\widetilde{op}}(\tilde{v}_i)_{i=1}^n$. Some examples of round-off error approximation functions for arithmetic operators are presented below. It is worth noting how the additional constraints are used in the division and in the square root to guarantee the validity of the output, and in the subtraction and arctangent to improve the precision of the error approximation. For example, as mentioned in [5], the floating point subtraction $\tilde{v}_1 \,\tilde{-}\, \tilde{v}_2$ can be exactly computed when $\tilde{v}_2/2 \leq x \leq 2 \,\tilde{*}\, \tilde{v}_2$. This property is captured by the error approximation function $\varepsilon_{\tilde{-}'}$ and corresponding constraint $\eta_{\tilde{-}'}$ shown below.

- $\varepsilon_{\tilde{+}}(r_1, e_1, r_2, e_2) := e_1 + e_2 + \frac{1}{2}\,ulp(|r_1 + r_2| + e_1 + e_2)$.
- $\varepsilon_{\tilde{-}}(r_1, e_1, r_2, e_2) := e_1 + e_2 + \frac{1}{2}\,ulp(|r_1 - r_2| + e_1 + e_2)\,\eta_{\tilde{-}}(\tilde{v}_1, \tilde{v}_2) := (\tilde{v}_2/2 > \tilde{v}_1) \vee (\tilde{v}_1 > 2\tilde{v}_2)$.
- $\varepsilon_{\tilde{-}'}(r_1, e_1, r_2, e_2) := e_1 + e_2$, $\eta_{\tilde{-}'}(\tilde{v}_1, \tilde{v}_2) := (\tilde{v}_2/2 \leq \tilde{v}_1 \leq 2\tilde{v}_2)$.
- $\varepsilon_{\tilde{*}}(r_1, e_1, r_2, e_2) := |r_1|e_2 + |r_2|e_1 + e_1e_2 + \frac{1}{2}\,ulp((|r_1| + e_1)(|r_2| + e_2))$.
- $\varepsilon_{\tilde{/}}(r_1, e_1, r_2, e_2) := \frac{|r_1|e_2 + |r_2|e_1}{r_2r_2 - e_2|r_2|} + \frac{1}{2}ulp\left(\frac{|r_1| + e_1}{|r_2| - e_2}\right)$, $\eta_{\tilde{/}}(r_1, r_2) := (r_2 \neq 0)$, and $\eta_{\tilde{/}}(\tilde{v}_1, \tilde{v}_2) := (\tilde{v}_2 \neq 0)$.
- $\varepsilon_{\tilde{-}}(r, e) := e$.
- $\varepsilon_{\widetilde{abs}}(r, e) := e$.
- $\varepsilon_{\widetilde{floor}}(r, e) := e + max(\lfloor r \rfloor - \lfloor r - e \rfloor, \lfloor r \rfloor - \lfloor r + e \rfloor) + \frac{1}{2}\,ulp(|\lfloor r \rfloor| + e)$.
- $\varepsilon_{\widetilde{sqrt}}(r, e) := \sqrt{e} + \frac{1}{2}\,ulp(\sqrt{r + e})$, $\eta_{\widetilde{sqrt}}(r) := (r \geq 0)$, and $\eta_{\widetilde{sqrt}}(\tilde{v}) := (\tilde{v} \geq 0)$.

- $\varepsilon_{\widetilde{sin}}(r,e) := min(2,e) + \frac{1}{2}\mathsf{ulp}(|sin(r)| + min(2,e)).$
- $\varepsilon_{\widetilde{cos}}(r,e) := min(2,e) + \frac{1}{2}\mathsf{ulp}(|cos(r)| + min(2,e)).$
- $\varepsilon_{\widetilde{atan}}(r,e) := e + \frac{1}{2}\mathsf{ulp}(atan(|r| + e)),\ \eta_{atan}(r,e) := (|r| \le e).$
- $\varepsilon_{\widetilde{atan}}{}'(r,e) := \frac{e}{min((r-e)^2,(r+e)^2)} + \frac{1}{2}\mathsf{ulp}(atan(|r|+e)),\ \eta_{atan}{}'(r,e) := (|r| > e).$

The fact that the previous definitions satisfy Formula (4) is formally proven in PVS and the proofs are electronically available in the NASA PVS Library.

3 Denotational Semantics

In this section, a denotational semantics for a declarative expression language that relies on the floating-point formalization presented in Sect. 2 is defined. This semantics computes a symbolic expression representing the round-off error of the program and collects the information needed to provide a certificate that guarantees its soundness.

In the following, the sets of arithmetic and boolean expressions over reals are denoted as $\mathbb{A}$ and $\mathbb{B}$, respectively. The floating point counterparts of $\mathbb{A}$ and $\mathbb{B}$ are denoted as $\widetilde{\mathbb{A}}$ and $\widetilde{\mathbb{B}}$, respectively. The expression language considered in this paper contains conditionals, let expressions, and function calls. Given a set Ω of pre-defined arithmetic floating-point operations, a set Σ of function symbols, and a denumerable set $\mathbb{V}$ of variables, $\widetilde{\mathbb{E}}$ denotes the set of program expressions, which syntax is given by the following grammar.

$$\widetilde{A} ::= \tilde{k} \mid x \mid \widetilde{op}(\widetilde{A}, \ldots, \widetilde{A}) \quad \widetilde{B} ::= true \mid false \mid \widetilde{B} \wedge \widetilde{B} \mid \widetilde{B} \vee \widetilde{B} \mid \neg \widetilde{B} \mid \widetilde{A} < \widetilde{A} \mid \widetilde{A} = \widetilde{A}$$
$$\widetilde{E} ::= \widetilde{A} \mid if\ \widetilde{B}\ then\ \widetilde{E}\ else\ \widetilde{E} \mid let\ x = \widetilde{A}\ in\ \widetilde{E} \mid \tilde{f}(\widetilde{A}, \ldots, \widetilde{A}) \tag{5}$$

where $\widetilde{A} \in \widetilde{\mathbb{A}}$, $\widetilde{B} \in \widetilde{\mathbb{B}}$, $\widetilde{E} \in \widetilde{\mathbb{E}}$, $\tilde{k} \in \mathbb{F}$, $x \in \mathbb{V}$, $\widetilde{op} \in \Omega$, and $\tilde{f} \in \Sigma$.

A program is defined as a set of *function declarations* of the form $\tilde{f}(x_1, \ldots, x_n) = \widetilde{E}$, where $x_1, \ldots, x_n$ are pairwise distinct variables in $\mathbb{V}$ and all free variables appearing in $\widetilde{E}$ are in $\{x_1, \ldots, x_n\}$. The natural number n is called the *arity* of $\tilde{f}$. Henceforth, it is assumed that programs are well-formed in the sense that for every function call $\tilde{f}(x_1, \ldots, x_n)$ that occurs in a program $\widetilde{P}$, a unique function $\tilde{f}$ of arity n is defined in $\widetilde{P}$. The set of programs is denoted as $\widetilde{\mathbb{P}}$.

The proposed semantics collects, for each program path, the corresponding path conditions (for both the real and the floating-point flow), and two *symbolic* arithmetic expressions representing (1) the value of the output assuming the use of real arithmetic and (2) an upper bound for the accumulated round-off error that the result might include due to floating-point operations. Furthermore, the semantics computes a symbolic proof of the correctness of the computed round-off error. The set of symbolic proofs that can be generated by the semantics is denoted by Π. The previous information is stored in a *conditional error bound*, which is a tuple on the form $(\eta, \tilde{\eta}, r, e, \pi)$ where $\eta \in \mathbb{B}$, $\tilde{\eta} \in \widetilde{\mathbb{B}}$, $r, e \in \mathbb{A}$, $\pi \in \Pi$, and such that $\eta \ne false$ and $\tilde{\eta} \ne false$. Intuitively, $(\eta, \tilde{\eta}, r, e, \pi)$ means that if the conditions η and $\tilde{\eta}$ are true, then the output of the ideal real numbers implementation of the program is r, and π is a formal proof that the round-off error of the floating-point implementation is bounded by e.

Both real and floating-point path conditions are collected in order to detect the presence of the program flow anomaly usually referred to as *unstable test*.

Definition 1 (Test Stability). *Let* $\mathbf{R_B} : \widetilde{\mathbb{B}} \to \mathbb{B}$ *be the function converting a floating-point expression to a real one, by simply replacing each operation on floating-point with the corresponding operation on reals and by applying* $\mathbf{R}$ *to the floating-point values.*

A conditional expression if $\tilde{\phi}$ *then* $\tilde{E}_1$ *else* $\tilde{E}_2$ *is said to be* unstable *when it exists an assignment for the variables in* $\tilde{\phi}$ *to* $\mathbb{F}$ *such that* $\tilde{\phi}$ *and* $\mathbf{R_B}(\tilde{\phi})$ *evaluate to a different boolean value. Otherwise the conditional expression is said to be* stable.

The presence of unstable tests makes the floating-point control flow different from the real arithmetic execution flow, and leads to unsound results when rounding errors provoke the unsound evaluation of conditionals. By separately collecting the information about real and floating-point flows, it is possible to consider the additional error of taking the incorrect branch in the cases in which the flows do not match. This guarantees a sound treatment of unstable tests in the proposed semantics.

Let $\mathbf{C}$ be the set of all conditional error bounds, and $\mathbb{C} := \wp(\mathbf{C})$ be the domain formed by sets of conditional error bounds, which is the support domain of the proposed semantics. An *environment* is defined as a function mapping a variable to a set of conditional error bounds, i.e., $Env = \mathbb{V} \to \mathbb{C}$. The empty environment is denoted as $\bot_{Env}$ and maps every variable to the empty set $\varnothing$.

The semantics of arithmetic expressions is a function $\mathcal{A} : \widetilde{\mathbb{A}} \times Env \to \mathbb{C}$ defined as follows, where $\sigma \in Env$, $x \in \mathbb{V}$, and $\phi_r, \phi_e : \mathbb{V} \to \mathbb{V}$ are two functions that associate to each variable x a fresh variable representing the real value and the error of x, respectively. Let $\widetilde{\text{op}}$ be an n-ary floating-point operator in Ω such that its real-valued counterpart is denoted as op. As stated in Sect. 2, it is assumed that there exists a function $\varepsilon_{\widetilde{\text{op}}}$ such that Formula (4) holds and let $\pi_{\widetilde{\text{op}}}(\pi_i)_{i=1}^n$ be a proof for that statement, which is defined in function of the proofs π_i corresponding to $\widetilde{\text{op}}$ operands. Furthermore, π_{cnst} and π_{var} are the proofs of Formula (4) for the constant and variable cases, respectively, which must be provided according to the formalization of Sect. 2.

$$\mathcal{A}[\![\tilde{k}]\!]_\sigma := \{(true, true, \tilde{k}, 0, \pi_{cnst})\} \tag{6}$$

$$\mathcal{A}[\![\mathbf{F}(k)]\!]_\sigma := \{(true, true, k, |k - \mathbf{F}(k)|, \pi_{cnst})\} \tag{7}$$

$$\mathcal{A}[\![x]\!]_\sigma := \begin{cases} \{(true, true, \phi_r(x), \phi_e(x), \pi_{var}(x))\} & \text{if } \sigma(x) = \varnothing \\ \sigma(x) & \text{otherwise} \end{cases} \tag{8}$$

$$\mathcal{A}[\![\widetilde{\text{op}}(\tilde{A}_i)_{i=1}^n]\!]_\sigma := \tag{9}$$

$$\bigcup \{(\bigwedge_{i=1}^n \eta_i \wedge \eta_{\text{op}}(r_i)_{i=1}^n, \bigwedge_{i=1}^n \tilde{\eta}_i \wedge \eta_{\widetilde{\text{op}}}(\tilde{A}_i)_{i=1}^n, \text{op}(r_i)_{i=1}^n, \varepsilon_{\widetilde{\text{op}}}(e_i)_{i=1}^n, \pi_{\widetilde{\text{op}}}(\pi_i)_{i=1}^n)$$

$$| \, \forall 1 \le i \le n \colon (\eta_i, \tilde{\eta}_i, r_i, e_i, \pi_i) \in \mathcal{A}[\![\tilde{A}_i]\!]_\sigma, \eta_{\text{op}}(r_i)_{i=1}^n \in \mathbb{B}, \eta_{\widetilde{\text{op}}}(\tilde{A}_i)_{i=1}^n \in \widetilde{\mathbb{B}},$$

$$\bigwedge_{i=1}^n \eta_i \wedge \eta_{\text{op}}(r_i)_{i=1}^n \ne false, \bigwedge_{i=1}^n \tilde{\eta}_i \wedge \eta_{\widetilde{\text{op}}}(\tilde{A}_i)_{i=1}^n \ne false\}$$

No rounding error is associated to a floating-point constant $\tilde{k}$, while the error of rounding a real constant k is the difference between its real value and its rounding. The semantics of a variable $x \in \mathbb{V}$ is composed of two cases. If x belongs to the environment, then the variable has been previously bound to an arithmetic expression $\tilde{A}$ through a let-expression. In this case, the semantics of x is exactly the semantics of $\tilde{A}$. If x is not in the environment, then x is a parameter of the function. Here, a new conditional error bound is added with two fresh variables, $\phi_r(x)$ and $\phi_e(x)$, representing the real value and the error of x, respectively. In the case of a floating-point arithmetic operation $\widetilde{op}$, the new error bound is obtained by applying $\varepsilon_{\widetilde{op}}$ to the errors and real values of the operands and the new conditions are obtained as the combination of the conditions of the operands. Predicates η_{op} and $\eta_{\widetilde{op}}$ represent the additional constraints needed when op and $\widetilde{op}$ are not total (as explained in Sect. 2). The proof for $\widetilde{op}$ is defined by merging $\pi_{\widetilde{op}}$ with the proofs of its operands.

Let $\mathbb{K} := \{\tilde{f}(x_1, \ldots, x_n) \mid \tilde{f} \in \Sigma, x_1, \ldots, x_n \in \mathbb{V}\}$ be the set of all possible function calls. An *interpretation* is a function $\rho \colon \mathbb{K} \to \mathbb{C}$ modulo variance. The set of all interpretations is denoted as *Int*. The empty interpretation is denoted as $\bot_{Int}$ and maps everything to the empty set. Given $\sigma \in Env$ and $\rho \in Int$, the semantics of program expressions, $\mathcal{E} : \widetilde{\mathbb{E}} \times Env \times Int \to \mathbb{C}$, returns the set of conditional error bounds representing an upper bound of the round-off error for each execution path, together with the corresponding conditions.

$$\mathcal{E}[\![\tilde{A}]\!]_\sigma^\rho := \mathcal{A}[\![\tilde{A}]\!]_\sigma \tag{10}$$

$$\mathcal{E}[\![let\ x = \tilde{A}\ in\ \tilde{E}]\!]_\sigma^\rho := \mathcal{E}[\![\tilde{E}]\!]_{\sigma[x \mapsto \mathcal{A}[\![\tilde{A}]\!]_\sigma]}^\rho \tag{11}$$

$$\mathcal{E}[\![if\ \tilde{B}\ then\ \tilde{E}_1\ else\ \tilde{E}_2]\!]_\sigma^\rho := \mathcal{E}[\![\tilde{E}_1]\!]_\sigma^\rho \Downarrow_{(\mathbf{R}_{\tilde{B}}(\tilde{B}), \tilde{B})} \cup \mathcal{E}[\![\tilde{E}_2]\!]_\sigma^\rho \Downarrow_{(\neg\,\mathbf{R}_{\tilde{B}}(\tilde{B}), \neg\tilde{B})} \cup \tag{12}$$

$$\bigcup \{(\eta_1 \wedge \eta_2, \tilde{\eta}_1, r_2, e_1 + |r_1 - r_2|, \pi_{un}(r_1, r_2, \pi_1)) \mid (\eta_1, \tilde{\eta}_1, r_1, e_1, \pi_1) \in \mathcal{E}[\![\tilde{E}_1]\!]_\sigma^\rho,$$

$$(\eta_2, \tilde{\eta}_2, r_2, e_2, \pi_2) \in \mathcal{E}[\![\tilde{E}_2]\!]_\sigma^\rho,\ \eta_1 \wedge \eta_2 \neq false\} \Downarrow_{(\neg\,\mathbf{R}_{\tilde{B}}(\tilde{B}), \tilde{B})} \cup$$

$$\bigcup \{(\eta_1 \wedge \eta_2, \tilde{\eta}_2, r_1, e_2 + |r_1 - r_2|, \pi_{un}(r_1, r_2, \pi_2))) \mid (\eta_1, \tilde{\eta}_1, r_1, e_1, \pi_1) \in \mathcal{E}[\![\tilde{E}_1]\!]_\sigma^\rho,$$

$$(\eta_2, \tilde{\eta}_2, r_2, e_2, \pi_2) \in \mathcal{E}[\![\tilde{E}_2]\!]_\sigma^\rho,\ \eta_1 \wedge \eta_2 \neq false\} \Downarrow_{(\mathbf{R}_{\tilde{B}}(\tilde{B}), \neg\tilde{B})}$$

$$\mathcal{E}[\![\tilde{f}(\tilde{A}_i)_{i=1}^n]\!]_\sigma^\rho := \bigcup \{(\eta \wedge \bigwedge_{i=1}^n \eta_i, \tilde{\eta} \wedge \bigwedge_{i=1}^n \tilde{\eta}_i, \bar{r}, \bar{e}, \bar{\pi}) \mid (\eta, \tilde{\eta}, r, e, \pi) \in \rho(\tilde{f}(x_1 \ldots x_n)),$$
$$\tag{13}$$

$$\forall 1 \leq i \leq n : (\eta_i, \tilde{\eta}_i, r_i, e_i, \pi_i) \in \mathcal{A}[\![\tilde{A}_i]\!]_\sigma,\ \bar{r} = r[\phi_r(x_1)/r_1, \ldots, \phi_r(x_n)/r_n],$$

$$\bar{e} = e[\phi_e(x_1)/e_1, \ldots, \phi_e(x_n)/e_n],\ \bar{\pi} = \pi[\phi_r(x_1)/r_1, \ldots, \phi_r(x_n)/r_n, \phi_e(x_1)/e_1,$$

$$\ldots, \phi_e(x_n)/e_n, \pi_{var}(x_1)/\pi_1, \ldots, \pi_{var}(x_n)/\pi_n],\ \eta \wedge \bigwedge_{i=1}^n \eta_i \neq false,\ \tilde{\eta} \wedge \bigwedge_{i=1}^n \tilde{\eta}_i \neq false\}$$

Intuitively, the semantics of the expression *let* $x = \tilde{A}$ *in* $\tilde{E}$ updates the current environment by associating to variable x the semantics of expression $\tilde{A}$.

The semantics of the conditional uses an auxiliary operator $\Downarrow$ for propagating new information in the conditions. Given $b \in \mathbb{B}$ and $\tilde{b} \in \widetilde{\mathbb{B}}$, $(\eta, \tilde{\eta}, r, e, t) \Downarrow_{(b, \tilde{b})} = (\eta \wedge b, \tilde{\eta} \wedge \tilde{b}, r, e, t)$ if $\eta \wedge b \neq false$ and $\tilde{\eta} \wedge \tilde{b} \neq false$, otherwise it is undefined.

The definition of $\Downarrow$ naturally extends to sets of conditional error bounds: given $C \subseteq \mathbb{C}$, $C \Downarrow_{(b,\tilde{b})} = \bigcup_{c \in C} c \Downarrow_{(b,\tilde{b})}$. Tests in conditionals need to be treated carefully to guarantee soundness. Consider the conditional *if $\tilde{B}$ then $\tilde{E}_1$ else $\tilde{E}_2$*. The semantics of $\tilde{E}_1$ and $\tilde{E}_2$ are enriched with the information about the fact that real and floating-point flows match, i.e., both $\tilde{B}$ and $\mathbf{R}_\mathbb{B}(\tilde{B})$ have the same value. If real and floating point flows do not coincide, the error of taking one branch instead of the other has to be considered. For example, if $\tilde{B}$ is satisfied but $\mathbf{R}_\mathbb{B}(\tilde{B})$ is not, the *then* branch is taken in the floating point computation, but the *else* would have been taken in the real one. In this case, the error is the difference between the real value of the result of $\tilde{E}_2$ and the floating point result of $\tilde{E}_1$. It is easy to show that this error is bounded by the round-off error of $\tilde{E}_1$ plus the difference between the real values of $\tilde{E}_1$ and $\tilde{E}_2$. The condition $(\neg\mathbf{R}_\mathbb{B}(\tilde{B}), \tilde{B})$ is propagated in order to model that $\tilde{B}$ holds but $\mathbf{R}_\mathbb{B}(\tilde{B})$ does not. The proof π_{un} formalizes the previous argumentation in terms of the formal development defined in Sect. 2.

The semantics of a function call combines the conditions coming from the interpretation of the function and the ones coming from the semantics of the parameters. Variables representing real values and errors of formal parameters are replaced with the symbolic expressions coming from the semantics of the actual parameters, and the proofs for the variables representing formal parameters are replaced by the proofs for the actual parameters.

The semantics of a program is a function $\mathcal{F} : \tilde{\mathbb{P}} \times Env \to \mathbb{C}$ defined as the least fixed point *(lfp)* of the immediate consequence operator $\mathcal{P} : \tilde{\mathbb{P}} \times Env \times Int \to \mathbb{C}$, i.e., given $\tilde{P} \in \tilde{\mathbb{P}}$, $\mathcal{F}[\![\tilde{P}]\!] := lfp(\mathcal{P}[\![\tilde{P}]\!]^{\perp Int}_{\perp Env})$, which is defined as $\mathcal{P}[\![\tilde{P}]\!]^\rho_\sigma(\tilde{f}(x_1 \ldots x_n)) := \mathcal{E}[\![\tilde{E}]\!]^\rho_\sigma$ for each function symbol $\tilde{f}$ defined in $\tilde{P}$ such that $\tilde{f}(x_1 \ldots x_n) = \tilde{E} \in \tilde{P}$. The least fixed point of $\mathcal{P}$ is guaranteed to exist from the Knaster-Tarski Fixpoint theorem [7]. In fact, it is easy to see that $(\mathbb{C}, \subseteq, \cup, \cap, \mathbf{C}, \varnothing)$ is a complete lattice and $\mathcal{P}$ is monotonic over $\mathbb{C}$, since at each iteration new conditional error bounds are added but not removed. When the program terminates in a finite number of steps for any possible input, this fixpoint computation converges in a finite number of steps. While this is a restrictive assumption in general, it is not unreasonable in avionics or embedded software, which tends to avoid recursion. However, in the future, the use of precise widening operators [8] on abstractions of this semantics will be explored in order to ensure the convergence for a wider variety of programs.

The semantics presented in this section allows for a static analysis that is compositional and parametric with respect to the functions used to approximate the round-off error of the arithmetic operations. Indeed, any floating-point operation $\widetilde{op}$ can be supported by this analysis, as long as an approximation error function $\varepsilon_{\widetilde{op}}$ satisfying Formula (4) is provided.

4   PRECiSA

PRECiSA (Program Round-off Error Certifier via Static Analysis) is a prototype implementation of the static analysis proposed in Sect. 3. PRECiSA accepts as input a floating-point program in the grammar defined in Sect. 3 and automatically generates an estimation of the floating-point round-off error together with proof certificates in PVS ensuring this estimation is correct.

Figure 1 depicts the functional architecture of PRECiSA. Given an input program, its semantics as defined in Sect. 3 is computed. This semantics is instantiated with the error approximation functions of the floating-operators from Sect. 2. Additionally, in order to improve the precision, PRECiSA distinguishes special cases in which the error estimation can be refined depending on the input. These cases include the subtraction $x \mathbin{\tilde{-}} y$ when $y\,/\,2 \leq x \leq 2 \mathbin{\tilde{*}} y$, and the multiplication for a non-negative power of 2, which can be computed exactly.

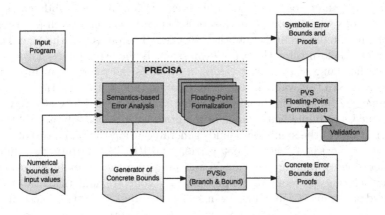

Fig. 1. PRECiSA architecture.

For each function $\tilde{f}$ in the input program, a set of conditional error bounds is generated. Each conditional error bound, corresponding to a possible computational flow of $\tilde{f}$, is then translated into a PVS lemma stating that, provided the conditions are satisfied, the floating-point value resulting from the execution of $\tilde{f}$ on floating-point values differs from the exact real-number computation by at most the round-off error approximation computed by the semantics. The translation of a conditional error bound $(\eta, \tilde{\eta}, r, e, \pi)$ into a PVS lemma is straightforward. The hypotheses of the lemma are η and $\tilde{\eta}$. The conclusion states that the difference between r and the output of $\tilde{f}$ using floating-point arithmetic is at most e. Since proving lemmas in PVS can be a tedious task and it often requires a high level of expertise, PRECiSA generates the proof script corresponding to each generated PVS lemma from the symbolic proof π.

PRECiSA computes round-off errors in symbolic form so that the analysis is modular and independent from the initial values of the input variables. As explained above, PRECiSA translates this symbolic information into PVS lemmas and proofs. Additionally, given some initial ranges for the input variables, PRECiSA computes concrete numerical estimations of these symbolic error expressions. Furthermore, it also generates PVS lemmas (and proof scripts) stating the correctness of such concrete bounds, and an additional lemma assuring the overall concrete round-off error of the function, independently from the chosen computational flow.

In order to compute the concrete numerical bounds, the branch-and-bound algorithm presented in [9] has been enhanced to support the symbolic error expressions produced by PRECiSA. This branch-and-bound algorithm relies on a parametric enclosure method for computing provably correct approximations of real-valued arithmetic expressions. PRECiSA currently uses interval arithmetic, but other enclosure methods such as Bernstein polynomials and affine arithmetic can be used since they are already defined in PVS [10,11]. The algorithm recursively splits the domain of the function into smaller subdomains and computes an enclosure of the original expression in these subdomains. The recursion stops when a precise enclosure is found, based on a given precision, or when the maximum recursion depth is reached. The output of the algorithm is a numerical enclosure for the error expression. If the error expression is undefined for the range of the input values, e.g., when the range of an input value includes zero and that value is used in a division, the algorithm returns an error. This enhanced branch-and-bound algorithm is specified and formally verified in PVS. Hence, the numerical bounds of the error expressions are provably sound concretizations of the symbolic bounds generated using the semantics of Sect. 3.

As shown in Fig. 1, the current version of PRECiSA outputs two different PVS files: one containing the lemmas and proofs on the symbolic error bounds and one including the lemmas and proofs on the concrete numerical error bounds computed assuming specific initial ranges for the input variables. These files can be automatically discharged in PVS with no user intervention.

The rest of this section illustrates the use of PRECiSA in the formal analysis of the Compact Position Reporting (CPR) algorithm, which is part of the Automatic Dependent Surveillance Broadcast (ADS-B) protocol. This protocol, which is a safety-critical component of advanced air traffic operational concepts, ensures that every aircraft automatically and periodically broadcast its current position and velocity vectors to nearby aircrafts and ground stations. The CPR algorithm is used to encode and decode the aircraft position (latitude and longitude). The standard organizations responsible for this protocol (RTCA in the US and EUROCAE in Europe) are currently studying reports of numerical stability issues in CPR. As part of the work presented in this paper, the authors have confirmed that under some circumstances, CPR may report incorrect aircraft positions that are several miles off of the actual position.

The CPR decoding function $rLat$ is presented below. This function recovers the current latitude of the aircraft starting from the received encoded latitude YZ and a given reference latitude $LatS$ (in degrees). The reference latitude, in general, corresponds to a previously decoded latitude.

$$j(LatS, \text{YZ}) = \widetilde{floor}((LatS \mathbin{\tilde{/}}(360 \mathbin{\tilde{/}} 59) \mathbin{\tilde{-}}(\text{YZ} \mathbin{\tilde{/}} 131072)) \mathbin{\tilde{+}} 0.5) \tag{14}$$

$$rLat(LatS, \text{YZ}) = 360 \mathbin{\tilde{/}} 59 \mathbin{\tilde{*}}(j(LatS, \text{YZ}) \mathbin{\tilde{+}}(\text{YZ} \mathbin{\tilde{/}} 131072)) \tag{15}$$

PRECiSA is able to differentiate the cases in which the accumulated error in the argument of the floating-point floor operation is large enough to make its result different from the ideal result for at least one unit. In cases where the accumulated error does not affect the result of the floor, PRECiSA computes a round-off error of 6.547117×10^{-14} on $rLat$ assuming double precision floating-point arithmetic and the following ranges for the inputs: $LatS \in [-90, 90]$ and $YZ \in [0, 131071]$. The symbolic bound is generated in 0.18 s and the concrete value is computed in 1.31 s. For these cases, it can be proved that the latitude decoded by the double precision floating-point procedure corresponds to its ideal definition.

On the contrary, when the accumulated error affects the result of the floor, PRECiSA computes an error bound of ≈ 6.1, which corresponds to several hundred nautical miles off with respect to the original position. The characterization of the input values to CPR that cause the floor operation to be unstable is still a matter of research.

5   Experimental Results

In this section, PRECiSA is compared in terms of accuracy and performance with the following floating-point analysis tools: Gappa (ver. 1.3.1) [12], Fluctuat (ver. 3.1376) [13], FPTaylor (ver. 0.9) [14] and Real2Float [15] (see Sect. 6 for a description of each tool). This comparison was performed using benchmarks taken from the FPTaylor repository. The selected benchmarks involve nonlinear expressions and polynomial approximations of functions, taken from well-known equations used in physics, control theory, and biological modeling. The experimental environment consisted of a 2.5 GHz Intel Core i7-4710MQ with 24 GB of RAM, running under Ubuntu 16.04 LTS. The benchmarks presented in this section and the corresponding PVS certificates are available as part of the PRECiSA distribution.

Table 1 shows the round-off error bounds computed by the aforementioned tools. Since FPTaylor offers two different modes for the analysis, only the best estimation obtained with either mode is reported in the table. Gappa and Fluctuat allow the user to manually provide hints to obtain tighter error bounds. However, for the sake of uniformity in the comparison, the table only shows error estimations that are fully automatically computed. For the same reason, for all examples and tools, input variables and constants are assumed to be real numbers. This means that they carry a round-off error that has to be taken into consideration in the analysis.

It can be seen in Table 1 that FPTaylor and PRECiSA produce more tight results than the other approaches. This is probably because both tools use accurate symbolic error expressions and optimization techniques to compute the numerical error bounds.

Table 1. Experimental results for absolute round-off error bounds (**bold** indicates the best approximation, *italic* indicates the second best.)

	Gappa	Fluctuat	Real2Float	FPTaylor	PRECiSA
carbonGas	2.61e−08	4.51e−08	2.21e−08	*8.06e−09*	**7.32e−09**
verhulst	4.18e−16	5.51e−16	4.66e−16	**2.47e−16**	*2.91e−16*
predPrey	2.04e−16	2.49e−16	2.51e−16	**1.59e−16**	*1.77e−16*
rigidBody1	**2.95e−13**	*3.22e−13*	5.33e−13	**2.95e−13**	**2.95e−13**
rigidBody2	*3.61e−11*	3.65e−11	6.48e−11	*3.61e−11*	**3.60e−11**
doppler1	2.02e−13	3.90e−13	7.65e−12	**1.58e−13**	*1.99e−13*
doppler2	3.92e−13	9.75e−13	1.57e−11	**2.89e−13**	*3.83e−13*
doppler3	1.08e−13	1.57e−13	8.59e−12	**6.62e−14**	*1.05e−13*
turbine1	8.40e−14	9.20e−14	2.46e−11	**1.67e−14**	*2.33e−14*
turbine2	1.28e−13	1.29e−13	2.07e−12	**1.95e−14**	*3.07e−14*
turbine3	3.99e+01	6.99e−14	1.70e−11	**9.64e−15**	*1.72e−14*
sqroot	5.71e−16	6.83E−16	1.28e−15	*5.02e−16*	**4.29e−16**
sine	1.13e−15	7.97E−16	6.03e−16	**4.43e−16**	*5.96e−16*
sineOrder3	*8.89e−16*	1.15E−15	1.19e−15	**5.94e−16**	1.11e−15

The times for the computation of the bounds in Table 1 are shown in Table 2.[4] It can be noticed that Gappa and Fluctuat are the fastest approaches. However, Gappa sometimes produces too coarse over-estimates (see for example turbine3 in Table 1) presumably because it uses interval arithmetic to compute the bounds. Unlike the other tools considered here, Fluctuat does not produce certificates for the soundness of its results.

PRECiSA, FPTaylor, and Real2Float show similar performance in half of the cases. However, in the other half, PRECiSA takes much longer in computing the bounds. This difference in the performance may be due to the fact that the calculation of the concrete bounds is performed inside the theorem prover. Conversely, the rest of the tools use specific developments that allow them to perform more efficiently. A possible enhancement for PRECiSA is to use a more performant tool to compute the bounds such as the Kodiak solver [16], a C++ implementation of the same branch and bound algorithm used by PRECiSA.

6   Related Work

Diverse techniques to estimate round-off error of floating-point computations can be found in the literature. Fluctuat [13] is a commercial analyzer that accepts as

---

[4] Times for PRECiSA do not include type-checking of the PVS formalization, which takes approximately 4 min. However, this type-checking only occurs once at the beginning of the same PVS session used to compute all the bounds in Table 1.

Table 2. Times in seconds for the generation of round-off error bounds. For PRECiSA the parameters used for the branch-and-bound search are shown next to the time in seconds as the pair (max depth, precision).

	Gappa	Fluctuat	Real2Float	FPTaylor	PRECiSA
carbonGas	0.152	0.025	0.815	1.209	3.830 (5, 10^{-9})
verhulst	0.034	0.043	0.465	0.812	0.789 (3, 10^{-17})
predPrey	0.052	0.031	0.735	0.916	0.477 (1, 10^{-17})
rigidBody1	0.086	0.029	0.494	0.877	0.653 (1, 10^{-12})
rigidBody2	0.112	0.024	0.287	1.115	0.565 (1, 10^{-7})
doppler1	0.057	0.025	5.998	3.026	107.696 (12, 10^{-14})
doppler2	0.069	0.029	5.993	3.008	26.520 (10, 10^{-13})
doppler3	0.063	0.029	5.970	21.927	45.875 (10, 10^{-14})
turbine1	0.165	0.028	67.960	2.906	110.272 (14, 10^{-15})
turbine2	0.100	0.026	3.972	1.939	7.145 (5, 10^{-14})
turbine3	0.130	0.026	67.460	3.430	351.022 (18, 10^{-16})
sqroot	0.281	0.024	0.712	1.157	0.343 (1, 10^{-14})
sine	0.145	0.025	0.948	1.296	6.023 (5, 10^{-17})
sineOrder3	0.114	0.026	0.304	0.847	1.616 (6, 10^{-17})

input a C (or ADA) program with annotations about input ranges and uncertainties, and produces bounds for the round-off error of the program expressions decomposed with respect to its provenance. Fluctuat provides support for iterative programs and unstable tests. It uses a zonotopic abstract domain [17] that is based on affine arithmetic. The prototype implementation presented in this paper is not competitive with Fluctuat in terms of speed. However, PRECiSA, which is publicly available under NASA's Open Source Agreement, provides a formal proof certificate of the correctness of the computed error estimation. The experimental evaluation shows that, for the considered benchmarks, both Fluctuat and PRECiSA provide similar results in terms of accuracy.

The tool FPTaylor [14] uses symbolic Taylor expansions to approximate floating-point expressions and applies a global optimization technique to obtain tight bounds for round-off errors. In addition, FPTaylor emits certificates for HOL Light [18], similarly to PRECiSA. Because of the technique used by FPTaylor, it is restricted to smooth functions. Therefore, it is not able to deal with non-derivable functions such as absolute value or floor, which are used, for example, in the CPR algorithm considered in Sect. 4. Unlike PRECiSA, which targets programs with conditional and function calls, FPTaylor is designed to analyze arithmetic expressions.

VCFloat [19] is a tool that automatically computes round-off error terms for numerical C expressions along with their correctness proof in Coq. This tool uses interval arithmetic to approximate the error bounds and generates validity conditions on the expressions. VCFloat computes the ulp by using the maximum exponent allowed in the floating-point representation, while PRECiSA computes the actual exponent for the maximum absolute value in the expression bounds, leading to more accurate estimations.

Real2Float[15] computes certified bounds for round-off errors by using an optimization technique employing semidefinite programming and sum of square certificates. Real2Float handles the ulp in the same way as VCFloat, which can result in coarser error approximations.

Gappa [12] computes enclosures for floating-point expressions via interval arithmetic. This enclosure method enables a quick computation of the bounds, but sometimes it can result in pessimistic error estimations. This tool also generates a proof of the results that can be checked in the Coq proof assistant. In Gappa, the bound computation, the certification construction, and their verification may require hints from the user. Thus, some level of expertise is required, unlike PRECiSA which is fully automatic.

Rosa [20] automatically compiles an ideal real number program to a floating-point one with the aim of minimizing the overall round-off error. In the same line, FPTuner [21] implements a rigorous approach to precision allocation supporting also mixed-precision.

7   Conclusion

In this paper, a static analysis technique for estimating floating-point round-off errors is presented. The analysis enables the automatic generation of formal proof certificates of the correctness of such estimations. The analysis enjoys several useful features. It is defined in a compositional way, which allows for an incremental, modular, and efficient treatment of the program being analyzed. It is fully automatic, thus no human intervention is required to generate and formally verify the error estimations. The technique supports the generation of formal certificates that can be checked by an external tool. The proposed static analysis is sound with respect to unstable conditions. In the literature, the *stable test hypothesis* is widely used to deal with this problem. However, this hypothesis may yield unsound results when the real flow does not correspond to the floating-point one. To the best of the authors' knowledge, the only other techniques that are sound with respect to unstable tests are the one presented in [22] for the Fluctuat analyzer and Rosa [20]. The proposed analysis is parametric with respect to floating-point precision and rounding mode. Finally, it can be extended with any floating-point operator provided the existence of a round-off error estimation that satisfies some basic properties.

The proposed technique is implemented in the prototype tool PRECiSA. PRECiSA is fully automatic and generates PVS certificates that guarantee the correctness of the error bounds with respect to the floating-point IEEE-754 standard. Furthermore, given concrete ranges for the input variables of a program, the numerical estimations computed by PRECiSA are provably sound over-approximations of the possible round-off error that can occur in the program.

The current implementation of PRECiSA supports single and double-precision floating-point formats and provides all the to-the-nearest rounding modalities introduced in the IEEE-754 standard. In the implementation of PRECiSA, the semantics-based analysis and the PVS floating-point formalization are completely independent from the numerical evaluation of the error expression. This means that different techniques can be used for the concrete bound estimation depending on the expression type and on the desired precision/efficiency trade-off. Currently, PRECiSA uses a branch-and-bound algorithm based on interval arithmetic. Preliminary experimental results are encouraging for the applicability of PRECiSA in the formal verification of software of interest to NASA.

The floating-point round-off error formalization presented in this paper is available as part of the NASA PVS Library (https://github.com/nasa/pvslib). It consists of more than 150 PVS theories and several new proof strategies. Although the framework can be implemented in any modern proof assistant, the choice of PVS for this research project is convenient for the following reasons. First, PVS is used in the verification and validation of algorithms and concepts developed under NASA's Safe Autonomous Systems Operations (SASO) Project such as separation assurance algorithms for unmanned aircraft systems [23]. These algorithms, which involve critical numerical computations, are used as test cases for the framework and tool proposed here. Second, the NASA PVS Library includes independently developed hardware-level [4] and high-level [5] formalizations of floating-point arithmetic, which are proved to be equivalent. The latter formalization is used and extended in this paper. Third, the NASA PVS Library also includes several formalizations of enclosure methods such as interval arithmetic [24], Bernstein polynomial basis [11], and affine arithmetic [10], which can be easily integrated in PRECiSA for computing concrete bounds of round-off errors. Finally, because of the automation support provided by PVS, no expertise in theorem proving is actually required to use the formalization presented in this paper.

The main drawback of the proposed approach is that it can generate large certificates for programs with nested conditionals. In fact, the number of conditional error bounds may grow exponentially in some cases due to the unstable tests handling (four different conditional error bounds may be generated for each conditional). In order to deal with this problem, an abstract semantics collapsing conditional error bounds produced after a given depth is being defined and will be integrated into PRECiSA in the near future. In this way, the number of elements in the semantics is reduced and consequently also the size of the generated proof certificate. Alternatively, the stable test hypothesis can be optionally enabled by the user in order to reduce the number of generated lemmas as done in most tools, although this may come at the cost of soundness. The support of recursion and loops will also be considered by defining abstractions on the domain of conditional error bounds and widening operators on these domains. Another future direction is the automatic generation of ACSL annotations related to round-off errors of C programs. The annotated program could then be automatically verified in a tool like Frama-C [25].

Acknowledgments. Research by the first two authors was supported by the National Aeronautics and Space Administration under NASA/NIA Cooperative Agreement NNL09AA00A.

References

1. de Figueiredo, L.H., Stolfi, J.: Affine arithmetic: concepts and applications. Numer. Algorithms **37**(1–4), 147–158 (2004)
2. Lorentz, G.G.: Bernstein Polynomials. Chelsea Publishing Company, London (1986)
3. Owre, S., Rushby, J.M., Shankar, N.: PVS: a prototype verification system. In: Kapur, D. (ed.) CADE 1992. LNCS, vol. 607, pp. 748–752. Springer, Heidelberg (1992). doi:10.1007/3-540-55602-8_217
4. Miner, P.: Defining the IEEE-854 floating-point standard in PVS. Technical report TM-1995-110167, NASA (1995)
5. Boldo, S., Muñoz, C.: A high-level formalization of floating-point numbers in PVS. Technical report CR-2006-214298, NASA (2006)
6. Harrison, J.: A machine-checked theory of floating point arithmetic. In: Bertot, Y., Dowek, G., Théry, L., Hirschowitz, A., Paulin, C. (eds.) TPHOLs 1999. LNCS, vol. 1690, pp. 113–130. Springer, Heidelberg (1999). doi:10.1007/3-540-48256-3_9
7. Tarski, A.: A lattice-theoretical fixpoint theorem and its applications. Pac. J. Math. **5**, 285–309 (1955)
8. Cousot, P., Cousot, R.: Abstract interpretation: a unified lattice model for static analysis of programs by construction or approximation of fixpoints. In: Proceedings of POPL 1977, pp. 238–252. ACM (1977)
9. Narkawicz, A., Muñoz, C.: A formally verified generic branching algorithm for global optimization. In: Cohen, E., Rybalchenko, A. (eds.) VSTTE 2013. LNCS, vol. 8164, pp. 326–343. Springer, Heidelberg (2014). doi:10.1007/978-3-642-54108-7_17
10. Moscato, M.M., Muñoz, C.A., Smith, A.P.: Affine arithmetic and applications to real-number proving. In: Urban, C., Zhang, X. (eds.) ITP 2015. LNCS, vol. 9236, pp. 294–309. Springer, Cham (2015). doi:10.1007/978-3-319-22102-1_20
11. Muñoz, C., Narkawicz, A.: Formalization of a representation of Bernstein polynomials and applications to global optimization. J. Autom. Reason. **51**(2), 151–196 (2013)
12. de Dinechin, F., Lauter, C., Melquiond, G.: Certifying the floating-point implementation of an elementary function using Gappa. IEEE Trans. Comput. **60**(2), 242–253 (2011)
13. Goubault, E., Putot, S.: Static analysis of numerical algorithms. In: Yi, K. (ed.) SAS 2006. LNCS, vol. 4134, pp. 18–34. Springer, Heidelberg (2006). doi:10.1007/11823230_3
14. Solovyev, A., Jacobsen, C., Rakamarić, Z., Gopalakrishnan, G.: Rigorous estimation of floating-point round-off errors with symbolic Taylor expansions. In: Bjørner, N., de Boer, F. (eds.) FM 2015. LNCS, vol. 9109, pp. 532–550. Springer, Cham (2015). doi:10.1007/978-3-319-19249-9_33
15. Magron, V., Constantinides, G., Donaldson, A.: Certified roundoff error bounds using semi definite programming. CoRR abs/1507.03331 (2015)
16. Smith, A., Muñoz, C., Narkawicz, A., Markevicius, M.: A rigorous generic branch and bound solver for nonlinear problems. In: Proceedings of SYNASC 2015. IEEE Computer Society Conference Publishing Services, September 2015

17. Goubault, E., Putot, S.: Static analysis of finite precision computations. In: Jhala, R., Schmidt, D. (eds.) VMCAI 2011. LNCS, vol. 6538, pp. 232–247. Springer, Heidelberg (2011). doi:10.1007/978-3-642-18275-4_17

18. Harrison, J.: HOL light: an overview. In: Berghofer, S., Nipkow, T., Urban, C., Wenzel, M. (eds.) TPHOLs 2009. LNCS, vol. 5674, pp. 60–66. Springer, Heidelberg (2009). doi:10.1007/978-3-642-03359-9_4

19. Ramananandro, T., Mountcastle, P., Meister, B., Lethin, R.: A unified COQ framework for verifying C programs with floating-point computations. In: Proceedings of CPP 2016, pp. 15–26. ACM (2016)

20. Darulova, E., Kuncak, V.: Sound compilation of reals. In: Proceedings of POPL 2014, pp. 235–248. ACM (2014)

21. Chiang, W., Baranowski, M., Briggs, I., Solovyev, A., Gopalakrishnan, G., Rakamarić, Z.: Rigorous floating-point mixed-precision tuning. In: Proceedings of POPL 2017, pp. 300–315. ACM (2017)

22. Goubault, E., Putot, S.: Robustness analysis of finite precision implementations. In: Shan, C. (ed.) APLAS 2013. LNCS, vol. 8301, pp. 50–57. Springer, Cham (2013). doi:10.1007/978-3-319-03542-0_4

23. Muñoz, C., Dutle, A., Narkawicz, A., Upchurch, J.: Unmanned aircraft systems in the national airspace system: a formal methods perspective. ACM SIGLOG News **3**(3), 67–76 (2016)

24. Daumas, M., Lester, D.R., Muñoz, C.: Verified real number calculations: a library for interval arithmetic. IEEE Trans. Comput. **58**(2), 226–237 (2009)

25. Kirchner, F., Kosmatov, N., Prevosto, V., Signoles, J., Yakobowski, B.: Frama-c: a software analysis perspective. Formal Asp. Comp. **27**(3), 573–609 (2015)

Classification Tree Method
with Parameter Shielding

Takashi Kitamura[1]([✉]), Akihisa Yamada[2], Goro Hatayama[3], Shinya Sakuragi[3],
Eun-Hye Choi[1], and Cyrille Artho[4]

[1] National Institute of Advanced Industrial Science and Technology (AIST),
Osaka, Japan
{t.kitamura,e.choi}@aist.go.jp
[2] Innsbruck University, Innsbruck, Austria
akihisa.yamada@uibk.ac.at
[3] Omron Social Solutions Co., Ltd., Kyoto, Japan
{goro_hatayama,shinya_sakuragi}@oss.omron.co.jp
[4] KTH Royal Institute of Technology, Stockholm, Sweden
artho@kth.se

Abstract. The Classification Tree Method (CTM) is a structured and
diagrammatic modeling technique for combinatorial testing. CTM can
express the notion of *"parameter shielding"*, the phenomenon that some
system parameters become invalidated depending on another system
parameter. The current form of CTM, however, is limited in its expressiveness: it can only express parameter shielding that depends on a single
parameter. In this paper, we extend CTM with parameter shielding that
depends on multiple parameters, proposing CTM$_{shield}$. We evaluate the
proposed extension on several industrial systems. The evaluation finds
that parameter shielding often depends on multiple parameters in real
systems, and the effectiveness of the extension.

1 Introduction

Testing is an important and often a necessary system development process for
assuring system quality in current industrial practice. *Combinatorial testing* is a
system testing technique, that effectively tests the interactions of parameters in
a system under test. Combinatorial testing derives, typically from specification,
a test model, which consists of a list of parameter-values and *constraints* over
them. Based on such test models, test suites are designed, that consider various
coverage criteria, such as t-way testing [1,2].

Figure 1 shows an example test model, which specifies an IC card system with
six parameters, each having two to three values: the *Age* of the card owner, the
Balance that is already charged in the card, whether *Credit Card (C.C.)* information is available or not, the *Charge Method (C.M.)* and *Charge Amount (C.A.)*
the owner specifies to the system, and the *Monthly Total (M.T.)* amount of
usage. The model also indicates *constraints* in logic formula, specifying *valid*
(and *invalid*) value combinations. The two constraints in the example model
specify the following specifications:

© Springer International Publishing AG 2017
S. Tonetta et al. (Eds.): SAFECOMP 2017, LNCS 10488, pp. 230–241, 2017.
DOI: 10.1007/978-3-319-66266-4_15

PARAMETERS	VALUES	CONSTRAINTS
Age	child, adult, senior	$\neg(C.C. = \text{with} \wedge Age = \text{child})$
Balance	>190€, ≤190€	$(C.M. = \text{c.c.} \Rightarrow C.C. = \text{with})$
Credit Card (C.C.)	with, without (w/o)	
Charge Method (C.M.)	cash, credit card (c.c.)	
Charge Amount (C.A.)	10€, 50€	
Monthly Total (M.T.)	>390€, ≤390€	

Fig. 1. A test model example for an IC card system; it consists of a parameter-values list (left) and a set of constraints (right).

- "An IC card owned by a child cannot have *Credit Card* information."
- "The *Charge Method* can be by credit card only if a *Credit Card* information is available."

Table 1 shows, as a test suite example, a 2-way test suite of the test model.

Table 1. A 2-way test suite for the test model of Fig. 1, which covers all valid value pairs but avoids invalid ones, e.g. $\langle C.C.=with,\ Age=child \rangle$, specified by the constraints.

No.	Age	Balance	C.C.	M.T.	C.M.	C.A.
1	child	>190€	w/o	≤390€	cash	10€
2	child	≤190€	w/o	>390€	cash	50€
3	adult	>190€	w/o	≤390€	cash	50€
4	adult	≤190€	with	>390€	c.c	10€
5	senior	>190€	with	≤390€	c.c	50€
6	senior	≤190€	w/o	≤390€	cash	50€
7	senior	>190€	with	>390€	cash	10€

A key challenge in applying combinatorial testing in real-world development is modeling, a. k. a. Input Parameter Modeling [2] or Input Domain Modeling [3]. Models in real-world systems often involve complex constraints on parameter-values. This makes modeling a time-consuming and error-prone task that requires experience and creativity of test experts.

Classification Tree Method (CTM) [4–6] is a structured and diagrammatic approach for the modeling problem. The main characteristic of CTM is that, using a tree-structured modeling language called *Classification Trees (CTs)*, is to be able to describe the notion of "Parameter shielding" concisely, which is a phenomenon that some parameters become invalided (i.e., *shielded*) if some specific values are (or are not) assigned to another parameter.

Suppose, for instance, the following specification SPEC1 is added to the system:

SPEC1: "Charging is allowed only if the *Balance* is below 190€."

Figure 2 shows a CTM model that expresses this specification using a tree structure. The tree structure expresses not only that (1) the relation between parameters and values, but also (2) *compositions* of parameters and (3) parameter shielding. The rounded rectangle node *Charge* combines *Charge Method* and *Charge Amount* of the previous example, and appears under value ≤190€ of *Balance*. This expresses that the two parameters become valid only when the *Balance* is below 190€, and become *invalid* (shielded) otherwise. Table 2 shows a 2-way test suite for the CTM model. Note that some parameters are assigned the *vain* value "—" when they are invalid. Note also that the test suite of Table 1 is not a valid 2-way test suite for the current model anymore, since, e.g., test case No. 1 in Table 1 is not executable under SPEC1.

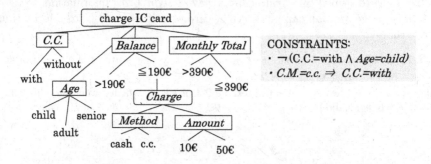

Fig. 2. A CTM test model for the IC card system that expresses SPEC1.

Table 2. A 2-way test suite for the model of Fig. 2 under SPEC1, where parameters *C.M.* and *C.A.* are shielded (as assigned the vain value '—') when *Balance* is >190€.

No.	Age	Balance	C.C.	M.T.	C.M.	C.A.
1	child	≤190€	w/o	≤390€	cash	10€
2	child	≤190€	w/o	>390€	cash	50€
3	child	>190€	w/o	>390€	—	—
4	adult	≤190€	with	>390€	c.c	10€
5	adult	≤190€	w/o	≤390€	cash	50€
6	adult	>190€	with	≤390€	—	—
7	senior	≤190€	with	>390€	cash	10€
8	senior	≤190€	with	≤390€	c.c	50€
9	senior	>190€	w/o	≤390€	—	—

Parameter shielding expressed in a tree structure is a unique and useful feature of CTM; however, its limitation is that it can only describe parameter shielding that depends on a single parameter-value. The reason is obvious: the dependencies of parameter shielding are expressed within the tree structure, and

Table 3. A valid 2-way test suite under SPEC2, where parameters *C.M.* and *C.A.* are shielded when either *Balance* is >190€ or *M.T.* is >390€.

No.	Age	Balance	C.C.	M.T.	C.M.	C.A.
1	child	≤190€	w/o	≤390€	cash	50€
2	child	≤190€	w/o	≤390€	cash	10€
3	child	>190€	w/o	>390€	—	—
4	adult	≤190€	with	≤390€	cash	10€
5	adult	≤190€	with	≤390€	c.c	50€
6	adult	>190€	with	≤390€	—	—
7	senior	≤190€	w/o	>390€	—	—
8	senior	≤190€	w/o	≤390€	c.c	50€
9	senior	≤190€	with	≤390€	cash	10€
10	senior	>190€	with	>390€	—	—

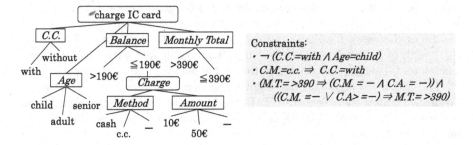

Fig. 3. A CTM test model for the IC card system uner SPEC2, which expresses a test model of the test suite in Table 3.

hence a parameter can only have one parent. In our case studies applying combinatorial testing and CTM to industrial systems, however, we often encountered a demand to express parameter shielding that depends on multiple parameter-values.

For instance, suppose SPEC1 is refined as in the following specification SPEC2:

> SPEC2: "Charging is allowed only if the *Balance* is below 190€ and *Monthly Total* usage is below 390€."

As the node *Charge* should be shielded depending on two (i.e., multiple) parameter-values, this is a typical example of the multi-dependent parameter shielding. Note this time that the test suite of Table 2 is not a valid 2-way test suite anymore, since, e.g., test case No. 2 is not executable under the refined specification SPEC2. A valid 2-way test suite under SPEC2 is as shown in Table 3. Further, it is now difficult to model SPEC2 concisely in CTM. The reason is, as explained, a tree node cannot have multiple parents.

A possible solution that CTM can do is to explicitly handle the vain values and complex constraints involving them as in Fig. 3. However, we assume such manipulations on test models makes themselves too complex and busy, losing conciseness, for engineers to creates and maintain, especially in dealing with industrial-scaled large systems.

In this paper, we propose CTM_{shield}, by extending CTM with parameter shielding that can depend on multiple parameter-values, or more generally an arbitrary logic formula. Figure 4 shows the basic idea of the extension, by showing an test model example in CTM_{shield} which expresses SPEC2. Observe that CTM_{shield} is extended with the additional description called *(parameter) shielding conditions*. Observe also that the shielding condition in Fig. 4 specifies SPEC2 directly, using the notation "$P \leftarrow_{shield} V$" to mean parameter-value V shields parameter P. In such a way, we aim to avoid explicitly handling the vain values and complex constraints to express parameter shielding, and thus to retain test models concise and readable. To evaluate the effectiveness of the proposed extension, we conduct experiments via case studies, where we applied combinatorial testing to test industrial systems in the railway domain, using CTM_{shield}. As summary, the experimental results showed that parameter shielding was used in 72% of the cases; CTM_{shield} was able to reduce the tree size by 7.13% and the length of constraints by 22.9% on average, compared with CTM of [7,8]. Therefore, CTM_{shield} contributes to saving human effort on modeling.

The paper is organized as follows. Section 2 mentions related studies. Section 3 clarifies the design of CTM_{shield}. Section 4 reports our experimental study to evaluate the effectiveness of the proposed extension. Section 5 states our plan for future work.

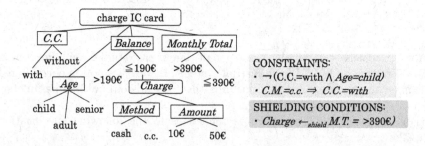

Fig. 4. A CTM_{shield} test model that expresses SPEC2 and hence is a test model of the test suite in Table 3.

2   Related Work

CTM has been recognized as a key technique in the field of combinatorial testing [2], and has been studied on various aspects. For example, Lehmann and Wegener [5] introduced constraints to the original CTM [7] to extend its expressiveness. Prioritizing test cases was studied for effective test design in the setting of CTM [6]. A test generation algorithm dedicated to CTM was developed in [8]. Also, experimental data in [8] indicate that the structured aspect of CTM reduces the lengths of constraints to be described. For industrial aspects, CTM has been used in industries of safety-critical domains: e. g., it is used in a standard test documentation in automotive industry [9]. Driven by industrial demand, tools to support CTM have been developed by several vendors [10].

The notion of parameter shielding in combinatorial testing has been studied in several different approaches. To our knowledge, the earliest work that is relevant for CTM is by Grochtmann [4]; however, its focus does not seem on parameter shielding but on diagrammatic approaches, as the phenomenon of parameter shielding was not mentioned. Chen et al. [11] first clarified and defined the notion of parameter shielding in the setting of Covering Arrays. which considers only unconstrained and unstructured models. They provided test generation algorithms for this special kind of Covering Arrays. Segall et al. take yet another approach of "common patterns" [12]. They identified several recurring properties in modeling as patterns, which are often hard to capture correctly, and supply solutions for them. The notion of parameter shielding is captured by one of their patterns, called "Conditionally-Excluded-Values" pattern. Zhao et al. developed a test generation tool of combinatorial testing, called CASCADE, which can handle shielding parameters explicitly [13] and its handling mechanism is basically same as the proposed solution in [12].

Our work differs from these works in that our contributions are to propose a modeling language by extending CTM with parameter shielding to advance CTM and evaluate its effectiveness via case studies.

3   Classification Tree Method with Parameter Shielding

This section proposes the modeling language CTM_{shield}, which extends CTM with the notion of parameter shielding. To be conscious about the extension, we first define the language for combinatorial testing, next that for CTM, and finally that for CTM_{shield}.

The definition of combinatorial testing, whose example is in Fig. 1, is as follows:

Definition 1 (Combinatorial testing). *A combinatorial testing model is a tuple $m = \langle P, V, \Phi \rangle$, where P is a set of* parameters, $V = \{V_p\}_{p \in P}$ *is a family of parameter-values, where V_p is the value domain of p, and constraints Φ are a set of Boolean formula over parameter-values.*

A *test case* is a value assignment to parameters in test model m. Formally, it can be defined as a function $\gamma : P \to V$ such that $\gamma(p) \in V_p$ for every $p \in P$. Note that a test case γ must satisfy all the constraints Φ (noted as $\forall \phi \in \Phi . \gamma \models \phi$ or $\gamma \models \Phi$).

A CTM test model consists of a *Classification Tree (CT)* and constraints. A CT consists of three kinds of nodes: *classifications*, which correspond to parameters in combinatorial testing; *classes*, which correspond to values; and *compositions*, a notion that does not appear in combinatorial testing.

Definition 2 (CTM). *A test model of CTM is a tuple* $m = \langle r, P, V, C, \uparrow, \Phi \rangle \in M$*, where* $\langle P, V, \Phi \rangle$ *forms a test model of combinatorial testing,* C *is a set of compositions,* $r \in C$ *is a root node, and* $\uparrow$ *is a function from* $P \cup C \backslash \{r\}$ *to* $V \cup C$ *that expresses a part of the child-parent relation of the tree structure of CT.*

As some parameters are shielded and assigned the vain value "—", a *test case* of CTM extends that of combinatorial testing as $\gamma : P \rightarrow \{-\} \cup V$, while inheriting $\gamma \models \Phi$. A parameter p is shielded, assigned "—", in a test case γ, if its nearest ancestor value is not chosen for the parameter in γ. For example, parameter $C.M.$ is shielded in test case No. 3 in Table 2, since its nearest ancestor value ">190€" is not chosen for the parameter $Balance$ in the test case.

Now, the definition of CTM$_{shield}$ is given as follows:

Definition 3 (CTM$_{shield}$). *A CTM$_{shield}$ model is a tuple* $m = \langle r, P, V, C, \uparrow, \Phi, \Phi_s \rangle \in M_s$*, where* $\langle r, P, V, C, \uparrow, \Phi \rangle$ *is a CTM model and* Φ_s *is a function from* $P \cup C$ *to Boolean formulas. We denote* $\Phi_s(n)$ *as the (parameter) shielding condition of* $n \in P \cup C$.

The definition of CTM$_{shield}$ extends that of CTM by the shielding conditions Φ_s. A test case of CTM$_{shield}$ also inherits that of CTM, including the condition of parameter shielding specified by the tree structure. Moreover, in CTM$_{shield}$ a parameter p in a test case is shielded by Φ_s when its shielding condition $\Phi_s(p)$ is satisfied by the test case.

In order to express Φ_s in practice, we take a list of pairs of form $p \leftarrow_{shields} \phi$ indicating that $\Phi_s(p) = \phi$, and assume $\Phi_s(q) = \text{FALSE}$ when q is not specified in the list. Note that a CTM model is a CTM$_{shield}$ model with an empty list of such specifications. Figure 4 is an example of CTM$_{shield}$, and Listing 1.1 shows a formulation of the test model in Fig. 4 according to Definition 3.

Listing 1.1. A formulation of the test model in Fig. 4 according to Definition 3.

```
1   r = { charge IC card (CICC)}
2   C= { Charge}
3   P = {C.C., Age, Balance, Method, Amount, Monthly Total (M.T.) }
4   V_C.C. = {with, without}, V_Amount = {10€, 50€}, V_Age = {child, adult, senior,
5   V_Balance = {>190€, ≤190€}, V_M.T. = {>390€, ≤990€ },
6   V_Method = {cash, c.c.}, V_C.A. = {10€, 50€},
7   ↑ = {(C.C., CICC), (Age, CICC), (Balance, CICC), (Charge, ≤190€), (Method, Charge),
8   (Amount, Charge)}
9   Φ = { ¬(C.C. = with ∧ Age = child), C.M. = c.c. ⇒ C.C = with }
10  Φ_s = { (>390€, Charge)}
```

4   Case Studies and Evaluations

This section reports our empirical studies to evaluate the effectiveness of the proposed extension, i.e., CTM$_{shield}$ extending CTM with parameter shielding, through case studies with industrial systems.

We determine the "effectiveness" of CTM$_{shield}$ by the conciseness of test models in CTM$_{shield}$ compared to those in CTM (the one dealt in [5,8]). More specifically, we measure the conciseness of models on their description complexity

Table 4. Summary of experimental results.

spec.	CTM_{shield} P/V	#N	$\|\Phi\|$	$l(\Phi)$	$\|\Phi_s\|$	$l(\Phi_s)$	CTM P/V	#N	$\|\Phi\|$	$l(\Phi)$	$\Delta^N_\%(\%)$	$\Delta^\Phi_\%(\%)$
e.g.1	$2^5 3^1$	22	3^2	6	3^1	3	$2^3 3^2 4^1$	24	$3^2 11^1$	17	8.3	47.1
A-1	$2^{14} 6^1$	58	3^3	9	4^2	8	$2^{10} 3^4 6^1$	62	$3^3 13^2$	35	6.3	51.4
A-2	$2^{15} 3^3 4^1 5^1$	76	3^2	6	4^1	4	$2^{14} 3^4 4^1 5^1$	77	$3^3 4^1$	13	1.3	23.1
A-3	$2^{23} 3^2$	93	3^8	24	$3^1 4^1$	7	$2^{18} 3^7$	98	$3^8 4^1 15^1$	43	5.1	27.9
A-4	$2^{19} 3^1 4^2$	103	3^4	12	4^3	12	$2^{15} 3^5 4^2$	107	$3^4 4^2 13^1$	33	3.7	27.3
A-6	2^{18}	71	3^8	24	4^6	24	$2^{10} 3^8$	79	$3^8 4^3 13^1 15^1$	64	10.0	25.0
A-5	$2^{19} 3^4 5^2 6^1 10^1$	112	3^{17}	51	4^4	16	$2^{16} 3^6 4^1 5^2 6^1 10^1$	116	$3^{17} 4^2 13^2$	85	3.4	21.2
A-8	$2^6 3^1$	27	0	0	4^2	8	$2^4 3^3$	29	4^2	8	6.7	0
A-7	$2^{17} 3^9 13^1 15^1 33^1$	159	0	0	4^7	28	$2^{12} 3^8 9^1 14^1 16^1 33^1$	169	4^7	28	4.1	0
A-9	$2^7 5^1$	36	3^4	12	3^1	3	$2^6 3^1 5^1$	37	3^5	15	2.6	0
A-10	$2^9 3^1$	39	3^1	3	5^1	5	$2^8 3^2$	40	$3^1 5^1$	8	2.4	0
A-11	$2^{10} 3$	46	3^1	3	4^1	4	$2^9 3^3$	47	$3^1 4^1$	7	2.1	0
A-12	$2^{37} 7^1$	139	3^4	12	4^3	12	$2^{34} 3^3 7^1$	142	$3^4 4^3$	24	2.1	0
A-13	$2^9 3^1$	31	0	0	0	0	$2^9 3^1$	31	0	0	0	0
A-14	$2^{16} 3^3$	67	0	0	0	0	$2^{16} 3^3$	67	0	0	0	0
A-15	$2^{10} 3^1$	42	0	0	0	0	$2^{10} 3^1$	42	0	0	0	0
A-16	$2^7 3^1$	25	0	0	0	0	$2^7 3^1$	25	0	0	0	0
A-17	$2^3 8^1$	23	0	0	0	0	$2^3 8^1$	23	0	0	0	0
A-18	2^3	17	0	0	0	0	2^3	17	0	0	0	0
A-19	2^{15}	58	0	0	0	0	2^{15}	58	0	0	0	0
										avg. of system A	4.2	14.7
B-1	$1^2 2^{17} 4^2$	65	$1^2 2^8 3^9 4^2$	0	4^5	20	$1^2 2^8 3^9 4^2$	87	$4^5 25^1 27^1$	72	10.2	72.2
B-2	$1^3 2^{43} 4^6$	165	$1^3 2^{16} 3^{27} 4^6$	0	$4^{17} 7^1$	75	$1^3 2^{16} 3^{27} 4^6$	220	$4^{15} 25^2 69^1$	179	12.2	58.1
B-3	$2^5 3^7$	43	$2^2 3^5 4^5$	18	4^4	16	$2^2 3^5 4^5$	58	$3^6 4^2 15^1 17^1$	58	13.6	41.4
B-4	$2^6 3^8$	50	$2^3 3^5 4^6$	27	4^5	20	$2^3 3^5 4^6$	63	$3^9 4^3 15^1 17^1$	71	14.1	33.8
B-5	$2^6 3^7 4^1$	51	$2^3 3^5 4^5 5^1$	33	4^5	20	$2^3 3^5 4^5 5^1$	64	$3^{11} 4^3 15^1 17^1$	77	13.8	31.2
B-6	2^{11}	33	$2^{10} 3^1$	0	4^1	4	$2^{10} 3^1$	49	4^1	4	2.0	0
										avg. of system B	11.0	39.4
										total avg.	7.13	22.9

in terms of the number of parameter-values and the length of constraints needed to describe the models. Our evaluation poses the following three research questions:

RQ1: How often is the parameter shielding condition used? What is its usage rate?

RQ2: How many tree nodes can CTM_{shield} reduce, compared with CTM?

RQ3: How much length of constraints can CTM_{shield} reduce, compared with CTM?

4.1 Setting

In the case studies, we applied combinatorial testing to functional testing of 25 system-level functions of the following two distinct industrial systems in railway domain, and in doing so we used CTM_{shield} for modeling the functions: 19 functions from a ticket gate system (system A) and 7 functions from a payment system (system B).

For comparison between CTM_{shield} and CTM, we also prepared test models in CTM. We prepare a program to translate test models in CTM_{shield} to equivalent ones in CTM; i.e., it handles complex manipulation of constraints and dummy nodes. For example, it inputs the CTM_{shield} test model in Fig. 4, and outputs the CTM test model in Fig. 3.

Next, we measure the following metrics of the test models in CTM_{shield} and CTM:

1. P/V: The size of parameter-values; this is expressed as $g_1^{k_1} g_2^{k_2} ... g_n^{k_n}$, which means that for each i there are k_i parameters that have g_i values, following [14, 15].
2. $\#N$: The number of nodes; this is the summation of the numbers of compositions, parameters, and values.
3. $l(\phi)$: The length of constraints ϕ, which is defined in a similar way as [16] as follows: $l(a) = 1$ for all atoms a, $l(\neg P) = 1 + l(P)$, and $l(P * Q) = 1 + l(P) + l(Q)$ where $*$ is a binary operator of $\wedge, \vee, \Rightarrow$, and $\Leftrightarrow$. E.g., $l(\underline{\neg_1 P_2 = v_{1_2} \vee_3 P_3 = v_{1_4}}) = 4$.

Since CTM_{shield} has an additional description component of parameter shielding conditions, we also measure the following two metrics for test models of CTM_{shield}:

4. $l(\Phi_s)$: The length of parameter shielding conditions Φ_s. As mentioned in Sect. 3 and exemplified in Fig. 4, a shielding condition is expressed using "$\leftarrow_{shield}$" in practice; e. g., "$P_1 \leftarrow_{shield} \neg P_2 = v_1 \vee P_3 = v_1$" to mean $\Phi_s(P_1) = \neg P_2 = v_1 \vee P_3 = v_2$", where P_1, P_2, P_3 expresses parameters and v_1 and v_2 values. Thus, we define the length of a shielding condition for parameter n by $l(\Phi_s(n)) + 2$, regarding $\leftarrow_{shield}$ as a binary operator. For example, $l(\Phi_s(P_1)) = l(\underline{\neg_1 P_2 = v_{1_2} \vee_3 P_3 = v_{1_4}}) + 2 = 6$
5. $|\Phi_s|$: The size of Φ_s in the form $1^{k_1} 2^{k_2} ... n^{k_i}$, which this time means there are k_i conditions whose length is n for each $n \in Nat$ while n^{k_i} are omitted if $k_i = 0$.

In order to quantitatively answer the research questions, from data about the test model of CTM (m_c) and that of CTM (m_s) for each function, we retrieve the following:

– the reduction rate of the number of nodes $\Delta_\%^N$:

$$\Delta_\%^N =: \frac{\#N^{m_c} - \#N^{m_s}}{\#N^{m_c}} \qquad (1)$$

– the reduction rate of constraint length $\Delta_\%^\Phi$:

$$\Delta_\%^\Phi =: \frac{l(\Phi^{m_c}) - (l(\Phi^{m_s}) + l(\Phi_s^{m_s}))}{l(\Phi^{m_c})} \qquad (2)$$

where $\#N^m$, $l(\Phi^m)$, and $l(\Phi_s^m)$ respectively mean the number of nodes, length of constraints, length of shielding conditions in test model m.

Note that $\Delta_\%^\Phi$ considers not only the length of constraints, but also the length of shielding conditions for test model in CTM_{shield} m_s. This is for a fair comparison. We expect (and will see) CTM_{shield} can in fact reduce the length of the constraints. However, this is achieved at the cost of describing the shielding conditions. To avoid such an unfair comparison, we designed in $\Delta_\%^\Phi$ to consider not only constraints length but also the length of shielding conditions in test models of CTM_{shield}.

4.2   Results and Observations

Table 4 summarizes the experimental results. The first column shows retrieved data from the test model example in CTM_{shield} in Fig. 4 and an equivalent test model in CTM in Fig. 3, whose main points are read as follows:

1. The CTM_{shield} test model in Fig. 4 has five parameters for two values and one parameter for three values, hence its P/V is expressed as $2^5 3^1$. On the other hand, the CTM test model in Fig. 3 has three parameters for two values, two for three values, and one for four values, hence its P/V is expressed as $2^3 3^2 4^1$.
2. The number of nodes in the CT in CTM is 24, while that in CTM_{shield} is 22. Thus, the number of nodes is reduced by 2 ($= 24 - 22$), and the node reduction rate ($\Delta_\%^N$) is 8.3%($= \frac{2}{24}$).
3. The constraint length of the CTM test model is 11, while that of CTM_{shield} is 6. We also take the description cost of shielding conditions for CTM_{shield} into account, as the length of shielding conditions which is 3. Thus, according to the definition, the reduction rate of constraint length ($\Delta_\%^\Phi$) is 47.1%($= \frac{(17-(3+6))}{17} = \frac{8}{17}$).

From the summary of the experimental results shown in Table 4, we answer the research questions as follows:

- **Answer for RQ1:** The shielding conditions were not necessarily used for all the cases; instead, they are used in 12 out of 19 cases (63.1%) for system A and in all the six cases (100%) for system B; hence 72% ($= 18/25$) in total of systems A and B.
- **Answer for RQ2:** For the cases where parameter shielding are used, the reduction rate of the number of tree nodes by CTM_{shield} ($\Delta_\%^N$) is on average 4.2% for system A and 11.0% for system B; 7.13% on the total average.
- **Answer for RQ3:** For the cases where parameter shielding are used, CTM_{shield} reduces the constraint length, compared with CTM, (i.e., $\Delta_\%^\Phi$) on average by 14.7% for system A, by 39.4% for system B; by 22.9% on the total average.

Note that all the test models for the functions in both systems are expressed as trees, from which we can consider structured and diagrammatic modeling approach of CTM is useful and effective in practice. Also, CTM_{shield} shows a higher effectiveness in system B than system A, from which we may consider that the effectiveness of using CTM_{shield} differs between systems. As shorter and simpler constraints reduce the human effort on modeling, we consider CTM_{shield} to be effective in real-world settings.

5   Conclusion and Future Work

This work tackled a modeling problem in combinatorial testing, which is a main concern for its use in real developments. We extend CTM, which have been studied and used as a practical modeling language in combinatorial testing, with parameter shielding, and proposed CTM_{shield}. Our experiments via case studies confirmed its effectiveness.

We plan to conduct more empirical studies to evaluate the effectiveness of CTM_{shield} when used to model industrial systems. We leave to future work a theoretical analysis of the proposed extension, such as consistency arguments with different formalisms for parameter shielding [11], theoretical analysis of effectiveness of the extension such as the maximum reduction of the number of nodes, the size of constraints per shielding condition, etc. We also plan to extend our combinatorial testing tool CALOT [8,17,18] with this feature of parameter shielding.

Acknowledgement. This work is partly supported by JST A-STEP grant AS2524001H.

References

1. Kuhn, D.R., Wallace, D.R., Gallo, A.M.: Software fault interactions and implications for software testing. IEEE Trans. Softw. Eng. **30**(6), 418–421 (2004)
2. Kuhn, R.D., Kacker, R.N., Lei, Y.: Introduction to Combinatorial Testing. CRC Press, Boca Raton (2013)
3. Ammann, P., Offutt, J.: Introduction to Software Testing. Cambridge University Press, Cambridge (2008)
4. Grochtmann, M.: Test case design using classification trees. In: Proceedings of STAR 1994 (1994)
5. Lehmann, E., Wegener, J.: Test case design by means of the CTE XL. In: Proceedings of EuroSTAR (2000)
6. Kruse, P.M., Luniak, M.: Automated test case generation using classification trees. Softw. Qual. Prof. **13**(1), 4–12 (2010)
7. Grochtmann, M., Wegener, J.: Test case design using classification trees and the classification-tree editor CTE. In: Proceedings of the of QW 1995 (1995)
8. Kitamura, T., Yamada, A., Hatayama, G., Artho, C., Choi, E.H., Do, N.T.B., Oiwa, Y., Sakuragi, S.: Combinatorial testing for tree-structured test models. In: Proceedings of QRS 2015, pp. 141–150. IEEE CPS (2015)
9. MODISTARC: OSEK/VDX operating system test plan version 2.0 (1999). http://www.osek-vdx.org/. Accessed 07 Mar 2016
10. Berner & Mattner: TESTONA ver.5.1.2 http://www.testona.net/en

11. Chen, B., Yan, J., Zhang, J.: Combinatorial testing with shielding parameters. In: Proceedings of APSEC 2010, pp. 280–289. IEEE CPS (2010)
12. Segall, I., Tzoref-Brill, R., Zlotnick, A.: Common patterns in combinatorial models. In: 2012 Proceedings of ICST 2012, Montreal, pp. 624–629. IEEE CPS (2012)
13. Zhao, Y., Zhang, Z., Yan, J., Zhang, J.: CASCADE: A test generation tool for combinatorial testing. In: Proceedings of ICSTW 2013, pp. 267–270. IEEE CPS (2013)
14. Cohen, D.M., Dalal, S.R., Fredman, M.L., Patton, G.C.: The AETG system: An approach to testing based on combinatiorial design. IEEE Trans. Softw. Eng. **23**(7), 437–444 (1997)
15. Garvin, B.J., Cohen, M.B., Dwyer, M.B.: An improved meta-heuristic search for constrained interaction testing. In: Proceedings of SSBSE 2009, pp. 13–22 (2009)
16. Büning, H.K., Lettmann, T.: Propositional Logic Deduction and Algorithms. Cambridge University Press, Cambridge (1999)
17. Yamada, A., Kitamura, T., Artho, C., Choi, E.H., Oiwa, Y., Biere, A.: Optimization of combinatorial testing by incremental SAT solving. In: Proceedings of ICST 2015, pp. 1–10. IEEE CPS (2015)
18. Yamada, A., Biere, A., Artho, C., Kitamura, T., Choi, E.: Greedy combinatorial test case generation using unsatisfiable cores. In: Proceedings of ASE 2016, pp. 614–624. IEEE CPS (2016)

Safety Analysis and Assessment

ErrorSim: A Tool for Error Propagation Analysis of Simulink Models

Mustafa Saraoğlu[1], Andrey Morozov[1(✉)], Mehmet Turan Söylemez[2], and Klaus Janschek[1]

[1] Technische Universität Dresden, Institute of Automation, Dresden, Germany
{mustafa.saraoglu,andrey.morozov,klaus.janschek}@tu-dresden.de
[2] Control and Automation Department, Istanbul Technical University, Istanbul, Turkey
turan.soylemez@itu.edu.tr

Abstract. This paper introduces a new lightweight tool for simulative error propagation analysis of Simulink models. The tool allows a user to inject different types of faults that are common for embedded control systems and analyze error propagation to critical system parts and outputs. The intended workflow comprises the following three steps: (i) setup faulty and critical blocks of a Simulink model, (ii) setup and run simulations, and (iii) observe and examine the obtained results. The tool is implemented in MATLAB using the callback block functions from the Simulink API. The graphical user interface allows the injection of several types of faults including computing hardware faults such as single and multiple bit-flips, sensor faults such as offsets, stuck-at faults, and a noise, and network faults such as time delays and packet drops. The fault occurrence and duration can be specified either with the classical reliability metrics like mean time to failure and mean time to repair, or failure rates with classical (normal, exponential, Poisson, Weibull etc.) or custom user-defined probability distributions. The error propagation to the selected critical blocks is reported with several statistical metrics including the mean number of errors, failure rate, and mean error value, as well as performance indexes such as integral squared error, integral absolute error, and integral time-weighted absolute error. The reported numerical results support standard reliability and safety assessment methods such as fault tree analysis and failure mode and effects analysis. The paper demonstrates the tool with a case study Simulink model of fault-tolerant control for a passenger jet.

Keywords: Dependability · Reliability · Safety · Fault injection · Error propagation · Model-based analysis · Simulink · Stability · Control

1 Introduction

Nowadays, the challenge is not only to design a fail-safe system but also, to verify and prove its safety and reliability properties. Safety critical hardware (HW) and software (SW) systems shall comply with relevant industrial standards based on

© Springer International Publishing AG 2017
S. Tonetta et al. (Eds.): SAFECOMP 2017, LNCS 10488, pp. 245–254, 2017.
DOI: 10.1007/978-3-319-66266-4_16

IEC 61508. Most of the big companies even have dedicated RAMS (Reliability, Availability, Maintainability, Safety), V&V (Verification and Validation), or QA (Quality Assurance) departments for this task.

Model-based approaches are widely used across safety-critical domains, especially for the control software development. They help to ensure consistency between a model and a production code and avoid bugs that could be introduced in case of conventional, manual programming. MATLAB Simulink [7] is the most common development environment that gives a lot of practical freedom and allows a designer to develop, modify and test a system in a fast and convenient way.

The certified development toolset [6], accompanied by detailed modeling guidelines [2,10] and extensive testing requirements, significantly reduces the number of systematic SW faults. However, the system stays vulnerable to different HW faults that have a random nature. The common types of these faults such as sensor faults, computing HW faults, and network faults are listed in the standards. The correct, failure-free operation of the system under the influence of these faults should be ensured and carefully examined. Therefore, we introduce ErrorSim, a new lightweight simulator of error propagation for Simulink models that allows the user to inject common HW faults and analyze error propagation to critical system parts and outputs.

2   Related Work

Fault injection is a group of methods for evaluation of system dependability properties [1]. These methods are highly recommended by industrial safety standards. A lot of different techniques have been developed in recent years.

Several good surveys of fault injection methods and tools [3,5,11,16] propose various classifications, based on injected fault types (HW/SW, transient/intermittent/permanent etc.), systems under evaluation (HW/SW/Hybrid), and fault injection methods (HW/SW/Model-implemented). ErrorSim supports the injection of different types of HW faults for evaluation of model-based HW/SW control systems implemented in Simulink using a model-implemented fault injection method.

Relevant model-implemented fault injection tools for SCADE and Simulink are introduced in [4,12–15]. MODIFI (MODel-Implemented Fault Injection) is the closest tool to ErrorSim. MODIFI also allows the injection of the HW faults such as single bit-flips and sensor faults into Simulink models. The main difference is that ErrorSim is a lightweight solution that works directly in the MATLAB environment without code generation, complex external setups, and any other third party tools or libraries. Also, our tool doesn't alter the original Simulink model with additional fault injection or error detection blocks. ErrorSim exploits Simulink callback block functions instead.

The advantage of the ErrorSim over the "native" Test Harnesses of the Simulink Test [8] is quite obvious. Our tool allows the injection of predefined common fault types in the fast and transparent manner without manual creation and setup of specific fault injectors and detectors. Also, ErrorSim reports the results using widely used reliability metrics.

3   Description of ErrorSim

ErrorSim is implemented in MATLAB and consists of two main logical parts that are responsible for fault injection and error detection. Figure 1 shows main steps of intended ErrorSim workflow.

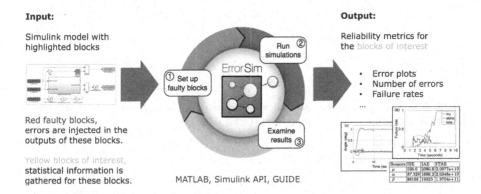

Fig. 1. Intended ErrorSim workflow comprises three major steps: (i) faulty blocks set-up, (ii) simulations, and (iii) result examination. (Color figure online)

Firstly, the user should open a Simulink model and mark faulty and critical blocks by changing their background colors to red and yellow respectively. After that, the user runs ErrorSim and perform the set-up of faulty blocks with the GUI shown in Fig. 2. *Fault type* and *fault injection method* should be specified for each faulty block, see Fig. 3. ErrorSim supports the following fault types defined in IEC 61508: sensor faults (offset, stuck-at fault, and noise), hardware faults (single and multiple bit flips), and network faults (drops and delays). The *fault injection method* is defined with two parameters: *event* and *effect*. The parameter *event* specifies a stochastic method for fault injection: failure probability, mean time to failure (MTTF), or failure rate distribution. The last option allows the user to define the fault injection using either classical normal, Weibull, gamma, exponential, Poisson, binomial or custom user-specified distributions. The parameter *effect* determines the duration of the fault. The following options are available: just once, constant time, infinite time, and mean time to repair (MTTR). A complete user-defined fault setup can be saved and loaded.

In the second step, ErrorSim performs one golden run followed by the user-defined number of simulations with fault injections. During the golden run, correct inputs of the critical (yellow) blocks are stored. During each faulty simulation, ErrorSim injects faults into the outputs of the faulty (red) blocks.

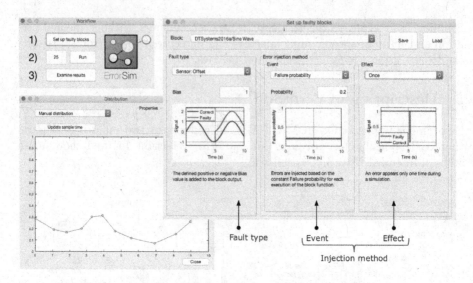

Fig. 2. The user interface for the faulty blocks set-up. The user selects and specifies a fault type and a fault injection method. (Color figure online)

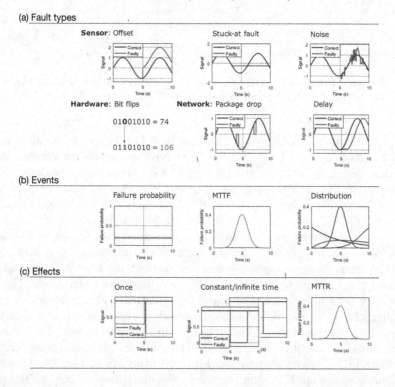

Fig. 3. Supported fault types and fault injection methods: supported fault types (a), events (b) and effects (c) for the definition of the fault injection method. (Color figure online)

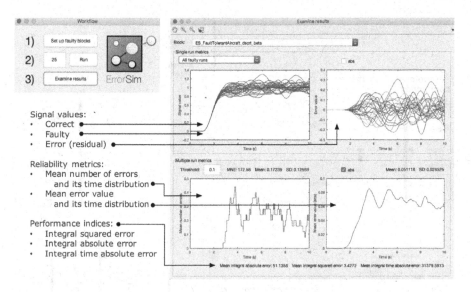

Fig. 4. The user interface with statistical information about the errors propagated to the critical blocks: signal values, reliability metrics, performance indices.

The inputs of the critical blocks are compared with the stored correct values of the golden run in order to detect errors. ErrorSim exploits the mechanism of block function callbacks to inject errors and store values.

In the third step, ErrorSim provides statistical information for each critical block (see Fig. 4): (i) the plots of correct, faulty, and error signals, (ii) common reliability metrics such as mean number of errors and error value as well as their time distributions, and (iii) widely used performance indices including integral squared error, integral absolute error, and integral time absolute error. The statistical information is presented with interactive MATLAB plots which are stored by ErrorSim.

4   Case Study

A Simulink model of a fault-tolerant control of a passenger jet [9], shown in Fig. 5, will be used in order to demonstrate ErrorSim's capabilities. The purpose of this example is to test and tune, state feedback parameters according to a cost function given in [9], in order to achieve better fault tolerance. The Simulink model is decomposed into several subsystems: a controller, a state-space model of an aircraft, wind disturbances, and sensors. We assume that three sensor signals that represent μ, α, and, β angles of an aircraft, suffer sensor faults. ErrorSim will examine how these faults affect system behavior. The faulty blocks from the Sensors subsystem are highlighted in red and the outputs to be analyzed (critical blocks) are highlighted in yellow in the Fig. 5.

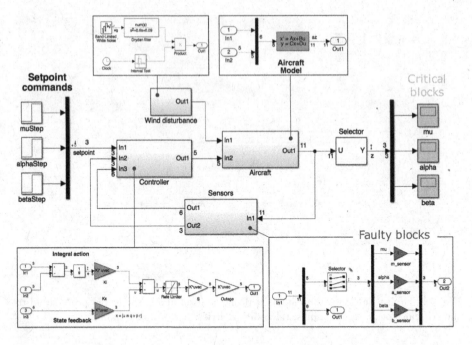

Fig. 5. Fault-tolerant passenger jet Simulink model, adopted from [9]. (Color figure online)

Three single-simulation experiments and one multiple-simulation experiment have been performed. Table 1 shows the *fault types* and *fault injection methods* for the single-simulation experiments. The plots in Fig. 6 demonstrate how the injected faults affect the system stability. The red, blue, and green curves represent μ, α, and, β angles of the system output. Figure 6(a) shows the output of a fault-free run. Figure 6(b) and (c) show that the system is able to tolerate the injected faults of Experiment 1 and Experiment 2 with minor deteriorations and steady state errors. Finally, Fig. 6(d) demonstrates that the system cannot tolerate the faults which are injected during Experiment 3 and becomes unstable.

Table 2 shows the *fault types* and *fault injection methods* for the multiple-simulation experiment with 50 faulty runs. Figure 7(a) shows how the average error values for all three parameters change over time. We can observe that β accumulates the error while the average error values of μ and α stay almost constant. This means that β is the most vulnerable angle to the injected faults. The right part of Table 2 also confirms this result with numerical performance indices such as integral squared error (ISE), integral absolute error (IAE), and integral time absolute error (ITAE).

ErrorSim allows the user to specify an error detection threshold. The error is registered if the difference between actual and correct values, is higher than this threshold. Two plots in Fig. 7(b) and (c) show the distribution of the average number of registered errors over time for two different thresholds. This average

Table 1. Fault setups of the three single-simulation experiments.

Experiment 1			
Sensors	Fault type	Fault injection method	
		Event	Effect
μ	Noise, %10	Failure probability, 0.03	Constant time, 1 s
α	Offset, +0.05	MTTF, 10 s	Constant time, 0.2 s
β	Stuck-at fault	Failure probability, 0.05	MTTR, 2 s
Experiment 2			
Sensors	Fault type	Fault injection method	
		Event	Effect
μ	Noise, %20	Failure probability, 0.1	Constant time, 1 s
α	Offset, +0.05	MTTF, 4 s	Constant time, 1 s
β	Stuck-at fault	Failure probability, 0.05	MTTR, 2 s
Experiment 3			
Sensors	Fault type	Fault injection method	
		Event	Effect
μ	Noise, %20	Failure probability, 0.1	Constant time, 1 s
α	Offset, +0.05	MTTF, 4 s	Constant time, 1 s
β	Stuck-at fault	Failure probability, 0.05	MTTR, 5 s

Table 2. The fault setup (left) and average values of performance indices (right) for the multi-simulation experiment with 50 runs.

Sensors	Fault type	Fault injection method		Performance indices		
		Event	Effect	ISE	IAE	ITAE
μ	Noise, %20	Failure probability, 0.05	Constant time, 1s	538.6	2090.8	2.0977e+10
α	Offset, +0.05	Weibull, a = 10, b = 5.2	Constant time, 1s	87.328	1699.2	2.0348e+10
β	Stuck-at fault	MTTF, 4 s	MTTR, 5 s	88168	19323	1.9704e+11

number can also be interpreted as a failure rate of the system. Figure 7(b) shows that, with a lower threshold (0.02), the failure rate of α tends to one after the first half of the simulation. However, this is not the case if the threshold is higher (0.05) which is shown in Fig. 7(c). This means that the errors of α are bounded and not critical.

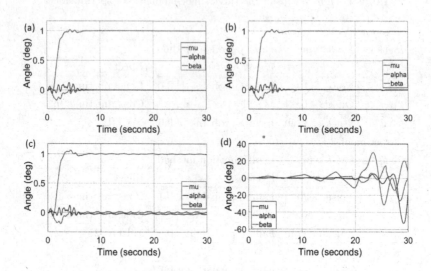

Fig. 6. Single-simulation experiments: a correct run (a), Experiment 1 (b), Experiment 2 (c), Experiment 3 (d). (Color figure online)

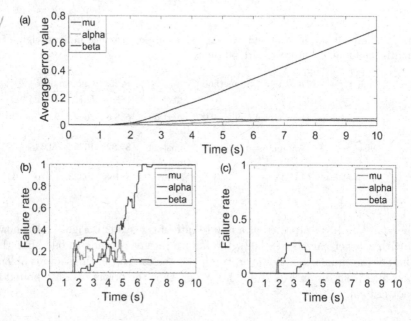

Fig. 7. Average error values for μ, α and β (a). Failure rates for μ, α and β: error thresholds 0.02 (b) and 0.05 (c).

5   Conclusion

The general technical description of ErrorSim, a new lightweight tool for error analysis of Simulink models, has been introduced in this paper. The key features have been demonstrated with a case study that shows how the tool can help to distinguish between critical and non-critical sensor faults for the closed-loop control system of a passenger jet. ErrorSim offers a variety of options for both fault injection and error detection, yielding numerical results which are helpful for the system dependability evaluation. ErrorSim has a transparent user interface and works directly in the MATLAB environment without any need for code generation, third-party libraries, or complex setup. The tool will be further developed and extended with new features and performance optimizations and aims to become a useful industrial tool.

References

1. Avizienis, A., Laprie, J.C., Randell, B., Landwehr, C.: Basic concepts and taxonomy of dependable and secure computing. IEEE Trans. Dependable Secure Comput. **1**(1), 11–33 (2004)
2. Fey, I., Müller, J.: Model-based design for safety-related applications (2008)
3. Hsueh, M.C., Tsai, T.K., Iyer, R.K.: Fault injection techniques and tools. Computer **30**(4), 75–82 (1997)
4. Joshi, A., Heimdahl, M.P.E.: Model-based safety analysis of simulink models using SCADE design verifier. In: Winther, R., Gran, B.A., Dahll, G. (eds.) SAFECOMP 2005. LNCS, vol. 3688, pp. 122–135. Springer, Heidelberg (2005). doi:10.1007/11563228_10
5. Kooli, M., Di Natale, G.: A survey on simulation-based fault injection tools for complex systems. In: 2014 9th IEEE International Conference on Design & Technology of Integrated Systems In: Nanoscale Era (DTIS), pp. 1–6. IEEE (2014)
6. MathWorks: IEC Certification Kit. http://www.mathworks.de/products/iec-61508/
7. MathWorks: Matlab & simulink: Simulink users guide r2016a (2016)
8. Mathworks: Develop, manage, and execute simulation-based tests (2017). https://www.mathworks.com/products/simulink-test.html
9. Mathworks: Fault-tolerant control of a passenger jet - matlab simulink example (2017). https://de.mathworks.com/help/control/examples/fault-tolerant-control-of-a-passenger-jet.html
10. Misra, A.: Sl sf modeling design and style guidelines for the application of simulink and stateflow. V1. 0, MIRA (2009)
11. Natella, R., Cotroneo, D., Madeira, H.S.: Assessing dependability with software fault injection: a survey. ACM Comput. Surv. (CSUR) **48**(3), 44 (2016)
12. Skarin, D., Vinter, J., Svenningsson, R.: Visualization of model-implemented fault injection experiments. In: Bondavalli, A., Ceccarelli, A., Ortmeier, F. (eds.) SAFECOMP 2014. LNCS, vol. 8696, pp. 219–230. Springer, Cham (2014). doi:10.1007/978-3-319-10557-4_25
13. Svenningsson, R., Vinter, J., Eriksson, H., Törngren, M.: MODIFI: a model-implemented fault injection tool. In: Schoitsch, E. (ed.) SAFECOMP 2010. LNCS, vol. 6351, pp. 210–222. Springer, Heidelberg (2010). doi:10.1007/978-3-642-15651-9_16

14. Vinter, J., Bromander, L., Raistrick, P., Edler, H.: Fiscade-a fault injection tool for scade models. In: 2007 3rd Institution of Engineering and Technology Conference on Automotive Electronics, pp. 1–9. IET (2007)

15. Vulinovic, S., Schlingloff, B.H.: Model based dependability evaluation for automotive control functions. In: Invited Session: Model-Based Design and Test, 9th World Multi-Conference on Systemics, Cybernetics and Informatics, Florida (2005)

16. Ziade, H., Ayoubi, R.A., Velazco, R., et al.: A survey on fault injection techniques. Int. Arab J. Inf. Technol. 1(2), 171–186 (2004)

Early Safety Assessment of Automotive Systems Using Sabotage Simulation-Based Fault Injection Framework

Garazi Juez[✉], Estíbaliz Amparan, Ray Lattarulo, Alejandra Ruíz, Joshué Pérez, and Huáscar Espinoza

TECNALIA Research & Innovation, Derio, Spain
{garazi.juez,estibaliz.amparan,rayalejandro.lattarulo,
alejandra.ruiz,joshue.perez,huascar.espinoza}@tecnalia.com

Abstract. As road vehicles increase their autonomy and the driver reduces his role in the control loop, novel challenges on dependability assessment arise. Model-based design combined with a simulation-based fault injection technique and a virtual vehicle poses as a promising solution for an early safety assessment of automotive systems. To start with, the design, where no safety was considered, is stimulated with a set of fault injection simulations (fault forecasting). By doing so, safety strategies can be evaluated during early development phases estimating the relationship of an individual failure to the degree of misbehaviour on vehicle level. After having decided the most suitable safety concept, a second set of fault injection experiments is used to perform an early safety validation of the chosen architecture. This double-step process avoids late redesigns, leading to significant cost and time savings. This paper presents a simulation-based fault injection approach aimed at finding acceptable safety properties for model-based design of automotive systems. We focus on instrumenting the use of this technique to obtain fault effects and the maximum response time of a system before a hazardous event occurs. Through these tangible outcomes, safety concepts and mechanisms can be more accurately dimensioned. In this work, a prototype tool called Sabotage has been developed to set up, configure, execute and analyse the simulation results. The feasibility of this method is demonstrated by applying it to a Lateral Control system.

Keywords: Fault Injection · Early safety assessment · Vehicle dynamics model

1 Introduction

Automated driving exhibits increasingly complex dependability challenges as the driver reduces his role in the control loop, and the vehicle must operate under exceptional situations, e.g. dealing with sensor noise. Fault Injection (FI) has been recognised as a potentially powerful technique for the safety assessment and corner-case validation of fault-tolerance mechanisms in manual and automated driving systems [1]. The major aim of performing FI is not to validate functionality, but rather to test the fault tolerance or probe how robust the vehicle is or their components are to arbitrary faults. The ISO 26262 standard [2] notably recommends its use across the validation and verification phases of the V-Cycle development process.

© Springer International Publishing AG 2017
S. Tonetta et al. (Eds.): SAFECOMP 2017, LNCS 10488, pp. 255–269, 2017.
DOI: 10.1007/978-3-319-66266-4_17

Despite the growing use of model-based tools in the design phases, FI is a technique that has seen little widespread use in early phases [3]. The potential benefits of using FI during pre-implementation phases of automotive systems range from providing an early evaluation up to a preliminary validation of safety concepts. In the specific case of manual driving, this could help determining (human-) controllability and fault tolerant time interval (FTTI) values in early design phases. FTTI is defined as the time-span in which a fault can be present in a system before a hazardous event occurs [2]. Concerning highly automated driving, we believe that FI could be applied for dimensioning monitoring functions by determining a system maximum response time before a hazardous event occurs.

This paper explores how to use model-based FI to assess safety properties of vehicle systems and how to augment vehicle simulation with appropriate fault models for safety determination. To address these concerns, a simulation-based FI framework (Sabotage) is coupled with the Dynacar vehicle simulator [4]. Dynacar includes a vehicle model (e.g. dynamics), an environment model (e.g. driving circuit) and pre-defined sensor and actuator model libraries for e.g. engine, transmission, steering system, and braking system. The added value of including vehicle and environment models is that the maximum time before the vehicle dynamics are unsafely affected can be identified. In other words, it allows quantitatively estimating the relationship of an individual failure to the degree of misbehaviour on vehicle level.

Our approach has been evaluated on a case study for the model-based design of a Lateral Control system. We have focused on automatically inserting fault injection model blocks (saboteurs), which represent failure modes, and forecast maximum system reaction times based on the critical lateral deviation (maximum lateral error). This value determines the required level of fault tolerance – e.g. redundancy or graceful degradation – without affecting vehicle safety. A good estimation of these values helps engineers to better define appropriate safety goals and requirements as main output of the safety concept [5].

The remainder of this paper is structured as follows. Section 2 presents the related state of the art. Section 3 introduces the Sabotage tool framework and how it can be used for an early safety assessment. Afterwards, Sect. 4 shows how the aforementioned method is applied to the Lateral Control case study. Finally, Sect. 5 presents conclusions and future work.

2   Related Work

Fault injection has been deeply investigated by both academia and industry as surveyed in [6] and described in [7]. The idea of using simulation-based FI in early design phases is not that widely spread. For instance, Svenningson [8] investigated the benefits of applying this technique on Simulink behavioural models, and Vinter et al. [9] developed a similar approach for the SCADE toolset. Even if failures can be derived, those effects and FTTI values cannot be estimated on vehicle level since no vehicle dynamics is considered. The closest to an investigation of simulation-based FI that integrated vehicle dynamics is presented in [10, 11]. Silveira et al. [10] implemented a seamless co-simulation approach that combines Matlab and CarSim for evaluating the fault impacts on vehicle stability. Also, Jones et al. [11] introduced a similar co-simulation solution using Matlab, CarMaker/TruckMaker and CRUISE tools. This work especially supports the determination of Automotive Safety Integrity Levels (ASIL) during the concept phase as per ISO 26262. The major drawback of these approaches is that the fault library and the solution are language dependent and the automation level could be further developed.

Concerning the use of FI across the range of abstraction levels of ISO 26262, most of the work has been done as a way of verifying the implemented safety mechanisms or safety requirements [12]. Only few works have emphasised its usage during early design phases. Pintard [3] developed guidance for applying FI on both sides of the ISO 26262's V-Cycle, including system and hardware pre-implementation phases; however, the aim of the author was not to develop a fault injection framework.

3 Overview of the Simulation-Based Fault Injection Approach

3.1 The Sabotage Tool Framework

Simulation-based fault injection is a technique that uses a series of high-level abstractions or models representing the system under study to evaluate and validate its dependability in early design phases. Thus the system is simulated on the basis of simplified assumptions to (a) predict its behaviour in the presence of faults, (b) to estimate the failure coverage and timing of fault tolerant mechanisms, or (c) to explore the effects of different workloads, i.e. different activation profiles. Applying FI provides remarkable benefits for designers. On the one hand, fault forecasting is achieved by performing an evaluation of the system behaviour with respect to fault occurrence or activation. On the other hand, as tackled in [14], FI is seen as a dynamic testing technique to achieve fault removal during the development phase of a system (verification, diagnosis, and correction).

Sabotage is a simulation-based fault injection tool framework based on the well-known FARM environment model [13]. The FARM model is composed of: (1) the set of Faults to be injected, (2) the set of Activations exercised during the experiment, (3) the Readouts to define observers of system behaviour, and (4) the Measures obtained to evaluate dependability properties. In the rest of this section, we describe the particularities of the proposed tool framework in light of the FARM constituents.

Figure 1 shows the Sabotage building blocks and the flow of models to perform a safety assessment during vehicle simulation in early design phases. The tightly-coupled simulation environment is constituted as follows: the Sabotage framework is used to set up, configure, run and analyse FI experiments. The Dynacar vehicle simulator [4], integrated as a Matlab/Simulink system function (S-function), includes models to represent some vehicle sensors, actuators and dynamics. An S-function is a computer language description of a Simulink block written in Matlab, C, C++, or Fortran. Besides, Dynacar provides a graphical user interface where the previously configured operational situations are observed. The model of the whole system is completed by including simulation models representing the Electronic Control Unit (ECU) functions (also known as controller model or control strategies). By co-simulating the three applications we are able to carry out a closed-loop modelling of the vehicle control system in the presence of faults.

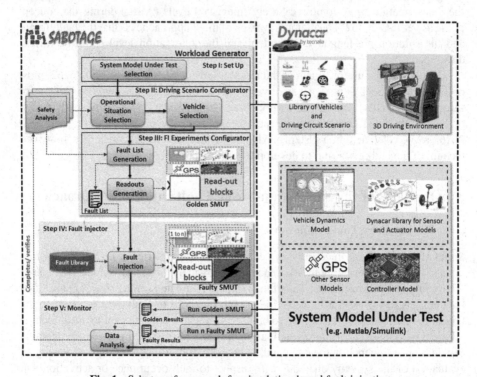

Fig. 1. Sabotage framework for simulation-based fault injection

The Sabotage framework operates as follows. First, a Workload Generator generates the functional inputs to be applied to the system model under test (SMUT). All these models are developed, for instance, using Matlab/Simulink. The Workload Generator consists of (i) selecting the system model under test, (ii) choosing the operational scenario from a driving circuit and environment scenario library, and (iii) configuring fault injection experiments, i.e. creating the fault list and deciding the read-out or observation points (signal monitors). Then a Fault Injector (for now implemented as Matlab code) uses both, the fault list and a fault model library (implemented as C code templates or XML), to create the saboteurs (S-functions) and generate as many Faulty SMUT as the designer needs. Once a fault free version of the SMUT (Golden) and at least one Faulty SMUT are available, the simulation environment is invoked through the Monitor (the Oracle implemented in Java). The Monitor not only runs experiments under the pre-configured vehicle scenario, but also compares and analyses the collected data.

Workload Generator. This block is in charge of three main activities: selecting the SMUT, choosing the most appropriate driving scenario, which represents the operational situation, and configuring fault injection experiments. Safety analysis provides the basis for specifying the operational situations (i.e. location, road conditions, environment conditions and the like). After that, the designer selects the vehicle and a driving circuit scenario that best symbolises those operational situations to be simulated. Dynacar manages a scenario catalogue that includes up to 150 configurable parameters, thus enabling the emulation of a wide range of vehicles and driving circuit scenarios. The *fault injection experiments configurator* block in Sabotage also addresses the inclusion of extra readout model blocks (signal monitors) in the target system (SMUT) to facilitate the logging process of output data.

Moreover, the activity of *fault list generation* creates a subset of faults that can be injected in a reasonable time but are still able to provide significant results. Our strategy to identify a representative fault subset is to use the target system malfunctions or failure modes, e.g. omission or commission, instead of injecting an exhaustive or random fault set. The kinds of faults in the subset include permanent, intermittent and transient faults.

Fault Injector. The fault list is used to produce a Faulty SMUT only in terms of reproducible and prearranged fault models. Fault models are characterised by a type (e.g. omission, frozen, delay, invert, oscillation or random), target location, injection triggering (e.g. driving circuit position or time driven), and duration. To create a Faulty SMUT, the Fault Injector injects an additional saboteur model block per fault entry from the fault list together with the associated fault models which are coded as templates in a fault library. Saboteurs are extra components added as part of the model-based design for the sole purpose of FI experiments. Algorithm 1 depicts a generic fault model for omission represented by a stuck-at last value.

```
Require:   input, pos,simutime,faultdur;
1          If pos== triggerpos then
2              Freeze=input;
3              enable=1;
4          While enable==1 && simutime<=faultdur do return freeze;
5          return input;
```

Algorithm 1. Stuck-at Last Value.

Monitor. After setting up the FI scenarios and having conceived the required amount of Faulty SMUT, the Monitor starts the simulation process. It tracks the execution flow of the Golden and Faulty simulation runs via *the readouts collection* activity. The Monitor compares Golden and Faulty SMUT results by the *data analysis* activity. The pass/fail criterion of the tests, which was established by the designer as part of Step III (cf. Fig. 1), is used to compute and finalise the results. This criterion includes different properties like the maximum acceptable distance from optimal path considering the vehicle behaviour is acceptable in terms of vehicle dynamics. This way, acceptable maximum system reaction times are obtained. In brief, we are able to report the corruption effects for fault forecasting and fault removal, as described in the next section.

3.2 Using Sabotage for an Early Safety Assessment

In this section, we explore a safety assessment process focused on supporting the creation and an early validation of a safety concept by using Sabotage. Figure 2 shows how the proposed approach can help to dimension the safety concept and to achieve its early safety validation. The approach is discussed in the following sequence in which the proposed safety assessment process is performed.

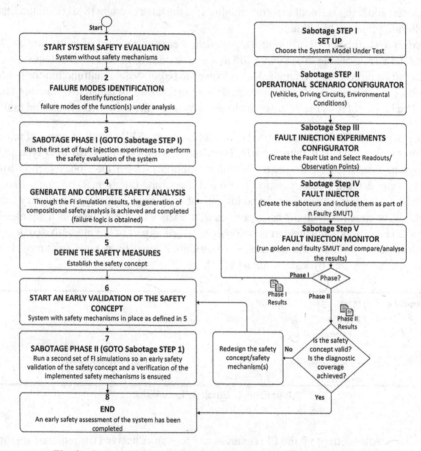

Fig. 2. Proposed early safety assessment flow by means of Sabotage

Sabotage Phase I: Start System Safety Evaluation. One assumption in this approach is that we start from existing system models (i.e. vehicle dynamics and system functions), which did not implement safety mechanisms before. The purpose of the process approach is to assist when creating the safety concept by including the vehicle dynamics. By applying this method, fault effects and the maximum response time of the system before a hazardous event occurs can be obtained. Furthermore, the severity of the injected failure modes can be quantified in terms of vehicle dynamics effect. Through these tangible outcomes, safety concepts and mechanisms can be more accurately dimensioned. Before completing any kind of fault injection simulation, the target system must be defined and its main functions and failure modes (e.g. omission) have to be stated. Likewise, a preliminary architecture is mandatory in order to know which functional failure modes could lead to system or vehicle failure and hazards.

By following the approach explained in Sect. 3.1, a first run of fault injection simulations needs to be configured. For that, the vehicle and the operational situations shall be specified to select the vehicle and the driving scenarios. Some typical situation scenarios that must be analysed are for example:

- Location: highway, urban;
- Road conditions: uphill, on a curve;
- Environment conditions: good conditions, heavy rain;
- Traffic situations: fluent;
- Vehicle speed (kph);
- Manoeuvres: parking, overtaking, lane keeping;
- People at risk: driver, passenger, pedestrians.

We foster the idea of complementing traditional safety analysis techniques by performing fault injection already at the concept phase. Those traditional analysis techniques include FMEA (Failure Modes and Effect Analysis), FTA (Fault Tree Analysis), DFA (Dependent Failure Analysis) or Preliminary Hazard Analysis (PHA). All of them require not only knowing the failure modes but also to have a clear vision of the failure effect. Yet sometimes those failure effects might not be clearly known in advance. Our approach aims at deriving potential effects or hazards based on the FI simulation results. As a starting point of such preliminary analysis, the malfunctions or failure modes are clearly identified in this process step. As a result of this activity, a fault list can be created by the Sabotage framework. This activity addresses the following questions:

- Where should the faults be injected?
- What is the most appropriate fault model representing the functional failure modes?
- How should the faults be triggered within the system?
- Where should the fault effect be observed?

After generating simulation settings and creating the fault list, Sabotage executes the Golden (fault free) and Faulty simulations, as described in Sect. 3.1. A set of scripts have been developed to achieve the required level of automation. The pass/fail criterion of the simulation is defined as part of the Workload (cf. Fig. 2 Sabotage Step III). The user can set that requirement as a vehicle dynamics property violation. The main goal of comparing the Golden versus Faulty SMUT is to obtain the required results in an automated way.

The results of the simulation experiments (c.f. Fig. 2 Phase I Results) can then complete the safety analysis and help dimensioning the safety concept through the maximum system reaction time. In other words, it can be used to better determine the required level of fault tolerance (e.g. redundancy or graceful degradation). In brief, Sabotage helps to identify those hazards (e.g. vehicle does not turn when it should) or to rank the failure modes with respect to fault occurrence. Dynacar is used to visually observe these system failures through its 3D virtual environment. To sum up, by using

FI approach, it is possible to get data in order to forecast how the system will behave under the effects of real faults for situations in which no previous data was available. Considering engineering needs to prove that fault reaction times are shorter than the FTTI, a good estimation of those values is relevant. This ensures that any fault reaction is completed before a hazardous event occurs.

Sabotage Phase II: Start an Early Validation of the Safety Concept. Once the model-based safety architecture has been defined, the designer can obtain an early validation of the implemented safety concept. For that, a second run of fault-injection is needed. After having the safety concept defined and its architecture designed as part of the system behavioural model, a second run of the FI simulations can be performed. This allows validating the safety of the system during early design phases. For instance, if the needed diagnostic coverage it is not achieved, the corresponding design part must be rebuilt. Furthermore, possible systematic faults or the robustness of the implemented safety mechanisms can be tested. In this second phase, the user can establish pass/fail criteria upon the defined safety goals and safety requirements.

4   Case Study: Automated Lateral Control

4.1   Automated Driving Control Architecture

After outlining the Sabotage FI simulation framework, the feasibility of this method is demonstrated by applying it to a Lateral Control system. It is worth mentioning that no safety was considered when modelling the system. For that reason, the Sabotage method is applied starting from Phase I (safety evaluation).

The Lateral Control system is part of a complete control architecture for automated driving developed in Matlab/Simulink. This automated control architecture consists of two main systems: Lateral and Longitudinal control. The Lateral Control is the responsible for steering the vehicle along the most appropriate trajectory depending on the vehicle and environment state. This automated function consists of three principal functions.

- Behavioural Planner: It selects the most convenient trajectory depending on the vehicle manoeuvre (i.e. lane keeping, lane changing and obstacle avoidance). Behavioural Planner is composed of another three sub-functions (i.e. Perception, Local Planner and Decision). The Perception function supplies information from the vehicle state sensors and environment state sensor as Differential GPS (DGPS). It has to be pointed out that no sensor fusion is considered in the current design. The Local Planner receives information from the environment sensors to obtain vehicle position. At last, the Decision function creates the optimal trajectory considering the manoeuvre that the vehicle shall perform.
- Trajectory Controller: Keeps the vehicle correctly on the trajectory. Knowing the lateral error, the angular error and the curvature of the path, Trajectory controller calculates the Variation Correction "C_v". The algorithm chosen for the evaluation of this design is the so-called Control Law algorithm and it is defined as formula (1).

$$C_v = K_1 * e_{lat} + K_2 * e_{ang} + K_3 * Curvature \qquad (1)$$

- The steering function: Controls the steering wheel to set the vehicle on the trajectory defined by Behavioural Planner. It obtains the input values from the Trajectory Controller.

4.2 Safety Evaluation of the Lateral Control System

Section 4.1 explains how the automated guidance must be performed synchronously with the longitudinal and lateral control. As functional safety is a crucial requirement, this section shows a safety evaluation for an existing preliminary Lateral Control System Behavioural Model. By performing the required simulations, the safety of the system is evaluated so that the most suitable safety concept is obtained. Hence, the following issues have been addressed:

- Simulation-based data acquisition with regards to component failure effects in the presence of real faults observed on vehicle level.
- Dimensioning the functional safety concept by applying the process explained in Sect. 3.2. This implies elaborating a fault tolerant Lateral Control system to avoid possible hazards and to ensure a high level of dependability through fail-operational behaviour or graceful degradation.

In Sect. 4.1, the main functions of the Lateral Control system have been introduced and the Malfunctions related to the Lateral Control system (cf. Fig. 2, Failure Modes Identification) consist of: Behavioural Planner (Unwanted Local Planner, Unwanted Perception, Unwanted Decision), Trajectory Controller (Omission, Commission) and Steering (Omission, Commission). These malfunctions or failure modes are necessary to derive a proper configuration of the required fault models (see Table 2, 2nd column). Those functional failure modes can be reproduced at system level (e.g. steering omission) or even as component level malfunctions (e.g. DGPS information omission). After completing that step, the step one of the first phase of Sabotage is applied. This requires the selection of the Lateral Control SMUT as the design-model for which the safety will be evaluated. In detail, the operational situation is specified: the speed of the vehicle is set to 45 kph maximum in a fluent urban traffic and performing a lane keeping manoeuvre on a curve at a city intersection.

With the aim of seeing the failure effects on vehicle level, Functional Failure Modes associated to the functions have been reproduced. The malfunctions are triggered while the vehicle is driving on a curve. In order to see system and vehicle level effects, functional failure modes related to the DGPS (Differential GPS) and the steering controller have been reproduced. The fault list (cf. Table 1) is specified as by following the template depicted in Sect. 3.1. Fault durations are randomly filled in as multiple of the simulator resolution (1 ms) and triggers are curve positions (X,Y).

Table 1. Example of a fault list generation

Component	Fault location (target signals)	Fault model	Fault duration	Fault trigger (X,Y)
DGPS	X,Y	FrozenLastValue	150 ms	10 m, 20 m
DGPS	X,Y	Delay	100 ms	20 m, 30 m
Steering ECU	Steering	FrozenLastValue	70 ms	30 m, 30 m

By employing the process described in Sect. 3.1, the saboteur blocks are automatically injected to the SMUT, through a custom Matlab script, which holds the proper configuration by means of the previously built up fault list. Together with the saboteurs, the read-out blocks are included as well. Then, the fault injection simulations are performed by triggering them at many driving circuit points on a curve to obtain the most critical ones (see Fig. 3).

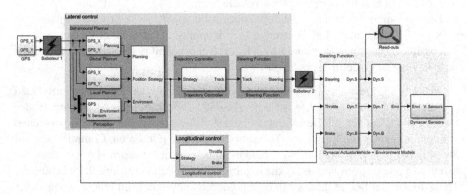

Fig. 3. Faulty system behavioural model

Table 2 lists the most relevant Potential Effects and Hazards obtained by FI simulation. For this purpose, the Lateral Control malfunctions are modelled by means of Fault Models which allow to obtain vehicle level effects and to get a more precise definition of the safety goals.

As depicted in Table 3, based on the identified hazards, appropriate safety goals have been derived. Figure 4 depicts how the maximum time before the vehicle dynamics are unsafely affected is obtained. More precisely, it illustrates a steering omission based on the Yaw Rate and the Lateral Error signals (observation points or read-outs).

Table 2. Hazard and potential effects obtained by FI simulation

Fault target	Fault model	Potential effects	Hazard
Steering	FrozenOutOfRange	Steering shaft is broken	Vehicle may perform a sudden steering and go out of control causing multiple collisions
	Frozen SteeringValueMax	Strong deviation of steering shaft position	Vehicle may perform an oversteering, spin and cause multiple collisions
	Frozen SteeringValueMin	Strong deviation of steering shaft position	Vehicle may perform an understeering and go out of control causing multiple collisions
	Frozen LastValue	Constant steering shaft position	Vehicle may depart lane due to blocked steering angle causing multiple collisions
Trajectory controller	Frozen LastValue	Constant Cv value	Vehicle may depart lane due to unwanted steering angle causing multiple collisions
	Frozen OutOfRange	Controller is saturated	Vehicle may depart lane due to unwanted steering angle causing multiple collisions
Behavioural planner	FrozenLastValue	The trajectory is not updated	Vehicle may follow a not updated trajectory
DGPS	Frozen DGPSLastValue	Behavioural planner is not updated	Vehicle may depart lane because of following an unwanted trajectory and cause multiple collisions
	Frozen RandomValue	Behavioural planner change the trajectory	Vehicle may perform a sudden steering, go out of control and cause multiple collisions

Table 3. Definitions of the lateral control safety goals

Safety goal ID	Safety goal definition
SG1	An unwanted steering angle shall be prevented
SG2	A sudden steering manoeuvre due to an unwanted trajectory shall be prevented
SG3	An unwanted behavioural planner shall be prevented

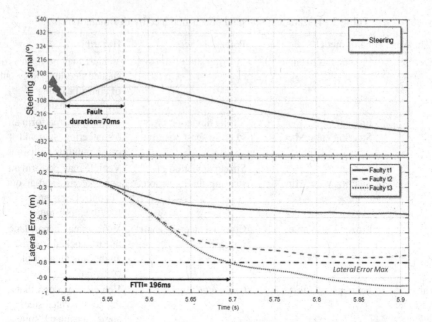

Fig. 4. Basis for FTTI calculation

To calculate the proper FTTI (Fig. 4) value by simulation, the maximum lateral error is taken into account as the pass/fail criterion. This value is analytically calculated using the formula (2). The following formula is used to determine where the vehicle dynamics is certainly affected:

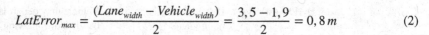

$$LatError_{max} = \frac{(Lane_{width} - Vehicle_{width})}{2} = \frac{3,5 - 1,9}{2} = 0,8\,m \tag{2}$$

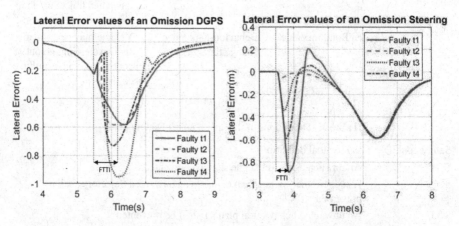

Fig. 5. Lateral error values for different steering and DGPS fault durations

Figure 5 depicts the collection of the results for faults introduced in X,Y DGPS signals and in the steering controller.

In addition, Table 4 represents how the FTTI values, the safety goals (Table 3) and the fault detection times (Fault duration) have been filled in based on FI experiments.

Table 4. Lateral control: hazard analysis

Function	Malfunction	SG	Safe state	FTTI (ms)	Fault duration (ms)
Steering	Commission	SG1	Ensure integrity of command execution	196	70
Trajectory controller	Commission	SG2	Graceful degradation and driver regains control	250	114
Behavioural planner	Commission	SG3	Graceful degradation and driver regains control	327	123

Table 5 lists the Functional Safety Requirements (FSR) based on FI simulations.

Table 5. Lateral control: definition of safety requirements

FRS	Related SG	Definition
FSR1	SG1	The system shall always assure that the yaw rate does not increase more than 16%
FSR2	SG1	The steering shall be fail-operational
FSR3	SG1	The operational state of the steering controller shall be monitored and reported to superordinate controller
FSR4	SG1	The system shall always assure that the range of the steering shall be between [−540, 540] degrees
FRS5	SG2	The system shall always assure that the LateralError value must be less than LateralErrorMax
FSR6	SG2	The system shall always assure that the Controller Cv parameter value is between [−1, 1]
FSR7	SG2	The operational state of the trajectory controller shall be monitored and reported to superordinate controller
FSR8	SG3	The trajectory shall be calculated based on the most appropriate manoeuvre (e.g. lane keeping, lane changing)
FRS9	SG3	The system shall assure that the new position (X_{t+1}, Y_{t+1}) of the trajectory based on vehicle speed shall not exceed more than 9% of the current position (X_t, Y_t)
FSR10	SG3	The system shall calculate its trajectory starting from the most appropriate manoeuvre (e.g. lane keeping, lane changing)
FSR11	SG3	The operational state of the behavioural planner shall be monitored and reported to superordinate controller

In the selection of safety concepts, the main outcome is that a redundant steering is necessary in order to achieve the required level of availability. The main reason is that a failure related to the steering shall be detected within 70 ms and the availability must be provided within 196 ms. Regarding failures coming from the Trajectory Controller, the detection time is established at 114 ms and the maximum system failure reaction time in terms of vehicle dynamics is 250 ms. Because of these timing results, graceful degradation might be sufficient in this case. Behavioural Planner malfunctions shall be detected in less than 123 ms and their effect on vehicle level controlled within 327 ms. The same applies to the Behavioural Planner for which graceful degradation might be sufficient.

5   Conclusion and Future Work

We have presented a simulation-based FI approach for an early safety assessment of automotive systems. Our approach has been evaluated in a case study for the model-based design of a Lateral Control system. From a novelty standpoint, we focused on determining of the fault detection time interval for permanent faults based on the maximum lateral error, as a vehicle dynamics property. A major strength of the method introduced in this paper is its usage during early design phases to evaluate the safety of the system. This allows dimensioning and trading-off between safety concepts and performs an early safety validation of the design. The uncertainty related to some automotive systems, such as an automated vehicle, makes traditional safety analysis methods definitely not sufficient, requiring additional virtual and simulation solutions. Forthwith, FI establishes itself as a way of completing and verifying previously carried out safety analyses. Given that analysing system reactions under the effects of real faults can a burden-some issue, these FI experiments arise as a viable solution.

Our future work spans the spectrum from relaxing the fault simulation constraints to instrumenting the automated assessment work. This includes: (1) adding the capability of automatically collapsing the injection of faults to generate optimised fault lists, (2) integrating with contract-based approaches, (3) connecting to other system modelling environments such as Papyrus/SysML, (4) linking to model-based safety analysis tools, and (5) comparing FI simulation results with the results of performing software fault injection for a model-car.

Acknowledgments. The authors have partially received funding from the ECSEL JU AMASS project under H2020 grant agreement No 692474, the UnCoVerCPS project under H2020 grant agreement No 643921 and MINETUR (Spain).

References

1. Koopman, P., Wagner, M.: Challenges in autonomous vehicle testing and validation. In: 2016 SAE World Congress (2016)
2. ISO 26262: Road vehicles – Functional safety, International Organisation for Standardisation (ISO) (2011)

3. Pintard, M.L.: Des analyses de securite a la validation experimentale par injection de fautes - le cas des systemes embarques automobiles. Ph.D, Institut National Polytechnique de Toulouse (2015)
4. Pena, A., Iglesias, I., Valera, J., Martin, A.: Development and validation of Dynacar RT software, a new integrated solution for design of electric and hybrid vehicles. In: EVS26 Los Angeles (2012)
5. Ruiz, A., Juez, G., Schleiss, P., Weiss, G.: A safe generic adaptation mechanism for smart cars. In: IEEE 26th International Symposium on Software Reliability Engineering (ISSRE), pp. 161–171, Gaithersbury, MD (2015). doi:10.1109/ISSRE.2015.7381810
6. Ziade, H., Ayoubi, R., Velazco, R.: A survey on fault injection techniques. Int. Arab J. Inf. Technol. 1(2), 171–186 (2004)
7. Benso, A., Di Carlo, S.: The art of fault injection. J. Control Eng. Appl. Inform. 13(4), 9–18 (2011)
8. Svenningsson, R.: Model-implemented fault injection for robustness assessment, Licentiate Thesis, Stockholm (2011)
9. Vinter, J., Bromander, L., Raistrick, P., Edler, H.: Fiscade - a fault injection tool for SCADE models. In: Automotive Electronics 2007 3rd Institution of Engineering and Technology Conference, pp. 1–9 (2007)
10. Silveira, A., Araujo, R., De Castro, R.: FIEEV: a co-simulation framework for fault injection in electrical vehicles. In: 2012 IEEE International Conference on Vehicular Electronics and Safety, ICVES 2012, pp. 357–362 (2012)
11. Jones, S., Armengaud, E., Böhm, H.: Safety simulation in the concept phase: advanced co-simulation toolchain for conventional, hybrid and fully electric vehicles. In: Fischer-Wolfarth, J., Meyer, G. (eds.) Advanced Microsystems for Automotive Applications 2014. Lecture Notes in Mobility, pp. 153–164. Springer, Switzerland (2014)
12. Folkesson, P., Ayatolahi, F., Sangchoolie, B., Vinter, J., Islam, M., Karlsson, J.: Back-to-back fault injection testing in model-based development. In: Koornneef, F., Gulijk, C. (eds.) SAFECOMP 2015. LNCS, vol. 9337, pp. 135–148. Springer, Cham (2015). doi: 10.1007/978-3-319-24255-2_11
13. Arlat, J., Aguera, M., Amat, L., Crouzet, Y., Fabre, J.C., Laprie, J.C., Martins, E., Powell, D.: Fault injection for dependability validation: a methodology and some applications. IEEE Trans. Softw. Eng. 16, 166–182 (1990). Fault injection for dependability validation: a methodology and some applications
14. Algirdas, A., Laprie, J.C., Randell, B., Landwehr, C.: Basic concepts and taxonomy of dependable and secure computing. IEEE Trans. Dependable Secur. Comput. 1, 11–33 (2004). doi:10.1109/TDSC.2004.2

Towards a Sensor Failure-Dependent Performance Adaptation Using the Validity Concept

Juliane Höbel[1]([✉]), Georg Jäger[2], Sebastian Zug[2], and Andreas Wendemuth[1]

[1] Institute for Electronics, Signal Processing and Communications Technology,
Otto-von-Guericke University, Magdeburg, Germany
{juliane.hoebel,andreas.wendemuth}@ovgu.de
[2] Institute for Intelligent Cooperating Systems, Otto-von-Guericke University,
Magdeburg, Germany
{jaeger,zug}@ivs.cs.uni-magdeburg.de

Abstract. Statically proving the adherence of a system to its safety requirements specified at design-time provokes overcautious systems with limited performance. Contrarily, dynamically assessing the quality of sensor observations at run-time enables adapting a system's performance accordingly while maintaining its safety. While this could be shown by Brade et al. [2] for a simulated scenario with one-dimensional sensors, we apply the proposed scheme, that is, the Validity Concept to 3D depth information. In this endeavour, we define a failure model covering the failure types *Noise*, *Outlier*, and *Illumination Artefacts*, define functions to estimate their severity at run-time and represent a 3D point cloud's quality in terms of validity information. Furthermore, we show that calculated *Validity Values* correlate with sensor failures impairing sensor observations and enable estimating the quality of subsequent applications.

1 Introduction

Nowadays, mobile robotic systems utilize the extensive knowledge of their dynamically changing environment to autonomously perform even complex tasks. While 3D depth cameras are widely used to obtain such extensive knowledge [1,8,9,13], they suffer from a variety of sensor failures (see Fig. 1), which highly depends on environmental conditions. In traditional systems, the threat which sensor failures pose on a system's safety is countervailed by implementing appropriate failure tolerance mechanisms at design-time while relying on these mechanisms at run-time. Thus, the safety strategy implemented is dictated by the most severe sensor failure possible. When considering context-dependent sensor failures, a system's safety strategy has to consider all possible scenarios in which the system may be situated at run-time. This will result in an overcautious system as the scenario-causing severe sensor failures may occur only infrequently but the system's performance is limited permanently. On the other hand, a system that maintains its safety by adapting its performance depending on the quality of available sensor

© Springer International Publishing AG 2017
S. Tonetta et al. (Eds.): SAFECOMP 2017, LNCS 10488, pp. 270–286, 2017.
DOI: 10.1007/978-3-319-66266-4_18

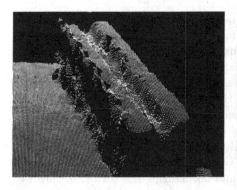 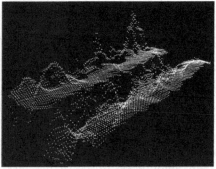

Fig. 1. Two 3D point clouds obtained by an *Intel RealSense F200* camera [11] observing an aluminium profile. In the left picture, *Outlier* failures are visible between the work-piece and the table. In the right picture, *Illumination Artefacts* occur at the edge of the work-piece.

observations would implicitly react to changing environmental conditions without permanently limiting its performance. An approach addressing this issue was proposed by Brade et al. [2] who elaborated key functions developed within the KARYON project [4] to implement a simulated autonomous car that adapts its velocity depending on the quality of available sensor observations. The key to this adaptation is the *Validity-Based Failure Algebra* [3], or in short, the *Validity Concept*, which introduces a validity-based quality measure of sensor observations applicable at design-time as well as at run-time. While the work of Brade et al. shows that a run-time performance adaptation is possible without sacrificing safety, the Validity Concept is tested solely with respect to one-dimensional distance sensors [2,3]. Contrarily, we apply the Validity Concept to the distance information of 3D depth cameras as a prerequisite to implementing a run-time performance adaptation. In this endeavour, we firstly introduce the core points of the Validity Concept in the following section and review the state of the art on modelling failures of 3D depth information in Sect. 3. While existing approaches address only separate failure types in their failure models, we introduce a sophisticated model in Sect. 4 and describe its usage for applying the Validity Concept. In Sect. 5, we evaluate our approach with respect to its intended usage, which is the implementation of a run-time performance adaptation. To test the approach with realistic data, we consider the *RoboCup@Work* league in which competitive teams are required to perform object classification and pose estimation both fast and safely [10]. Finally, we conclude our work in the last section and describe possible future work.

2 Validity-Based Failure Algebra

In this section, we introduce the core points of the Validity-Based Failure Algebra proposed by Brade et al. [3]. While the concept enables us to assess the quality of sensor data consistently at design-time and at run-time, we focus on the latter with respect to its usage for a run-time performance adaptation. The Validity-Based Failure Algebra aims at describing the confidence that an application can have in certain sensor data. In this endeavour, Brade et al. presume a failure model that describes a sensor's failure characteristics by a set of m failure types, $\{(A, p) | A \in \mathbb{R}, p \in [0, 1]\}$. Each of these failure types is considered to cause a maximal failure amplitude A occurring with a likelihood p. Brade et al. abstract this information by defining the *Failure Vector* $\vec{f}$ in which each element is associated with one failure type, see Fig. 2. The values of the corresponding elements are determined by assigning the failure type's maximal failure amplitudes A_l ($l \in \{0, 1, ..., m\}$) and normalizing the vector. In this way, the value of each element F_l is the failure type's share on the summed maximal failure amplitude. In a subsequent step, the elements are multiplied with the counter-probabilities $(1 - p_l)$ to determine the *Validity Shares* f_l that form the elements of the *Validity Vector* $\vec{v}$. Due to this multiplication, the *Validity Shares* are restricted to the range of $f_l \in [0, F_l]$. While the *Validity Vector* is initialised with static design-time knowledge, its purpose is to inform about the failure types impairing a sensor observation at run-time. Therefore, a separate *Validity Vector* is associated with each observation provided by a sensor at run-time and is updated whenever additional run-time knowledge about the severity of failure types is available. Brade et al. consider detectors recognising occurrences of considered sensor failure types and filters as *Processes* of a subsequent processing chain that produce such run-time knowledge. However, one can generalise this idea by defining that each *Process* altering the sensor data also updates its associated *Validity Vector*, see Fig. 2. To provide a more condensed quality measure besides the *Validity Vector*, Brade et al. additionally define the *Validity Value v* as the sum of all *Validity Shares* f_l of the vector $\vec{v}$. Due to its relation to the *Failure Vector*, the *Validity Value* ranges between 0 and 1, where 1 indicates correct sensor observations and 0 indicates severe sensor failures. Brade et al. [2] utilize this reduced quality measure to realize their run-time performance adaptation. At design-time, different performance levels of a system are defined. For each level, the system is simulated with increasingly severe sensor failures. By monitoring the severity of sensor failures in relation to the system's safety, a minimum *Validity Value* at which the system behaved safely is determined. This proven safety is used at run-time where the highest possible level of performance is inferred from the *Validity Value* of available sensor data. In this way, the system's performance is adapted at run-time while its safety is maintained.

3   State of the Art

The Validity Concept enables monitoring the quality of sensor data at run-time by abstracting the failure model of a considered sensor. As we aim for applying the concept to 3D depth cameras, we review the state of the art on modelling their failures in this section. We focus on the most common techniques:

- In Stereo Vision, a scene is observed from two different perspectives to utilize the displacement of features for triangulation [5].

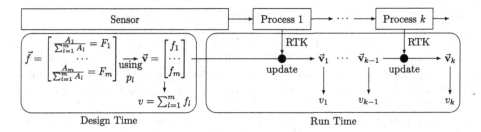

Fig. 2. Overview of the Validity Concept of Brade et al. [3]. RTK is the abbreviation of *Run-Time Knowledge*, which is produced by any *Process* applied to a sensor's output.

- Structured Light projects a pattern on a scene and exploits the observed displacement of the pattern for triangulation too [14].
- Time-of-Flight (ToF) cameras illuminate a scene with modulated light and measure the phase shift of reflected light to calculate a scene's depth [19].

All these sensing techniques provide 3D depth information of an observed scene, also called (3D) point clouds. Despite their differences, we identified the error sources of common failure types in the literature causing common failure types. An overview of this relation is shown in Table 1 and is discussed in Subsect. 3.1. In a concluding subsection, we review failure models considering these failure types and assess their applicability to the Validity Concept.

Table 1. Overview of error sources of sensing techniques for 3D depth information and their associated data-centric failure types.

Failure type	Triangulation-based		Time-of-Flight
	Structured light	Stereo vision	Continuous wave
Noise	Quantization [24]	Quantization [5]	Non-uniform illumination [6]
	Numerical errors [24]		Inaccurate measuring time [6]
	Object surface [14]		
	Mislocating features [24]	Mislocating features [5]	
	Lighting condition [14]	Lighting condition [14]	
	Motion Bblur [15]	Motion blur [23]	Motion blur [20]
Outlier	Exceptional high/low	Exceptional high/low	
	reflectivity of surfaces [22]	reflectivity of surfaces [22]	
	Strong sun light [14]	Strong sun light [14]	
	Object edges [6,22]	Object edges [6,22]	
Illumination	Multiple light reception [9]		Multiple light reception [6]
Artefacts	Object edges [14]		
Offset	Parallel projection model [24]	Perspective projection model [7]	Emitted light modulation model [6]
	Incorrect calibration [13,19]	Incorrect calibration [13,19]	Incorrect calibration [13,19]
	Inaccurate camera design [24]	Inaccurate camera design [24]	Inaccurate camera design [24]
			Integration-time value [6]
Gaps	Shadowing or	Shadowing or	Shadowing or
	occluding effects [12,19]	occluding effects [12]	occluding effects [12]
	Absorbing surfaces [12]		

3.1 Failure Types and Error Sources

By taking a data-centric perspective, we identified five failure types common to all sensing techniques presented. These failure types are *Noise, Outlier, Illumination Artefacts, Offset,* and *Gaps.* In this subsection, we associate these failure types with the error sources reported in the literature for each of the presented methods, see Table 1.

Noise failures are random inaccuracies continuously affecting the 3D points. In the case of triangulation-based methods, usual error sources are lighting conditions [14], numerical errors [24], and motion blurring [6]. ToF cameras exhibit this failure type when the scene is non-uniformly illuminated by their projectors [6]. While a 3D point affected by a *Noise* failure still relates to an actual object in the observed scene, *Outlier* failures are points that cannot be accounted to a real object anymore. In that manner, the definition of an *Outlier* failure in this context contrasts with the traditional one. While these potentially introduce large inaccuracies, their occurrences are connected with the spatial situation of the observed scene. Hence, common sources of these failures are edges of surfaces [6,22], along with strong sunlight [14], and surfaces with exceptionally high or low reflectivity [22]. While the failure type *Illumination Artefact* is similar to an *Outlier* failure, it usually affects multiple, neighbouring points. Due to this characteristics, the affected points form long-tailed but flat clusters. The failure type is caused by indirect illumination originated from concavity of an object or sharp edges [14]. Another common failure type is *Gaps* that are missing depth information. These occur inherently due to discretising a scene into 3D points as well as shadowing or occluding effects [19]. In the case of the Structured Light approach, this failure type can be caused by surfaces absorbing infrared light too [12]. Finally, the *Offset* failure describes constant offsets in depth information. It is usually caused by incorrect calibration parameters [14,19,24], inaccurate camera design [24], or the usage of inadequate models for calculating the depth information (parallel projection model [24], perspective projection model [7], emitted light modulation model [6]).

3.2 Failure Models

The last subsection dealt with failure types that abstract the error sources of the individual sensing techniques. Hence, the failure models addressing these failure types apply to 3D depth information in general. Consequently, in this section, we review such failure models.

A detailed representation of the *Noise* failure is provided by Rauscher et al. [19]. They assume a Gaussian random failure with a mean value of zero and describe the standard deviation by a polynomial function over the measured depth. Such a distance-related *Noise* failure model is commonly used and is applied in [14] too. Another definition is provided by Pauly et al. [18] along with an approach to reduce noisiness and model *Gaps* using the point density in 3D depth information. Despite their detailed failure representation, they neglect considering the remaining failure types. Yang et al. [24], on the other hand, not only address quantisation errors and dislocated features as sources of *Noise* failure, but also the parallel projection model as a source of *Offset* failures. The approach of [9] investigated short-range and long-range effects as causes for *Illumination Artefacts* but lack an explicit description of this failure type. Likewise, the failure type *Outlier* is separately modelled in [25] exploiting the local neighbourhood of single points in a 3D point cloud. Finally, *Offset* failures are modelled in [14] to manage incorrect calibrations.

While the presented approaches model the failures of 3D depth information in detail, they solely focus on a subset or individual failure types. When considering the run-time usage of failure models, it is reasonable to omit the *Offset* failures as they are usually compensable by appropriate calibration at design-time. Furthermore, *Gaps* failures highly depend on the object observed and are therefore intractable to model in general. On the other hand, the failure types *Noise*, *Outliers*, and *Illumination Artefacts* cannot be neglected. Nonetheless, a failure model comprising these three failure types could not be found in the literature. Hence, the current state of the art does not provide failure models covering all relevant failure types to be used in the Validity Concept.

4 Applying the Validity Concept to 3D Depth Information

While we showed in Sect. 2 that using the Validity Concept requires an appropriate failure model, the last section demonstrated the lack of such a model for 3D depth information. Consequently, in this section, we will define a failure model and utilize it to apply the Validity-Based Failure Algebra to 3D point clouds. Furthermore, we will discuss the definition, severity estimation, and validity calculation of each failure type in a separate subsection but start with a general discussion about challenges arising when applying the Validity Concept to 3D point clouds. For that, we will define the set P which represents a 3D point cloud extended with validity information:

$$P = \{(\vec{p}_i, \vec{v}_i, v_i) \mid \vec{p}_i \in \mathbb{R}^3_{\geq 0}, \ \vec{v}_i = [f_{i1} \ f_{i2} \ \cdots \ f_{im}]^T, \ 1 \leq i \leq n\} \quad (1)$$

The set P of size n associates a *Validity Vector* $\vec{v}_i$ and a *Validity Value* v_i to each measurement point $\vec{p}_i$. The *Validity Vector* comprises the *Validity Shares* $f_{i_1}, ..., f_{i_m}$, which represent the current severity estimation of their associated failure types. In Sect. 3, we identified five failure types of which only *Noise*, *Outlier*, and *Illumination Artefacts* are relevant at run-time. Hence, here we consider $m = 3$ failure types, where f_{i_1} maps to *Noise*, f_{i_2} maps to *Outlier*, and f_{i_3} maps to *Illumination Artefacts*. As a consequence, applying the Validity Concept to 3D point clouds requires determining the *Validity Shares* f_{i_1}, f_{i_2}, and f_{i_3} for each point in P.

As defined by Brade et al. [3], these represent the currently estimated severity of a failure type in relation to its maximal severity F_l, where l encodes the failure type, see Sect. 2. Furthermore, the *Validity Shares* f_l are initialised using the failure types' occurrence probabilities p_l. Brade et al. extract these values statically from a sensor's failure model. However, the failure types considered in this paper are highly context-dependent [14,19]. Therefore, statically defining a failure type's maximum severity as well as its probability of occurrence is deemed to be correct solely for a specific context, but cannot be considered as generally correct.

To address these challenges, we argue for excluding the static knowledge. Instead, we apply the Validity Concept by providing so-called distance-related *Belief Functions*. Their purpose is two-fold. On the one hand, they estimate the relative severity of failure types as the distance between the actual sensor data and its estimated ideal value at run-time, and, on the other hand, they transform the identified severities into their respective *Validity Shares*. As this calculation directly constitutes the quality assessment of sensor data, an engineer has to consider the application's safety requirements when designing this function. Furthermore, as the *Belief Functions* directly calculate the *Validity Shares* f_l at run-time, the requirement for static knowledge of F_l or p_l is circumvented for assessing sensor data. However, as defined by Brade et al., the values of F_l also serve as range limitations in which the *Validity Share* f_l varies ($f_l \in [0, F_l]$), see Sect. 2. Due to the inherent uncertainty of static knowledge about the failure types considered, we do not rely on these values but assign equal ranges to each failure type. In the same way, we considered the $m = 3$ failure types, each *Validity Share* shall be in the range of $f_{i_1}, f_{i_2}, f_{i_3} \in [0, 1/3]$. In summary, applying the Validity Concept to 3D point clouds requires defining the failure types *Noise*, *Outlier*, *Illumination Artefacts*, and the functions to estimate their severity as well as their *Belief Functions*. These aspects of each considered failure type are discussed in the following subsections.

4.1 Noise

In this subsection, we will provide a definition of the *Noise* failure type and a *Belief Function* to estimate its severity and to calculate its *Validity Share* f_{i_1}.

In literature, the failure type *Noise* is considered to be random inaccuracies of sensor data occurring continuously [18]. While there are several models of this failure type [19], we will refer to Pauly et al. [18] who define a confidence measure estimating the noisiness of a single point in P. The measure quantifies the deviation of a considered point $\vec{p}_i$ from a plane defined by its neighbouring points. For defining this measure, Pauly et al. start by calculating the covariance matrix $\mathbf{C}_i$ of each point $\vec{p}_i \in P$ [18]:

$$\mathbf{C}_i = \sum_{j=1}^{n} \vec{p}_{ij} \vec{p}_{ij}^T \phi_i(\|\vec{p}_{ij}\|) \tag{2}$$

where $\vec{p}_{ij} = \vec{p}_i - \vec{p}_j$ is the distance between the considered point $\vec{p}_i$ and its neighbouring point $\vec{p}_j$. Furthermore, the radial Gaussian function $\phi_i(\|\vec{p}_{ij}\|)$ defines the neighbourhood of point $\vec{p}_i$ and reflects the assumption that point $\vec{p}_j$ is part of the same plane as point $\vec{p}_i$ only when the distance to each other is small.

However, the presence of *Noise* influences the calculated covariance matrix itself, resulting in a disturbed confidence measure. Hence, Pauly et al. propose to reduce the *Noise* by defining another covariance matrix Ω_i of point $\vec{\mathbf{p}}_i$ with a restricted neighbourhood [18]:

$$\Omega_i = \sum_{j=1}^{k} (\vec{\mathbf{p}}_j - \vec{\mathbf{p}}) \cdot (\vec{\mathbf{p}}_j - \vec{\mathbf{p}})^T \tag{3}$$

where k defines the number of neighbouring points of $\vec{\mathbf{p}}_i$, and $\vec{\mathbf{p}}$ is the geometric centre of the neighbourhood. Using a second matrix Ω_j for a neighbouring point $\vec{\mathbf{p}}_j$, Pauly et al. adapt the neighbourhood-function [18]:

$$\phi_{ij}' = \phi_i\left(\sqrt{\vec{\mathbf{p}}_{ij}^T \vec{\mathbf{p}}_{ij} + tr(\Omega_i) + tr(\Omega_j)}\right) \tag{4}$$

This function is used to modify (2) and to calculate a corrected matrix C_i' [18]:

$$\mathbf{C}_i' = \sum_{j=1}^{n} \vec{\mathbf{p}}_{ij} \vec{\mathbf{p}}_{ij}^T \phi_{ij}' + \Omega_i \cdot \sum_{j=1}^{n} \phi_{ij}' + \sum_{j=1}^{n} \Omega_j \cdot \phi_{ij}' \tag{5}$$

Due to the definition of each point $\vec{\mathbf{p}}_i \in \mathbb{R}^3_{\geq 0}$, $\mathbf{C}_i'$ is a 3×3 matrix, yielding 3 eigenvectors with eigenvalues λ_i^1, λ_i^2 and λ_i^3. The two eigenvectors yielding the highest eigenvalues are assumed to define the plane from which the noisiness of a point is measured. Finally, Pauly et al. represent the noisiness of a point $\vec{\mathbf{p}}_i$ with their confidence measure [18]:

$$\bar{\lambda}_i = \lambda_i^{min}/(\lambda_i^1 + \lambda_i^2 + \lambda_i^3) \tag{6}$$

where λ_i^{min} represents the minimum eigenvalue of these three. As a consequence, $\bar{\lambda}_i$ is always in the range of $[0, 1/3]$. Furthermore, as λ_i^{min} quantifies the distance of point $\vec{\mathbf{p}}_i$ from the estimated plane, values of $\bar{\lambda}_i$ close to 0 indicate a high confidence, that is, a low noisiness, while increased values indicate reduced confidence, which is increased noisiness. This interpretation is in contrast to the definition of *Validity Shares*, where high values indicate high confidence. Hence, we apply the following *Belief Function* to convert the confidence measure of Pauly et al. into the *Validity Share* f_{i_1}:

$$f_{i_1} = 1/3 - \bar{\lambda}_i \tag{7}$$

4.2 Outlier

In contrast to the *Noise* failure type, an observation is considered as an *Outlier* when it lies outside the overall pattern of a distribution [17]. Albeit, this failure type is rather infrequent, it impairs sensor data more severely. To detect whether a point $\vec{\mathbf{p}}_i$ is an *Outlier*, we define a confidence interval and estimate the failure's severity as its distance to the interval border. In this endeavour, we start by calculating the average distance of a point $\vec{\mathbf{p}}_i$ to its k-nearest neighbours as:

$$\mu_i = \frac{1}{k} \sum_{j=1}^{k} \|\vec{\mathbf{p}}_{ij}\| \tag{8}$$

Similar to the last subsection, the values of $\|\vec{\mathbf{p}}_{ij}\|$ may be corrupted by *Noise* failures. As these disturb the values of μ_i, we utilize the approach of Pauly et al. to reduce the noisiness once again. However, this time we directly utilize the Ω-matrices (see (3)). Using the matrices Ω_i and Ω_j, the calculated distance between $\vec{\mathbf{p}}_i$ and $\vec{\mathbf{p}}_j$ is corrected by assuming a random distribution and calculating its expected value $E[\|\vec{\mathbf{p}}_{ij}\|]$. As this expected value is determined by the traces of the matrices Ω_i and Ω_j, the corrected average distance μ_i' is given by:

$$\mu_i' = \frac{1}{k} \sum_{j=1}^{k} E[\|\vec{\mathbf{p}}_{ij}\|] = \frac{1}{k} \sum_{j=1}^{k} \sqrt{\vec{\mathbf{p}}_{ij}^T \vec{\mathbf{p}}_{ij} + tr(\Omega_i) + tr(\Omega_j)} \tag{9}$$

By assuming that the distances μ_i' are distributed normally over the set P, we define the confidence interval $[\mu_P - s \cdot \sigma_P; \mu_P + s \cdot \sigma_P]$ using the mean μ_P and standard deviation σ_P over all distances μ_i'. The parameter s controls the width of the confidence interval and is to be specified with respect to an application's safety requirements as well as its tolerance to *Outlier* failures. The interval itself defines the pattern of the distribution. Following the definition [17], a point $\vec{\mathbf{p}}_i$ is an *Outlier* if it is outside the interval. However, points for which $\mu_i' < \mu_P - s \cdot \sigma_P$ are characterised by being close to their neighbouring points and likely to being a part of a cluster, which is a pattern itself. Therefore, those points are not considered to be *Outliers*. Contrarily, a point $\vec{\mathbf{p}}_i$ for which $\mu_i' > \mu_P + s \cdot \sigma_P$ is separated from the pattern and is consequently deemed as an *Outlier*. Finally, by abbreviating the upper border as the threshold $t_O = \mu_P + s \cdot \sigma_P$, we define the *Belief Function* as an exponential function:

$$f_{i_2} = \begin{cases} 1/3 & : \mu_i' \leq t_O \\ 1/3 \cdot e^{-(\mu_i' - t_O)^2 / t_O^{a_O}} & : \mu_i' > t_O \end{cases} \tag{10}$$

with $a_O \in \mathbb{R}_{>0}$. The term $-(\mu_i' - t_O)^2$ squares the estimated severity $(\mu_i - t_O)$ and multiplies it with -1 to ensure function values between 0 and 1. By scaling these values linearly with $1/3$, the *Outlier's Validity Share* f_{i_2} is within its range $[0, 1/3]$. In this case an exponential mapping between the estimated severity and the *Outlier's Validity Share* is applied to account for the special characteristics of an *Outlier*: its commonly severe occurrences. Due to the exponential mapping, the slope of the *Belief Function* rapidly declines. Finally, the parameter a_O also tunes the slope of the *Belief Function* and can therefore be used by an engineer to adjust the severity assessment of *Outliers* with respect to an application's safety requirement.

4.3   Illumination Artefacts

While points affected by *Outliers* show no relation to each other, *Illumination Artefacts* affect clusters of points. Such a cluster forms a plane that is oriented parallel to the view of the camera. Therefore, points on this plane should, if they were real, hide other points from the view of the camera. However, their presence in P, despite not being able to be observed by the camera, leaves no other conclusion than deeming those points as *Illumination Artefacts*. In endeavouring to detect those points, Fuchs et al. [8] propose comparing the angle between vector $\vec{c}$, which is the camera's line of sight, and the vector defined by the two neighbouring points $\vec{p}_i$ and $\vec{p}_j$. If the angle is greater than $\pi - t_I$, where t_I is a threshold for which Fuchs et al. propose a value of $t_I = 0.087$, $\vec{p}_i$ is assumed to be an *Illumination Artefact*. However, since they consider only a single neighbouring point $\vec{p}_j$, this decision is not robust to noisy data. Contrarily, we have to anticipate *Noise* failures and therefore adapt the approach. We start with the *Noise*-reduced covariance matrix C_i' of point $\vec{p}_i$, see (5). As a covariance matrix is always symmetric and positive semi-definite, its eigenvectors span an orthonormal space. Therefore, the two eigenvectors yielding the highest eigenvalues span a plane while the eigenvector yielding the lowest eigenvalue is the normal vector $\vec{n}_i$ of this plane. In case the point $\vec{p}_i$ is affected by *Illumination Artefacts*, the estimated plane is parallel to the line of sight of the camera $\vec{c}$, implying that the angle β_i between $\vec{c}$ and the normal $\vec{n}_i$ is close to 90° (or $\frac{\pi}{2}$ in radiant). The angle β_i is calculated by:

$$\beta_i = \vec{n}_i \cdot (\vec{c} - \vec{p}_i)/|\vec{n}_i| \cdot |\vec{c} - \vec{p}_i| \qquad (11)$$

Using the angle β_i, a point $\vec{p}_i$ is considered as an *Illumination Artefact* if its corresponding angle β_i is greater or equal to $\frac{\pi}{2} - t_I$. By assuming a neighbourhood of k points instead of relying on a single neighbouring point, this adapted version is more tolerant to *Noise* failures. Finally, incorporating the threshold t_I in the *Belief Function* allows transforming the angle β_i into the corresponding *Validity Share*:

$$f_{i_3} = \begin{cases} 1/3 & : \ \beta_i < \frac{\pi}{2} - t_I \\ 1/3 \cdot e^{-\beta_i^2/\frac{\pi}{2}a_I} & : \ \beta_i \geq \frac{\pi}{2} - t_I \end{cases} \qquad (12)$$

where $a_I \in \mathbb{R}_{>0}$ allows an engineer to tune the slope of the *Belief Function*. We also used an exponential mapping for this function because of the similarity of *Illumination Artefacts* to the *Outlier* failure type.

4.4   Validity of Points and Point Clouds

The previous considerations were focused on single points $\vec{p}_i$. However, when processing 3D point clouds, it is common to isolate regions of interest based on *segmentation* [21]. These regions R are all subsets of the overall point cloud P ($R \subseteq P$). The included points share characteristics such as corresponding to the same object. Similar to a point $\vec{p}_i$ of a point cloud P, a region R can be attributed with a *Validity Vector* $\vec{v}_R$ and a *Validity Value* v_R as well. As this requires fusing the validity information of all points $\vec{p}_i \in R$, there are several options. In applications where the validity of a single point $\vec{p}_i$ is relevant to its safety, it is feasible to form the *Validity Vector* $\vec{v}_R$ using the minimum values of the *Validity Shares*. Contrarily, applications that might be robust to failures of a single point would act overcautiously when using this option. In such case, forming the vector $\vec{v}_R$ using the median of *Validity Shares* would be another option. On the one hand, this option is robust to exceptionally low or high *Validity Shares* but, on the other hand, it is unable to represent slight changes in their values. Therefore, to limit the effect of exceptionally low or high *Validity Shares* while reflecting also slight changes in their values, we use the mean of the *Validity Shares*:

$$f_{R_l} = \frac{1}{|R|} \cdot \sum_{i=1}^{|R|} f_{i_l} \tag{13}$$

where $l \in \{1, 2, 3\}$. Hence, the *Validity Shares* f_{R_l} are the average of the corresponding *Validity Shares* f_{i_l} of the points $\vec{p}_i \in R$. As the *Validity Shares* f_{R_l} form the *Validity Vector* $\vec{v}_R$, the *Validity Value* v_R is the sum of its elements. Furthermore, since R may be equal to P, the *Validity Vector* $\vec{v}_P$ and the *Validity Value* v_P of a complete 3D point cloud P are obtained in the same way.

5 Evaluation

To evaluate the approach presented with respect to its utilization in a run-time performance adaptation, we need to consider two different aspects: First, we need to show that the *Validity Value* v_P adequately represents the quality of 3D point clouds. Second, we need to show that the *Validity Vector* $\vec{v}_P$ of sensor data and its elements f_{P_l} allow inferring the quality of an application's output data from the quality of its input data. This is a mandatory prerequisite for defining different levels of performance at design-time and to safely switch between them at run-time. In Subsect. 5.2, we analyse the first aspect using real and simulated sensor data from the *RoboCup@Work* league. To examine the second aspect, in Subsect. 5.3, we reuse the sensor data and additionally assume the tasks of object classification and position estimation. In the next subsection, however, we start by describing the experimental setup of the evaluation.

5.1 Experimental Setup

Simulated and real 3D depth information were acquired for the evaluation. We simulated 3D point clouds, consisting of 400 points each, by assuming a planar surface of $1\,m \times 1\,m$, with a distance of $1.2\,m$ to a virtual camera. To match this with a realistic scenario, the x and y components of points are distributed normally $\mathcal{N}(0, 1)$ as proposed by Pauly et al. [18]. To obtain real sensor data, we studied a scenario from the *RoboCup@Work* league with an *Intel RealSense F200* [11] camera. The camera observed two different aluminium profiles separately from a fixed position. The first was of size $20\,mm \times 20\,mm \times 100\,mm$, while the second was of size $40\,mm \times 40\,mm \times 100\,mm$. Both were placed on a table with a distance of $0.35\,m$ to the camera. Figure 1 shows two examples of point clouds obtained from this scene. To derive *Validity Shares* for evaluating the approach, we parametrised the *Belief Functions*, using $a_O = a_I = 2$. Concerning the *Outlier* failure type, we additionally used a value of $s = 1.2$ to specify its confidence interval, see Subsect. 4.2. We implemented the presented approach in

C++ using the Robot Operating System (ROS) Kinetic [16] on Ubuntu 16.04. To evaluate the computation time t_c, we executed the algorithms on 15 real point clouds on an Intel Core i5-4200U CPU with 3.8 GiB of main memory. Each of these point clouds contains 5561 points $(+/-33)$. Furthermore, by reconsidering the parameters of the *Belief Functions* (see Sect. 4), we assume that only the parameter k has a major effect on t_c. Therefore, we varied k from $\{8, 16, 24\}$. Using this configuration, the mean t_c to determine the *Validity Shares* and the *Validity Value* is 1.11 s $(k = 8)$, 2.71 s $(k = 16)$, and 5.1 s $(k = 24)$. These results show a linear effect of increasing k on t_c. To decrease t_c, a GPU-based real-time processing can be an alternative.

5.2 Correlation of Validity Values and Failure Severities

In this subsection, we analyse the acquired data with hypothesis tests to show that the *Validity Value* v_P correlates with the failure amplitude and likelihood of the failure types *Noise*, *Outlier*, and *Illumination Artefacts*. We design seven tests (see Table 2) where T_1 and T_2 show that the *Validity Value* v_P reflects increased failure amplitudes of *Noise* and *Outlier* failures. Similarly, tests T_3, T_4, and T_5 evidence that increasing likelihood of occurrence of failure types causes a reduction in the *Validity Value*. Finally, tests T_6 and T_7 also show this relation but use

Table 2. Overview of parameters of failure injection (p_l: Occurrence probability of failure type, A: Failure amplitude of failure type in $[mm]$) to generate *Control Samples* and *Paired Samples* of hypothesis tests and the tests' results.

Test: Considered failure type	Control samples	Paired samples	Test result $\alpha = 0.05$)
Failure severity - Simulated data			
T_1: *Noise*	$p_1 = 1.0$ $A_1 \sim \mathcal{N}(0, 10)$	$p_1 = 1.0$ $A_1 \sim \mathcal{N}(0, 15)$	$p_{T_1} = 0.0 < \alpha$
T_2: *Outlier*	$p_2 = 0.05$ $A_2 \sim \mathcal{U}(100, 200)$	$p_2 = 0.05$ $A_2 \sim \mathcal{U}(300, 500)$	$p_{T_2} = 0.0 < \alpha$
Occurrence probability - Simulated data			
T_3: *Noise*	$p_1 = 0.05$ $A_1 \sim \mathcal{N}(0, 20)$	$p_1 = 0.1$ $A_1 \sim \mathcal{N}(0, 20)$	$p_{T_3} = 0.0 < \alpha$
T_4: *Outlier*	$p_2 = 0.05$ $A_2 \sim \mathcal{U}(200, 500)$	$p_2 = 0.1$ $A_2 \sim \mathcal{U}(200, 500)$	$p_{T_4} = 0.0 < \alpha$
T_5: *Illumination artefacts*	$p_3 = 0.33$ $\beta_i = \frac{\pi}{2}$	$p_3 = 0.5$ $\beta_i = \frac{\pi}{2}$	$p_{T_5} = 0.0 < \alpha$
Occurrence probability - Real data			
T_6: *Outlier*	$p_2 = 0.0$ $A_2 = 0.0$	$p_2 = 0.12 \pm 0.007$ $A_2 \sim \mathcal{U}(> 0, 20)$	$p_{T_6} = 0.03 < \alpha$
T_7: *Illumination artefacts*	$p_3 = 0.0$ $A_3 = 0.0$	$p_3 = 0.03 \pm 0.01$ $A_3 \sim \mathcal{U}(> 0, 10)$	$p_{T_7} = 0.01 < \alpha$

real sensor data instead of simulated sensor data. For testing these hypotheses, we applied paired two-sample Student's t-tests (effect size $d = 0.5$, statistical power of 0.9) to the simulated data and independent two-sample Student's t-tests (effect size $d = 0.7$, statistical power of 0.9) to the real sensor data. For all tests, the significance level α was set to 0.05. As required by the tests' type, two sets (*Control Samples* and *Paired Samples*) of 44 *Validity Values* v_P have to be generated for each test. For tests using simulated data (T_1, T_2, T_3, T_4, and T_5), we calculated these values from 3D point clouds in which only the currently considered failure type was injected using the parameters stated in Table 2. For the tests using real sensor data (T_6 and T_7), the *Validity Values* of the *Control Samples* were calculated from point clouds generated by manually removing all failures while *Validity Values* of the *Paired Samples* were calculated from point clouds generated by removing all unconsidered failure types. Thus, the samples differ only in the number of occurrences of the considered failure type. The test itself evaluates whether the mean of the differences between both sets is different from zero, which is the case when the test's statistic (p_{T_t}-value, where t encodes the test's number) is less than the significance level α. As seen in Table 2, we obtained this result for each test, which evidences that the differences in the *Validity Values* between both samples are not random. Hence, as these differences were caused by increasing the likelihood or the failure amplitude of failure types, the *Validity Value* v_P of a 3D point cloud adequately represents its quality.

5.3   Correlation of Application Quality and Input Validity Values

To show that the quality of an application's output data can be inferred from the *Validity Shares* of its input data, we examine the tasks of object classification and position estimation from the *RoboCup@Work* league as examples. We apply these tasks to the real sensor data and associate the quality of their output data with *Validity Vectors* of their input data. We visualise this association for each

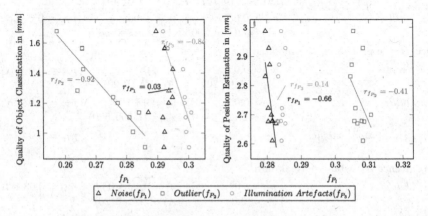

Fig. 3. The quality of applications depending on the *Validity Shares* f_{P_1}, f_{P_2}, and f_{P_3}. Corresponding trend lines are shown along with Pearson's correlation coefficient.

Validity Share of these vectors by fitting a linear model in a least-squares manner. Additionally, linear correlations are revealed when the calculated correlation coefficient $r_{f_{P_l}}$ is close to ± 1. The results are shown in Fig. 3. In this work, the applied object classification is based on the *Ensemble of Shape Function (ESF)* descriptor [1] for *RoboCup@Work* objects with a weak geometric structure. The *ESF* descriptor is a high-dimensional signature of an object's cluster of points, which describes information about the cluster's geometry, and is stored in a feature vector. As we consider solely the first aluminium profile for this task, we obtain a single reference feature vector. At run-time, a similar feature vector is extracted from a point cloud and is classified using the k-nearest neighbours (NN) algorithm. In contrast to other classification algorithms, e.g. Deep Neural Networks, k-NN directly provides a quality score by evaluating the Euclidean distance between the newly classified feature vector and the reference feature vector. The larger the distance to the reference vector, the less likely the feature vector is a member of the object and the lower the quality of the application. We applied this classification task to 11 real point clouds. As shown in the left diagram in Fig. 3, the *Validity Shares* of *Outlier* and *Illumination Artefacts* exhibit strong linear correlations to the application's quality, their correlation coefficients are close to -1. Contrarily, the *Noise* failure is uncorrelated, which complies with the literature [1] in which this method is considered to be robust to *Noise* failures. Variations of the application's quality are caused by *Outlier* and *Illumination Artefacts*, affecting the test data along with *Noise*.

Similar to the object classification, we used the approach of *ESF* for estimating the position of the classified object. We assessed this task, utilizing the Euclidean distance of the estimated position from the correct position. For this task, we used 11 point clouds obtained from the second aluminium profile. The results are shown in the right diagram in Fig. 3. While the *Validity Shares* of *Noise* and *Outlier* exhibit moderate correlations, *Illumination Artefacts* prove to be uncorrelated. The lack of correlations may have three reasons. First, our approach does not adequately model the quality of 3D point clouds, which would contradict Subsect. 5.2. Second, the considered failure model does not contain all the relevant failure types. As our failure model neglects the *Gaps* and *Offset* failures, these could cause variations in the task's quality that may not be reflected by the *Validity Shares*. Third, the information represented by the input data is not sufficient to correctly estimate the position of the object. Such insufficient information is not indicated by the *Validity Shares* since this is not the purpose of the Validity Concept. Finally, we could identify relevant correlations between the values of the *Validity Shares* and the quality of the object classification, showing that our approach is feasible for estimating an application's quality. According to Sect. 2, this is mandatory for implementing a run-time performance adaptation in future work. However, as a similar statement cannot be made for the second task, the reasons mentioned should be investigated in future analysis.

6   Conclusion and Future Work

In this work, we applied the Validity Concept introduced by Brade et al. [3] to 3D point clouds provided by camera-based sensor systems. For this, we defined a failure model covering *Noise*, *Outlier*, and *Illumination Artefacts*, derived methods to estimate their severity, and proposed *Belief Functions* to derive validity information for each point of a 3D point cloud. Fusing this information to obtain validity information for a complete 3D point cloud enabled us to show that the proposed approach adequately represents the quality of such sensor data. Regarding the task of object classification, we could correlate the *Validity Shares* of real 3D point clouds to the quality of the task's output data. Following the Validity Concept, this correlation can be used to implement a run-time performance adaptation in future work. For instance, one could apply filters to mitigate present failure types, depending on the quality of the current sensor data. Hence, filtering the sensor data would be afforded only in case of low quality, while otherwise, the effort is saved. Depending on the number of applied filters, various levels of performance can be defined. While the safety of a system should be guaranteed on all of these levels, one should contemplate that *Validity Shares* solely provide information about failure types defined by an underlying failure model. Thus, it is a system engineer's obligation to guarantee a sufficiently complete failure model. In fact, without correlation to the *Validity Shares* of its input data, such an incomplete failure model could have caused the quality of the position estimation task to be inconsistent. Consequently, in future work, the incompleteness of failure models, along with the other mentioned reasons, shall be investigated using different scenarios and different applications. This also provides opportunities to address additional research questions, such as: Which fusing methodologies (see Subsect. 4.4) are applicable with respect to varying strict safety policies? To which kind of systems is the Validity Concept (in general and with respect to 3D depth information) applicable? Furthermore, the presented failure model is motivated by the failures of different sensing techniques and therefore aims at the failures of 3D depth information in general. However, the failure model and its application to the Validity Concept has been investigated only in reference to a single experiment. Thus, while the generality of the approach can be assumed, in future work, it has to be examined in more detail.

References

1. Aldoma, A., Marton, Z.C., Tombari, F., Wohlkinger, W., Potthast, C., Zeisl, B., Rusu, R.B., Gedikli, S., Vincze, M.: Tutorial: Point cloud library: three-dimensional object recognition and 6 dof pose estimation. IEEE Robot. Autom. Mag. **19**(3), 80–91 (2012)
2. Brade, T., Jäger, G., Zug, S., Kaiser, J.: Sensor- and environment dependent performance adaptation for maintaining safety requirements. In: Bondavalli, A., Ceccarelli, A., Ortmeier, F. (eds.) SAFECOMP 2014. LNCS, vol. 8696, pp. 46–54. Springer, Cham (2014). doi:10.1007/978-3-319-10557-4_7

3. Brade, T., Zug, S., Kaiser, J.: Validity-based failure algebra for distributed sensor systems. In: 2013 IEEE 32nd International Symposium on Reliable Distributed Systems (SRDS), pp. 143–152. IEEE (2013)
4. Casimiro, A., Kaiser, J., Schiller, E.M., Costa, P., Parizi, J., Johansson, R., Librino, R.: The karyon project: predictable and safe coordination in cooperative vehicular systems. In: 2013 43rd Annual IEEE/IFIP Conference on Dependable Systems and Networks Workshop (DSN-W), pp. 1–12. IEEE (2013)
5. Das, S., Ahuja, N.: Performance analysis of stereo, vergence, and focus as depth cues for active vision. IEEE Trans. Pattern Anal. Mach. Intell. **17**(12), 1213–1219 (1995)
6. Foix, S., Alenya, G., Torras, C.: Lock-in time-of-flight (tof) cameras: a survey. IEEE Sens. J. **11**(9), 1917–1926 (2011)
7. Fooladgar, F., Samavi, S., Soroushmehr, S.M.R., Shirani, S.: Geometrical analysis of localization error in stereo vision systems. IEEE Sens. J. **13**(11), 4236–4246 (2013)
8. Fuchs, S., May, S.: Calibration and registration for precise surface reconstruction with time-of-flight cameras. Int. J. Intell. Syst. Technol. Appl. **5**(3–4), 274–284 (2008)
9. Gupta, M., Agrawal, A., Veeraraghavan, A., Narasimhan, S.G.: A practical approach to 3d scanning in the presence of interreflections, subsurface scattering and defocus. Int. J. Comput. Vision **102**(1–3), 33–55 (2013)
10. Hochgeschwender, N., Kammel, R., Kraetzschmar, G., Nowak, W., Norouzi, A., Schnieders, B., Zug, S.: Robocup@work rulebook. http://www.robocupatwork.org/download/rulebook-2017-01-24.pdf. Accessed 17 Feb 2017
11. Intel: Intel realsense f200 camera (2015). http://www.intel.co.uk/content/www/uk/en/support/emerging-technologies/intel-realsense-technology/intel-realsense-cameras/intel-realsense-camera-f200.html. Accessed 15 Feb 2017
12. Jain, R.C., Jain, A.: Analysis and Interpretation of Range Images. Springer, New York (2012)
13. Jecić, S., Drvar, N.: The assessment of structured light and laser scanning methods in 3d shape measurements. In: 4th International Congress of Croatian Society of Mechanics (2003)
14. Khoshelham, K., Elberink, S.O.: Accuracy and resolution of kinect depth data for indoor mapping applications. Sensors **12**(2), 1437–1454 (2012)
15. Konig, S., Gumhold, S.: Image-based motion compensation for structured light scanning of dynamic surfaces. Int. J. Intell. Syst. Technol. Appl. **5**(3–4), 434–441 (2008)
16. Koubaa, A.: Robot Operating System (ROS). SCI, vol. 707. Springer, Cham (2017)
17. Moore, D.S., McCabe, G.P.: Introduction to the Practice of Statistics. WH Freeman/Times Books/Henry Holt & Co., New York (1989)
18. Pauly, M., Mitra, N.J., Guibas, L.J.: Uncertainty and variability in point cloud surface data. In: Symposium on Point-Based Graphics, vol. 9 (2004)
19. Rauscher, G., Dube, D., Zell, A.: A comparison of 3D sensors for wheeled mobile robots. In: Menegatti, E., Michael, N., Berns, K., Yamaguchi, H. (eds.) Intelligent Autonomous Systems 2013. AISC, vol. 302, pp. 29–41. Springer, Cham (2016). doi:10.1007/978-3-319-08338-4_3
20. Schmidt, M., Jähne, B.: Efficient and robust reduction of motion artifacts for 3d time-of-flight cameras. In: 2011 International Conference on 3D Imaging (IC3D), pp. 1–8. IEEE (2011)

21. Shapiro, L., Stockman, G.C.: Computer Vision: Prentice Hall, Upper Saddle River (2001)
22. Sotoodeh, S.: Outlier detection in laser scanner point clouds. Int. Arch. Photogram. Remote Sens. Spat. Inf. Sci. **36**(5), 297–302 (2006)
23. Wang, W., Wang, Y., Huo, L., Huang, Q., Gao, W.: Symmetric segment-based stereo matching of motion blurred images with illumination variations. In: 19th International Conference on Pattern Recognition, ICPR 2008, pp. 1–4. IEEE (2008)
24. Yang, Z., Wang, Y.F.: Error analysis of 3d shape construction from structured lighting. Pattern Recogn. **29**(2), 189–206 (1996)
25. Zhang, Z.: Iterative point matching for registration of free-form curves and surfaces. Int. J. Comput. Vision **13**(2), 119–152 (1994)

SMT-Based Synthesis of Fault-Tolerant Architectures

Kevin Delmas[(⊠)], Rémi Delmas, and Claire Pagetti

ONERA/DTIM, 2 av. E. Belin, 31055 Toulouse, France
{kevin.delmas,remi.delmas,claire.pagetti}@onera.fr

Abstract. Safety-critical systems must satisfy safety requirements ensuring that catastrophic consequences of combined component failures are kept below a certain probability occurrence threshold. Therefore, designers must define a hardened architecture of the system, which fulfils the required safety level by integrating safety mechanisms. We propose an automatic SMT-based synthesis methodology to harden an initial architecture for a given safety objective. The proposed ideas are experimented on an avionics flight controller case-study and several benchmarks.

1 Introduction

The design and development of safety critical applications must satisfy stringent dependability requirements. In the avionics domain for instance, the correctness of applications must be proven or at least argued to the certification authorities. To help the designers achieve that goal, several avionics standards are available such as the ARP-4754 [1]. Following these guidelines, any avionics function is categorized according to the severity of its loss and subject to qualitative and quantitative safety requirements.

1.1 Design-Space Exploration Problem

During the design, a *preliminary functional architecture* of a system is designed as a combination of sub-functions providing the expected functionality. This architecture is then analysed to check if the high-level safety requirements are fulfilled assuming some properties (such as failure independence). Such an analysis is done on a *dysfunctional model*, that is, a component-based description of the architecture giving the *failure modes* (the observable effects of a failure) produced by the system in the context of *failure events* (the cause of a failure). If the analysis fails, the designer must propose a *hardened* architecture, that is, a modified architecture enriched with some safety mechanisms.

The automatic architectural optimization of fault-tolerant systems (also called *design space exploration* or *exploration problem*) generally relies on *component substitution i.e* substituting a component by a safer version [2,3] to generate new architectures (called *candidates*). The safer versions available for a component (called *alternatives* of the component) are instances of well-formed

© Springer International Publishing AG 2017
S. Tonetta et al. (Eds.): SAFECOMP 2017, LNCS 10488, pp. 287–302, 2017.
DOI: 10.1007/978-3-319-66266-4_19

safety design patterns of proven efficiency [4,5]. The patterns that can be used to harden an architecture are often chosen depending on the designer's expertise, the expected safety increase and by considering the impact on the design of non-functional criteria (such as CPU consumption, temporal performance, etc.).

1.2   Contribution

The main steps of the existing design space exploration approaches (detailed in Sect. 7) are the followings:

(1) choose and replace some system's components by safety patterns. This requires in particular that designers must identify which are the relevant components and the relevant patterns to use;
(2) assess the resulting candidate. This requires computing the *structure function* (a Boolean function indicating if the candidate fails) and the safety indicators such as the reliability;
(3) if the result is compliant with the safety objectives, then the candidate is a solution of the exploration problem, otherwise discard the candidate and restart from 1.

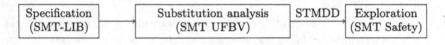

Fig. 1. SMT-based resolution method overview

We propose a Satisfiability Modulo Theory (SMT) based design space exploration method, detailed in Fig. 1, which improves the exploration process by:

Specification encoding the system's model and safety requirements in the standardized language SMT-LIB [6] which allows to use off-the-shelf SMT solvers for analysis and exploration;

Substitution Analysis assessing a priori the effect of substituting a component by a pattern. This means computing for all pairs (component, pattern) some safety values by an automatic analysis based on the resolution of SMT problems using the Uninterpreted Functions and BitVector theory (UFBV). Moreover, at the end of this stage, we provide a *MDD* (Multi-Valued Decision Diagram) – named STMDD for System Trace MDD – usable to compute the safety indicators of any potential candidate;

Exploration integrating the STMDD in a theory of our design called *Safety*. Thus exploration is performed by an SMT solver which uses the *Safety* theory for candidate assessment. This assessment is based on the safety values directly computed from the STMDD. Moreover if the result is not compliant with the safety objectives, the set of selected pairs (component, pattern) causing the non conformity is removed from the exploration space.

Thus, instead of performing a safety assessment from scratch for each candidate, we compute the MDD only once. Furthermore, if the candidate is not compliant with the safety objectives, the exploration space is drastically reduced thanks to the conflict clauses generated by the *Safety* theory solver. However, we must assess all pairs (component, pattern) during the preprocessing phase. This is not really an issue, since the number of failures for one component or one pattern is small (around 2 or 3) compared to the number of failures of a complete architecture.

We first recall some basics on safety assessment in Sect. 2 and then formalize the exploration problem in the *many sorted first order logic* (MSFOL).

2 Reminder on Safety Analysis

The system designer must build a dysfunctional model (simply called *model*) encoding the system behaviour in the presence of failures.

2.1 Assumptions

We assume that the occurrence probability of basic failure events is known and that the dysfunctional model satisfies the following properties: (1) **Static**: A dysfunctional state does not depend on the order of failure events occurrence; (2) **Non repairable**: A failed component cannot return to a working state; (3) **Closed**: The system behaviour depends only on failure events; (4) **Exponential law**: The failure events are independent and their probability of occurrence is modelled by an exponential distribution. (5) **Substitution**: The component substitutions preserve the initial component's interface. The hypotheses 1 and 5 allow us to leverage powerful analytic methods to compute minimal cutsets, prime implicants and reliability values. Indeed dynamic systems would require stochastic methods (e.g. [7]) which are less easily amenable to be handled with satisfiability solvers. Moreover, the hypotheses 2–4 define a classic safety assessment context for static systems [8].

Dysfunctional model is an abstract representation of the system that describes its behaviour in the presence of failures. Let us first remind the safety-related terminology.

Definition 1 (Terminology). *Let C be a component, then: (1) a failure F of C is the inability of C to provide a function; (2) failure modes FM of C are the observable effects of the failure F; (3) a failure condition FC is $FC = \bigvee_i FM_i$ where FM_i are failure modes; (4) a failure event e is the cause of a failure F.*

A model can be modular and hierarchical. Moreover, the user can constitute packages of components definitions that can be reused, instantiated and manipulated. However, due to the lack of space, we consider only the flat models and conduct the analysis at the component level.

Let us name the different entities of a dysfunctional model as follows: (1) $\mathcal{C}$ are the components or pattern instances; (2) $\mathcal{E}$ are the failure events; (3) $\mathcal{F}$ are the flows *i.e* the inputs and outputs of components that carry the failure modes generated by components' failure events; (4) $\mathcal{V}$ are the possible failure modes.

*Example 1 (*ROSACE*).* We introduce a running example that is a simplification of an open-source avionics control engineering case study ROSACE defined in [9]. This control chain manages the longitudinal motion of a medium-range civilian aircraft in *en-route* phase. Figure 2a shows the architecture of ROSACE, which is composed of four components. Three filters (F_{Vz}, F_{Va}, F_q) receive and filter some sensors values namely the vertical speed V_z, the true airspeed V_a and the pitch rate q. The filtered signals (V_{af}, V_{zf} and V_{qf}) are used by the airspeed controller C_{Va} to monitor V_a by sending throttle command δ_{thc} to the engines.

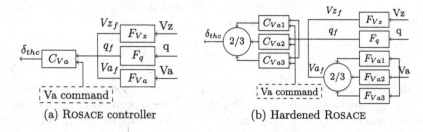

(a) ROSACE controller   (b) Hardened ROSACE

Fig. 2. ROSACE overview

In ROSACE, the components are $\mathcal{C} = \{C_{Va}, F_{Va}, F_{Vz}, F_q\}$. The failure modes $\mathcal{V}$ of all components are 1. erroneous data (E) caused by the failure event $C.e$; 2. omission of data (L) caused by the failure event $C.l$; where C is the component's name. The failure events are $\mathcal{E} = \{C_{Va}.e, C_{Va}.l, F_q.e, F_q.l, F_{Va}.e, F_{Va}.l, F_{Vz}.e, F_{Vz}.l, e, l\}$.

2.2 Safety Analysis

This section is a brief introduction to safety analysis, which is detailed in [8]. For static systems, safety assessment is based on the system's *structure function*. This Boolean function over the system's failure events, called φ, returns a Boolean indicating whether the failure condition is true or not.

Example 2 (Structure function). The structure function φ of ROSACE for the failure condition: *"the output δ_{ec} of* ROSACE*is lost or erroneous"* is:

$$\varphi_{Rosace} = F_{Va}.e \vee F_{Va}.l \vee C_{Va}.e \vee C_{Va}.l \vee (F_q.e \vee F_q.l) \wedge (F_{Vz}.e \vee F_{Vz}.l)$$

The reliability is defined as the probability that φ becomes true within a given operation time. Since the reliability computation cannot be performed without failure events probabilities, we assume that these probabilities are defined by the user before the exploration process.

Definition 2 (Reliability). *Let S be a model, e a failure event and t_e the random variable modelling the instant where e occurs. Then the reliability $R_e(t)$ (resp. the unreliability $\overline{R_e}(t)$) is the probability that e does not occur (resp. occurs) during the time interval $[0,t]$ knowing S is functional at $t = 0$. By abuse of language we write $p(e)$ (resp. $p(\overline{e})$) for $p(t_e \leq t)$ (resp. $p(t_e > t)$).*

$$\forall t \in \mathbb{R}^+, R_e(t) \stackrel{def}{=} p(\overline{e}) = 1 - p(e) = 1 - \overline{R_e}(t)$$

Example 3 (Reliability). Let us assume that the failure rate of ROSACE's events is $10^{-5}h^{-1}$ then the unreliability after one hour is $\overline{R}(1) \simeq 4.10^{-5}$.

Another safety indicator is the set of minimal sets (MCS) of events needed to trigger a given failure condition. For static systems, these sets are the prime implicants of φ, [10], *i.e* conjunctions of failure events or their negation.

Definition 3 (Prime Implicants (PI)). *Let S be the system model, φ the structure function and p a subset of literals built over the system's failure events. p is a prime implicant iff: (1) $\bigwedge_{l \in p} l \Rightarrow \varphi$ and (2) $\forall (l \in p), \bigwedge_{l' \in p \setminus \{l\}} l' \not\Rightarrow \varphi$.*

Example 4 (PI). The prime implicants of φ_{Rosace} are $\{\{F_{Va}.e\}, \{F_{Va}.l\}, \{C_{Va}.e\}, \{C_{Va}.l\}, \{F_{Vz}.e, F_q.e\}, \{F_{Vz}.e, F_q.l\}, \{F_{Vz}.l, F_q.e\}, \{F_{Vz}.l, F_q.l\}\}$.

The so-called minimal cutsets (mcs) are the restriction of prime implicants to positive literals [10]. So the minimal cardinality of an mcs is the minimal number of positive literals belonging to a prime implicant of φ.

2.3 Hardened Architecture

An hardened architecture must satisfy safety objectives. For ROSACE, the failure condition δ_{thc} *is lost or erroneous* is HAZ according to the ARP-4754, thus: (1) the loss must be triggered by at least two independent failures; (2) the failure rate must be lower than $10^{-7}h^{-1}$ (per flight hour). In the sequel we approximate this requirement by the mean failure rate, *i.e*, the reliability divided by the exposition time. ROSACE does not fulfill the requirement, since there are single points of failures (see example 4), therefore a hardening is mandatory. For instance designers can instantiate a triplication pattern (replication of component together with a two-out-of-three voting), as depicted in Fig. 2b. In the sequel, we show how to model and solve the exploration problem automatically.

3 System Modelling: Illustration on Rosace

The system model is encoded as a Satisfiability problem over *many sorted first order logic* (MSFOL) described with the SMT-LIB standardized language [6]. An SMT problem is a **S**atifiability problem over a set of logic formula **M**odulo a set of **T**heories [11]. In the following sections, we use the **U**ninterpreted **F**unctions and fixed size **Bit**V**ectors theories, known as UFBV in the SMT-LIB standard and the algebraic datatypes (tuples for instance). Basically, the SMT modelling of a system contains (1) sort and function definitions (said interpreted) which describe components' behaviours, (2) function declarations (said uninterpreted *i.e* without a body definition) representing the unknowns of the satisfiability problem, (3) assertions *i.e* the formula that must be satisfied.

A sort can be seen as a type, and some built-in sorts are provided by SMT-LIB such as Boolean and bitvectors of fixed but arbitrary large size. Our modelling is based on two kinds of sorts: (1) the bitvectors sorts representing the failure modes of $\mathcal{V}$, (2) the tuple sorts gathering several values when components have several outputs. For ROSACE, the failure modes of $\mathcal{V}$ are represented by a *bitvector sort* t of size two declared using (declare $-$ sort t ($\_$ BitVec 2)). For each failure mode, a bitvector constant is defined.

```
(declare-sort t (_ BitVec 2))   (define-const E t #b10)
(define-const L t #b01)         (define-const empty t #b00)
```

The following command illustrates the definition of a tuple type `Tuple2` which can be built using mkTuple2 constructor and its first (resp. second) fields are accessed through `fst` (resp. `snd`) function.

```
(declare-datatype Tuple2 () ((mkTuple2((fst t) (snd t)))))
```

A component $c \in \mathcal{C}$ is encoded as an interpreted function defined using (define $-$ fun). The function's inputs are both the inputs and the failure events of c whereas the function's outputs are those of c. When the component has several outputs, the values are gathered in a tuple sort `TupleX`. In the sequel, the failure modes generation and propagation modelling is based on the following built-in operators: (1) the `let` binder which defines an expression *expr* where local identifiers x1,...,xn respectively equal to expr1,...,exprn are used to define `expr`; (2) the conditional selection operator (`ite` b e1 e2) which stands for *if* b *then* e1 *else* e2; (3) the classic operators over bitvectors. Thus for ROSACE, the models of a filter F (like F_{V_a}, F_{Vz} and F_q) and C_{V_a} are:

```
(define-fun F ((e Bool) (l Bool)) t (ite e E (ite l L empty)))
(define-fun CVa ((e Bool) (l Bool) (Vzf t) (qf t) (Vaf t)) t
 (ite e E (ite l L (ite (= Vaf E) E (ite (= Vaf L) L
   (ite (and (= Vzf E) (= qf E)) E
    (ite (and (= Vzf L) (= qf L)) L empty)))))))
```

The system is also encoded by an interpreted function which composes its sub-component's functions. So for ROSACE, the main system is:

```
(define-fun Rosace
   ((CVa.e Bool)(CVa.l Bool) (Fq.e Bool) (Fq.l Bool)
    (FVa.e Bool) (FVa.l Bool) (FVz.e Bool) (FVz.l Bool)) t
   (let ((Vaf (F FVa.e FVa.l)) (Vzf  (F FVz.e FVz.l))
       (qf  (F Fq.e Fq.l)))
      (CVa CVa.e CVa.l Vzf qf Vaf )))
```

Eventually the failure condition fc is translated as an interpreted function on the system outputs returning a Boolean (also called a *predicate*) if and only if fc occurs.

```
(define-fun fc ((deltaThc t)) Bool (not (= deltaThc empty)))
```

Uninterpreted functions are declared using (`declare − fun`). For instance we declare an unknown structure function `phi`.

```
(declare-fun phi (Bool Bool Bool Bool Bool Bool Bool Bool) Bool)
```

Assertions must be Boolean formulas, and are added by (`assert a`). A formula is any Boolean expression composed of predicate calls, Boolean connectives, *term* equalities and quantifiers. The quantifiers are used as shown below:

```
(forall ((x1 T1)...(xn Tn)) boolExpr)
(exists ((x1 T1)...(xn Tn)) boolExpr)
```

A forall (resp. exists) is true whenever boolExpr is true for all (resp. for some) $x1, \ldots, xn$. A *term* is a constant `v` or a function call (`f t1...tn`) where each argument `ti` is a term of appropriate sort w.r.t the function signature. For instance we can ensure that `phi` is true if and only if the failure condition is true as follows:

```
(assert (forall
 ((CVa.e Bool)  (CVa.l Bool) (Fq.e Bool) (Fq.l Bool)
  (FVa.e Bool) (FVa.l Bool) (FVz.e Bool) (FVz.l Bool))
 (= (phi CVa.e CVa.l Fq.e Fq.l FVa.e FVa.l  FVz.e FVz.l)
    (fc (Rosace CVa.e CVa.l Fq.e Fq.l FVa.e FVa.l FVz.e FVz.l)))))
```

Solving an SMT problem means: *finding a definition for uninterpreted functions which satisfies the assertions.* These definitions are called a *model* of the problem. The (`check − sat`) command asks the solver to find a model of the SMT problem. If the answer is SAT a model can be obtained using the (`get − model`) command. Otherwise the problem is UNSAT and an unsatisfiability proof can, optionally, be generated. Let us introduce the usage of the MSFOL system's model for design space exploration.

4   Component Traces

In this section we detail how the impact of a single component substitution on safety indicators (*i.e* the reliability and the minimal cardinality of the mcs) is computed in a preprocessing phase before design-space exploration.

4.1   Safety Patterns

We recall that safety patterns are generic safety mechanisms of proven efficiency used to harden an architecture. For instance, on the right hand side, the COM/-MON (command and monitoring) pattern is composed of two redundant components that work in hot redundancy, computing a same value. A comparator checks if the outputs are coherent, if so the consolidated value is forwarded, otherwise no output is provided. This pattern is coded in SMT-LIB as DupF.

```
                    (define-fun DupF
                      ((F1.e Bool) (F1.l Bool)
                       (F2.e Bool) (F2.l Bool)) t
                      (let ((out1 (F F1.e F1.l))
                            (out2 (F F2.e F2.l)))
                        (ite (= out1 empty) out1 L)))
```

4.2 Flow-Based Analysis

Replacing a component by a pattern that may have different failure events and propagation rules invalidates the system's structure function and requires to recompute it. This can become the main computational bottleneck of design-space exploration. We propose a new representation based on failure modes observed on the component interfaces, called *component traces*. The corresponding safety indicators are shown below on the table on the right. For instance, in the left Figure below, FM_2 is observed on B output and results from the event combination $\{A.e_1, B.e_2\}$. If instead, we represent this behaviour by the failure modes observed on the component's interface, it becomes $(B, \{(in, FM_1), (out, FM_2)\})$. We argue that a substitution is supposed to prevent some failure modes but not to add new ones. That is why, the failure modes produced by the safety pattern are often a subset of those produced by the initial component. Thus the analysis performed on the initial failure modes observed on the component's interface can be reused after the substitution.

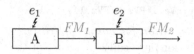

	event-based	flow-based
	event occurrence	component trace
	$p(e)$ where e is an event	$p(tr)$ where tr is a trace
	structure function φ	system trace MDD

4.3 Component Trace Definition

A *component trace* is a valuation of the component's inputs and outputs for some (combination of) event occurrence. These traces are computed by solving SMT problems as illustrated in the Example 5.

Example 5 (Component Trace). Let us consider a filter F of ROSACE with one output named *out*. Then the traces of F are the failure modes observed on its outputs *out* resulting from some failure events e or l. Thus a valuation $\{(out, X)\}$ is a trace of F if and only if the below SMT problem is SAT. For F the possible traces are $\{\{(out, E)\}, \{(out, L)\}, \{(out, \emptyset)\}\}$.

```
(declare-const e Bool) (declare-const l Bool)
(assert(= (F e l)  X))
```

4.4 Computing Safety Indicators on Component Traces

To properly define safety indicators on component traces, we compute $trig_c$ which gives the events valuations of the component c producing a given trace. The function $trig_c$ is computed by solving an SMT problem for each possible component trace tr, whose models provide the events valuations producing tr.

Example 6. Let us consider again a filter F of ROSACE, the event valuations producing the trace $\{(out, E)\}$ are the models of the following SMT problem, *i.e* $\{\{(e, true), (l, true)\}, \{(e, true), (l, false)\}\}$ that is simplified to $trig_F(\{(out, E)\}) = \{(e, true)\}$.

```
(declare-const e Bool)   (declare-const 1 Bool)
(assert (= (F e 1) E))
```

We introduce for each trace tr the notion of *trace probability* $prob_c(tr)$ (resp. *cardinality* $card_c(tr)$) as the probability associated with $trig_c(tr)$ (resp. the minimum cardinality of minimal cutsets of $trig_c(tr)$). In practice the BDD encoding $trig_c(tr)$ is first computed and then the classic computation methods are applied [10]. This BDD is local to a single component and hence remains quite small.

Example 7 (Safety indicators on component traces). For $tr = \{(out, E)\}$ of F_{V_a}, the probability (resp the cardinality) is $prob_{F_{V_a}}(trig_{F_{V_a}}(tr)) = p(e) = 0.01$ (resp. $card_{F_{V_a}}(trig_{F_{V_a}}(tr)) = min(|\{e\}|) = 1$).

4.5 Component Traces and Substitutions

A component can be replaced by components taken from a set of alternative components. For each alternative, we compute and store the *prob* and *card* values in an array as shown in the Example 8. If an initial component trace is infeasible after a substitution, the *prob* (resp. *card*) default value 0 (resp. $+\infty$) is stored.

Example 8 (Component traces and substitutions). If F_{Va} can be substituted by DupF, the analysis of DupF traces give $trig_{DupF}(out, E) = \{\{F_{Va1}.e, F_{Va2}.e\}, \{F_{Va1}.l, F_{Va2}.l\}\}$ with a cardinality of 2 and a reliability of 0.0002. Figure below shows the array for F_{Va}.

$\{(out, E)\}$			$\{(out, \emptyset)\}$			$\{(out, L)\}$		
	F	DupF		F	DupF		F	DupF
card	1	2	*card*	0	0	*card*	1	2
prob	10^{-2}	2.10^{-4}	*prob*	.98	.9996	*prob*	10^{-2}	2.10^{-4}

5 System Trace MDD

5.1 System Trace Definition (STMDD)

Intuitively, a *system trace*, for a given failure condition, gathers all component traces (interface flow valuations) consistent with the system definition and realizing a given failure condition. Such system traces are called *dangerous system traces*. For space efficiency, dangerous traces are encoded as an Multi-valued Decision Diagram [12], called System Trace MDD (STMDD), where variables are components and edges indicate which component trace occurred. In the sequel, the set of dangerous traces of a system encoded by a STMDD is named T.

Example 9 (System trace). A dangerous system trace of ROSACE for the failure condition: *"no failures modes are observed on the output δ_{thc} of ROSACE"*, is $\{(F_{Va}, \{(out, E)\}), (F_{Vz}, \{(out, \emptyset)\}), (F_q, \{(out, \emptyset)\}), (C_{Va}, \{(Vaf, E), (Vzf, \emptyset), (qf, \emptyset), (out, E)\})\}$.

Example 10 (STMDD). Let us assume that the filters can be substituted by DupF and the controller by DupC, then the STMDD (where paths to zero terminal are dismissed) for ROSACE is shown in Fig. 3 where only F_{Va} and C_{Va} can fail.

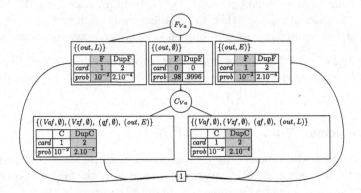

Fig. 3. STMDD of ROSACE

The property 1 states that the STMDD and structure function characterize the same set of system events valuations, allowing to use the STMDD φ's BDD to assess the system safety indicators.

Property 1. *Let s be a system, fc a failure condition, φ be the structure function of s for fc and T be the dangerous system traces represented by the STMDD of s for fc then $\phi \Leftrightarrow \varphi$ where $\phi = \bigvee_{tr \in T} \bigwedge_{c \in C, \ tr' \in tr \wedge tr' \in trace(c)} trig_c(tr')$.*

As said previously, we want to use the STMDD of a system s to compute the safety indicators of any system s' obtained by substituting a component c by another component c' in s. Thus the set of dangerous system traces of s must be included in the one of s'. This property holds if the set of c' traces is a subset of the corresponding traces of c. We call such a substitution an *acceptable* one. This component traces inclusion boils down to prove that the following problem is UNSAT.

```
(assert (exists ((in1 tin1)...(inn tinn)(o1 tout1)...(om toutm)
      (e1 Bool)...(ek Bool) (e1' Bool)...(ek' Bool))
    (and (= (f_c' e1'...ek in1...inn) (mkTupleM o1...om))
      (not (= (f_c e1...ek in1...inn) (mkTupleM o1...om))))))
```

To conclude, the STMDD can be used to compute the safety indicators of any candidate obtained by acceptable substitutions of the initial system's components.

5.2   Computing Safety Indicators on STMDD

We now detail how safety indicators are computed over the STMDD. Since two distinct system traces cannot be triggered for the same system's events valuation, the Boolean functions associated with the system traces are pairwise incompatible. Moreover the events associated with two distinct component traces within a given system trace are independent. Therefore, the below formula gives the unreliability of a system encoded by a STMDD representing a set of dangerous system traces T where sub_c is the selected substituting component for c.

$$\overline{R} = \sum_{tr \in T} \quad \prod_{\substack{c \in \mathcal{C}, \\ tr' \in tr \wedge tr' \in trace(c)}} prob_{sub_c}(tr') \tag{1}$$

In the same way, the minimal cardinality of cutsets is equal to the minimal number of events needed to produce any dangerous trace of the system. Thus, the minimal cardinality of system's cutsets is the minimal cardinality among trace tree paths.

$$\min_{cs \in MCS}(|cs|) = \min_{tr \in T} \left(\sum_{\substack{c \in \mathcal{C}, \\ tr' \in tr \wedge tr' \in trace(c)}} card_{sub_c}(tr') \right) \tag{2}$$

Example 11. If F_{Va} remains unchanged and C_{Va} is replaced by DupC then the dimmed *card* and *prob* cells of the ROSACE STMDD (see Fig. 3) are used in the Eqs. 1 and 2 to compute the safety indicators. Hence, we have $\min_{cs \in MCS}(|cs|) = min(1, 2, 2, 1) = 1$ and $\overline{R} = 0.01 + 0.98(2 \times 0.0002) + 0.01 \simeq 0.02$.

6   SMT-Based Exploration

To solve the design-space exploration problem with SMT solvers, we define here the *Safety* theory which provides predicates over safety requirement satisfaction.

6.1   Safety Theory

SMT solvers decide the satisfiability of a set of MSFOL formulas called assertions. These assertions contain *atomic* formulas, that is, either a Boolean variable or a theory predicate handled by its associated theory solver. Thus we introduce the Safety theory and its solver which handle the safety requirement predicates using the analysis of the system's STMDD. So, this theory relies on the sort `TraceTree` and the sort `Sub` to model the problem. A value of `Sub` determines which substitutions are applied and a value of `TraceTree` is the SMT-LIB encoding of the STMDD. The predicates of the Safety theory are (`choose Sub` Int) true if the ith substitution is applied, (`isSafeCard stt req`) and (`isSafeR stt req`) true if the minimal cardinality of the mcs (resp. the reliability) computed on `stt` is greater or equal to `req`.

6.2 SMT Encoding of Exploration Problem

The exploration problem is then encoded as a SMT problem, as the one generated for ROSACE shown below. It contains: 1. a constant declaration of sort Sub per initial component which encodes substitution selection (here sC_{Va} and sF_{Va}); 2. a constant definition of sort TraceTree representing the STMDD (here a STMDD node contains a list of triplets (subtree, cardinality array, unreliability array)); 3. an assertion ensuring that exactly one substitution is chosen per component; 4. the safety requirements added through isSafeCard and isSafeR predicates.

```
(declare-const sFVa Sub) (declare-const sCVa Sub)
(define-const one TraceTree leaf)
(define-const CVaNode TraceTree (node
 (cons (mkTuple3 one cardCVaE rCVaE)
   (cons (mkTuple3 one cardCVaL rCVaL) nil))))
(define-const FVaNode TraceTree (node
 (cons (mkTuple3 one cardFVaE rFVaE)
  (cons (mkTuple3 one cardFVaL rFVaL)
   (cons (mkTuple3 CVaNode cardFVaEmpty rFVaEmpty) nil )))))
(assert (exactly1 (choose sCVa 0) (choose SCVa 1)))
(assert (exactly1 (choose sFVa 0) (choose SFVa 1)))
(assert (safeCard FVaNode 3)) (assert (safeR FVaNode 0.999999999))
```

Thanks to the commands (check − sat) and (get − model) the solver explores the design space using the Safety theory and eventually answers either SAT and then gives a valid candidate or UNSAT and generates a proof.

6.3 Experimental Setup

To evaluate our approach, we modelled several design-space exploration problems, and benchmarked our SMT-based method against an evaluation version of HIPHOPS [13], which uses genetic algorithms for design-space exploration. Systems were modelling using a DSL called KCR from which the SMT-LIB encodings used in this paper are generated automatically. The KCR DSL and algorithms presented in this paper are fully implemented in the KCR *analyser* tool[1] based on the Z3 SMT solver [14] with associated benchmarks. The considered benchmarks are: 1. the complete ROSACE case study (where all components can fail); 2. the FUEL system given as example with the HIPHOPS tool[2]; 3. the HBS system, model of a hybrid breaking system [see Footnote 2]; 4. the QUAD-COPTER system, model of a semi automatic drone navigation manager. For each component, a dozen of alternatives extracted from [5] are modelled.

---

[1] Available at http://www.onera.fr/en/staff/kevin-delmas?page=1.
[2] Available at http://hip-hops.eu/index.php.

6.4 Experiments

The Table 1 presents the exploration time to find any candidate fulfilling the safety requirements. These requirements are a combination of a cardinality requirement, *i.e*, any failure condition must occur in a triple failure context and an unreliability requirement, *i.e*, the unreliability after one hour must be less or equal to 10^{-5} or 10^{-9}. Since HIPHOPS cannot consider cardinality requirements, the comparison is only based on the reliability requirement. For all benchmarks, the experiments demonstrate that our SMT-based method solves the problem faster by several orders of magnitude than genetic-based approach. This efficiency is due to the fast safety assessment offered by the STMDD. Indeed HIPHOPS must compute the unreliability from scratch for each of evaluated candidate which is time consuming. Moreover the generation of conflict clauses during exploration prevents to generate systems which have been already assessed in contrary to HIPHOPS exploration process which is only directed by the breeding/selection process of the genetic algorithm. Nevertheless, contrary to HIPHOPS, our tool is not able to optimize multi-costs criteria, this limitation is discussed in the conclusion.

Table 1. Exploration time with KCR and HIPHOPS

	$min_{cs \in MCS}(|cs|)$	$\overline{R}(1)$							
		FUEL		HBS		ROSACE		QUADCOPTER	
		10^{-5}	10^{-9}	10^{-5}	10^{-9}	10^{-5}	10^{-9}	10^{-5}	10^{-9}
KCR (s)	-	9.45	0.063	1.68	0.78	4.38	4.7	0.43	0.48
HIPHOPS (s)	-	52.33	36.35	7.13	7.19	$> 10^3$	$> 10^3$	$> 10^3$	$> 10^3$
KCR (s)	3	0.117	0.059	0.66	0.62	4.07	4.45	0.33	0.28

7 Related Works

To harden an architecture, there are mainly two steps: first perform safety assessment on candidates, second use these results to select and generate candidates.

7.1 Selection and Generation

The authors of [2,3] classify the selection and generation techniques in two main families: evolutionary-based approaches, e.g. [13,15] and constraint-based approaches, e.g. [16–18].

According to [2] evolutionary approaches, more precisely genetic algorithms, are the most widely used techniques. These algorithms breed numerous alternative evolutions of an initial architectural design while continuously assessing their fitness according to quantitative fault-tolerance properties and various other non-functional aspects encoded as numerical criteria. They attempt to enumerate the Pareto-front of the solution space to propose all possible design trade-offs to the user. For instance, the genetic-based exploration is currently implemented in the commercial tool HIPHOPS [13]. Nevertheless, these approaches can neither ensure the optimality of found architectures nor prove that a problem does not admit any solutions.

The constraint-based methods like [16,17] rely on constraints solvers to find a valid and optimal candidate. For instance, the mixed-integer linear programming (MILP) is largely used [16,19] to model the exploration problem. But these approaches often imply some strong assumptions on the considered system's model and the possible substitutions. For instance, the approach of [16] is focused on serial systems where each component can be replaced by a set of redundant components. Our work is inspired by the approach of [20] and the associated tool System Configuration Toolkit (SCP), which encodes the system's components by the properties it ensures (expressed as SMT predicates) and which are asserted iff the component is chosen. The SMT solver must then choose which component's properties are needed to assert a given global goal. This approach does not address specifically a safety assessment but suggests a component-based translation of system to SMT problem and encourages the use of custom theories, as the one we developed in this paper, to assert domain-specific properties. Eventually, the methods presented in [21,22] address the design space exploration of an automated air traffic controller under quantitative and qualitative safety requirements. More precisely, the exploration is performed by an exhaustive enumeration of the candidates and the assessment is based on a contract-based model checking. Nevertheless the combinatorial explosion of the design space prevents us to use such enumerative methods for the large-scale systems.

This paper is also inspired by our previous work [18] on an iterative constraint-based method for solving the exploration problem. More precisely, this method selects the architecture substitutions needed to obtain a compliant architecture. This procedure was based on a hardening loop composed of the following steps: (1) *Safety assessment*: a safety analysis decides if the current architecture satisfies the safety requirements with dedicated tools such that CECILIA-OCAS [23], (2) *Hardening*: if an hardening is needed, the new substitution selection is given by solving a Pseudo-Boolean problem that ensures that the new selection improves system's safety. (3) *Substitution*: The substitutions are processed and the resulting architecture is used in a new iteration. This *Assessment, Hardening, Substitution* process is repeated until an architecture satisfying the safety requirements is obtained. The main improvement brought by the proposed SMT-based method is to directly find the solution by solving an SMT problem that encodes completely the exploration problem.

7.2   Assessment of a Candidate

The classic safety assessment methods are based on *Binary Decision Diagram* (BDD) [24] representation of φ [25]. Thus the usage of BDDs to compute the safety indicators during exploration seems to be a relevant choice. However during exploration, a new candidate is generated by substituting a component by another one. So new failure events can appear, invalidating the current structure function, forcing its regeneration from scratch after each substitution.

8 Conclusion

Summary. This paper introduced the STMDD and associated safety assessment algorithms, as well as the *Safety theory*, which allows encoding design-space exploration as an SMT problem. This approach allowed us to solve the design-space exploration problem several orders of magnitude faster that more traditional approaches based on evolutionary algorithms on the considered benchmarks.

Ongoing Works. The current work focuses on the enhancement of exploration theory presented in Sect. 6. Indeed the current theory cannot indicate to the solver a promising substitution choice. This information can help the solver to generate relevant candidates and reduce the exploration time.

Future Works. As mentioned in the introduction, the safety designer must consider safety requirements but also some cost functions to build a safe and cheap architecture. We will, in a not too distant future, propose a formulation of the exploration problem capable of optimizing cost functions using available SMT/SAT optimization techniques such as Max-SAT [26].

References

1. SAE: Aerospace Recommended Practices 4754a - Development of Civil Aircraft and Systems (2010)
2. Grunske, L., Lindsay, P., Bondarev, E., Papadopoulos, Y., Parker, D.: An outline of an architecture-based method for optimizing dependability attributes of software-intensive systems. In: Lemos, R., Gacek, C., Romanovsky, A. (eds.) WADS 2006. LNCS, vol. 4615, pp. 188–209. Springer, Heidelberg (2007). doi:10.1007/978-3-540-74035-3_9
3. Aleti, A., Buhnova, B., Grunske, L., Koziolek, A., Meedeniya, I.: Software architecture optimization methods: a systematic literature review. IEEE Trans. Softw. Eng. **39**(5), 658–683 (2013)
4. Kehren, C., Seguin, C., Bieber, P., Castel, C., Bougnol, C., Heckmann, J.P., Metge, S.: Architecture patterns for safe design. In: AAAF 1st Complex and Safe Systems Engineering Conference (CS2E 2004), pp. 21–22. Citeseer (2004)
5. Armoush, A.: Design patterns for safety-critical embedded systems. Ph.D. thesis, RWTH Aachen University (2010)
6. Barrett, C., Fontaine, P., Tinelli, C.: The SMT-LIB standard–version 2.5 (2010)
7. Bozzano, M., Cimatti, A., Tapparo, F.: Symbolic fault tree analysis for reactive systems. In: Namjoshi, K.S., Yoneda, T., Higashino, T., Okamura, Y. (eds.) ATVA 2007. LNCS, vol. 4762, pp. 162–176. Springer, Heidelberg (2007). doi:10.1007/978-3-540-75596-8_13
8. Villemeur, A.: Reliability, Availability, Maintainbility and Safety Assessment. Wiley, Chichester (1992)

9. Pagetti, C., Saussié, D., Gratia, R., Noulard, E., Siron, P.: The ROSACE case study: from simulink specification to multi/many-core execution. In: 2014 IEEE 20th Real-Time and Embedded Technology and Applications Symposium (RTAS), pp. 309–318. IEEE (2014)

10. Rauzy, A.: Mathematical foundations of minimal cutsets. IEEE Trans. Reliab. 50(4), 389–396 (2001)

11. Barrett, C.W., Sebastiani, R., Seshia, S.A., Tinelli, C.: Satisfiability modulo theories. Handb. Satisfiability 185, 825–885 (2009)

12. Srinivasan, A., Ham, T., Malik, S., Brayton, R.K.: Algorithms for discrete function manipulation. In: 1990 IEEE International Conference on Computer-Aided Design, ICCAD-1990, Digest of Technical Papers, pp. 92–95. IEEE (1990)

13. Adachi, M., Papadopoulos, Y., Sharvia, S., Parker, D., Tohdo, T.: An approach to optimization of fault tolerant architectures using hip-hops. Softw. Pract. Exp. 41(11), 1303–1327 (2011)

14. de Moura, L., Bjørner, N.: Z3: an efficient SMT solver. In: Ramakrishnan, C.R., Rehof, J. (eds.) TACAS 2008. LNCS, vol. 4963, pp. 337–340. Springer, Heidelberg (2008). doi:10.1007/978-3-540-78800-3_24

15. Walker, M., Reiser, M.O., Tucci-Piergiovanni, S., Papadopoulos, Y., Lönn, H., Mraidha, C., Parker, D., Chen, D., Servat, D.: Automatic optimisation of system architectures using EAST-ADL. J. Syst. Softw. 86(10), 2467–2487 (2013)

16. Amari, S.V., Dill, G.: Redundancy optimization problem with warm-standby redundancy. In: 2010 Proceedings-Annual Reliability and Maintainability Symposium (RAMS), pp. 1–6. IEEE (2010)

17. dos Santos Coelho, L.: An efficient particle swarm approach for mixed-integer programming in reliability-redundancy optimization applications. Reliab. Eng. Syst. Saf. 94(4), 830–837 (2009)

18. Delmas, K., Delmas, R., Pagetti, C.: Automatic architecture hardening using safety patterns. In: Koornneef, F., Gulijk, C. (eds.) SAFECOMP 2015. LNCS, vol. 9337, pp. 283–296. Springer, Cham (2015). doi:10.1007/978-3-319-24255-2_21

19. Messaoud, S.: Optimal Architecture Synthesis for Aircraft Electrical Power Systems. Ph.D. thesis, University of California Berkeley (2013)

20. Peter, S., Givargis, T.: Component-based synthesis of embedded systems using satisfiability modulo theories. ACM Trans. Des. Autom. Electron. Syst. (TODAES) 20(4), 49 (2015)

21. Mattarei, C., Cimatti, A., Gario, M., Tonetta, S., Rozier, K.Y.: Comparing different functional allocations in automated air traffic control design. In: Formal Methods in Computer-Aided Design (FMCAD), pp. 112–119. IEEE (2015)

22. Gario, M., Cimatti, A., Mattarei, C., Tonetta, S., Rozier, K.Y.: Model checking at scale: automated air traffic control design space exploration. In: Chaudhuri, S., Farzan, A. (eds.) CAV 2016. LNCS, vol. 9780, pp. 3–22. Springer, Cham (2016). doi:10.1007/978-3-319-41540-6_1

23. Dassault: Cecilia OCAS framework (2014)

24. Bryant, R.E.: Symbolic boolean manipulation with ordered binary-decision diagrams. ACM Comput. Surv. (CSUR) 24(3), 293–318 (1992)

25. Rauzy, A.: Binary decision diagrams for reliability studies. In: Misra, K.B. (ed.) Handbook of Performability Engineering, pp. 381–396. Springer, London (2008)

26. Hansen, P., Jaumard, B.: Algorithms for the maximum satisfiability problem. Computing 44(4), 279–303 (1990)

Safety and Security

A Lightweight Threat Analysis Approach Intertwining Safety and Security for the Automotive Domain

Jürgen Dürrwang[1]([✉]) [iD], Kristian Beckers[2]([✉]), and Reiner Kriesten[1]([✉])

[1] Institute of Energy Efficient Mobility (IEEM), University of Applied Sciences,
Moltkestrs. 30, 76133 Karlsruhe, Germany
{duju0001,krre0001}@hs-karlsruhe.de
[2] Software Engineering, Technical University Munich (TUM),
Boltzmannstr. 3, 85748 Garching, Germany
beckersk@in.tum.de

Abstract. The automotive industry relies increasingly on computer technology in their cars, which malicious attackers can exploit. Therefore, the Original Equipment Manufacturers (OEMs) have to adopt security engineering practices in their development efforts, in addition to their safety engineering efforts. In particular, information assets that can undermine safety have to be identified and protected. Assessing the safety relevance of specific information assets is best done by safety engineers, who, unfortunately, often do not have the security expertise to do so. In this paper, we propose a technique for identifying information assets and protection goals that are relevant for safety. Our method is based on security guide-words, which allow a structured identification of possible attack scenarios. The method is similar to the Hazard and Operability Study (HAZOP) in safety for eliciting possible faults. The similarity of the approach shall ease the effort for non-security engineers to identify information assets and protection goals to allow an exchange between safety and security mindsets. In contrary to other proposed methods, we performed an evaluation of our technique to show their practical application. In our evaluation with a total of 30 employees of an automotive supplier and employees of the University of Applied Sciences in Karlsruhe, results show that all non-security engineers achieved for precision, productivity and sensitivity, on average, higher values than the security control group.

Keywords: Safety and security co-analysis · Functional safety · Automotive security · Threat analysis

1 Introduction

Modern automobiles host more than 50 Electronic Control Units (ECUs) which contain and implement a total of up to 100 million code lines [3] to control

© Springer International Publishing AG 2017
S. Tonetta et al. (Eds.): SAFECOMP 2017, LNCS 10488, pp. 305–319, 2017.
DOI: 10.1007/978-3-319-66266-4_20

safety-critical functionality. This fact and the close interconnectivity of automotive ECUs open up new possibilities to attack these systems [9], which impair the safe operation of the vehicle. To counter these attacks a holistic approach to security by design has to be applied, starting with a threat analysis in the early development phase. Such analyses are broadly applied in classical IT but are rarely used in the automotive domain. Also security engineers who have knowledge in automotive are rare. In contrast, analyses addressing functional safety are mandatory. For this purpose, hazard analysis and risk assessment compliant to ISO 26262 [6] is applied. The ISO 26262 identifies malfunctions in electric or electronic components of passenger cars which can cause harm of human life. During the analysis, hazards are identified and mapped to the car's operational situations to determine the values: severity, the occurrence of operational situation and controllability. Afterwards, these values are used to calculate the Automotive Safety Integrity Level (ASIL) deriving safety requirements. However, security requirements remain unconsidered.

While security and safety look similar at first glance, the "execution details" differ drastically and require a fundamentally different mindset. For instance, safety engineers do not think about changing assumptions as physics remain static, whereas thinking about changing assumptions is an essential requirement for a security engineer. Thus, we argue that safety and security analysis must not be conducted by the same persons. On the other hand, for a intertwined safety and security analysis, safety engineers have to be trained to conduct the tasks together with security experts. Because safety engineers have the domain knowledge but may not be security experts. Conversely, security engineers often do not know about safety and have less experience in the automotive safety domain but need information assets and protection goals for their work. Therefore, a method is needed to allow safety engineers defining information assets and protection goals so that security engineers can take over. In this paper, we propose a methodology that is based on so-called security guide-words [15]. The method can be used by safety engineers to identify information assets and protection goals that are relevant for safety. Based on this, security engineers can perform further security analysis and develop protection concepts. In particular, the contributions of this paper are the following:

- The Security Guide-word Method (SGM), **an approach that can be used to reuse existing safety analysis artefacts to identify security assets and protection goals**. SGM is tailored to minimize the integration effort in typical automotive engineering processes.
- An **evaluation of SGM based on a study** that was conducted based on a set of 30 professionals from security and safety divisions of an automotive engineering company and a control group from academia.

The paper is structured as follows: Sect. 2 summarises threat analyses approaches for the automotive domain including approaches to combine safety and security, followed by our proposed methodology in Sect. 3. Afterwards, we give an evaluation of SGM, presenting our hypotheses, the performed study, and achieved results. Section 5 discusses the study results and the significance of our statements. Lastly, Sect. 6 summarises our outcomes and shows further work on SGM.

2 Related Work

Several approaches for threat analysis exist. In particular, for the automotive domain, the Society of Automotive Engineers (SAE) guidebook J3061 [12] provides security guidelines in compliance with the ISO 26262 standard. The guideline summarises recommended security practices and suggests for threat analyses: Attack Tree Analysis (ATA) as a counterpart to Fault Tree Analysis (FTA), Microsoft's STRIDE, and the E-Safety Vehicle Intrusion Protected Applications (EVITA) project using dark-side scenarios in combination with ATAs. Additionally, EVITA propose the Threat and Operability Analysis (THROP) based on the well-known HAZOP method, which uses guide-words for the analysis. HAZOP was originally developed for the chemical industry and transferred to automotive as analysis approach for functional safety. Unfortunately, EVITA provides no structured approach which reuses artefacts of a safety analysis and is further particularly extensive and complex. Furthermore, their presented guidewords do not reflect the behaviour of an attacker.

A further holistic approach for co-analysis of safety and security for automotive is the Combined Harm Assessment of Safety and Security for Information Systems (CHASSIS), which applies use cases and sequence diagrams to identify safety and security requirements. During a brainstorming session with engineers of both domains and the application of HAZOP, potential misuses of the system are identified [14]. Even though CHASSIS applies HAZOP, no guide-words are presented in its guideline. Moreover, the approach proposes a widely separate safety and security analysis with few information exchange between both worlds [14].

We also based our method on HAZOP and its application of guide-words. Especially the capability of the application on embedded systems [7] was an important pre-step for adopting HAZOP in the automotive domain. Further, Winther et al. [15] presented the "security-HAZOP" approach combining safety and security analysis for Information and Communication Technology (ICT)-systems. While our approach is also based on HAZOP, we differ from other approaches by using HAZOP to interface safety and security processes together instead of only security or only safety. Furthermore, compared to the related work we provide a rigorous evaluation of the approach based on its intended real world users.

3 SGM Approach

We propose an application of our SGM in an early development phase of a modern car, based on the work of Winther et al. [15]. In particular, we consider an application in the hazard and risk analysis according to ISO 26262 as feasible. The required steps are illustrated in Fig. 1.

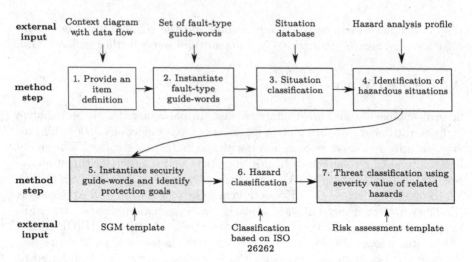

Fig. 1. Security Guide-word Method (SGM) steps during hazard analysis in compliance to ISO 26262.

Subsequently, Step 1–4 and Step 6, which are part of the well-known safety process, are briefly explained. Step **5** and **7** explain in detail the extensions by our SGM (see the highlighted steps in Fig. 1). We further explain the process based on a running example that is shown in Fig. 2.

Step 1 - Provide an Item Definition: The initial step of our approach starts with an item definition as required by ISO 26262. We consider a context diagram extended by data flows as sufficient and easiest for this task. The diagram includes high level architecture information, describing the involved

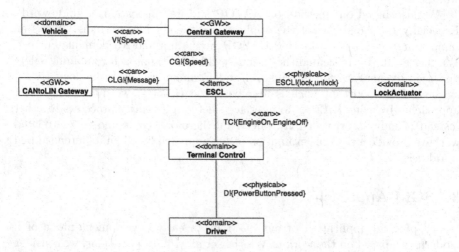

Fig. 2. Context diagram of ESCL-System based on our work in [1].

entities namely ECUs, gateways(GWs), bus systems and domains surrounding it, e.g., the driver. Furthermore, the diagram includes any data and information flow between the entities, which are known by that time. The context diagram used in this work is presented in Fig. 2. As notation for our example we use the UML4PF [4] profile extension.

Figure 2 represents an Electronic Steering Column Lock (ESCL)-System for locking the steering column of a car. Therefore, it is a part of the anti-theft device of a modern car. The ESCL-System has two main requirements *R1: The steering column shall be locked when the driver wants to immobilise the vehicle* and *R2: The steering column shall be unlocked, when the driver wants to drive.* Given the requirements of the item under analysis we know its basic functionality and its environment.

Step 2 - Instantiate Fault-Type Guide-Words: We consider a set of so-called *fault-type guide-words* inspired by the HAZOP standard [5] as appropriate for safety analysis. The set contains words like *no, unintended, early, late, more, less, inverted, intermittent, after, other than* and *part of.* The set of guide-words is not unique and can be extended by domain specific words and helps developers to consider all relevant faults by focussing on typical problems. As an example we use Fig. 2 and the defined requirements from Step 1 (*R1, R2*) to identify faults listed in Table 1.

Table 1. Identified faults related to the context diagram in Fig. 2

Fault-ID	Fault
1	Unintended lock
2	No lock

Step 3 - Situation Classification: In this step, a hierarchically organized list of operational situations is created. The list is often reused from previous analyses, since operational situations change only little over time. Each situation has to be rated as relevant or not for the actual item under analysis. Therefore, the requirements of the item and its context diagram can help to reduce the total set of situations. From the safety point of view, special situations like maintenance is not considered, but we deem them as also important for security. Hence, a consideration of maintenance and workshop situations makes sense for protection goal identification and thus for the analysis.

Step 4 - Identification of Hazardous Situations: For each fault and function combination all situations that could lead to a potential hazard are identified in the list of situations being relevant. The effect of a hazard is described on the vehicle level and its consequences are listed in a table. For the given example we list the following hazards in Table 2.

Table 2. Identified hazards

ID	Hazard
1	Loss of steering control while driving on highway
2	Loss of steering control while cornering fast
3	Steering will not lock if vehicle is parked
...	...

Step 5 - (SGM) Instantiate Security Guide-Words and Identify Protection Goals: In this step, we insert our security analysis approach by applying the automotive security guide-words. The guide-words are derived from existent attacks on modern vehicles [11] and thus, they represent the malicious intent of the attacker. We derived ten guide-words namely *disclosure, disconnection, delay, deletion, stopping, denial, trigger, insertion, reset,* and *manipulation*. Moreover, for each presented guide-word, protection goals can be derived and broken down to the Confidentiality, Integrity, and Availability (CIA) triad which is well-known in the security domain. This enables security engineers to understand safety issues under the view of security. Thus, an ideal interface between the safety and security mindsets is created. For a structured collection of protection goals we provide an analysis template for the application of guide-words, which is presented in Table 3.

Table 3. SGM template

Threat-ID	Fault-ID	Can be triggered by	Signal or function	Component or subsystem	Entry point
T-ID	F-ID	(1)	(2)	(3)	(4)

Even though SGM is used to identify protection goals and information assets, we decided to call the first column in Table 3 a Threat-ID due to the fact that each row represents a security threat which security engineers can directly understand. The second column contains a Fault-ID which belongs to the protection goal. It further points to the relevant fault identified during the safety analysis (see Table 1). In particular, the columns contain: (1) one of the security guide-words representing the type of malicious action, (2) one signal or function existent in the given context diagram, (3) the component or subsystem, which processes the signal or provides the function, and lastly (4) the entry point of the manipulation. Furthermore, column 2–4 represent the protection goal identified by the safety engineer. If we apply the template to the ESCL-System shown in Fig. 2, we can identify the information assets and protection goals and list them in Table 4.

Table 4. SGM template for ESCL-System in Fig. 2 (Fault-ID 1:=*unintended lock*).

Threat-ID	Fault-ID	Can be triggered by	Signal or function	Component or subsystem	Entry point
1	1	Triggering	Lock function	ESCL	CAN
2	1	Reset	-	ESCL-ECU	Physical, CAN
3	1	Manipulation	ESCL!{lock, unlock}	ESCL	Physical
4	...	...	...	...	...

For example we can read Threat 1 in Table 4 as: *Unintended lock can be triggered by triggering the lock function of ESCL on Controller Area Network (CAN)*.

Step 6 - Hazard Classification: For each hazard identified by the analyst values for severity, exposure of operational situation and controllability are defined in compliance to ISO 26262. Based on these estimations, the ASIL is determined using a matrix provided in ISO 26262 Part 3. The provided matrix allows a calculation in five ASILs increasing from QM, A, B, C to the highest level D. Except for level QM, safety goals are derived and recorded for the corresponding ASIL.

Step 7 - (SGM) Threat Classification Using the Severity Value of Related Hazards: We rank identified threats by reusing artefacts of the safety analysis. In particular, we select the associated Fault-ID for each Thread-ID in Table 3. Then we collect those hazards which may directly occur because of this selected fault. Finally, we pick the highest ASIL of all hazards in regard to the fault. We consider this worst-case approach as reasonable as we have to assume that attackers will trigger their attack in the most dangerous situation. At this point, our method finishes (Fig. 1). But for a holistic approach we want to show the next safety step demanded by ISO 26262 and also the next step which is done by a security engineer representing the security requirements elicitation.

Step 8 - (Safety) Functional Safety Concept: For each recorded safety goal of Step 6 safety requirements are derived leading to functional safety concept demanded by ISO 26262. For this purpose a structured procedure is given by the standard.

Step 8 - (Security) Security Requirements Elicitation: A downstream step of our approach is to formulate security requirements based on the identified protection goals of Step 5. As an example we show a threat and requirement pair in Table 5. The identified threat shall allow security engineers to identify and design suitable security countermeasures against it. In particular, security engineers use established security methodologies to assess the threat occurrence probability and the impact of a successful attack. For instance, to assess the threat shown in Table 5, a security engineer has to determine the likeliness of an attacker being able to get access to the CAN bus. Note, that this mapping was not part of our experiment but is added here to explain how threats will be used to elicit security requirements by security experts.

Table 5. From threats to requirements

Threat	Security requirement
An attacker can cause an unintended lock of the steering column wheel by triggering the lock function of the component lock actuator on bus system CAN	The lock function of the component lock actuator on bus system CAN has to be protected from unauthorised access

Besides, the presented SGM approach focuses on security for safety, we consider an extension to other aspects of security e.g. privacy, as feasible. To do so, the set of guide-words has to be supplemented by new words derived from a security expert for the relevant scope. At this point, we will further point out that the presented approach supports a security analysis from a safety view. Hence, the approach does not replace a holistic security in depth analysis including aspects like financial risk, reputation, etc.

4 Evaluation

The goal of the SGM method is to allow safety engineers to identify relevant protection objectives and assets. In this section, we evaluate whether the SGM method provides results that are comparable to results of regular security engineers. We evaluate this question by carrying out a study conducted with 30 safety and security engineers of an automotive company and full-time employees of a university. We divided our evaluation of the SGM into two main parts. In part one, we used a questionnaire for background assessment of our participants to determine their skills. In part two, we conducted the empirical evaluation of SGM with the participants to test our hypotheses.

4.1 Hypotheses

Our primary hypothesis states that SGM enables safety engineers to identify information assets and protection goals in the same manner as security engineers can identify. To confirm this, we analysed how well non-security engineers can find protection goals and how many of them are correct with respect to expert assessments. Accordingly, we derived three test-hypotheses from our primary hypothesis regarding to the metrics: precision (PPV), productivity (PRO), and sensitivity/recall (TPR). Additionally, we also reported the efficiency of our method, but we did not formulate a respective test-hypothesis. The reason is a lack of comparative values.

To consider one of the test-hypotheses to be correct the associated null-hypothesis has to be rejected. In order to evaluate the defined null-hypothesis we counted the True Positives (TP) of the instantiated fields. Two security experts, who did not participate in the experiment, classified the instantiated fields as TP if the identified protection goals were correct. Moreover, instantiated fields which were marked as false by the two security experts are False Positives (FP). The number of fields instantiated by our participants are called Fields Initiated (FI). The total number of fields that can be instantiated by the participants are called Number of Fields (NF). For each test-hypothesis (H_1) we formulated an associated null hypothesis (H_0), which we tested.

Our prime interest is the precision (PPV) of our participants in order to assess the applicability of our method. We defined the relation between FP and TP as follows: $PPV = TP/(TP + FP)$. Our hypothesis is that correct results are pre-dominant on average.

For pre-dominancy, we defined a value of more than 80%. The value is not arbitrarily chosen, but based on previous research of Scandariato et al. [13]. The authors used this threshold to measure TP when applying the Microsoft STRIDE threat analysis technique. As a result, we formulated the related null hypothesis as follows:

$$H_{0,Saf}^{PPV} : \mu\{PPV = TP/(TP + FP)\} \leq 0.80$$

In the same manner, we defined productivity (PRO) as the relation of the number of fields instantiated to the total number of fields that can be instantiated by the participants including FP: $PRO = FI/NF$. We are interested in how many fields our participants instantiated and we formulated our related null hypothesis accordingly:

$$H_{0,Saf}^{PRO} : \mu\{PRO = FI/NF\} \leq 0.80$$

Hence, we consider it as possible that non-security engineers, on average, are able to produce protection goals of at least 80%, which describes the alternative hypothesis. Furthermore, we assume that non-security engineers can achieve at least the same degree of sensitivity (recall) as the security group. Therefore, we formulated the related null hypothesis for sensitivity (TPR=TP/(TP+FN)) as follows:

$$H_{0,Saf}^{TPR} : \mu\{TPR_{Saf}\} \leq \mu\{TPR_{Sec}\}$$

As we are not able to measure False Negatives (FN) directly, we decided to replace FN with the number of not-found protection goals in the practical experiment and thus, we used FN := NF − FI to formulate our null hypothesis.

4.2   Study Design

Our study design is based on the work of Scandariato et al. [13] and our previous study [2]. Therefore, we structured the study into three phases. The first phase contains a short introduction to functional safety and automotive security. We explained the relation between safety and security incidents to our participants and how they can influence each other. Furthermore, we explained the terms safety and security and their fundamental differences. This was necessary, because the groups *novice* and *safety* did not work on security topics before. Afterwards, we handed out a questionnaire to all participants, assessing their knowledge. The questionnaire is split into two parts. The first part is a self-assessment of the following topics: automotive software engineering, functional safety, automotive bus systems, real-time systems, security as well as hazard and threat analysis. The participants selected out of five experience levels ranging from unskilled to expert. In the second phase we asked questions regarding all topics mentioned previously. This allowed us to validate the self-assessment. We also assessed the flow experience of the participants during the experiment using the scale of Rheinberg et al. [10]. A comprehensive analysis of the background assessment and all used questionnaires are publicly available [8].

We started the practical task with an introduction of the Security Guideword Method (SGM) (slides are available under [8]). Afterwards, we asked the participants to apply the method to a real world example. The example was carefully selected to ensure a complexity that can be managed within a time frame of up to 15 min. We used the ESCL-System in Fig. 2.

4.3 Participants

Three different groups of people participated in our empirical evaluation. We were able to enlist security and safety experts from an automotive supplier and full-time employees of the University of Applied Science in Karlsruhe[1]. Table 6 shows a detailed overview of our participants.

Table 6. Participants for SGM evaluation.

	No SGM	SGM	Participants
Team *security*	X	-	9
Team *novice*	-	X	7
Team *safety*	-	X	14
Overall full time employees participating in the experiment			$\sum$ 30

Group one consists of 9 security engineers of an automotive supplier, group two of 7 novices in safety and security from the University and group three of 14 safety engineers from the same automotive supplier as the security engineers. As team *novice* consist of doctoral students coming from working areas which are not related to safety and security, they have never done a safety or security analysis before. Therefore, we requested team *novice* and team *safety* to work on the task with the SGM and for comparison, team *security* to work without the SGM.

---

[1] Note that these full time employees are doing a PhD, as well. In contrast to scholarship students they not exclusively work on their PhD.

4.4   Study Results

As stated above, we measured Fields Initiated (FI), True Positives (TP) and False Positives (FP) for each group. The achieved values and distributions are summarized in the following Whisker-Plots (see Figs. 3a, b and 4).

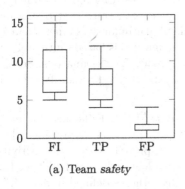

(a) Team *safety*

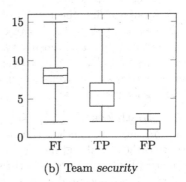

(b) Team *security*

Fig. 3. Results for Fields Initiated (FI), True Positives (TP) and False Positives (FP) of the team *safety* and *security*.

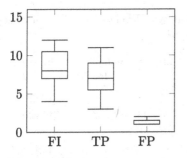

Fig. 4. Results for FI, TP and FP of the team *novice*

Table 7. Measured means for the team: *security*, *safety* and *novice*.

	Security	Safety	Novice
Precision	78.29%	84.75%	83.33%
Productivity	51.85%	57.14%	56.19%
Sensitivity	40.74%	48.09%	47.61%
Efficiency	31.111	34.29	33.71
FI	7.778	8.57	8.43

Figures 3a, b and 4 show the distribution of the measured values for FI, TP and FP. We observed similar results for team *safety* and team *novice*, which indicates consistent results considering both groups using the SGM. In particular both groups achieved higher medians for TP than team *security*, as well as lower minima of FI and TP. We consider this an indicator for the fact that team *safety* and team *novice* had domain knowledge concerning safety, which team *security* was lacking.

The maximum number of protection goals (FI) identified by team *novice* was 12, the minimum was 4 and the median was 8. They further identified a maximum of 11 correct protection goals (TP), a minimum of 3 and a median of 7. For FI team *safety* (Fig. 3a) achieved a maximum number of 15 and a minimum number of 5. For the median the team achieved 7.5 protection goals. Team *safety* identified a maximum number of 12 TP, a minimum number of 4 and for the median the team identified 7 correct protection goals. In contrast, team *security* (Fig. 3b) identified a median of 8 for protection goals (FI) which is slightly better than the result of team *safety* with an achieved value of 7.5. Moreover, team *security* identified a maximum number of 12 protection goals (TP) and a minimum of 2. For the median the team achieved 6 correct protection goals which represents a lower value than the values achieved by team *safety* and *novice*. Considering the results of Table 7, we can state that teams *safety* and *novice* performed better because of their continuously higher means for precision, productivity, and sensitivity. We assume this is based on the following two facts. Firstly, SGM uses a structured approach for the analysis. Secondly, SGM enables engineers to reuse their domain knowledge to identify protection goals and information assets.

Testing Hypotheses ($H_{0,Saf}^{PPV}$, $H_{0,Saf}^{PRO}$ and $H_{0,Saf}^{TPR}$). Following the analysis of FI, TP and FP, we checked the validity of our proposed hypotheses. Therefore, we used the calculated means for precision, productivity and sensitivity of group *safety* (Table 7) to perform three independent right sided t-Tests. Based on these results we accepted or rejected the hypotheses defined in Sect. 4.1. As already mentioned, to accept a hypothesis (H_1) we have to reject the related null hypothesis (H_0). Table 8 shows the results of the performed t-Tests.

Table 8. Results for right sided t-Tests with a significance level of $\alpha = 10\%$. All values listed in the second column are derived from Sect. 4.1.

Hypothesis	Accepted μ (for H_1)	State H_0	t-value	p-value of t-Test for H_0	State H_1
Precision (PPV)	>80%	Rejected	1.6875	0.057	*Accepted*
Productivity (PRO)	>80%	*Accepted*	1.4695	0.998	Rejected
	>51.85%	*Accepted*	−3.7101	0.203	Rejected
Sensitivity (TPR)	>40.74%	Rejected	0.8587	0.082	*Accepted*

As Table 7 shows, team *safety* achieved for productivity a value of 57.14% leading to acceptance of the null hypothesis $H_{0,Saf}^{PRO}$ and thus to rejection of our hypothesis for productivity (see Table 8). Related to our hypothesis that non-security engineers can reach at least the same degree of productivity as security engineers by applying of SGM, we decided to perform a further t-Test for $H_{0,Saf}^{PRO}$. As second threshold we used 51.85% which is the measured mean of team *security*. Even though the achieved mean of 57.14% of team *safety* is higher than the value of team *security*, the performed t-Test states that we have to accept the null hypothesis $H_{0,Saf}^{PRO}$ again. Thus, we have to reject the assumed hypothesis that safety engineers can reach the same degree of productivity as security engineers.

In contrast, we can directly reject null hypothesis $H_{0,Saf}^{PPV}$ and $H_{0,Saf}^{TPR}$ without a second test. In particular, for team *safety* and precision (PPV) we measured a mean of 84.74%, which is greater than the defined threshold of 80%. Furthermore, for sensitivity (TPR) we measured a mean of 48.09% which is also a higher value than the defined threshold of 40.74% (see Table 8) achieved by the security team. Considering the fact that for both hypotheses the calculated p-values are smaller than α, we reject the null hypothesis $H_{0,Saf}^{PPV}$ and $H_{0,Saf}^{TPR}$. Consequently, we accept our hypothesis that non-security engineers can achieve at least 80% for precision (PPV) and we can accept the hypothesis that non-security engineers can achieve at least the same level of sensitivity (TPR) as well as security engineers using our SGM.

Furthermore, the results in Table 7 indicate that the proposed SGM enables engineers with less security knowledge to identify correct protection goals and information assets which further shows that a combined safety & security analysis is possible by non-security experts. This statement seems feasible by the consistently higher means in column 3 and 4 of Table 7. Additionally, we discovered that almost all participants started with protecting goals that have a high safety impact. We discovered this insight by evaluating the type of malfunction used in the SGM template. We measured a higher number of protection goals related to malfunction 1 (unintended lock) as related to malfunction 2 (no lock). In particular, malfunction 1 results in the highest number of hazards in our sample solution. Furthermore, we analysed three values regarding the flow experience [10] of our participants measured in parallel to the experiment [8]. In particular, team *safety* responded that they felt more in work-flow, had fewer concerns, and felt less challenged as team *security*.

Summing up, we can state that safety engineers are able to achieve at least the same degree of precision and sensitivity as the security engineers by using the SGM. Hence, we consider it as feasible that safety engineers are able to identify correct protection goals and information assets supporting a security analysis by applying SGM. Moreover, our methods allows safety engineers to reuse artefacts of a previously performed safety analysis.

5   Threats to Validity

In this section, we discuss threats to validity of our study regarding the four validity classes proposed by Wohlin et al. [16].

Construct validity: The measures made for the experiment in terms of precision, productivity and sensitivity might not be representative for measuring the applicability of the method. There might be better measures than ours but when we investigated further analysis work in the field [13], we did not identify any method which is more precise than the one used in this publication.

Conclusion validity: For our experiment, we had only 21 non-security participants enrolled in the study reducing the significance of our statistical evaluation and the stated hypotheses. However, all participants had automotive background through their daily work or their bachelor and master studies which is shown by the results in our assessment background [8]. Moreover, we had 14 safety engineers as participants working daily on safety issues which distinguished us from other previously performed evaluations. But most of all, it is a particular challenge to gather a large sample group of this type that is highly representative for the target audience.

Internal validity: A threat to the internal validity is that we conducted the experiment with participants having less knowledge in security and who may felt overwhelmed with the task which reduces the meaningful application of the SGM. However, we analysed the already mentioned values regarding the flow experience [10] of our participants and team *safety* responded that they felt more in work-flow, had fewer concerns, and felt less challenged as team *security*.

External validity: In this study we had a single group of non-safety engineers (*novice*) conducting the experiment which do not correspond to the desired target group of safety engineers. However, we decided to publish the results of this group to discuss them. Furthermore, group *novice* showed background [8] knowledge in the automotive domain and therefore we consider them as representative, too. Additionally, the possibility exists that some safety engineers heard about security topics during their daily work or in presentations affecting the measurement. Nevertheless, we consider that neither team *safety* nor team *novice* can be regarded as security experts. This assumption is confirmed by the background assessment of team *safety* and team *novice* [8].

6   Conclusions and Future Work

In this work, we proposed to use existing security guide-words for the identification of protection goals and information assets in the automotive domain in order to create a common interface between safety and security. Our new approach allows a structured identification of protection goals and information assets by reusing artefacts of the ISO 26262 hazard analysis. The method will reduce the effort of threat analyses of automotive systems by the distribution of tasks to safety and security engineers. In particular, safety engineers will now be able to produce protection goals that security engineers can directly understand and adopt for their security analyses. Moreover, it is conceivable that SGM will be a part of a security development life-cycle in automotive as proposed in SAE J3061 [12]. This is further supported by the fact that SGM is based on HAZOP, which is well-known in the automotive domain. Furthermore, we contributed an empirical evaluation of our approach with a total number of 30 participants. To be precise, 14 safety engineers, 9 security engineers, and 7 full-time employees of the University of Applied Sciences in Karlsruhe participated in our experiment. Two groups applied SGM and achieved a precision above 80% within a 15 min time frame for identification of protection goals and information assets of a typical ISO 26262 item. Hence, the next steps will be to improve the approach by including item attributes to better assist safety engineers. Therefore, we want to use more details picked from the context diagram to preselect guide-words for the engineers. This will further reduce the effort for the analyst and it might be possible that their task can be done with computer-aid e.g. using an expert or recommender system. Besides, we will also conduct additional studies with a higher number of safety engineers together with our automotive partners. For this purpose, we want to set-up a online survey including a short introduction to the topic, an introduction to the ESCL example and a practical task which can also be done online. We hope that this will give us access to a greater number of safety engineers for a more significant validation.

Acknowledgements. We thank the anonymous reviewers for their inspiring comments. This work has been developed in the project SAFE ME ASAP (reference number: 03FH011IX5) that is partly funded by the German ministry of education and research (BMBF) within the research programme ICT 2020.

References

1. Beckers, K., Dürrwang, J., Holling, D.: Standard compliant hazard and threat analysis for the automotive domain. Information **7**(3), 36 (2016). http://www.mdpi.com/2078-2489/7/3/36
2. Beckers, K., Holling, D., Côté, I., Hatebur, D.: A structured hazard analysis and risk assessment method for automotive systems-a descriptive study. Reliab. Eng. Syst. Safety **158**, 185–195 (2016)
3. Charette, R.N.: This car runs on code (2009). http://spectrum.ieee.org/transportation/systems/this-car-runs-on-code. Accessed 12 Feb 2016
4. Hatebur, D., Heisel, M.: A UML profile for requirements analysis of dependable software. In: Schoitsch, E. (ed.) SAFECOMP 2010. LNCS, vol. 6351, pp. 317–331. Springer, Heidelberg (2010). doi:10.1007/978-3-642-15651-9_24
5. IEC: Hazard and Operability Studies (HAZOP studies). ISO/IEC 62882, International Electrotechnical Commission (IEC) (2005)
6. ISO: ISO 26262 - Road Vehicles - Functional Safety (2011)
7. Wei, J., Matsubara, Y., Takada, H.: HAZOP-based security analysis for embedded systems: case study of open. In: 2015 7th International Conference on Electronics, Computers and Artificial Intelligence (ECAI), pp. SSS-1–SSS-8 (2016)
8. Jürgen, D.: Evaluation security guideword experiment. http://www.home.hs-karlsruhe.de/~duju0001/Evaluation_SGM/. Accessed 13 Mar 2017
9. Miller, C., Valasek, C.: A survey of remote automotive attack surfaces (2014)
10. Rheinberg, F., Vollmeyer, R., Engeser, S.: Die Erfassung des Flow-Rrlebens (2003)
11. Ring, M., Dürrwang, J., Sommer, F., Kriesten, R.: Survey on vehicular attacks - building a vulnerability database. In: 2015 IEEE International Conference on Vehicular Electronics and Safety (ICVES), pp. 208–212 (2015)
12. SAE: Cybersecurity guidebook for cyber-physical vehicle systems (2016). http://standards.sae.org/wip/j3061/. Accessed 12 Apr 2016
13. Scandariato, R., Wuyts, K., Joosen, W.: A descriptive study of Microsoft's threat modeling technique. Requirements Eng. **20**(2), 163–180 (2015)
14. Schmittner, C., Ma, Z., Schoitsch, E., Gruber, T.: A case study of FMVEA and CHASSIS as safety and security co-analysis method for automotive cyber-physical systems. In: Proceedings of the 1st ACM Workshop on Cyber-Physical System Security, pp. 69–80 (2015)
15. Winther, R., Johnsen, O.-A., Gran, B.A.: Security assessments of safety critical systems using HAZOPs. In: Voges, U. (ed.) SAFECOMP 2001. LNCS, vol. 2187, pp. 14–24. Springer, Heidelberg (2001). doi:10.1007/3-540-45416-0_2
16. Wohlin, C., Runeson, P., Höst, M., Ohlsson, M.C., Regnell, B., Wesslén, A.: Experimentation in Software Engineering. Springer Science & Business Media, Heidelberg (2012)

A Security Architecture for Railway Signalling

Christian Schlehuber[1]([⊠]), Markus Heinrich[2], Tsvetoslava Vateva-Gurova[2],
Stefan Katzenbeisser[2], and Neeraj Suri[2]

[1] DB Netz AG, Frankfurt, Germany
christian.schlehuber@deutschebahn.com
[2] Department of Computer Science, TU Darmstadt, Darmstadt, Germany
{heinrich,katzenbeisser}@seceng.informatik.tu-darmstadt.de,
vateva@deeds.informatik.tu-darmstadt.de, suri@cs.tu-darmstadt.de

Abstract. We present the proposed security architecture Deutsche Bahn plans to deploy to protect its trackside safety-critical signalling system against cyber-attacks. We first present the existing reference interlocking system that is built using standard components. Next, we present a taxonomy to help model the attack vectors relevant for the railway environment. Building upon this, we present the proposed "compartmentalized" defence concept for securing the upcoming signalling systems.

1 Introduction

The state of the art in safety-critical railway signalling typically entails the use of monolithic interlocking systems that are often proprietary, expensive and not easily exchangeable. Consequently, the transition to more cost-effective and growth-oriented open networks is desired that can also utilize commercial off-the-shelf (COTS) hardware and software, provided the safety requirements are met.

These drivers have led Deutsche Bahn (DB) to explore transforming its signalling infrastructure using open networks and COTS to reduce cost and maintenance overhead. At the same time, the risk of cyber-attacks introduced by open networks and COTS needs to be explicitly addressed to avoid any compromise of safety. This work documents DB's ongoing experience in developing new signalling architectures that by-design decouple safety and security functionalities.

In this context, we first present a taxonomy of attacks outlining the potential cyber-threats relevant to protecting a railway signalling system. Consequently, utilizing the actual layout of the currently used German railway command and control system, we propose a security architecture that explicitly delineates safety and security, and will be deployed by DB in Germany's new interlocking systems (ILS) to address security concerns. The architecture is compartmentalized into zones and conduits following IEC 62443 [6]. Thereby we regard the German prestandard DIN VDE V 0831-104 [2] which is a guideline to apply IEC 62443 to the railway signalling domain with respect to the very strict safety requirements.

© Springer International Publishing AG 2017
S. Tonetta et al. (Eds.): SAFECOMP 2017, LNCS 10488, pp. 320–328, 2017.
DOI: 10.1007/978-3-319-66266-4_21

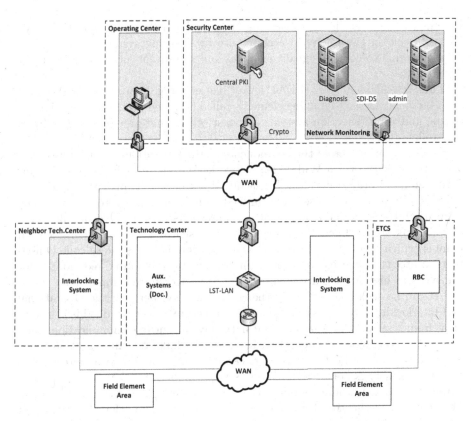

Fig. 1. Architecture of a typical signalling network.

2   Current Interlocking Network Architecture

The reference architecture, as currently deployed by DB, is divided into three layers: *Operational Layer, Interlocking Layer* and the *Field Element Area.*

The *Operational Layer* (upper blocks of Fig. 1) consists of an Operating Center and a Security Center. The Operating Center is responsible for the central monitoring and controlling of the system and is equipped with central switching points. The Security Center provides security services to the system such as security monitoring of certain communication channels and management of the Public Key Infrastructure (PKI). As depicted in Fig. 1, the communication between the Operational Layer and the Interlocking Layer of the reference architecture is encrypted. The Security Center has the same or higher security requirements compared to the rest of the components.

The *Interlocking Layer* (middle blocks in Fig. 1) provides the safety logic of the system. The main components of the Interlocking Layer are the Technology Center and the interface to the European Train Control System (ETCS), as depicted in Fig. 1. The Technology Center is comprised of the ILS and auxiliary systems (e.g., needed for documenting the actions of the ILS). The ILS plays a central role in the reference architecture by ensuring system's safety given its critical role to control signals, switches and to prevent any conflicting train movements.

The *Field Element Area* (FEA) (lowest blocks in Fig. 1) provides the interface to the actual trackside signalling elements called field elements. These are signals, points, and train detection systems amongst others that are steered by Object Controllers (OC).

Communication across the components of the Operational and Interlocking layers takes place over a Wide Area Network (WAN) through the use of Standard Communication Interfaces. Typically, the Rail Safe Transport Application (RaSTA) Protocol [3] is used as a unified communication protocol for all the defined interfaces. RaSTA targets at guaranteeing safety in the communication of railway systems. Each RaSTA-network is assigned a network identification number which is unique within the given transport layer. A safety code is used to guarantee the integrity of the transmitted messages. Required redundancy for the system's high availability is omitted in Fig. 1 to reduce complexity.

As can be seen in Fig. 1, only the communication between the Operational and Interlocking Layers of the reference architecture is encrypted. This is insufficient from a security perspective, and naturally the entire communication chain across the Technology Center, the FEAs and the linking communication interfaces need to be protected. However, enhancing the presented architecture in terms of security is not a trivial task, as various operational and compatibility constraints make introducing innovations to the interlocking system rather cumbersome. A complicating factor being re-ensuring that no safety violations get introduced with any security related changes (i.e. proving freedom of interference). In a normal computational environment, addressing security issues might require rapid patching and frequent updates. However, for the safety-critical railway environment any changes to a critical infrastructure, such as the signalling system that might affect the safety of the system, require explicit approval by the National Safety Authority. This can take significant time and exacerbates the timely reaction to security risks. In addition, the limited hardware resources in the signalling system do not allow deploying widely-used security solutions that are computationally intensive. Moreover, it is expected that deployed systems are used over a long operational lifetime (typically decades) and also provide strong timeliness response guarantees. All of these constraints need to be explicitly addressed when proposing a security-oriented signalling system architecture.

3   Railway Security Assessment

In order to propose a security architecture, this section presents the prerequisites needed for defending signalling infrastructure and also elucidates the capabilities of attackers against which the signalling system needs to be protected. To systematically tackle the problem of enhancing security in interlocking systems, we first provide a taxonomy of the attacks relevant for the railway environment.

Given the physically large spatial scattering of the railway infrastructure, it is infeasible to install physical protection comparable to a limited area factory premise. Access control and plant security, as important elements in a factory's security concept, do not apply to the full extent across the railway system. Only some parts – for example the interlocking computer – reside in a building that offers physical perimeter protection, while others (e.g., the field elements) lie unprotected along the railtracks.

In addition, we need to ensure safety and high availability of railway signalling systems. This is tightly coupled with the timeliness requirements of critical communication between network entities. In cases where we cannot preclude attacks, it is necessary to install monitoring systems that can detect ongoing attacks. For setting up a proper security concept we first need to define the capabilities of the attacker we want to defend the system against. In the railway signalling community it is widely recognized that some security incidents are already covered by the established safety functions.

The design of DB's security architecture follows the standard IEC 62443 [6] and the German prestandard DIN VDE V 0831-104 [2]. They classify the strength of attackers according to their (financial) resources, their motivation, and their knowledge. With the attacker strength in mind, we capture attacks that can be performed in a taxonomy that scopes the applicable security measures.

A taxonomy can facilitate enhancing security, as it can represent the diverse attack scenarios that threaten the railway signalling system, and also allows to consider future threats. While sophisticated attack scenarios have been considered by the taxonomies in [4,5,7–9] as well, most of them go beyond attack vectors and include information on the targeted system [4,8] that can be as detailed as software versions. However, unlike contemporary taxonomies built on full information access, we consider the systems from the operator perspective and do not know beforehand which technology the vendors use to meet the requirements. Thus, we are constrained to only model generic requirements of the systems.

Figure 2 outlines our approach to categorize threats. On the top level we distinguish across directed and undirected attacks. This is justified by the following assumption: It is impossible for undirected attacks to cause an unsafe state in the signalling system, as they will typically not circumvent the existing safety measures. However, this class of attacks may affect the availability of the system.

Since casualties could be the consequence, we consider impersonation as the most severe attack (i.e. an attacker being able to forge authentic messages of a network entity such as a OC or the ILS computer itself). As in any other network that comprises standard components, all known and unknown vulnerabilities pose a threat to the system in case they are exploited. Thus, vulnerabilities must be regarded in an attack model. Due to the scattered physical layout of the network it is prone to many kinds of information gathering attempts, and network entities like the field elements are difficult to protect against physical tampering. Although confidentiality is not an important target of signalling security, some information like cryptographic keys that are used to protect entities

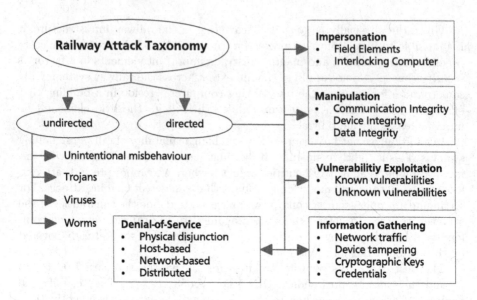

Fig. 2. A railway attack taxonomy.

and communication channels, as well as account credentials, need to be kept secret. A compromised key would enable more severe attacks on the system, for example impersonation. This interconnection shows that a holistic approach is needed to secure railway signalling and neither perimeter protection nor isolated solutions will suffice. Orthogonal to the presented threats are denial-of-service attacks where no comprehensive countermeasure exists. The signalling systems mitigate this threat by utilizing redundancy and avoiding single points of failure. We do not explicitly depict redundancy in Figs. 1 and 3, though all signalling relevant communication is performed over at least two separate channels provided by RaSTA. Entities such as the Security Center (from Fig. 1) also exist redundantly.

4   New Security Architecture for Interlocking Systems

For safety-related railway systems, the dominant requirements are integrity, timely delivery of critical messages and system availability. To ensure this, a Reliability, Availability, Maintainability, and Safety (RAMS) lifecycle has been introduced by EN 50126 [1] to make the current signalling systems resilient to internal faults and human error. However, EN 50126 does not consider attackers or malware that constitute a growing threat to all industrial control systems, including railway signalling systems. Thus, enhanced security mechanisms are needed, provided their potential to detrimentally affect safety and availability is explicitly delineated. This makes it infeasible to introduce standard "commercial" anti-malware and anti-virus systems into an ILS network, as the side effects are not easily discernible to be controlled.

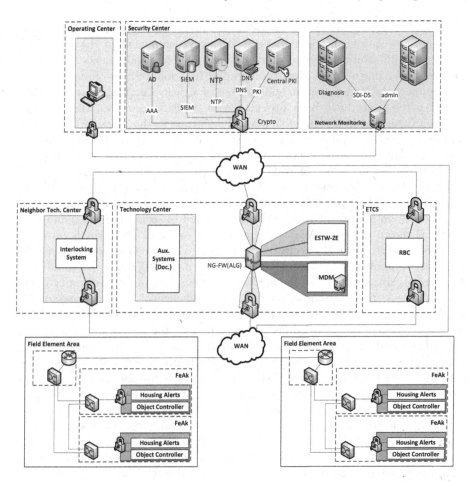

Fig. 3. Proposed Security Architecture for interlocking systems of DB. (Color figure online)

Based on the developed attack model taxonomy, a security architecture for the new interlocking technology was engineered. The security engineering process is based on the standard IEC 62443-3-3 [6] with guidance taken from DIN VDE V 0831-104 [2]. According to the general system design the signalling system has been partitioned into functional blocks e.g., Object Controllers (OC) and ILS (see Fig. 3). The reference architecture is additionally divided into zones and conduits, where each zone is logically or physically defined [6]. According to IEC 62443 each object within the architecture being hardware, software, user, etc. is assigned to exactly one zone or to exactly one conduit. A zone (colored areas) is a grouping of assets that have common security requirements which is expressed as a Security Level (SL) that is assigned to each zone. Conduits are the communication channels between zones with both the same and different security requirements.

A risk analysis yielded SLs of 2 or 3 for every zone. Based on these SLs, the security requirements were defined for every component of the system to ensure the fulfilment of a defence-in-depth concept. The requirements range from password changing abilities over cryptographic functions to a set of requirements that support the later detection and analysis of attacks e.g., logging capabilities.

After the zones have been provided with security measures, the conduits between them remain a vulnerable point. In contrast to the zones, IEC 62443-3-3 does not contain guidance on how to secure conduits. Over our requirements and taxonomy process two types of conduits have been identified, namely: (a) conduits connecting zones of equal SL, and (b) conduits connecting zones of different SLs. Conduits which only have unidirectional data flow could also be considered, but these are only a subtype of one of the former described conduits.

The system layout of Fig. 1 has been extended to secure the zones and conduits, as shown in Fig. 3. Again, redundancy is omitted. The FEA is provided in more detail to show the security application. Multiple OCs are presented as there are a number of field elements to steer in a single FEA. For redundancy, they are organized in a ring topology with switches (angular boxes) and routers (round boxes). The relation between OC and field element is usually one-to-one. Security boxes have been added to every OC (depicted as locks) in the FEA within a junction box (labelled FeAk). They provide the system with encryption capabilities and the possibility for basic filtering and DoS prevention rules. The capabilities are required for securing conduits between zones with equal SLs. The boxes are based on a ruggedized and hardened hardware platform. As they are completely separated from the safety functionality, they can be applied as a replacement of switch components in the interlocking network and even be introduced during system upgrades. The security terminates in the security box, thus the safety hardware need to be protected by physical measures. The FEA junction boxes are thus physically protected by "housing alerts" that trigger an alarm to prohibit attackers from tampering with the system.

In the Technology Center, a termination point for the field element encryption has been introduced. Also, several zones with different SLs have to be connected, e.g., the interlocking system has to be connected to the maintenance and data management subsystem (MDM) with different SL.

To tackle this challenge, an application layer gateway (ALG) has been introduced as a central entity of the Technology Center. This device is configured to only allow desired connections between zones. Via packet inspection mechanisms malicious code can be identified. If zones of different SL are connected, the allowed communication can be limited via white-list filtering on different layers. If anomalous behaviour is detected the ALG reports this to the Security Operation Center (SOC), where an operator can decide what actions have to be taken. In certain cases the separation of a zone from the rest of the network (quarantine) may be needed, which then can be realized by the ALG. Upon the detection of new attack scenarios the operator also has the possibility to change the rule set and filtering of the ALG to mitigate the new attack.

On the operational layer the SOC has been extended by a Security and Information Event Management (SIEM) system besides elements for system management, such as PKI, domain name service, network time server, and a directory service. The SIEM system aggregates information from every component and analyses it for possible attacks. If it detects a possible attack the security operator is informed, starts with further investigation on the issue, and finally performs some action to solve it.

As the provisioning of security requires the application of tools and methods on a sustained basis, a process based approach is implemented to ensure a constant level of security. For this a patch management process has been developed. Changes to components are first checked in a simulated environment for quality assurance before they are applied to the operational components. For a rapid reaction to attacks, the rule sets of the ALG and security boxes can be altered to mitigate the vulnerability until a patch can be applied. Furthermore, processes for incident management and an Information Security Management System (ISMS) have been implemented. Upon the detection of an anomaly it is checked against a database of known incidents and relevant actions are applied. For unclassified anomalies, forensics are performed to determine the relevant reaction. After solving the incident, the findings are used as input for the ISMS to enhance the security processes.

By having added security features to the communication channel of the safety building blocks, the architecture allows to control that strict safety requirements such as availability and timeliness are still met. The communication channel is transparent to the safety system such that the security blocks can be updated independently and without affecting the safety homologation process. The decoupling of safety and security still requires to make the physical gap between them as small as possible (e.g., on the same circuit board), to avoid attacks just behind the security component.

5   Conclusion

The existing interlocking architecture provides insufficient security against cyber-attacks. To overcome this, DB plans to deploy the presented security architecture in Germany's new ILS to mitigate security risks without detrimentally impacting the system's safety. The presented security concept includes monitoring and information systems as well as basic security building blocks such as cryptography support and filtering. It ensures security not only cross the Operational and Interlocking layers but also provides security functions for the Technology Center and the Field Element Areas. In addition, processes are established to ensure the correct handling of incidents and functional requirements to each building block in order to help build security enabled components.

Acknowledgements. Research supported in part by EC CIPSEC GA 700378.

References

1. CENELEC: EN 50126: Railway applications - The specification and demonstration of Reliability, Availability, Maintainability and Safety (RAMS) (1999)
2. DKE: Elektrische Bahn-Signalanlagen - Teil 104: Leitfaden für die IT-Sicherheit auf Grundlage der IEC 62443 (DIN VDE V 0831-104) (2014)
3. DKE: Electric signalling systems for railways - Part 200: Safe transmission protocol according to DIN EN 50159 (DIN VDE V 0831-200) (2015)
4. Hansman, S., Hunt, R.: A taxonomy of network and computer attacks. Comput. Secur. **24**(1), 31–43 (2005). doi:10.1016/j.cose.2004.06.011
5. Howard, J.D., Longstaff, T.A.: A common language for computer security incidents. Technical report SAND98-8667, Sandia Natl Lab, (1998). doi:10.2172/751004
6. Intl. Electrotechnical Commission: IEC 62443 Industrial communication networks - Network and system security. IEC 62443, November 2010
7. Meyers, C., Powers, S., Faissol, D.: Taxonomies of cyber adversaries and attacks: a survey of incidents and approaches. Lawrence Livermore Natl. Lab. **7**, 1–22 (2009). doi:10.2172/967712
8. Simmons, C., Shiva, S., Bedi, H., Dasgupta, D.: Avoidit: A cyber attack taxonomy. In: Annual Symposium on Information Assurance, pp. 2–12 (2014)
9. Weber, D.J.: A taxonomy of computer intrusions. Ph.D. thesis, MIT (1998)

Systematic Pattern Approach for Safety and Security Co-engineering in the Automotive Domain

Tiago Amorim[1(✉)], Helmut Martin[2], Zhendong Ma[3], Christoph Schmittner[3], Daniel Schneider[4], Georg Macher[5], Bernhard Winkler[2], Martin Krammer[2], and Christian Kreiner[6]

[1] Technische Universität Berlin, Berlin, Germany
buarquedeamorim@tu-berlin.de
[2] VIRTUAL VEHICLE Research Center, Graz, Austria
{helmut.martin,bernhard.winkler,martin.krammer}@v2c2.at
[3] Austrian Institute of Technology, Vienna, Austria
{zhendong.ma,christoph.schmittner}@ait.ac.at
[4] Fraunhofer Institute for Experimental Software Engineering, Kaiserslautern, Germany
daniel.schneider@iese.fraunhofer.de
[5] AVL List GmbH, Graz, Austria
georg.macher@avl.com
[6] Institute for Technical Informatics, Graz University of Technology, Graz, Austria
christian.kreiner@tugraz.at

Abstract. Future automotive systems will exhibit increased levels of automation as well as ever tighter integration with other vehicles, traffic infrastructure, and cloud services. From safety perspective, this can be perceived as boon or bane - it greatly increases complexity and uncertainty, but at the same time opens up new opportunities for realizing innovative safety functions. Moreover, cybersecurity becomes important as additional concern because attacks are now much more likely and severe. Unfortunately, there is lack of experience with security concerns in context of safety engineering in general and in automotive safety departments in particular. To remediate this problem, we propose a systematic pattern-based approach that interlinks safety and security patterns and provides guidance with respect to selection and combination of both types of patterns in context of system engineering. The application of a combined safety and security pattern engineering workflow is shown and demonstrated by an automotive use case scenario.

Keywords: ISO 26262 · SAE J3061 · Engineering workflow · Safety pattern · Security pattern · Automotive

1 Introduction

Future applications in the automotive domain will be highly connected. They will rely on interacting functionalities exchanging data via various networking channels, and storing or receiving their operational data in or from the cloud. On the one hand, there is enormous potential in these new types of cyber-physical-system (CPS) applications

© Springer International Publishing AG 2017
S. Tonetta et al. (Eds.): SAFECOMP 2017, LNCS 10488, pp. 329–342, 2017.
DOI: 10.1007/978-3-319-66266-4_22

and services, which are bound to revolutionize the automotive domain, as we know it today. On the other hand, ensuring safety and security of next-generation automotive systems is a significant and comprehensive challenge that needs to be addressed before promising visions can become reality and an economic and societal success story.

Today, practitioners in the automotive domain are well experienced to deal with safety aspects during CPS development. However, there is a lack of knowledge on how to handle related security aspects, because the knowledge is either just non-existent or, maybe even more often, distributed over different organizational units in a company and thus not easily accessible.

Given the tight interconnection and the mutual impact of safety and security aspects, we argue that there is a need for a combined engineering approach enabling safety and security co-engineering. Moreover, given the present lack of experience in safety and security co-engineering, we think that providing additional guidance to engineers would be highly beneficial.

In this paper, we specifically focus on the proper and due consideration of the security aspect within a safety engineering lifecycle, which is one particularly urgent problem related to the aforementioned challenge. Consequently, we propose a systematic pattern-based and ISO 26262-oriented approach for safety and security co-engineering in the automotive domain. Through the use of patterns, we hope to close the security knowledge gap by harvesting its manifold benefits: conservation and reuse of design knowledge, best practices and tested solutions, reuse of architectural artifacts enabled by abstraction, cross-domain exchange of solution concepts, etc. Apart from the systematic interlinking of safety and security patterns, we elaborate how these patterns can be specified and maintained.

2   Background and Related Work

This section provides background knowledge about architectural patterns in general, safety patterns, security patterns, safety and security co-engineering, and current relevant automotive guidance for safety and cybersecurity.

2.1   Relevant Automotive Guidance for Safety and Cybersecurity

ISO 26262 – "Road Vehicles – Functional Safety" [1] is an automotive domain-specific safety standard. It provides a structured and generic approach for the complete safety lifecycle of an automotive E/E system including design, development, production, service processes, and decommissioning. ISO 26262 recommends requirements and techniques for system, software, and hardware design to achieve functional safety of E/E systems. For instance, the *Usage of established design patterns* is recommended (i.e. "+") for all ASIL levels for each sub-phase of software development, as described in Subsect. 4.4.7 of Part 6. Concerning security, the first edition, released in 2011, does not consider it explicitly neither there is any support or guidance. The second edition, to be released mid-2018, is expected to provide some notes regarding the interaction of safety and security activities.

SAE J3061 [10] is a cybersecurity process framework for the development lifecycle of in-car systems. It provides guidance on best practice methods and techniques for secure system development tailored to the automotive domain by using a corresponding V model, as defined in ISO 26262. In J3061, safety and security interaction points are defined to coordinate the two engineering processes.

2.2 Safety and Security Co-analysis and Co-engineering

In our view, safety & security co-analysis refers to methods and techniques that can be used to identify safety hazards and security threats. Safety & security co-engineering refers to engineering activities that consider both safety and security and their interactions in the development lifecycle. Co-analysis includes activities in the early stage of the development lifecycle, e.g. in the requirements engineering as well as the design phase. Co-engineering considers all phases of the lifecycle, in which co-analysis is an integral part.

In the context of automotive domain, existing co-analysis methods Hazard Analysis and Risk Management (HARA) is standardized in ISO 26262 for safety, which can be extended with security Threat Analysis and Risk Assessment (TARA) method, as mentioned in SAE J3061 to identify cybersecurity risks [15]. Other proposals include Failure mode and Vulnerability Effect Analysis (FMVEA) [4] and Security Aware Hazard Analysis and Risk Assessment (SAHARA) [16] that aim at combining both safety and security analysis in parallel. A safety and security co-engineering approach should include all engineering activities in the automotive system development lifecycle according to relevant standards such as ISO 26262 and SAE J3061 based on the V-model [17].

2.3 Architectural Patterns

Patterns are used to solve similar problems with a general and universal solution. A well-known and proven solution for a specific problem is generalized so that it can be reused for similar recurring problems in other projects. Alexander describes the concept of using architecture patterns to solve similar problems in different projects [9].

The concept of patterns is used in many different domains including hardware and software. A good and very well-known reference is the book by Gamma et al. [11] (also known as the Gang of Four), which had a significant impact on making the pattern approach popular for software development. The book includes some general background and concepts as well as a collection of concrete patterns for object-oriented software design.

The state-of-the-art provides a few dozen safety architecture patterns [2, 3], with some being just a variation of simpler ones. Armoush introduced in his PhD thesis [3] new safety patterns and provides a collection of existing safety patterns and a characterization of the main pattern representation attributes for embedded systems patterns (e.g. Name, Type, ID, Abstract, Context, Problem, Structure,...). These patterns are mostly based on the work of Douglas [12, 13] for hardware patterns and on Pullum [14] for software fault tolerance techniques brought into pattern notation for software patterns.

Safety patterns usually include some kind of hardware redundancy, multiple channels with voters, or sanity checks [2]. They can address software or hardware issues and they allow systems to remain fully functional or to bring them to a safe state. Describing existing patterns, but the ones used in the presented case study, is out of the scope of this work.

Security engineering is an iterative and incremental process. Security patterns can be seen as the essence of sound security designs and best practices from an existing body of knowledge that can be used to solve security problems in new scenarios. During the security engineering process, security patterns can be used in requirements analysis and design to eliminate security flaws and provide additional information for security validation. Security patterns have attracted the attention of both academic researchers and industry [5]. The main focus of existing work is on the construction (including representation, classification, and organization) and application of security patterns. Security patterns are represented as textual templates or combined with UML models, in a hierarchically layered architecture or in a searchable pattern library. Security patterns have been proposed for requirements engineering, software system design such as web services, and Service-Oriented Architectures [6]. Open Security Architecture[1] is a community-based online repository of security control patterns based on the ISO 27000 information security standard family for enterprise IT systems, in which patterns are represented as text and graphical architecture designs in a consistent template. In recent years, security patterns have also been proposed for cyber-physical systems [7].

3   Methodology

Although patterns address specific problems, the context in which a pattern is applied influences how it should be applied. Therefore, more than a catalogue of patterns, practitioners require a workflow to systematically guide their efforts when using patterns to tackle safety and security problems. We propose a safety and security pattern engineering lifecycle that aims at combining the two engineering processes for pattern identification and design and allows for the necessary interaction and balancing of safety and security concerns.

3.1   Pattern Engineering Lifecycle

The Pattern Engineering Lifecycle is the approach proposed in this paper to help engineers selecting and applying safety and security patterns to develop safe and secure systems. The Pattern Engineering Lifecycle is meant to be used in unison (and tightly integrated) with the usual safety and security engineering approaches. It therefore does not substitute established approaches but rather enhances them with further tasks. The approach is suitable to be used with all existing patterns as well as ones to be developed.

---

[1] http://www.opensecurityarchitecture.org.

The lifecycle takes place at the end of the *Product Development: System level* phase of the V-Model framework of ISO 26262 [1]. At this point, the *Functional* and *Technical Concept* are fully developed and both are used as input for the lifecycle. The output of the lifecycle is then consumed by the next phases of the V-Model, namely *Product Development: Hardware level* and *Software level.*

The lifecycle is divided into three main phases happening one after the other in a waterfall fashion (cf. Fig. 1). The first phase, Safety Pattern Engineering, comes before Security Pattern Engineering, the second phase. The rationale for this is that the approach explicitly focuses on "security for safety" (i.e., safety concerns are the main engineering drivers) and that security should start working when the final architecture is almost finished. Also, in general, further changes in the architecture might open new vulnerability points or might not be properly covered by mechanisms already implemented. However, security measures can influence system properties that can alter safety. For this reason, we introduce the Safety and Security Co-Engineering Loop, the third phase of the lifecycle. The loop prevents safety-motivated changes from creating unforeseen vulnerabilities and security-motivated changes from jeopardizing safety characteristics of the system. Each of these phases will be described in detail in the next paragraphs.

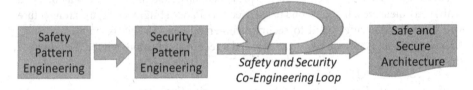

Fig. 1. Pattern engineering lifecycle

Safety Pattern Engineering. Safety Pattern Engineering involves safety-related tasks and is composed of three main tasks (cf. Fig. 2), which will be described in the following paragraphs.

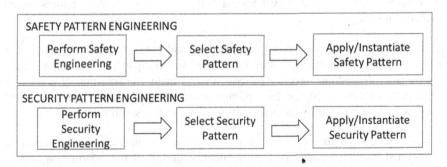

Fig. 2. Safety pattern engineering and security pattern engineering tasks

Perform Safety Engineering. As described above, patterns are used to tackle specific problems; therefore, we need to have a good understanding of the system and the context in order to select and apply patterns appropriately. The workflow starts with established safety engineering approaches and techniques that need to be carried out until Safety Requirements (Functional or Technical) are available.

Select Safety Pattern. The decision about which pattern best fits a specific system should be analyzed taking into account the problem to be addressed and the context of the system. Besides, there are a few trade-offs that one needs to take into consideration when choosing an architectural pattern, such as costs (hardware, development effort) or standardization. The Safety Requirements guide safety engineers into selecting a safety. Current state-of-the-art [3, 12, 13] provides many patterns with detailed information about the impact in the system in the view of different dimensions (e.g. Cost, Reliability, Safety). There might be cases that no pattern is suitable for the discovered problems, thus the engineer needs to come up with an ad-hoc solution.

Apply/Instantiate Safety Pattern. The engineers should apply the safety pattern to the architecture, performing required changes on the architecture or on the pattern. Using the pattern "as-is" is usually not possible and some adaptation might be required. The updated system architecture is the prerequisite for the next task.

Security Pattern Engineering. In the previous phase, the architecture was updated with safety measures. In the second phase, Security Pattern Engineering, the architecture will be analyzed with regard to security vulnerabilities. The weak points are to be addressed by applicable security patterns and a secure architecture will be the output of this phase.

Perform Security Engineering. In this step, Security Engineering is performed on the existing system context such as functional requirements, results of Safety Engineering, and intermediate architectural design of the system, including the safety patterns. Established Security Engineering methods and techniques such as attack surface analysis, attack trees, and threat modeling can be used to identify vulnerabilities and threats. The results of this task leads to security measures that either mitigate potential threats or reduce the risks to an acceptable level. Special attention is given to vulnerabilities caused by safety patterns.

Select Security Pattern. The security engineers should give priority to the selection of re-usable security solutions from well-established security patterns for mitigating the security risks. If multiple security patterns are available, the selection of a security pattern is then a design decision that optimizes cost-benefit. Similar to the selection of safety patterns, if no security pattern is available, an ad-hoc solution is applied.

Apply/Instantiate Security Pattern. In this step, the instantiated security pattern is incorporated into the existing system architecture design. If the information how to integrate is not available in the pattern description, the security engineers should adapt the security pattern to the specific system context and requirements.

Safety and Security Co-engineering Loop. After the initial two phases of the Pattern Engineering Lifecycle, the Safety and Security Co-Engineering Loop starts. In this phase, lightweight versions of safety pattern engineering and security pattern engineering take place one after the other until no extra modification is required in the architecture. The fact that they are performed as a lightweight version means that the focus is on checking those aspects that experienced alteration and their respective influence on the overall system.

The Loop starts with the safety pattern engineering task requiring safety engineers to analyze how the newly added security patterns might impact the system safety. Some security architecture strategy might impair, for example, the communication time between components, causing a command to arrive late. Also in this task, the results of the first security pattern engineering phase help the safety engineers to identify further points of failure that could be caused by an attack. The initial safety pattern might require some modification to add extra safety.

On the other hand, if the newly proposed safety mechanisms imply new vulnerabilities or changes in the attack surface, the security engineers should detect, assess, and propose new solutions. This is what happens during the security pattern engineering performed in the lightweight version. This goes on like a cycle and stops when the system fulfills the desired safety and security requirements. Updating supporting documentation and updating the architecture are also tasks to be performed.

4   Implementation of Pattern Engineering Approach

In the following section, the technical implementation of the approach shall be demonstrated on an automotive case study.

4.1   Use Case Description

Our automotive use case example of a connected electrified hybrid powertrain is a combination of one or more electric motor(s) and a conventional internal combustion engine, which is currently the most common variant of hybrid powertrains. The variety of powertrain configuration options increases the complexity of the powertrain itself as well as the required control systems, which include software functions and electronic control units. With the integration of connectivity features, further novel vehicle functionalities and new business models can be discovered. Therefore, we focus on an integral part of every connected hybrid powertrain, the battery management system (BMS), and its functionalities related to the connection to the external world; in this case especially the connections with the charging unit.

In this paper, we investigate a specific use case scenario of the connected hybrid powertrain use case: charging of the battery system by connecting it with an external charging unit. Figure 3 left shows the most relevant elements: battery satellite modules, battery management system, CAN communication, the charging interface, and the external charging unit.

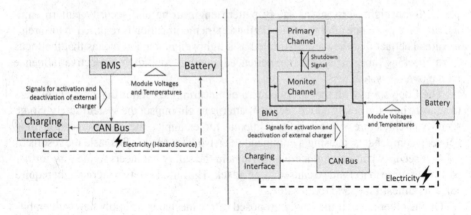

Fig. 3. **Left**: Automotive Battery Use Case, **Right**: Architecture with the safety pattern applied

4.2 Application of the Approach

In this subsection, we apply the Pattern Engineering Lifecycle in the use case scenario presented in the previous subsection. The concept phase is considered in this example.

4.2.1 Safety Pattern Engineering

Perform Safety Engineering. We describe in the following a small summary of the results of this task up to the level of Functional Safety Requirements:

Hazard: Wrong estimation of charging status.

Comment: The battery of electric vehicles can be very dangerous in case of over-charging, even causing explosions. If the charging status of a battery is estimated wrongly, extra energy might be supplied, leading to a hazardous situation.

Operational situation: Parking

Comment: The hazard will only happen while charging, and this can only be performed while the car is parked. This hazard might also occur while driving when architectures with regenerative systems are considered.

Hazard classification:

- Severity: 3 ‖ Exposure of frequency: 4 ‖ Controllability: 2
- Resulting hazard ASIL: [C]
- Safety goal: Estimate correct status of cycle while charging.
  - Safe state: Disconnect HV battery, Alert driver.
- Functional Safety requirement: Detect Failure and errors from BMS.

Select Safety Pattern. The results from Safety Engineering describe two possible safe states for the system that are compliant with the Safety goal. The "Disconnect HV battery" measure would cut off the power supply, the source of the hazard. The "Alert driver" measure would issue a warning to the driver. The car will be in parking mode if the hazard occurs (operational situation: Parking); therefore, full functionality in case of fault occurrence is not required.

We should apply to the architecture a pattern that helps fulfilling the Functional Safety Requirement "Detect Failure and errors from BMS". We selected the Monitor-Actuator Pattern [12] (cf. Fig. 3 Right) which provides heterogeneous redundancy. This pattern adds to the architecture a monitoring channel that detects possible faults and triggers the primary channel to enter its fail-safe state. The Monitor-Actuator Pattern is suitable to systems with low availability requirements and addresses the problem of finding an appropriate mechanism for detecting failures or errors without incurring higher costs.

Apply/Instantiate Safety Pattern. The Monitor-Actuator Pattern was instantiated as depicted in Fig. 3. Only changes to the BMS component were made.

4.2.2   Security Pattern Engineering

Perform Security Engineering. In this context, Security Engineering follows the initial definition of a safety pattern to identify potential security vulnerabilities, threats, and risks in order to find appropriate countermeasures and apply corresponding security patterns. In this example, we use the threat modeling methodology [8], in which a system is modeled in a data flow diagram (DFD). When modeling the functional blocks from the safety pattern (cf. Fig. 3.) in a DFD, a few transitions and extrapolations occur. First, since threat modeling assumes that attacks happen when data flow from one process (i.e., a software component that takes input and either produces output or performs an action) to another, the logic signal flows in the safety pattern need to be translated into directional data flows according to the software architecture implementing this safety logic. Therefore, additional components are added such as the "CAN bus" process, which represents the communication bus in the in-car system. Second, the trust boundaries need to be defined in the DFD in order to identify attacks originating from data flows across trust boundaries. As a result, the charging interface is split into two parts: an in-car charging interface and the corresponding interface at the charging station. The interface on the charging station is modeled as an external interactor outside the "In-car system" trust boundary. There can be different levels of trust boundaries. In this case, we assume that attacks can only originate from outside the "In-car system" boundary. Third, at the system level, security has an influence on components beyond the scope of the safety pattern. Since the communication between the primary and monitor channel and the charging interface goes through the CAN bus, and the powertrain unit is connected to the same bus, the security of the charging interface also influences the security of the powertrain unit. Thus even though the two safety modules cannot be attacked directly due to the unidirectional data flows, there are risks that an attacker might use the system charging function to attack the powertrain unit. Figure 4 shows the modeled architecture in DFD using the Microsoft Threat Modeling Tool.

The security analysis provides a list of threats according to the STRIDE method. In our case, the threats we identified are the communications from the external charging interface to the CAN bus that is responsible for establishing and maintaining communications for charging control. An attacker can use the in-car charging interface as an entry point by compromising the external charging interface or tampering with the communications between the interfaces to inject malicious content into the CAN bus.

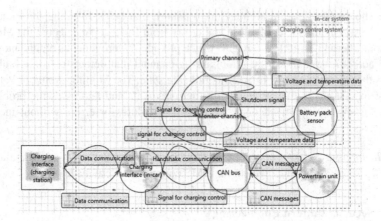

Fig. 4. Threat modeling of architecture (Tool: MS Threat Modeling Tool 2016)

Select Security Pattern. One possible solution is to add a security gateway between the external unit and the internal CAN bus as shown in Fig. 5. The security gateway is a security pattern that is placed between an unprotected internal network and untrusted external entities when communication to the outside is inevitable. As a repeatable solution, the security gateway is not limited to the charging interface. It can be applied to any communication between the CAN bus and untrusted external devices. In general, it controls the network access to the internal ECUs according to predefined security policies and can also inspect packet content to detect intrusion attempts and anomalies. It can also serve as an endpoint for secure communication with external entities that implement network or application level securities. In this way, it adds security protection and segments the system without fundamentally changing the existing in-car system architecture.

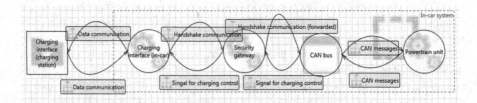

Fig. 5. Security Gateway as a security pattern (Tool: MS Threat Modeling Tool 2016)

Apply/Instantiate Security Pattern. In Fig. 5, we see the altered architecture with the Security Gateway module. Beyond the many benefits, a security gateway might introduce latency into the communication, which is a subject of safety impact analysis.

4.2.3   Safety and Security Co-engineering Loop

First Safety Pattern Engineering Iteration. With the inputs from previous tasks we perform a HAZOP analysis to identify potential anomalies in the provision of the service

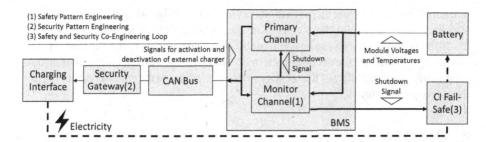

Fig. 6. Architecture after the first Iteration of safety and security co-engineering

controlling the Charging Interface (cf. Table 1). The focus is thus on the changes performed to the architecture by the security engineers.

Table 1. HAZOP Guideword analysis of the architecture.

Function: Command to the charging interface to stop charging		
Guideword	Possible causes	Possible consequences
Commission	–	–
Omission	The Gateway blocks a message to stop charging. Message gets corrupted	The Charging Interface keeps providing energy to the battery
Early	–	–
Late	The extra processing time required slows the reaction time of the components	Battery is charged for a couple of hundreds of milliseconds more than required
Value High	–	–
Value Low	–	–

Based on the analysis we identified failure modes Omission and Late as potential causes of a hazard (cf. Table 1). Other potential failure modes are not relevant for this scenario. As input from the Security Pattern Engineering phase, we get the information that the Security Gateway adds a small latency to the communication between the Charging Interface and the BMS. This small delay can cause a minor amount of extra charging in the battery which is not a source of hazard.

From the input received from the previous phase, we also discovered that the safety functions on the charging interface will not suffice in the case of a hacker attack. To tackle this issue a Charging Interface fail-safe device connected to the Monitor channel was integrated (cf. Fig. 6). Of course, one obvious drawback in this solution is the extra cost incurred due to extra hardware and installation.

First Security Pattern Engineering Iteration. The changes in the architecture neither create new vulnerabilities nor jeopardize the current mechanisms already in place. Since further modification of the architecture was not required, the Loop reaches an end. After finalization of the safety and security pattern engineering activities, the design can be reviewed to check whether all applied patterns can co-exist and whether there is no unwanted influence. While there is a direct review of the design with the applied patterns after each iteration, a final check can ensure the soundness of the design. It was decided to add the Security Gateway as an additional component in the system, to not only ensure that safety pattern and the security pattern do not interfere with each other, but also to support the maintainability of the security solution. Updates to the gateway do not impact the safety pattern directly.

5   Discussion

The availability of recurring process steps, based on automotive industry standards, results in faster and cheaper product development while fulfilling the need for intangible product properties, namely safety and security. This means that if, for instance, a safety (architectural) pattern is selected to address a specific safety requirement, additional information and guidance with respect to neuralgic aspects from a security point of view is needed. These might be subject to further security analyses and the application of an additional security (architectural) pattern might be warranted. The security pattern, in turn, can have a safety impact, which is again explicitly specified.

The decision about which pattern fits best for a specific system should be analyzed taking into account the problem to be addressed and the context of the system. Besides, there are a few trade-offs that one needs to take into consideration when choosing an architectural pattern, such as costs (e.g. available hardware, development effort) or standardization. These trade-offs are project specific can also involve managerial decisions.

As stated, safety and security engineering are very closely related disciplines and their synergy can be fostered when their similarities are recognized and adequate interactions are established correctly.

6   Conclusion and Future Work

This paper focused on the selection, combination, and application of safety and security patterns. The introduction of the Pattern Engineering Lifecycle provided a systematic way of safety- and security-related pattern engineering process steps to development, and included already existing work products, such as the results of safety analyses. The Safety and Security Co-Engineering Loops helped to align these activities systematically. It benefits from tight integration of safety- and security-related process steps, which requires increased exchange of information between them.

An industrial use case demonstrated the practical realization of our approach: the architecture of an automotive battery system was described in a semi-formal way, including identification of its main components, physical interconnections, and flows of information. Within the Safety Pattern Engineering step, the "Monitor-Actuator Pattern" was selected as an appropriate measure for detecting failures originating from the BMS. Within the Security Pattern Engineering step, the "Security Gateway Pattern" was selected to protect the CAN bus from attacks on the Charging Interface. During the Safety and Security Co-Engineering Loop, the conducted HAZOP analysis identified additional modifications to the overall system. As result, a dedicated risk reduction measure was proposed to enhance the integrity due to combination of the two patterns. Finally, the complete system was presented after the first iteration of the introduced Safety and Security Co-Engineering Loop.

With the presented approach, we aimed to derive the manifold benefits from patterns inherent to their nature. This is a mean for accelerating the application of adequate safety and security co-engineering in the automotive domain. In particular, we showed a way to remediate the lack of security knowledge and facilitate easier and more informed integration of these two "separate" yet interfering disciplines. Future work should investigate an advanced model-based tool support for the proposed steps of the approach with interfaces to existing external tools.

Acknowledgment. This work is supported by the EU projects EMC^2 and AMASS. Research leading to these results has received funding from the EU ARTEMIS Joint Undertaking under grant agreement n° 621429 (project EMC2), EU ECSEL Joint Undertaking under grant agreement n° 692474 (project AMASS), and from the COMET K2 - Competence Centres for Excellent Technologies Programme of the Austrian Federal Ministry for Transport, Innovation and Technology (bmvit), the Austrian Federal Ministry of Science, Research and Economy (bmwfw), the Austrian Research Promotion Agency (FFG), the Province of Styria, and the Styrian Business Promotion Agency (SFG), the German Federal Ministry of Education and Research (BMBF), grant "CrESt, 01IS16043".

References

1. International Organization for Standardization: ISO 26262 - Road vehicles– Functional safety, Part 1–10. ISO/TC 22/SC 32 - Electrical and electronic components and general system aspects (2011)
2. Preschern, C., Kajtazovic, N., Kreiner, C.: Building a safety architecture pattern system. In: Proceedings of the 18th European Conference on Pattern Languages of Program, p. 17. ACM (2015)
3. Armoush, A.: Design patterns for safety-critical embedded systems, Doctoral dissertation, RWTH Aachen University (2010)
4. Schmittner, C., Ma, Z., Schoitsch, E., Gruber, T.: A case study of FMVEA and CHASSIS as safety and security co-analysis method for automotive cyber-physical systems. In: Proceedings of the 1st ACM Workshop on Cyber-Physical System Security. ACM (2015)
5. Schumacher, M.: Security Engineering with Patterns: Origins, Theoretical Models, and New Applications, vol. 2754. Springer, Heidelberg (2003)
6. Delessy, N.A., Fernandez, E.B.: A pattern-driven security process for SOA applications. In: Third International Conference on Availability, Reliability and Security, ARES 2008, pp. 416–421. IEEE, March 2008
7. Petroulakis, N.E., Spanoudakis, G., Askoxylakis, I.G., Miaoudakis, A., Traganitis, A.: A pattern-based approach for designing reliable cyber-physical systems. In: Global Communications Conference (GLOBECOM), pp. 1–6. IEEE, December 2015
8. Shostack, A.: Threat Modeling: Designing for Security. Wiley, Hoboken (2014)
9. Alexander, C., Ishikawa, S., Silverstein, M., Ramió, J.R., Jacobson, M., Fiksdahl-King, I.: A Pattern Language, pp. 311–314. Gustavo Gili, Barcelona (1977)

10. SAE International: J3061 - Cybersecurity Guidebook for Cyber-Physical Vehicle Systems (2016)
11. Vlissides, J., Helm, R., Johnson, R., Gamma, E.: Design Patterns: Elements of Reusable Object-Oriented Software. Addison-Wesley, Reading (1995). 49(120), 11
12. Douglas, B.: Real-Time Design Patterns: Robust Scalable Architecture for Real-Time Systems. Pearson, Essex (2002)
13. Douglas, B.: Design Patterns for Embedded Systems in C. Elsevier, Amsterdam (2010)
14. Pullum, L.L.: Software Fault Tolerance Techniques and Implementation. Artech House Inc, Norwood (2001)
15. Macher, G., Armengaud, E., Kreiner, C., Brenner, Schmittner, C., Ma, Z., Martin, H., Krammer, M.: Integration of Security in the Development Lifecycle of Dependable Automotive CPS. Handbook of Research for Cyber-Physical Systems Ubiquity. IGI Global (2017)
16. Macher, G., Sporer, H., Berlach, R., Armengaud, E., Kreiner, C.: SAHARA: a security-aware hazard and risk analysis method. In: Design, Automation Test in Europe Conference Exhibition, pp. 621–624 (2015)
17. Schmittner, C., Ma, Z., Gruber, T., Schoitsch, E.: Safety and Security Co-engineering of Connected, Intelligent, and Automated Vehicles. ERCIM News #109 (2017)

Author Index

Printed in the United States
By Bookmasters